MCSE Windows® 20 Professional For Dum

CW01617401

New Since Windows NT 4.0

These software components are new or drastically changed with Windows 2000 Professional, making them likely candidates for the exam:

- Network and Dial-Up Connections (Chapters 6 and 13)
- Encryption (Chapter 3)
- Disk quotas (Chapter 3)
- Dynamic disks (Chapters 3 and 7)
- FAT32 (Chapter 3)
- Windows File Protection and SFC (Chapter 15)
- Remote Installation Service (Chapter 4)
- SysPrep (Chapter 4)
- Microsoft Management Console (Chapter 2)
- Plug and Play (Chapter 9)
- ACPI power management (Chapter 9)
- Multiple display support (Chapter 8)
- Accessibility options (Chapter 5)
- Group Policy (Chapter 11)
- Offline files and folders (Chapter 12)

Hardware

- Universal Serial Bus (USB) is an external daisy chain bus that uses only one interrupt.
- FireWire (IEEE 1394) is like USB, but faster.
- Multiple displays work with AGP or PCI adapters only.
- Only administrators can install Plug-and-Play devices where the user must specify driver location.
- View hardware details in System Information under the Computer Management console.
- Fix resource conflicts in Device Manager.

Installation

- Minimum hardware: P133 CPU, 16MB RAM, 120MB disk (140MB for a new installation).
- Upgrading into an old Windows folder preserves old settings.
- Installing to a new folder gives flexibility and a dual-boot option.
- Setup Manager helps create a custom installation script (UNATTEND.TXT).
- SysPrep lets you clone systems without duplicating SIDs. Requires clients have same # of CPUs, disk controller, and power management.
- Remote Installation Services (RIS) clients need to see a DHCP server (or relay agent) and domain controller in order to boot.
- You can now partition and format disks from within Setup.
- WINNT32.EXE upgrades Windows 9*x* and NT, WINNT.EXE upgrades, Windows 3.*x*, and DOS.

System Recovery

- Get back to previous control set with Last Known Good boot.
- Save and restore Registry and (optionally) system files with System State option in NTBACKUP.
- Emergency Recovery Diskette (ERD) contains list of system files with checksums.
- Recovery Console boots to text mode command line interface if Windows 2000 can't boot normally.
- Copy files, enable and disable services in Recovery Console.

MCSE Windows® 2000 Professional For Dummies®

Cheat Sheet

Networking

- NetBEUI, IPX/SPX, and TCP/IP are "big three" protocols but Active Directory requires TCP/IP.
- Almost all settings (including TCP/IP) now on a per-connection basis in Network and Dial-Up Connections folder.
- Key TCP/IP concepts are IP address, subnet mask, default gateway, DHCP, WINS, and DNS.
- DNS is Active Directory namespace and now "dynamic" (clients update database automatically when IP data changes).
- Automatic Private IP Addressing (APIPA) for SOHO network with TCP/IP but no DHCP.
- IPCONFIG /ALL reports IP configuration details at command prompt.
- Virtual Private Networking supported with PPTP, L2TP, and IPSec protocols for secure access over Internet.
- Multilink combines devices for more bandwidth.
- Internet Connection Sharing lets one PC share link with others.

Group Policy and Security

- Computer policies (pre-logon) and user policies (post-logon).
- Hierarchical system: domain policies override local policies.
- View local policies with Local Security Policy console and GPEDIT.MSC.
- View domain policies with Active Directory Users and Computers tool pointing to a domain controller.
- Security Templates and Security Configuration and Analysis console snap-ins work with INF templates.
- Windows 2000 "power users" roughly equivalent to NT4 "users."
- Don't use local users & groups (stored in local Registry) in domain environment.
- Stricter Registry access controls than NT4.
- NTFS ("file-and-folder") permissions restrict local and network access to NTFS disks.
- Shared folder permissions restrict network access to any disk or printer.
- "Deny" permission always overrides any other.

Test-Taking Tips

- For a non-adaptive test, answer easy questions first; mark long or tough ones to come back to later; and answer every question.
- For an adaptive test, do your level best on each question before proceeding.
- Get lots of paper to draw diagrams and at least two pencils.
- Take every last minute coming to you.
- Tile exhibit windows with question windows to make a split screen.
- Watch out for the number of answers requested ("best answer," "all that apply," and so on).

Hungry Minds™

Cheat Sheet $2.95 value. Item 0653-6.
For more information about Hungry Minds, call 1-800-762-2974.

MCSE Windows® 2000 Professional FOR DUMMIES®

MCSE Windows® 2000 Professional FOR DUMMIES®

by Glenn Weadock, MCSE

Hungry Minds™

Best-Selling Books • Digital Downloads • e-Books • Answer Networks • e-Newsletters • Branded Web Sites • e-Learning

New York, NY ◆ Cleveland, OH ◆ Indianapolis, IN

MCSE Windows® 2000 Professional For Dummies®

Published by
Hungry Minds, Inc.
909 Third Avenue
New York, NY 10022
www.hungryminds.com
www.dummies.com

Library of Congress Control Number: 00-101094

ISBN: 0-7645-0653-6

Printed in the United States of America

10 9 8 7 6 5 4

1B/SY/QZ/QR/IN

Distributed in the United States by Hungry Minds, Inc.

Distributed by CDG Books Canada Inc. for Canada; by Transworld Publishers Limited in the United Kingdom; by IDG Norge Books for Norway; by IDG Sweden Books for Sweden; by IDG Books Australia Publishing Corporation Pty. Ltd. for Australia and New Zealand; by TransQuest Publishers Pte Ltd. for Singapore, Malaysia, Thailand, Indonesia, and Hong Kong; by Gotop Information Inc. for Taiwan; by ICG Muse, Inc. for Japan; by Intersoft for South Africa; by Eyrolles for France; by International Thomson Publishing for Germany, Austria and Switzerland; by Distribuidora Cuspide for Argentina; by LR International for Brazil; by Galileo Libros for Chile; by Ediciones ZETA S.C.R. Ltda. for Peru; by WS Computer Publishing Corporation, Inc., for the Philippines; by Contemporanea de Ediciones for Venezuela; by Express Computer Distributors for the Caribbean and West Indies; by Micronesia Media Distributor, Inc. for Micronesia; by Chips Computadoras S.A. de C.V. for Mexico; by Editorial Norma de Panama S.A. for Panama; by American Bookshops for Finland.

For general information on Hungry Minds' products and services please contact our Customer Care Department within the U.S. at 800-762-2974, outside the U.S. at 317-572-3993 or fax 317-572-4002.

For sales inquiries and reseller information, including discounts, premium and bulk quantity sales, and foreign-language translations, please contact our Customer Care Department at 800-434-3422, fax 317-572-4002, or write to Hungry Minds, Inc., Attn: Customer Care Department, 10475 Crosspoint Boulevard, Indianapolis, IN 46256.

For information on licensing foreign or domestic rights, please contact our Sub-Rights Customer Care Department at 212-884-5000.

For information on using Hungry Minds' products and services in the classroom or for ordering examination copies, please contact our Educational Sales Department at 800-434-2086 or fax 317-572-4005.

For press review copies, author interviews, or other publicity information, please contact our Public Relations Department at 317-572-3168 or fax 317-572-4168.

For authorization to photocopy items for corporate, personal, or educational use, please contact Copyright Clearance Center, 222 Rosewood Drive, Danvers, MA 01923, or fax 978-750-4470.

About the Author

Glenn Weadock is president of Independent Software, Inc., a consulting firm he founded in 1982 after graduating from Stanford University's engineering school. One of the country's most popular technical trainers, Glenn has taught Windows to thousands of students in the United States, United Kingdom, and Canada in more than 180 seminars since 1988. He has written six intensive two-day seminars for Data-Tech Institute, including Windows on NetWare and Supporting and Troubleshooting Windows 98, and has written and presented four Data-Tech computer videos.

Glenn is the author of *MCSE Windows 98 For Dummies, Small Business Networking For Dummies* and co-author of *Windows 98 Registry For Dummies, Windows 95 Registry For Dummies,* and *Creating Cool PowerPoint 97 Presentations,* all from IDG Books Worldwide, Inc. Glenn is a member of the Association for Computing Machinery and the American Society for Training and Development.

Dedication

To all those who study hard, not just to do better, but to do a better job.

Author's Acknowledgments

I thank my wife, Emily Weadock, for her assistance and my agent, Mike Snell, for his representation. Thanks also to the technical editors at Sento. It's been a pleasure to work with all of you.

Publisher's Acknowledgments

We're proud of this book; please register your comments through our Online Registration Form located at `http://my2cents.dummies.com`.

Some of the people who helped bring this book to market include the following:

Acquisitions, Editorial, and Media Development

Project Editor: Pat O'Brien

Acquisitions Editor: Judith Brief

Copy Editor: Christine Berman

Technical Editor: Gerry Routledge

Media Development Editor: Megan Decraene

Associate Permissions Editor: Carmen Krikorian

Editorial Manager: Rev Mengle

Media Development Manager: Heather Heath Dismore

Production

Project Coordinator: Amanda Foxworth

Layout and Graphics: Amy Adrian, Joe Bucki, Gabriele McCann, Tracy K. Oliver, Kristin Pickett, Jill Piscitelli, Brent Savage, Jacque Schneider, Brian Torwelle, Julie Trippetti, Jeremy Unger

Proofreaders: Laura Albert, Susan Moritz, Carl Pierce, Marianne Santy, Jeannie Smith

Indexer: Sharon Hilgenberg

General and Administrative

Hungry Minds, Inc.: John Kilcullen, CEO; Bill Barry, President and COO; John Ball, Executive VP, Operations & Administration; John Harris, Executive VP and CFO

Hungry Minds Technology Publishing Group: Richard Swadley, Senior Vice President and Publisher; Mary Bednarek, Vice President and Publisher, Networking; Walter R. Bruce III, Vice President and Publisher; Joseph Wikert, Vice President and Publisher, Web Development Group; Mary C. Corder, Editorial Director, Dummies Technology; Andy Cummings, Publishing Director, Dummies Technology; Barry Pruett, Publishing Director, Visual/Graphic Design

Hungry Minds Manufacturing: Ivor Parker, Vice President, Manufacturing

Hungry Minds Marketing: John Helmus, Assistant Vice President, Director of Marketing

Hungry Minds Production for Branded Press: Debbie Stailey, Production Director

Hungry Minds Sales: Michael Violano, Vice President, International Sales and Sub Rights

Contents at a Glance

Cartoons at a Glance

By Rich Tennant

"Well, shoot — Microsoft left SneakerNet off the exam requirements again."

page 9

"Look, I've told you the story of 'OSI and the Seven Layers' twice this week already."

page 137

page 209

"I guess you could say this is the hub of our network."

page 43

"Well kid, if your certification is as impressive as your cover letter, you've got a big future with this gang."

page 317

"OH, I THINK WE'VE FOUND OUR MAN."

page 371

"ACCORDING TO THIS RESUME YOU'VE DONE A LOT OF JOB-HOPPING."

page 385

Fax: 978-546-7747
E-mail: richtennant@the5thwave.com
World Wide Web: www.the5thwave.com

Table of Contents

Introduction

You hold in your hands a quick, no-nonsense guide to passing the Windows 2000 Professional MCP/MCSE test. This introduction covers the book's purpose, style, and organization, and describes the icons I use to guide you through the text.

About This Book

One of the many ways in which the computer industry shows its relative youth is the lack of an organized system of credentials for technical professionals. This situation makes life needlessly difficult for managers and job seekers alike. Managers have a hard time qualifying job applicants, and applicants have a hard time explaining just what it is that they know without getting overly technical.

Manager: So, Andy, tell me, what are your areas of computer knowledge?

Applicant (hesitating): Well, I'm mainly into TCP/IP, DHCP, DNS, HTML, DHTML, XML, and C++. That is, recently.

Manager (confused): I see. Well, well, that all sounds fine. But do you know anything about networking, Web design, or programming?

For businesses looking to hire technical consultants, the problems are similar. As the computer business grows exponentially in importance with each passing year, the need for some system of credentials has increased dramatically. In typical fashion, the computer industry has utterly failed to get together on a single, industry-wide certification program for software expertise, so the larger individual vendors (most notably Microsoft, Novell, and Cisco) offer their own programs.

Many certifications now exist for computer professionals, such as the Certified NetWare Engineer (CNE) from Novell and the "A+" designation for hardware technicians. As Microsoft has increased its dominance on the desktop and has made inroads in the server market, the MCSE (Microsoft Certified Systems Engineer) certification has grown in importance, making it the most desired professional certification in today's PC industry.

"Installing, Configuring, and Administering Microsoft Windows 2000 Professional," that is, Exam #70-210, is one of the required tests in the Windows 2000 track that computer professionals can pursue towards obtaining MCSE certification. The Windows NT 4.0 track remains an option as I write this, but it is slated for expiration at the end of calendar 2001. So many aspiring MCSEs will follow the newer Windows 2000 track in order to enjoy the MCSE credential for the longest possible time.

Exam #70-210 also conveys the somewhat less exalted certification of MCP, or Microsoft Certified Professional. For those who want to put three letters after their names instead of four, this is the test to take if you already use Windows 2000 at home or at work.

Whatever your particular goal, *MCSE Windows 2000 Professional For Dummies* is the only book you need to pass the test.

What this book is

This book's goal is simply to help you pass the Windows 2000 Professional certification test while investing as little study time as possible. (Time is of the essence; pass this test, and you've got six more to go to get your MCSE.) As a result, this book isn't as chatty as other *...For Dummies* books you may have read. The style is get-to-the-point. Although I do throw in the occasional zinger or chuckle to enliven the (we may as well admit it) often-dry material, the jokes stay out of your way.

Also because of the time factor, I personally don't like the approach in which you first read a 1500-page tome covering the material (much of it irrelevant) in excruciating detail, then also buy and read and learn by rote a 200-page collection of bullet items to use for "cramming" right before the exam. That approach is inefficient if your primary goal is to get certified, although book publishers love it because they get to sell twice as many books.

MCSE Windows 2000 Professional For Dummies is designed to be the only book you need to read on the subject if you want to pass the test. This book does three things:

- It gives you enough technical explanation so that you can understand the various key technology concepts.
- It gives you enough sample questions in each chapter so that you can assess your own readiness and identify areas that need more work.
- It lets you do some "cramming" right before the test by providing practice tests in print and hundreds of sample questions on the enclosed CD.

Feel free to consult other books to supplement this one if you want to increase your odds still further, or if you need to know more about Windows 2000 Professional than the exam covers. But if your goal is to pass the exam in the minimum time and with minimum effort, this book's all you need.

Most of you know by now that the *...For Dummies* series has grown beyond introducing computer basics to rank novices. Titles like the one you now have in front of you are clearly designed for a professional readership. How can that make sense? Simple. The hallmarks of the *...For Dummies* book series are clear writing, good organization, lighthearted irreverence, respect for the reader, and value for the dollar. Those are important attributes for a test-prep book.

I've added to the mix the same commitment to accuracy that gained my earlier book, *MCSE Windows 98 For Dummies*, wide recognition as the most error-free book available on that exam. I built a test network of four PCs running various versions of Windows, including Windows 2000 Professional and Windows 2000 Server, so that I could test everything in this book against reality.

So, your friends may rib you about buying one of these yellow-and-black titles, but let me encourage you to zing them back when you get your MCSE many weeks (and dollars) before they do.

I've tried to make this the book about the Windows 2000 Professional test that I'd want if I were preparing to take it. I hope you'll tell me how you like this book, and how I can make it better for the next edition. You can reach me through my company's Web site, which is at `http://www.i-sw.com`.

What this book isn't

First off, this book isn't a "preview" based on someone's guess about what the test will look like (or on beta software code). This book is based on Microsoft's published objectives list and on multiple takings of the exam by yours truly. Also, it is based on "golden code" — I'm writing this on a PC running the commercial version of Windows 2000 Professional. This fact means that we are not the first book to market on this particular subject, but the publisher and I will not rush a product like this out the door unless we're confident that it's as relevant and accurate as it needs to be.

This book also isn't an encyclopedia of Windows 2000 Professional information. It only contains stuff that I think you'll need to know on the exam. Therefore, this book is not, or at least should not be, your last stop on the way to Windows 2000 mastery. Passing the test is the first milestone en route to Windows 2000 guru-hood, not the last. You'll need to read other materials, work (and experiment) with the product, and converse with other Windows 2000 experts (for example, on public Internet newsgroups) to gain true practical expertise.

This book isn't a rehash of a text on the Windows NT 4.0 Workstation exam. Windows 2000 is similar to Windows NT 4.0 Workstation in many ways (the newer product's original name was "Windows NT 5.0"), but Windows 2000 has lots of new stuff in it, including a healthy dollop of Windows 98 technology. I wrote this book from the ground up to be 100 percent specific to Windows 2000.

Finally, this book is not a guarantee. If you read it carefully, you should pass the first time you take the test. If you don't, you may not. I can't control whether you study this book earnestly and seriously, or out of the corner of your eye while you are watching *Attack of the Killer Mutant Ninja Hamsters*. I *can* try to do a good job presenting the material you'll need to know in a clear and concise way, and that's been my goal.

Who you are

MCSE Windows 2000 Professional For Dummies is for actual or aspiring computer professionals. I don't make a lot of assumptions in these pages about you or your business, but the few assumptions I do make are as follows:

- You have some prior experience with computers, and you've logged some hours in the air flying Windows 98, 95, or NT 4.0.
- You have better things to do than to read a thousand-page epic on the Windows 2000 certification test.
- You want to pass the certification test on the first try.
- You'd like to pick up some tips in the course of studying for the exam that you'll actually be able to use in real life, once you get a cool job with the help of your MCP or MCSE status.

If this sounds like you, read on!

Who I am

The value of any book depends on the experience of the author, so you should want to know just who the heck is writing this book. I've run a computer consulting business, Independent Software, Inc., since 1982, and I've been a seminar developer and instructor since 1988. As a consultant, I normally work with large organizations on rolling out and supporting Windows technologies, although for a change of pace I provided consulting services and testimony in the Microsoft antitrust trial for about a year. My seminars target the professional technical market, and have included intensive 2-day courses on Windows 3.0, 3.1, 95, 98, and (now) 2000.

An MCSE myself, I've taken more Microsoft exams than I care to remember. I've received MCP status for all versions of Windows since 3.1, and I've also passed various weird limited-time Microsoft tests, such as "Windows 95 Migration Specialist." In addition, I've been a Windows 2000 beta tester for about the last 20 years. (OK, it only seemed that long!)

I've written a few other books on Windows before this one. *Windows 2000 Registry For Dummies, Windows 98 Registry For Dummies,* and *Windows 95 Registry For Dummies* make the inscrutable Registry database at least moderately scrutable. *Bulletproofing Windows 98, Bulletproofing Windows 95,* and *Bulletproofing NetWare* are more technical books in the McGraw-Hill series that I created, focusing on reliability.

How This Book Is Organized

Microsoft publishes a list of *objectives*, or *skills*, for each test in the MCSE series. (You can find them, at this writing, at `www.microsoft.com/Mcp/exam/stat/SP70-210.htm`.) I've designed this book to follow that list. (In a few cases, I've juggled topics so they fit where they make a bit more sense, and in other cases, I've added material that does not appear on the objective list but that shows up on the exam.)

As with most *...For Dummies* books, you can dip in and out of specific chapters according to where you are in your studies and what level of knowledge you already have about particular subjects. You can certainly read this book cover to cover, but each chapter is designed to give you all the information you need on a specific topic and not leave you hanging if you haven't read the entire book up to that point.

Part I: The Backdrop

In Part I, I answer the following burning questions: 1) What's the Windows 2000 Professional test all about? and 2) What are the basics of Windows 2000 Professional that you must know to profitably study the rest of the book? I recommend that everyone read Chapter 1. If you already have a fair amount of hands-on experience with Windows 2000 Professional, skim Chapter 2, and if you see anything that looks new or unfamiliar, read it.

Part II: Planning, Installation, and Basic Configuration

Part II is where you should start if you have to take the test tomorrow and you plan to read all night to get ready. (Not the recommended strategy, by the way.) Chapter 3 deals with file systems: FAT, FAT32, and NTFS. Chapter 4 covers the actual installation, automation options, uninstall procedures, and dual-boot setups. Chapter 5 covers language, localization, and desktop setup issues. Chapter 6 deals with networking protocols, with a decided emphasis on TCP/IP.

Part III: Installing and Configuring Hardware

Windows 2000 Professional brings many new hardware-related features to the table (oops, I mean "desktop"), so Part III looks at them in the detail you'll need. Chapter 7 deals with disks, tapes, and printers. Chapter 8 covers displays and other input/output devices. Chapter 9 focuses on portable computing hardware, including power management and wireless communications.

Part IV: Configuring and Managing Resource Access

In Part IV, I walk you through the essentials of using Windows 2000 to control resource access in a network. Chapter 10 covers resource access on the local machine, exploring concepts of users and groups. Chapter 11 explores the various access restrictions that you can apply to shared folders and NTFS disks, and shows how to share and monitor resources. Chapter 12 examines the core concepts of "IntelliMirror:" the Registry, user profiles, offline folders, and the new Windows Installer service. And Chapter 13 covers resource access via the special case of Dial-Up Networking.

Part V: Tuning and Troubleshooting Windows 2000

Part V shows you, in Chapter 14, how to monitor Windows 2000's performance using the built-in tools — and how to optimize that performance. Chapter 15 covers the key troubleshooting techniques you'll need to correct the more common Windows 2000 problems, and discusses the various methods for recovering a Windows 2000 system that has become damaged.

Part VI: The Part of Tens

The Part of Tens is a standard feature of *...For Dummies* books, and this one is no different. Chapter 16 offers ten test-taking tips that have nothing to do with Windows 2000 but everything to do with passing the exam.

Part VII: Appendixes

The first appendix is a practice test that you can take shortly before the actual exam, to refresh the main points, fill in any gaps in your knowledge, and get you comfortable with the probable format of the actual test questions. The last is a description of the software goodies on the enclosed CD-ROM.

Chapter Structure

You may be familiar with other books in the *...For Dummies* series, but the MCSE books share some design features that don't appear in non-MCSE titles. You'll appreciate their usefulness as you work your way through the chapters, but here's a capsule description of those features.

Page One

The first page of each chapter presents the exam objectives covered by the chapter, along with a brief two- or three-paragraph introduction to the subject matter. If you're in a major hurry, you can use each chapter's first page to focus your attention on the subjects you know least well, and skip chapters covering material you already know.

Quick Assessment

Immediately after the first page is a quick assessment test covering the exam objectives for that chapter. If you get every question right, you may not even need to read the chapter; you should jump to the end and take the "Prep Test." If you miss a few of the quick assessment questions, which is the more normal scenario, you can flag the chapter sections that you should focus on with particular zeal. Little "sticky notes" appear next to the quick assessment questions to help you match the questions with their associated objectives.

Labs, tables, and graphics

Throughout the main part of each chapter are various labs, tables, and graphics to help you study. *Labs* are simply sequences of numbered steps that you can perform on an actual Windows 2000 PC (assuming you have access to one) in order to grasp a subject more fully. *Tables* are columnar lists of information that would be awkward if presented in paragraph form.

Graphics are either screen snapshots of actual Windows 2000 systems or line drawings that illustrate specific points. These features aren't unique to MCSE books, but we do use them a bit more heavily here than in our other titles.

Prep Test

Each chapter of exam material ends with a "prep test" that is designed to look and feel like a chunk of the actual exam. Of course, there's no guarantee that the prep test questions will actually appear on the test, but they're great for double-checking that you really understand the chapter material. They also have value in preparing you for the format of questions that Microsoft likes to use in the real test.

Icons Used in This Book

Several graphical icons highlight certain kinds of material:

Use this icon to avoid a *gotcha* — a common trap or pitfall, either in test-taking technique or in understanding some aspect of Windows 2000.

These are tips to save you time when preparing for, or actually taking, the certification exam.

This icon points out a bit of knowledge that's worth committing to your long-term memory because it's likely to appear in the test.

Short suggestions, hints, and bits of useful information appear next to this icon.

Add this fact to your vocabulary . . . or else!

That's it for this Introduction. Stand up, stretch, pour yourself a cup of tea, and come back when you're ready to start prepping for a successful exam.

Part I
The Backdrop

"Well, shoot—Microsoft left SneakerNet off the exam requirements again."

In this part . . .

You may have never taken a Microsoft certification exam before. You may have never studied Windows 2000 Professional in detail before. In either case, this part's for you. This part may also be for you if you could use a refresher on exam procedure or on Windows 2000 itself.

Every Dummies book is what editors like to call a "non-linear" read; that is, you can dip in and out of different sections as needed, when needed (sort of a literary salad bar). This part is a little bit of an exception. You really should read it, or at least skim over it, before diving into the rest of the book.

Chapter 1 goes over the look and feel of MCSE exams so you have a good sense of what to expect when you walk into that testing room. This chapter also presents Microsoft's objective map for exam #70-210, cross-referenced to chapters in this book. Chapter 2 is a technology primer that outlines key features of the operating system.

Chapter 1

The Windows 2000 Professional Test

In This Chapter

- Finding out how the Windows 2000 Professional test fits into the Microsoft certification scheme
- Getting familiar with testing procedures
- Understanding the test's style and format
- Discovering the list of skills Microsoft says you need to know to pass the test
- Picking up a few hints about test-taking

Microsoft Exam #70-210, which has the catchy name *Installing, Configuring, and Administering Microsoft Windows 2000 Professional*, helps fulfill certification requirements for the following "degrees":

- Microsoft Certified Professional
- Microsoft Certified Professional + Internet
- Microsoft Certified Trainer
- Microsoft Certified System Engineer
- Microsoft Certified System Engineer + Internet

You can read a lot more detail on these (and other) Microsoft certification programs in Appendix C. For now, just know that by passing this test, you not only gain the right to add the MCP certification to your résumé, you also pass a core requirement of the MCSE certification's Windows 2000 track.

If you're familiar with the NT 4.0 MCSE track, please take note. You *must* take Exam #70-210 to achieve Windows 2000 MCSE status, and the Windows 95, 98, and NT Workstation exams don't count for anything toward your Windows 2000 MCSE. This is a change from the NT track, which permitted a choice: You could take a test on Windows 95, Windows 98, or NT Workstation 4.0 to fulfill the workstation exam requirement. That isn't true for the Windows 2000 track.

Is the Windows 2000 Professional exam the only one you want to take? If an MCP is good enough for your needs, 99% of this book remains relevant for you despite the "MCSE" in the title. Your MCP designation will have a longer life if you achieve it with the Windows 2000 Professional exam as opposed to the Windows 98 or Windows NT 4.0 Workstation exams.

If you aspire to MCSE certification, taking the Windows 2000 exam as your first test makes sense.

- You may already know Windows 2000 as a user, so you won't have to start from scratch to know it as a technician.
- You don't have to know much about some challenging Windows 2000 Server topics, such as Active Directory, to pass the Windows 2000 Professional exam.

Having said that, I'm here to tell you that the Windows 2000 Professional test is significantly harder than the Windows 98 test, and that one was no piece of cake! So don't take it lightly, even if you do take it first.

About the Exam

When it comes to MCSE exams, you have to master *both* the style and substance aspects of the tests if you hope to pass them. This section lays out the key points in both categories, but first, a few words on procedure.

Procedure

You should know about a few formalities and procedural issues before diving into the exam.

Signing up

Microsoft exams are delivered by two organizations: Sylvan Prometric and Virtual University Enterprises (VUE). The usual procedure is to get in touch with one of these organizations (either by phone or Web site) at least one day in advance of the test, make payment arrangements (credit cards are okay), and set up a time and a place. Here's some contact information:

- **Sylvan Prometric (`www.prometric.com`, `www.2test.com`):** 800-755-EXAM (from the U.S. and Canada), 410-843-8000 (from anywhere)
- **NCS Virtual University Enterprises (`www.vue.com/ms`):** 888-837-8616 (from the U.S. and Canada), 612-995-8800 (from anywhere)

TIP

Two things can save you trouble when you take the exam:

- Provide a zip code or postal code and let the customer representative find the testing location nearest you. The shorter the drive, the fresher you'll be when you walk into the testing center.
- Call the testing center directly for detailed directions.

Plan to arrive about 15 minutes before test time. At Sylvan Prometric centers, you must normally present two forms of identification, at least one with a photograph on it. You also have to sign a form and a sign-in sheet, which takes a few minutes. However, if you're late, don't fret; depending on how busy the testing center is, you may still be able to slide on in and take your test.

After you sign in, you receive a few sheets of scratch paper and a couple of pencils, and the proctor asks to see your forearms and palms to make sure you haven't made a body part into a human cheat sheet with a Rapidograph technical pen.

Okay, nobody really asks to see your skin. And anyway, scribbling on your epidermis or hiding papers down your pants wouldn't help you, because most test sites have TV cameras watching your every move. Don't be offended by this; video monitoring is a good way to ensure that someone else doesn't gain an unfair advantage over you by cheating.

Agree or go home

As your session at the testing center starts, you have to agree to a statement written by Microsoft that says things like "I agree not to use my belt-buckle spy camera to make screen shots of this test, which I will then sell on the Internet for big bucks." As an honest, upright citizen, you will most likely click the Agree button and move on. (If you want to actually read the agreement, doing so takes no time off the actual exam clock.)

Easy questions that (alas) don't count

You're likely to see a timed questionnaire before the graded test questions. Your answers provide various marketing data to Microsoft. The meter isn't really running during this questionnaire, as the 15 minutes don't count against the 90 minutes you have for the "real" test. So, you can take your time, but I recommend that you blast through the questionnaire quickly without paying a lot of attention. Save your brain cells for the questions that count.

My personal opinion is that if Microsoft wants marketing data, they should pay you, not the other way around. I normally check box "A" on every answer.

Call for comments

At the end of your exam, after you click the Finish button, you have an opportunity to comment on the test. I always feel that this part is premature; I'd like to know whether I passed before telling Microsoft whether its test is excellent or no darned good.

If you do feel strongly about some aspect of the test, then by all means, let your feelings be known. Otherwise, skip this part. You may need to get out of the testing center as quickly as possible, for reasons I explain in a minute.

Signing off

At the end of the test, you find out whether you passed. The two bars at the top of the page indicate the required score and your score.

On some tests, the report breaks down your performance by category, so you can spend a little time reviewing where you did well and where you could have done better. That information may be useful as you study for other exams, if you're en route to your MCSE, or if you need to take the Windows 2000 test again to pass. If the report doesn't break down your performance by category, and if you failed, then you need to read the next section, "Rerun readiness."

After the test, you can click either Exit or Print another report. (One report prints automatically.) Printing one or two extra reports as file copies is a good idea; you can give one to your boss, keep one for your own file, frame another, and so on. You'll most likely have to get the printouts from an administrator after you leave the test center.

Rerun readiness

If you have to take the exam again, increase your odds of success:

1. Leave the testing center.
2. Head for the nearest desk and chair.
3. Whip out a pen and notebook (or notebook computer).
4. Write down as much as you can remember about the questions you just faced — especially the tough ones.

Do this while the material is still fresh in your mind. You're not likely to see all the same questions again next time, but you're likely to see some of them, and if you make some post-mortem notes, you can focus your study time and increase your odds of passing next time.

Style

Knowing something about an exam's design can help get you comfortable with the format in advance, so here are a few words on what you can expect to see after you sign in at the test center.

Microsoft is free to modify the exam format whenever and however it wants. As I write this, the two styles that Microsoft uses are

- "Classic" multiple choice
- Adaptive

This section discusses both. Don't make the assumption that the exam is one style or the other, despite what you may see on various MCSE-related Web sites. Microsoft is known to change a test's style midway through its life cycle. Upon its initial release to the public, Exam #70-210 uses a classic multiple choice format: 50 questions, 90 minutes, and a minimum passing grade of 62 percent.

Choose from multiples

The "classic" MCSE test is a closed-book, multiple-choice exam (no bringing your well-worn copy of this book, and no essay questions such as "Describe the probable impact of Windows 2000 on world history, in 500 words or less"). Computers are well suited for grading multiple-choice tests, and it *is* nice to get your grade right away.

Just because the exam is multiple choice doesn't mean that you can ignore the question format. A common pitfall is giving only one answer when the question calls for multiple answers.

You can usually tell by the graphical element next to the answers:

- If they're circles (radio buttons), only one answer is right.
- If they're squares (check boxes), maybe more than one answer is right.

Be very aware whether the question calls for the best answer, two answers, three answers, "all that apply," or whatever the case may be. I recommend marking questions that expect more than one answer for later review (see "Skipping to success" later in this chapter) because of their inherent trickiness. (Bear in mind that if your test is the adaptive type, you can't mark questions for review. See the section "Adapting to adaptive tests" later in this chapter.)

Some of the questions are pretty long, and they sometimes give you more information than you really need. I'm in favor of reading through these long paragraphs once and only once, noting the key facts (and maybe even drawing a picture) on your scratch paper. This way, you won't have to read those long spiels multiple times.

A graphic example

Some of the questions involve a graphical screen, either as part of the question (the screen is called an *exhibit*) or as the way to provide the answer (the screen is called a *simulation*).

When a graphic is an exhibit, don't skip over it! You can click a button at the question's main screen to show the exhibit, but overlooking the button is possible. Most often, the test question exhibits show a simplified network diagram illustrating the hypothetical setup you're being quizzed about.

Consider looking at the exhibit before even reading the question. That way, you already have a mental picture of the question's premise. You can look at the exhibit as often as you want.

When a graphic is the vehicle for *providing* an answer, it's normally a screen shot of a dialog box or property sheet. The cursor turns into a riflesight icon, and you must point-and-click at the check box(es) or radio button(s) on the dialog box to answer the question. (The inclusion of such dialog boxes and property sheets on the test is one reason I include plenty of screen shots in this book.)

Although no one who can talk about it really knows how accurate you have to be for your answer to register with the test engine, take your time and click right in the middle of the check box or radio button.

No point losing points for poor pointing.

You may also see questions in which you must click one or more computer icons in a network diagram to convey your answer. I've taken some MCSE tests that even ask you to drag-and-drop little graphical boxes saying things like "Application Server" and "Router" onto specific computers in a network diagram. Don't be surprised to see one or two of these drag-and-drop questions on the test.

So, although most of the exam questions and answers don't involve pictures, know how to deal with those that do. By the time you take the test, Microsoft may cook up some other clever graphical exam elements, but at least you'll be aware of the ones in this section, if you encounter them.

Skipping to success

In the classical multiple-choice test style, you can skip any questions you don't immediately understand, and come back to them later. That's actually a good practice. Because your grade in a classical-style test depends solely on the percentage of questions you answer correctly, you need to make sure that you answer as many questions as you can. An unanswered question may as well be wrong; you only get points for questions you answer, and answer correctly.

So, if a question stumps you, go ahead and make your best guess, but "mark" the question for later review by clicking the Mark button on the test screen. Then move on to the next question. After you're done with the first pass through all the questions, you get a review screen that shows the questions you've marked. A click of the mouse takes you back to ponder further on those knotty problems. You may run out of time before you can study all the questions you marked, but at least you're not missing the opportunity to score on questions that you can quickly answer correctly.

If your test uses the classic style, *use every last minute you have coming to you*. You may very well finish in less than the allotted 90 minutes, especially if you've done a great job preparing by studying this book carefully. So apply these rules:

- Take the time to go back and review questions that you marked, especially those asking for multiple answers.
- Look for keywords in the test questions that may offer a clue that you missed on first glance.
- Draw diagrams.
- For questions that you don't understand well, use the process of elimination to improve your odds.

Adapting to adaptive tests

Adaptive, or "hybrid" tests, have two parts:

- A regular, what-percent-did-you-get-right part
- An adaptive part

Unfortunately, you don't necessarily know where the dividing line is between the two parts, so you may have to treat the whole test as if it is adaptive, unless Microsoft gives you some clues in the testing instructions.

Okay — so what does "adaptive" mean? An *adaptive* exam grades based on the hardest question you can answer on the subject matter of the test. You encounter a series of questions of increasing difficulty. Each question depends on the previous answer: If you got the previous answer correct, then you get a harder question, but if you got it wrong, then you get an easier question. The questions "adapt" to your answers.

Pace yourself using the on-screen clock. Adaptive tests don't have as many questions, so you can allow yourself more time per question than on a classic-style test. However, you typically don't know in advance how many questions you'll receive. What I usually do is take the average of the maximum and minimum number of questions (the test tells you this information) and calculate the approximate amount of time you should spend per question using that number.

You don't have the luxury of marking and reviewing questions on an adaptive exam: You have one shot at each question. So the test-taking style is very different indeed from the "classic" test in which your grade depends solely on the percentage of questions you answer correctly. Here are two suggestions for taking an adaptive test:

- Go slowly and carefully.
- Do your best on each question, skipping none of them.

Substance

This section deals in more detail with exam content. First, I present the formal Microsoft test objectives, then I offer a few subjective comments.

Testing by objectives

When the "real" part of the test begins, you deal with exam questions designed to test your knowledge in a wide variety of areas. Microsoft publishes objectives, or "skill areas," for each MCP exam on its Web site under `www.microsoft.com/mcp`. (These objectives appear elsewhere, too, sometimes in somewhat different form, as in the *Microsoft Windows 2000 Professional MCSE Training Kit*, which you don't need to buy now that you have this book.) In the following sections, I provide Microsoft's objective list for the Windows 2000 Professional exam at this writing, along with a cross-reference to the relevant chapter in this book.

This book's organization doesn't match the organization of the objective list for the good reason that the objective list's organization is (in my humble opinion) a confusing mess. I've rearranged the flow of subjects for easier learning. For example, what do you do when you set up a new PC? You typically choose a file system, install the operating system, install the networking software, and get all your hardware working. Later, you set up users and groups, define access permissions, set up user profiles, and the like. Typically, the last things you do are to optimize the performance of your system and troubleshoot anything that isn't working. That's the organization of this book.

The formal list is subject to change at any time, so you may want to see whether Microsoft has added or removed topics by checking the Web site. However, don't take the list of objectives as gospel. Some exam questions don't relate to the stated objectives, and, conversely, any given exam may not cover every stated objective. If I spend some time on a subject that doesn't explicitly appear in the objective list at the start of the chapter, you can assume that I saw one or more exam questions covering that subject!

Installing Windows 2000 Professional

- Perform an attended installation of Windows 2000 Professional. (See Chapter 4.)
- Perform an unattended installation of Windows 2000 Professional. Methods include using Windows 2000 Server Remote Installation Services (RIS), using the System Preparation Tool, and creating unattended answer files by using Setup Manager. (See Chapter 4.)
- Upgrade from a previous version of Windows to Windows 2000 Professional. Methods include applying update packs to installed software applications and preparing a computer to meet upgrade requirements. (See Chapter 4.)
- Deploy service packs. (See Chapter 4.)
- Troubleshoot failed installations. (See Chapter 15.)

Implementing and Conducting Administration of Resources

- Monitor, manage, and troubleshoot access to files and folders. Methods include configuring, managing, and troubleshooting file compression. (See Chapter 3.)
- Monitor, manage, and troubleshoot access to files and folders. Methods include controlling access to files and folders by using permissions and optimizing access to files and folders. (See Chapter 11.)
- Manage and troubleshoot access to shared folders. Methods include creating and removing shared folders, controlling access to shared folders by using permissions, and managing and troubleshooting Web server resources. (See Chapter 11.)
- Connect to local and network print devices. Methods include managing printers and print jobs, controlling access to printers by using permissions, connecting to an Internet printer, and connecting to a local print device. (See Chapter 7.)
- Configure and manage file systems. Methods include converting from one file system to another file system, and configuring file systems by using NTFS, FAT32, or FAT. (See Chapter 3.)

Implementing, Managing, and Troubleshooting Hardware Devices and Drivers

- Implement, manage, and troubleshoot disk devices. Methods include installing, configuring, and managing DVD and CD-ROM devices; monitoring and configuring disks; monitoring, configuring, and troubleshooting volumes; and monitoring and configuring removable media, such as tape devices. (See Chapter 7.)
- Implement, manage, and troubleshoot display devices. Methods include configuring multiple-display support and installing, configuring, and troubleshooting a video adapter. (See Chapter 8.)
- Implement, manage, and troubleshoot mobile computer hardware. Methods include configuring Advanced Power Management (APM) and configuring and managing card services. (See Chapter 9.)
- Implement, manage, and troubleshoot input and output (I/O) devices. Methods include monitoring, configuring, and troubleshooting I/O devices, such as printers, scanners, multimedia devices, mouse, keyboard, and smart card reader; monitoring, configuring, and troubleshooting multimedia hardware, such as cameras; installing, configuring, and managing modems; and installing, configuring, and managing USB devices. (See Chapter 8.)
- Implement, manage and troubleshoot input and output (I/O) devices. Methods include installing, configuring, and managing Infrared Data Association (IrDA) devices, and installing, configuring, and managing wireless devices. (See Chapter 9.)
- Update drivers. (See Chapter 15.)
- Monitor and configure multiple processing units. (See Chapter 14.)
- Install, configure, and troubleshoot network adapters. (See Chapter 6.)

Monitoring and Optimizing System Performance and Reliability

- Manage and troubleshoot driver signing. (See Chapter 15.)
- Configure, manage, and troubleshoot the Task Scheduler. (See Chapter 14.)
- Manage and troubleshoot the use and synchronization of offline files. (See Chapter 12.)
- Optimize and troubleshoot performance of the Windows 2000 Professional desktop. Methods include optimizing and troubleshooting memory performance; optimizing and troubleshooting processor utilization; optimizing and troubleshooting disk performance; optimizing and troubleshooting network performance; and optimizing and troubleshooting application performance. (See Chapter 14.)
- Manage hardware profiles. (See Chapter 9.)

- Recover systems and user data. Methods include recovering systems and user data by using Windows Backup; troubleshooting system restoration by using Safe Mode; and recovering systems and user data by using the Recovery Console. (See Chapter 15.)

Configuring and Troubleshooting the Desktop Environment

- Configure and manage user profiles. (See Chapter 12.)
- Configure support for multiple languages or multiple locations. Methods include enabling multiple-language support; configuring multiple-language support for users; configuring local settings; and configuring Windows 2000 Professional for multiple locations. (See Chapter 5.)
- Install applications by using Windows Installer packages. (See Chapter 12.)
- Configure and troubleshoot desktop settings. (See Chapter 5.)
- Configure and troubleshoot fax support. (See Chapter 7.)
- Configure and troubleshoot accessibility services. (See Chapter 5.)

Implementing, Managing, and Troubleshooting Network Protocols and Services

- Configure and troubleshoot the TCP/IP protocol. (See Chapter 6.)
- Connect to computers by using dial-up networking. Methods include connecting to computers by using a virtual private network (VPN) connection; creating a dial-up connection to connect to a remote access server; connecting to the Internet by using dial-up networking; and configuring and troubleshooting Internet Connection Sharing. (See Chapter 13.)
- Connect to shared resources on a Microsoft network. (See Chapter 11.)

Implementing, Monitoring, and Troubleshooting Security

- Encrypt data on a hard disk by using Encrypting File System (EFS). (See Chapter 3.)
- Implement, configure, manage, and troubleshoot local Group Policy. (See Chapter 11.)
- Implement, configure, manage, and troubleshoot local user accounts. Methods include implementing, configuring, managing, and troubleshooting auditing; implementing, configuring, managing, and troubleshooting account settings; implementing, configuring, managing, and troubleshooting account policy; creating and managing local users and groups; and implementing, configuring, managing, and troubleshooting user rights. (See Chapter 10.)
- Implement, configure, manage, and troubleshoot local user authentication. Methods include configuring and troubleshooting local user accounts, and configuring and troubleshooting domain user accounts. (See Chapter 10.)
- Implement, configure, manage, and troubleshoot a security configuration. (See Chapter 12.)

Hints that may help

Here are a few tips to smooth your way to Microsoft certification:

- Although the formal list of objectives is incredibly wide-ranging, expect a heavy focus on features that are new since Windows NT 4.0 Workstation. For example, you can bet the exam includes questions on Plug and Play, power management, personalized menus, Active Directory, dynamic disks, file protection, encryption, safe mode boot, recovery console, management consoles, and so on.

  I try to highlight such features in each chapter to help you focus on them.
- Know Windows 2000 Server features before taking the Windows 2000 Professional test. You don't have to know how to set up DHCP, DNS, WINS, and Active Directory on the server to pass Exam #70-210, but you should have an understanding of those technologies as Windows 2000 Server implements them. Microsoft always throws in a fair dose of networking material in its workstation operating system exams.
- Most people learn best by doing. Therefore, if at all possible, set yourself up a little test network consisting of at least one Windows 2000 Professional PC and one Windows 2000 Server PC. You can use an old and slow "leftover" computer for the server PC if you're just using it for educational purposes. (Don't go slower than a Pentium 200 with 64MB of RAM.)
- After you pass the test, reward yourself! Buy that CD you've been wanting, go to the movies, pick up some real French champagne — do whatever you do for fun.

From a psychological standpoint, rewarding yourself for passing each test gives you positive reinforcement for the next test. But that's not why you should do it. Good work deserves celebration. When I finish this book, for example, I plan to buy a brand new, bright red Porsche Boxster. (Assuming, of course, that I can convince my publisher that covering the down payment would be a great way to reward a hardworking author.)

Chapter 2

Fundamentals of Windows 2000

In This Chapter

- Getting to know the members of the Windows family tree
- Mastering the basics of the Windows 2000 architecture (non-Ph.D. version)
- Finding out what sets Windows 2000 apart from Windows NT Workstation 4.0

None of the material in this chapter is on the exam. However, all of the material in this chapter is on the exam.

What I mean is this: You need a good basic understanding of the Windows 2000 history and architecture to deal with some of the detailed questions that presume such an understanding. For example, you may encounter a question that asks about the relative merits of Windows 2000 versus Windows NT Workstation or Windows 98 when it comes to installing Plug and Play hardware. (2000 and 98 support Plug and Play, but NT doesn't.) For another example, you may be expected to understand what the HAL is. (It's the *Hardware Abstraction Layer,* a key component of the Windows 2000 Professional operating system that determines, among other things, power management and Plug and Play capabilities.)

My suggestion is that you get comfortable with this information before you move on to the detailed chapters. I keep it brief and avoid arcane topics that probably won't surface on the exam.

Comfortable with the information that I present in this chapter? You're ready to move on to specific exam preparation in the remainder of the book. Still not sure of yourself after poring over this chapter a couple of times? Look for a good general book on Windows 2000, such as *Windows 2000 Professional For Dummies,* or *Windows 2000 Secrets.*

Windows Operating Systems

This section explains where Windows 2000 falls within the Windows product family. In a nutshell, Windows 2000 combines many of the benefits of both its ancestors, Windows 98 and Windows NT 4.0. To be thorough, however, I have to begin this section with a quick look at Windows 3.*x*.

The Windows 3.x clan

Windows 3.*x* (that is, Windows 3.0, Windows 3.1, Windows for Workgroups 3.1, and Windows for Workgroups 3.11) is still in use worldwide. Microsoft describes all Windows 3.*x* products as operating *environments* rather than operating systems, because Windows 3.*x* doesn't entirely replace MS-DOS. Windows 3.*x* is 16-bit software, and application programs written for Windows 3.*x* are (with rare exceptions) also 16-bit software.

Windows 3.1 brought the PC user the following key elements:

- A graphical user interface using drop-down menus, dialog boxes, program icons and groups, and (to some extent) a drag-and-drop metaphor
- A platform for applications that can use more memory than 640K
- A vehicle for running multiple applications simultaneously *(cooperative multitasking)* and for rapidly switching between applications loaded in memory *(task switching)*
- An environment where all programs use a single set of print and screen drivers
- A structure for exchanging data more easily between programs

Windows for Workgroups 3.1 introduced peer networking. Its successor, Version 3.11 (late 1993), was a much more stable and versatile network client than its predecessors.

Windows 3.*x* and DOS machines use the old 8.3 file-naming convention, and therefore can't see the full name of a shared folder on a Windows 2000 PC if that folder's share name exceeds the 8.3 limit.

The Windows 9x clan

Windows 95 (August 1995) and its successor, Windows 98 (June 1998), bring 32-bit capabilities to the Intel-and-compatible PC, along with a heavily revised user interface. Windows 9*x* (as the exam may refer to versions 98 and 95 collectively) focuses on compatibility, whereas Windows NT and Windows 2000 focus on security and reliability.

Design goals

The nine key goals of the Windows 9*x* design team tell you nearly all you need to know about where Windows 9*x* fits in regard to Windows 3.*x*, NT, and 2000. The goals are:

- **Compatibility.** If you have an old DOS device driver that loads in CONFIG.SYS or AUTOEXEC.BAT, chances are excellent that you can use that device with Windows 9*x*. Need to run an old 16-bit Windows 3.1 application? It probably runs fine under Windows 9*x*, too.
- **Performance.** Windows 9*x* was designed to perform well under low memory conditions, so its designers had to forgo the extra layers of memory protection that make NT and 2000 more reliable.
- **Robustness.** Windows 9*x* is more reliable than Windows 3.*x* (fewer crashes and lockups), and less reliable than NT or 2000.
- **Better setup and configuration.** Windows 9*x* autodetects a wide variety of hardware during setup, in large part thanks to the Plug and Play standard. You can install Windows 9*x* from a network server as well as a CD-ROM, and the Batch Setup tool helps you script LAN-based installations. As for configuring the software, Windows 9*x* control panels use the Registry database for most system settings, centralizing such settings but adding to system complexity.
- **Better user interface.** The Start button, taskbar, and property sheet made their debut in Windows 95, along with dozens of other user interface (UI) changes and a new emphasis on the right mouse button. Windows 98 makes few changes to the core UI of Windows 95, although the Web View of folders and the Active Desktop add a new Internet look.
- **Protected mode design.** Nearly everything in Windows 9*x* runs in the Intel processor's "protected mode," which affords better reliability, as opposed to the "real mode" that DOS software uses.
- **Support for 32-bit applications.** Windows 9*x* can run 32-bit applications, conferring upon them goodies such as a private memory space, preemptive multitasking, and multithreaded execution. However, Windows 9*x* does not use 32-bit software through and through; many modules are still 16-bit code.
- **Better client and workgroup functionality.** Windows 9*x* contains the peer-to-peer networking capabilities introduced by Windows for Workgroups, adding peer services for Novell networks, too. Microsoft also provides better support for multiple concurrent networks, 32-bit network components at every level, a more modular design, and better speed.
- **Better mobile computing support.** From Dial-Up Networking to the Direct Cable Connection and Briefcase, Windows 9*x* makes life easier on road warriors who need to connect to office or public networks.

Versions

The important distinctions that you should know for the exam, and for real life, are between the original Windows 95, Windows 95 "OSR2," Windows 98, and Windows 98 Second Edition (see Table 2-1). (You can check the version number for all Windows 9*x* products by right-clicking the My Computer icon, choosing Properties, and looking at the version on the General tab.)

Table 2-1 Windows 9*x* Versions

Version	*Distinguishing Features*
4.00.950	Original Windows 95 product
4.00.950a	Windows 95 with Service Pack 1, which corrected mostly minor bugs
4.00.950B, 4.00.950C	OSR2, or OEM Service Release 2 Windows 95 variant that added the FAT32 file system and (with "C") USB support
4.10.1998	Windows 98, mainly a bug fix release with some handy new utilities
4.10.2222A	Windows 98 Second Edition, more bug fixes and Internet Connection Sharing

The Windows NT/2000 clan

Windows NT and Windows 2000 can both function as workstation operating systems or as server operating systems. In either situation, Microsoft recommends these products for situations in which security and reliability take precedence over maximum hardware and software compatibility.

Reliability and security

Reliability in the NT platform is achieved through various architectural characteristics, including the following:

- Support for only 32-bit device drivers. 16-bit drivers and Windows 9*x*-style VxDs (virtual device drivers) are a major source of Windows 9*x* and 3.*x* crashes.
- Total hardware protection (software is never allowed to communicate directly with a device) via a Hardware Abstraction Layer, or HAL.
- Restricted list of approved hardware devices compared to Windows 9*x* (see HCL.TXT in the SUPPORT directory of the Windows 2000 CD-ROM for the Hardware Compatibility List).

Windows 2000 and NT have their own self-contained security system (users, passwords, permissions, rights, and so on). This is in sharp contrast to Windows 9*x*, which offers only relatively weak share-level security or which can leverage the security capabilities of NT or NetWare.

The price of progress

Microsoft has said for a long time that the NT product line is its long-term, strategic platform. Nevertheless, NT and its successor, Windows 2000 (formerly Windows NT 5.0!), have not made Windows 9*x* obsolete, nor are they likely to do so anytime soon. The main reason is that for many customers, a move to NT or Windows 2000 means abandoning some older software and hardware. In order to provide enhanced reliability and security, the NT/2000 product line sacrifices compatibility with some legacy devices and programs. Windows 2000 and NT operating systems don't support DOS-style device drivers, and they don't support all 16-bit Windows programs.

Here's a quick check for legacy issues:

- If an exam question refers to 16-bit software, remember that Windows 98 provides a greater likelihood of compatibility than Windows NT or Windows 2000.
- If a question refers to "real-mode device drivers," or "legacy device drivers," know that Windows 2000 doesn't support them at *all*. They're the kind of device drivers that load via CONFIG.SYS or AUTOEXEC.BAT.

What NT4 and 2000 have in common

You should understand the basic differences between the NT/2000 products and the Windows 9*x* products. Here are some of the key common features of NT/2000:

- Full 32-bit operating system.
- High reliability. All applications and the operating system itself run in protected memory areas.
- Preemptive multitasking for all applications, providing generally better performance running 32-bit software. Windows 9*x* uses the less sophisticated *cooperative* multitasking for 16-bit applications.
- Support for symmetrical multiprocessing; that is, multiple CPUs in the same box. Windows 2000 Professional supports machines having either one processor or two processors. Other versions of Windows 2000 support more.
- High-performance file system (NTFS) with transaction logging and file-level security. Windows 9*x* only offers folder-level security.
- Incompatibility with real-mode device drivers and with software that tries to "speak" directly to hardware devices.

What's New about 2000?

What's new with Windows 2000? That's a hugely important question, because the exam tends to focus on these new features.

Windows 2000 flavors

First, the family tree has some new (and renamed) leaves. Windows 2000 isn't really one product, it's four:

- Windows 2000 Professional (the successor to Windows NT Workstation)
- The Windows 2000 Server family, which is available in three flavors:
  - Windows 2000 Server (the basic package)
  - Windows 2000 Advanced Server (successor to Windows NT Server, Enterprise Edition)
  - Windows 2000 Datacenter Server

Windows 2000 Professional is sometimes described as Windows NT 4.0 Workstation plus Plug and Play and power management. That's reasonably accurate for a one-sentence description, but Windows 2000 offers a lot more than that. (Weighing in at over 600 megabytes of disk space, it should!)

Windows 2000 represents a combination of the Windows 9*x* and NT product lines in the following ways:

- Tight security is available but you don't have to use all the security features.
- Compatibility with DOS and DOS games is better than NT but still not as good as 9*x*.
- Reliability is very good but ease of use is near that of Windows 9*x*.
- Workgroup networking and client/server networking are both supported.
- Works on more hardware than NT4 (largely thanks to Plug and Play) but less than Windows 9*x*.

Without question, Windows 2000 is more nearly "Windows NT 5.0" than it is "Windows 99," but the new operating system borrows much of the user interface and hardware support technology from Windows 98.

The remainder of this section compares Windows 2000 Professional to its nearest cousin, Windows NT 4.0 Workstation. The new goodies break out into the following categories:

- Active Directory
- IntelliMirror
- Active Desktop and Internet software
- Security
- Usability
- Hardware
- Deployment
- Management

Each category is covered in the following sections.

Active Directory

One of the most important new features of Windows 2000, at least for network users, is *Active Directory* (AD). AD is supposed to act like a master Rolodex for your whole network: It contains details on all network resources, from users and groups to printers and programs. Actually, AD is a bit more like a security guard holding a master Rolodex, because AD also handles access control. AD uses constructs to organize the network, such as

- Forests
- Trees
- Domains
- Organizational units
- Groups

The Active Directory model simplifies the earlier Windows NT 4.0 networking model in some ways.

- **All domain controllers are peers.**

  The concept of primary and backup domain controllers is gone.

- **Trust relationships are transitive.**

  That is, if domain A trusts domain B and B trusts C, then A trusts C. This simplifies network design and administration.

- **A single database contains the entire network directory, instead of a collection of databases.**

  The network directory data moves out of the Registry and into a more extensible, scalable, and speedy structure.

Many of the benefits of Windows 2000 are possible only when a combination of Windows 2000 Servers and Windows 2000 Professional clients interact in the context of Active Directory.

Other exams in the Windows 2000 track zero in on AD, but you can bet you'll see some related material on Exam #70-210.

IntelliMirror

IntelliMirror is a marketing term for a collection of technologies designed to let users move more freely around the network and on the road while maintaining their own settings, preferences, applications, and documents. Here are two key advantages:

- My Documents is included in user profiles.
- Users can designate folders as "available offline."

The network impact of offline folders and frequent synchronization can be significant. Chapter 12 looks closely at IntelliMirror.

Active Desktop and Internet software

Windows 2000 includes the Internet Explorer 5 Web browser with the operating system and also provides a "Web view" option for folders and for the desktop itself. The Web view feature lets users specify an HTML file, with whatever objects you want to include (ActiveX, Java, and so on), to appear as the desktop or folder background. The Web objects occupy a layer underneath the typical desktop and folder icons.

Web view also allows you to specify that:

- Selectable objects should appear underlined, as they do on a Web page.
- Moving a cursor over an object highlights it.
- Single-clicking a highlighted object activates it, instead of double-clicking.
- Thumbnails of selected data files appear in a separate windowpane.

Active Desktop lets you plop an entire Web page onto the desktop as well, in which case you can tell Windows 2000 how often you'd like it to be updated. Active Desktop also includes a number of enhancements not related in any functional way to Internet technologies, such as new support for drag-and-drop operations on the taskbar.

The "single Explorer" aspect of Windows 2000 means that you can

- Invoke a Web-browsing window from a Windows Explorer screen by typing the URL (Uniform Resource Locator) into the address bar.
- Switch between the local view and the browser view by using the Back and Forward buttons.

  Most of the menu bar buttons change between the two views, which is why I put "single Explorer" in quotes when introducing this list.

Microsoft has brought Internet technology into the help system, too, by making HTML documents the starting point instead of RTF (Rich Text Format) documents. HTML Help

- Functions like the Windows 98 help engine.
- Lets application vendors add graphics more easily.

Windows 2000 Professional comes with a variety of other Internet-related software, such as

- Outlook Express.
- NetMeeting.
- Internet Information Server (IIS).
- Indexing Service. This is an IIS feature (off by default) that accelerates local drive searches.

Security

Windows 2000 updates and expands security options.

- **The Kerberos security protocol replaces the older, slower NTLM mechanism for LAN communications.**

  Kerberos is the big news in Windows 2000 security.
- **Encryption joins the NTFS file system.**

  Users can encrypt data files so no one else can open or modify those files.
- **The TCP/IP protocol that underlies Internet applications is improved.**
- **Communication is more secure with new support for**
  - IPsec (secure IP)
  - L2TP (Layer 2 Tunneling Protocol)

- **The default access control restrictions for the file system and the Registry are stricter for Windows 2000 than for Windows NT Workstation 4.0.**
- **A *regular* user account in NT may need to be upgraded to a *power* user account in Windows 2000 to perform the same tasks and run the same applications.**
- **Windows 2000 supports hardware-based authentication devices, such as "smart cards."**

  These are common in the military and are becoming popular in the corporate world.

Usability

Windows 2000 makes a number of strides forward (and a couple backward) compared to the NT 4.0 platform when it comes to usability, but the user interface isn't much different from that of Windows 98 — just a few evolutionary improvements.

Dialog boxes

Various dialog boxes have been refined in Windows 2000, such as the Open, Save As, Logon, and Shut Down dialog boxes. These improvements are generally of the incremental, evolutionary nature. If you see any dialog boxes on the exam, you should find the changes intuitive and easy to grasp.

New wizards

The Network Connection wizard is the most important new one in Windows 2000 Professional (Windows 2000 Server has lots and lots of new wizards).

New to Microspeak? A "wizard" is a guided sequence of steps that helps the user accomplish a common task.

AutoComplete and MRU lists

Many Windows 2000 dialog boxes automatically complete fields as the user begins typing them.

AutoComplete creates convenience for some and security holes for others. The list of Most Recently Used (MRU) lists has grown very long indeed, including even individual fields on Web site forms, and Microsoft has not provided a mechanism for clearing them all. Where the security and privacy of user computing aren't important, AutoComplete and the proliferation of MRU lists save users time while going about daily tasks.

Personalized menus

After a period of time, Windows 2000 begins hiding menu selections that users have not chosen. The Start menu and its cascading submenus show only recently used choices, hiding others beneath a chevron character that, if clicked, shows (after a delay) all the menu options.

Organizations must weigh the potential convenience of disappearing menu options against the potential confusion and delays it can introduce. Personalized menus may be easily disabled via a dialog box, policy setting, or Registry setting.

Hardware

The big news when it comes to hardware support is in

- Power management
- Plug and Play
- Device and bus support
- Driver signing

Power management

Windows 2000 manages PC power much differently than Windows NT 4.0. In fact, power management is tied very closely to Plug and Play. Two acronyms come into play here:

- **APM,** or Advanced Power Management, is an older standard that was less than rigorous and therefore inconsistently implemented. Most PCs built before 1999 use APM if they offer any power management features at all.
- **ACPI,** or Advanced Configuration and Power Interface, is a newer standard that is more completely defined. Windows 2000 much prefers ACPI to APM. ACPI is a better-defined standard that gives more control to the operating system and less to the BIOS.

On ACPI machines, Windows 2000's better power management makes it a viable, and even convenient, operating system for notebook computers that meet Windows 2000's hardware requirements — something that could never truly be said about Windows NT 4.0 Workstation. Standby and hibernate modes are both supported.

Plug and Play

Windows 2000 builds on the Plug and Play support in Windows 98. It puts to shame the limited add-in Plug and Play support that you could retrofit to Windows NT Workstation 4.0. Windows 2000 does a pretty good job of detecting and configuring most Plug and Play hardware.

Modems and COM ports are unhappy exceptions — you must usually detect these devices manually, via the Phone and Modem Options control panel or the Add New Hardware wizard.

Improvements include

- Eliminating resource assignment spreadsheets, which were required by Windows NT 4.0.
- Reducing the likelihood that the operating system won't be able to boot because of hardware problems.

PCs designed to the ACPI specification work *much* better with Plug and Play.

New devices and buses

Windows 2000 supports a variety of new (to the NT platform) devices and buses, including:

- **Universal Serial Bus (USB)**

  A single daisy-chained cable to connect keyboards, speakers, scanners, mice, monitors, and other devices to a PC port. The port only uses one interrupt.
- **FireWire (IEEE 1394)**

  Transfer rates are high enough to handle consumer electronic devices, such as camcorders and VCRs.
- **DVD**

  The standard read-only flavor is supported. DVDs can hold video, audio, and computer data on the same disc.
- **Digital scanners and cameras**

  Digital scanners and cameras even have their own control panel icon.
- **Multiple displays**

  Graphics professionals and power users can connect extra monitors to make larger continuous desktops.

  The feature is limited to AGP and PCI adapters. Even then, not all models work.

With respect to disk drive management, Windows 2000 brings three new items to the table.

- The space-saving FAT32 file system introduced in Windows 95 OSR2 comes with Windows 2000, along with a one-way conversion utility.
  - Windows 2000 supports FAT32 on any partition, including the boot partition.
  - FAT32 lets you create much larger disk partitions than FAT16 but remains less secure and reliable than NTFS.
- Windows 2000 introduces *version 5* of *NTFS*, the NT File System.This is the recommended file system for Windows 2000. It provides
  - File-and-folder security
  - Extensible volumes
  - Support for multiple-disk stripe sets
  - Encryption (but not simultaneously with compression)
  - Compression (but not simultaneously with encryption)
- Windows 2000 now includes a basic *disk defragmenter*.

Driver signing

Windows 2000 provides a new level of authentication called *driver signing*. Microsoft brands a *digital signature* into the core operating system files and drivers that it ships with Windows 2000.

- Windows 2000 can tell when a program installation tries to replace one of those core files with a version not "signed" by Microsoft.
- Administrators can control whether any given PC can accept unsigned drivers.

The *Windows File Protection* background program watches system files and replaces them if necessary with "known good" versions from a special "hip pocket" folder named DLLCACHE.

Deployment

Windows 2000 makes several changes to installation and deployment.

Interactive installations

The Windows 2000 installation process is improved in some ways over that for Windows NT 4.0 and Windows 9*x*, and regresses in other ways.

Here are some positive aspects of the new installation procedure:

- Fewer reboots
- Better (although not perfect) "clumping" of question-and-answer screens
- Better overall hardware detection than Windows NT 4.0
- More wizards to ease setup chores (especially valuable in Server)

On the minus side, customers have less choice about which accessories, applets, and options should be installed.

- The familiar "typical," "custom," and "minimal" installation options are gone.
- The only area in which an interactive user can choose components to install is in the networking area.

The lack of flexibility afforded to customers in this area is one reason the hardware requirements are dramatically higher for Windows 2000 than for Windows 98 or even NT 4.

Automated installations

Microsoft has introduced two new options for automated deployment of the Windows 2000 operating system:

- **Remote Installation Service (RIS)**

  With RIS, a server can install Windows 2000 onto a PC that doesn't even have an operating system on it.
- **SysPrep**

  Use this with disk-cloning software such as Ghost or Drive Image. SysPrep helps create the master image, and your cloning software duplicates it.

The usual scripted installation options using "answer files" are still available, too.

New migration paths

You can now upgrade a Windows 95 or 98 system to Windows 2000. A direct upgrade path from the 9*x* platform to Windows NT 4.0 never existed. Having said that, the upgrade path from Windows NT 4.0 to Windows 2000 is likely to be smoother, due to the greater similarities between the two operating systems.

Management

Microsoft says that it's focusing on TCO (Total Cost of Ownership) these days, and administrators may be able to reduce TCO with certain new Windows 2000 features.

Group Policy

Policies are a mechanism for implementing and controlling the various other types of Windows 2000 security, not a new type of security themselves. Policies can be

- Local only
- Network-based only (using Active Directory)
- Both local and network-based

Think of policies as the "rules of the house" that set forth all the security restrictions (both machine-specific and user- and group-specific) that you've chosen to implement.

After an administrator sets policies, policies automatically modify the Registry (applying security, user-interface consistency, or both) at

- Boot time
- Logon time
- Periodic refresh intervals

Technically, Windows 2000 policies work differently on

- Standalone machines
- Computers in a solely Windows 2000 network
- Computers in mixed-mode networks with Windows NT 4.0 clients

Winning the award for most awkward name for a software utility, Microsoft calls the Windows 2000 implementation of policies "Group Policy."

- The Local Group Policy utility runs on local workstations.
- The Group Policy property sheets are included in the various Active Directory administrative tools on a Windows 2000 server.

Automatic IP Addressing

Automatic IP Addressing allows Windows 2000 PCs to assign themselves IP addresses if no address server exists on the network. (Windows 98 also offers this capability.) That's handy for computers on purely private networks, that is, networks that don't need to connect to the public Internet.

Microsoft Management Console

Windows 2000 uses a new kind of control panel in addition to the older *.CPL files. This new variation is called *Microsoft Management Console*, or *MMC* for short. Microsoft used MMCs in a few products (such as its Internet server software) before Windows 2000, and it seems to be the way the company is moving.

MMC is a little like a standard car chassis within which software developers can put whatever engine they want. The framework has some consistent elements, but the contents of any given MMC window may vary greatly. One nice feature of MMC is that it enables administrators to build their own customized consoles with whatever "snap-ins" they find most useful.

Windows Update

Windows 98's Windows Update migrates intact to Windows 2000. This feature allows a user to connect to a Microsoft Web site that downloads ActiveX controls to the PC. Those programs then scan the software environment, consult a central Microsoft server, and present recommended downloads to the user, even organizing them by priority (critical, nice-to-have, etc.).

WARNING!

With users free to run Windows Update at random times and free to choose whichever updates they deem appropriate, administrators, technicians, and troubleshooters can't know in advance just what updates any given PC may contain. You can disable Windows Update through the Group Policy tool, discussed in Chapter 11.

Windows Installer

The new Windows Installer model attempts to bring some order to the chaos of application installation. Some key elements of Windows Installer technology include the following:

- Organized "package" file format that lists application actions in a structured and organized manner
- One-click installation repair capability
- Full uninstall capability (including Registry entries)

Understanding the Windows 2000 Architecture

This section presents a very concise overview of the Windows 2000 architecture for those of you unfamiliar with Windows NT 4.0. (The underlying architecture is very similar between the two operating systems.)

The three "multi's" — multitasking, multithreading, and multiprocessing

If you're a computer user with a working knowledge, the following list is a valuable clarification of terms that are used randomly in the computing world, but have very specific meanings:

- *Multitasking* runs multiple programs at the same time.

  Actually, the computer *seems* to be doing multiple things at once but is really slicing up CPU (Central Processing Unit) time into tiny amounts and distributing it to multiple activities.

  Windows 9*x*, NT, and 2000 use a clever system called *preemptive* multitasking.

  - The operating system figures out in advance how much CPU time each program gets when its turn comes around (that job is handled by the scheduler).
  - The operating system can jump in and suspend a piggish application instead of waiting for it to yield control.

- Windows 3.*x* can multitask, but only in a fairly unsophisticated manner known as *cooperative* multitasking. In that model, programs are expected to be good citizens, periodically yielding control of the computer to other programs. Windows 3.*x* has no way of "giving the hook" to a program that's hogging the stage.
- *Multithreading* means that a single program can create (or *spawn*) several threads of execution that proceed simultaneously. For example, a word processor may spawn a spell-check task in a separate, independent thread, while another thread performs document repagination at the same time. Windows 9*x*, NT, and 2000 support multithreading.
- *Multiprocessing* means that the operating system can use more than one CPU.

Windows 2000 and NT support multiprocessing, but Windows 9*x* does not.

  - Windows 2000 Professional supports machines having either one or two CPUs.
  - Windows 2000 Server supports up to four CPUs (more with vendor-specific support). Windows 2000 Advanced Server supports up to 8, and Datacenter Server up to 32.

- The type of multiprocessing supported by Windows 2000 is *symmetric* (the acronym is SMP); each CPU is the same and has access to the same memory. Many operating system tasks still run only on the first CPU in a multi-CPU system.

User mode and kernel mode

Any given program or thread in Windows 2000 runs in either *user mode* or *kernel mode.*

- **User mode is safer, slower, and further removed from the underlying hardware.** Applications run in user mode.
- **Kernel mode is riskier, faster, and closer to the hardware.** Core operating system functions run in kernel mode, such as
  - Memory management
  - File system management
  - Device driver management

Virtual memory

Every loaded 32-bit program in a Windows 2000 environment thinks that it has access to a 4GB address space, half of which it can use for its own code, and half of which is reserved for operating system code (the API). However, Windows 2000 and all Windows applications can only use a maximum of 4GB physical memory on the entire PC. The way in which Windows lets multiple programs think that they can each see the entire 4GB is through *memory mapping.*

At any given moment, Program X isn't using its entire 4GB memory space, so Windows can present to Program X only the memory that it's using at that moment. Think of an analogy: Most banks couldn't pay all depositors their entire balance at the same moment, but they could give each depositor a portion of his or her balance over the span of a typical day. So, in a sense, your bank accounts are virtual money. No wonder people still hide cash in coffee cans or under the mattress.

Even after parceling out physical memory on an as-needed basis in this elaborate shell game of memory mapping, sometimes physical memory (RAM) becomes exhausted. (That's likely to occur faster with Windows 2000 than with Windows NT 4.0, partly because Windows 2000 needs more RAM to hold all the extra Internet software that loads at startup.) When an application demands more memory than Windows can find in physical RAM, Windows 2000 grabs a chunk of disk space to use as *virtual memory*, also known as the *pagefile*. Disks are much slower than RAM, but the principle is that a system that runs slowly is better than one that stops entirely.

Windows 2000 manages the swapfile size automatically, shrinking and expanding it as needed, in the default configuration.

You have a couple of options to maximize performance:

- Specify a higher minimum pagefile size yourself to reduce Windows 2000 overhead (processor and disk time spent expanding the pagefile to meet demand).
- Place the pagefile on your fastest local hard drive for better speed.

Dynamic Link Libraries

Dynamic Link Libraries, or *DLLs,* are files that (typically) contain program code. A program or the Windows 2000 operating system itself can load a DLL into memory on an as-needed basis. The DLL concept lets you run programs with less RAM than would be required if all programs loaded every bit of code they needed, every time they started.

Much of Windows 2000 itself is in the form of DLLs, and most Windows applications use DLLs, too. Many Windows programs call upon DLLs in Windows to accomplish certain tasks; such DLLs go by the name of *system DLLs*.

The DLL model has presented some problems in the past. Microsoft often updates and modifies system DLL files between version releases of Windows. Application software developers sometimes "redistribute" specific versions of system DLLs, under license from Microsoft, so that the application knows that the PC is using a recent-enough version of the system DLLs for the application to work correctly. However, sometimes application installation routines overwrite newer DLLs with older ones, which can cause other applications that need the newer DLLs to break. Conversely, other times, a newer DLL may not work with an older program that needs an older version of that DLL. So both newer *and* older DLLs can create problems.

The new System File Checker utility, Windows File Protection, and the Windows Installer model have features designed to reduce DLL problems. Make sure you understand their purposes!

Hardware abstraction

The layer of Windows 2000 that communicates directly with the PC's hardware is called the *HAL,* or Hardware Abstraction Layer. Windows 2000 chooses an appropriate HAL for a given PC during the early stages of the installation program, based on factors such as

- CPU type
- Number of CPUs
- Power management support in the BIOS

The HAL design, which "abstracts" the underlying hardware from the rest of the Windows 2000 operating system, allows Windows 2000 to run on non-Intel processors. However, for various economic and political reasons, Windows 2000's ability to run on non-Intel processors is much less of a factor than it might have been. Therefore:

You probably won't see any exam questions on non-Intel processors.

You can't change the HAL without reinstalling Windows 2000. (The only exception: If you add a second CPU, you can change the HAL by updating the computer's "driver" in the System control panel's Device Manager.)

If you're not comfortable with the information that I present in this chapter, before continuing, you may want to spend a little time with the Windows 2000 help system, targeting the areas that seem a little fuzzy.

Part II
Planning, Installation, and Basic Configuration

The 5th Wave By Rich Tennant

"I guess you could say this is the hub of our network."

In this part . . .

Somebody once said that computer software can't be considered truly user-friendly until setting up a PC becomes as simple as setting up a toaster. If Windows 2000 Professional is a toaster, it's a nuclear-powered one with ten thousand moving parts! Setting up Windows 2000 correctly is no simple task, and this beefy part covers the initial work you're likely to do when setting up Windows 2000 Professional — whether for one user or for an entire worldwide corporation. The focus here is on software setup; Part III deals with hardware.

Chapter 3 covers choosing and using the file system, no simple task because Windows 2000 lets you choose from three options. Chapter 4 runs through a typical interactive installation and also discusses automated installation options, a favorite exam topic. Chapter 5 covers user environment settings such as language, locale, and accessibility options. Chapter 6 looks at setting up network cards and lower-level networking software pieces.

Chapter 3

Planning the File System

Exam Objectives

- Choosing between FAT16, FAT32, and NTFS file systems
- Discovering compression and encryption capabilities
- Getting a handle on dynamic disks
- Converting from one file system to another

Windows 2000 supports more file systems than any other Microsoft operating system, and each file system has its own set of features and foibles. Choosing the appropriate file system for a given situation is an important part of using Windows 2000 successfully, and it's also an important part of the certification exam. (Other aspects of managing disks appear in Chapter 7.)

Quick Assessment

Configure file systems by using NTFS, FAT32, or FAT

1 Microsoft recommends the use of ______ on PCs that will dual-boot with an earlier version of Windows.

2 NTFS version ______ in Windows 2000 is the new version of the NTFS file system in Windows NT Workstation 4.0.

3 The FAT32 file system allows Windows 2000 to use partitions up to 2 ______ in size.

4 NTFS gives administrators greater control over access permissions by providing ______ and ______ security.

Convert from one file system to another file system

5 To convert an NTFS partition to FAT32, use the command ______.

Configure, manage, and troubleshoot file compression

6 If you move a compressed file to a different folder on the same disk, and that folder is uncompressed, the moved file is ______ (compressed or uncompressed).

7 If you compress a folder on an NTFS partition, you cannot also ______ that folder.

8 The control panel that lets you make compressed files visible is the ______ control panel.

Encrypt data on a hard disk by using Encrypting File System (EFS)

9 The Encrypting File System uses public and private ______.

10 An encrypted file stays encrypted as long as it stays on an ______.

Answers

1 *FAT or FAT32.* See the sections "FAT" and "FAT32" for details.

2 *Five.* Windows NT uses NTFS 4. The "NTFS" section explains the differences.

3 *Terabytes.* (Good name for a lady crocodile.) See "FAT32" for more.

4 *File, folder.* (Also acceptable is "file, directory.") Miss this one? Read the "NTFS" section.

5 *No such command exists.* Trick question (you may as well see them here first!). See the "Converting from One File System to Another" section if this one eluded you.

6 *Compressed.* The section "Copying and moving" lays out these sorts of rules.

7 *Encrypt.* See "Setting compression on files or folders" if you missed this one.

8 *Folder options.* This one's new with Windows 2000.

9 *Keys.* The "Encryption" section elaborates.

10 *NTFS disk.* Again, the "Encryption" section has the details.

File System Choices

The file system determines how the operating system organizes disk space. Which file system you choose has implications for security, speed, efficiency, reliability, recoverability, and compatibility. You must choose a file system before you format a disk partition (on a regular, "basic" disk) or volume (on a "dynamic" disk — see the section "Basic versus dynamic disks" later in this chapter).

Microsoft's operating systems have presented a variety of file systems, most of which are incompatible with each other, as shown in Table 3-1:

Table 3-1 Windows Versions and File System Support

Operating System Version	*FAT?*	*FAT32?*	*NTFS?*
Windows 95 (original release and OSR1)	Y	N	N
Windows 95 (OSR2 and higher)	Y	Y	N
Windows 98	Y	Y	N
Windows NT 4.0	Y	N	Y

Windows 2000 gives you three choices for a file system: FAT16 (or plain old FAT as it's sometimes called), FAT32, and NTFS — more specifically, NTFS Version 5.

You're allowed to choose different file systems for different partitions or volumes on the same computer. For example, on a dual-boot computer, you may want to use FAT for the C drive (so that you can boot to Windows 98 or Windows 2000), FAT32 for the D drive (which would contain Windows 98), and NTFS for the E drive (which would contain Windows 2000). Note also that, in this example, the logical drives C, D, and E could all reside on a single physical disk.

Lab 3-1 shows you how to see which file system is in use for a given logical drive.

Lab 3-1 Checking the File System in Use

1. **Double-click the My Computer icon on the desktop.**
2. **Right-click the icon for the logical drive that you want to check.**
3. **Choose Properties.**

   The General tab of the computer property sheet appears.

4. **Look at the third line down.**

   It should say "File system: FAT," "File system: FAT32," or "File system: NTFS."

The above method works for Windows NT 4.0 and Windows 9*x*, also. Another method that's unique to Windows 2000 is to run the Disk Management console "plug-in," as detailed in Lab 3-2.

Lab 3-2 Running the Disk Management Utility

1. **Right-click the My Computer desktop icon.**
2. **Choose Manage.**
3. **Click the Disk Management icon in the left window pane.**

   You can see the file systems listed in the diagram on the right. For those of you familiar with Windows NT Workstation 4.0, you've just discovered the Windows 2000 version of the NT Disk Administrator utility.

If an exam question asks whether DOS, Windows 3.*x*, or Windows 9*x* can "see" a FAT32 or NTFS partition over a network — for example, when connecting as a client to a Windows 2000 PC that is sharing its files as a server — the answer is yes. The Windows 2000 PC "serves up" FAT32 and NTFS disks in a way that disguises, or abstracts, their underlying file system.

FAT

FAT, also known as FAT16, is the most compatible file system in the PC world. It works with DOS, Windows 3.*x*, Windows 9*x*, Windows NT, and Windows 2000.

The Windows 2000 setup program uses FAT to format the system partition if both

- NTFS isn't chosen; and
- The disk is less than or equal to 2GB in size.

However, FAT has limitations that are more serious as disk drives (and the operating systems, applications, and data files that those drives contain) have become larger:

- A FAT partition can be no larger than 4GB (gigabytes) on Windows 2000 (and NT 4.0). That means, in turn, that a drive letter (such as C or D) can't be larger than 4GB, because a logical drive must reside on no more than one partition.

  Windows 95 and 98 only let you set up 2GB FAT partitions.

- With larger hard drives, the FAT *cluster* — that is, the smallest chunk of disk space that the operating system can allocate — also must become larger. Otherwise, too many clusters would exist for the file allocation table to track. (Remember, FAT is a 16-bit structure with limited size.) Larger clusters, in turn, waste more disk space, especially with lots of small files.

Microsoft recommends FAT only in dual-boot systems or where you need compatibility with a DOS boot diskette.

FAT32

Microsoft's update of the FAT16 file system is FAT32, which made its debut in Windows 95 OSR2 and which uses 32-bit structures.

The Windows 2000 installation program will automatically use FAT32 if you say "no" to NTFS and if the disk to be formatted is larger than 2 GB.

FAT32 brings the following advantages:

- A FAT32 partition can theoretically be 2TB (terabytes) in size, where 1TB = 1,024GB.

  That's a lot of space, a fact that explains why Microsoft refers to FAT32 as "large disk support" when you run the FDISK partitioning program. Now, if you're upgrading from a Windows 95 or 98 machine, Windows 2000 will use FAT32 partitions of larger than 32GB if they already exist. However, Windows 2000 doesn't let you create a *new* FAT32 partition larger than 32GB. Even so, that's still much larger than the FAT16 limitation of 4GB.
- FAT32 can be used on a PC set up to dual-boot between Windows 2000 and Windows 98, or between Windows 2000 and Windows 95 OSR2.
- Because FAT32 is a 32-bit structure that can therefore handle larger data sets, the cluster size can stay low — 4KB on drives up to 8GB in size (see Table 3-1).

  Smaller clusters mean less wasted space. Conversion to FAT32 can increase the free space on disk by as much as 25 percent.
- The 4KB cluster size that FAT32 uses matches up more neatly with the Windows 2000 memory management scheme.

  Many applications can load into memory more rapidly from a FAT32 partition.

Table 3-2 Cluster Sizes under FAT16 and FAT32

Size of Partition	*Cluster Size, FAT16*	*Cluster Size, FAT32*
Up to 511MB	8KB	Not available
512MB to 1023MB	16KB	4KB
1024MB to 2GB	32KB	4KB
2GB to 8GB	Not available	4KB
8GB to 16GB	Not available	8KB
16GB to 32GB	Not available	16KB

FAT32 has limitations that may make it inappropriate in some cases:

- FAT32 doesn't work on disks smaller than 512MB in size.

  I know, such drives are rare now, and Windows 2000 itself doesn't fit in less than 600MB or so. Still, you should know this fact for the exam.

- Without third-party software, FAT32 isn't readable by MS-DOS, Windows 3.*x*, Windows NT, or early sub-versions of Windows 95 (4.00.950 and 4.00.950a) running on the same PC.

  That rules out FAT32 on the C drive for systems that must dual-boot to one or more of those operating systems.

- FAT32 may create problems for older disk utilities designed for FAT16. Not many of these utilities are around anymore, but it's something to double-check.
- Some older applications may be able to "see" only 2GB per drive letter, even on a FAT32 system.

FAT32 partitions don't permit compression, but that's usually not too big a deal because FAT32 partitions are more space-efficient than FAT16 partitions to begin with.

Windows 2000 supports FAT32 on any partition, including the system partition (that is, the one from which the computer boots). As with FAT, Microsoft recommends FAT32 only for PCs that must dual-boot with older Windows versions.

NTFS

NTFS, or "NT File System," is Microsoft's recommended file system for Windows 2000 if you are not setting up a dual-boot system.

The suggested minimum size for an NTFS disk is 10MB. NTFS can't be used on floppies.

NTFS basics

NTFS isn't nearly as compatible with other operating systems as FAT16; in fact, NTFS only works with Windows NT and Windows 2000. Heck, it's not even completely compatible between those two operating systems, as this section explains later. However, the goodies that you get with NTFS include the following:

- **Extra security.** With NTFS, you can control access at the folder level and at the file level. (Microsoft therefore often calls NTFS access control "file- and folder-level security." You also see the terms *file security* and *directory security* in this context.) I call NTFS access control "extra" security because it is in addition to the access controls that you can set when you share a folder ("share security").
- **More flexible compression.** You can specify particular files or folders to compress. With FAT16, you must compress an entire drive, all or nothing.
- **Better performance on large drives.** FAT disks slow down on large drives; NTFS disks slow down too, but not as much.
- **Larger disk sizes.** Microsoft recommends NTFS for disk sizes up to 2TB. (Microsoft also states that the theoretical upper limit for NTFS is "much higher" than 2TB.) However, Microsoft strongly advises using NTFS rather than FAT32 for partitions larger than 32GB.
- **Larger file sizes.** The maximum size of a file on a FAT disk is 2GB; on a FAT32 disk, 4GB; and on an NTFS disk, file size is limited only by the size of the disk.

New NTFS perks

Windows 2000's version of NTFS isn't identical to Windows NT Workstation 4.0's version. Windows 2000 uses NTFS 5, while NT uses NTFS 4. The new version, NTFS 5, supports the following new features:

- **Quotas.** Administrators can limit the amount of disk space used by a given user on a given partition or volume. Chapter 7 examines disk quotas in detail.

  This feature is a bigger deal for Windows 2000 Server, but you can still use it on the Professional product.

- **Encryption.** For additional security, users can encrypt files that are then off-limits to anyone who logs onto the machine with a different account.
- **Change journal.** The operating system tracks all changes (that is, filename, time of change, and type of change, but not the actual changed data) made to the file system in the change journal.

  Again, this feature is more important for the server product, but services and applications on the Professional product can use it, too. The feature is off by default.
- **Mount points.** A mount point lets you map an entire physical disk onto a folder on another disk.

  For example, if you add a second hard drive (one that you would normally designate D) to a PC, you can assign that new drive to the folder `C:\Newdata`. The user will never need to use the D drive letter. Chapter 7 explains how to use mount points.
- **Sparse files.** A sparse file is a file with lots of "air" in it, like a spreadsheet with data in cells A1 and Z100 but nothing in between. NTFS 5 lets application developers specify files as sparse, so the sparse files can occupy much less disk space than they would (for example) under FAT or FAT32.

On a dual-boot machine, NT can't "see" an NTFS 5 partition unless you have updated the PC to run NT Service Pack 4 or higher. Service Pack 4 installs an updated NTFS.SYS file system driver that can understand NTFS 5 partitions. (However, the new features that NTFS 5 makes possible, such as disk quotas, are inoperable when you boot to Windows NT Workstation 4.0.) Therefore, the following tip is worth remembering:

INSTANT ANSWER

If you plan to install Windows 2000 onto a machine presently running Windows NT Workstation 4.0, and you plan to make that machine dual-boot, upgrade to Service Pack 4 or higher before you install Windows 2000. Windows 2000 automatically converts any NTFS 4 partitions that it finds to NTFS 5.

Focus on NTFS 5

This section takes a closer look at some of the new goodies Microsoft built into NTFS Version 5, namely, compression, encryption, and dynamic disks. These are very likely subjects for exam questions!

Compression

Compression lets you reduce the amount of space on disk that a file or folder occupies. NTFS compression is *transparent*; that is, After you've designated a file as compressed, you don't need to expand it manually before you can use it again. NTFS automatically handles that, as well as the recompression after you've edited and saved the file. Any Windows or DOS program that can run under Windows 2000 can work with compressed files. If you designate a *folder* as being compressed, then when you create a new file inside that folder or copy an existing file into that folder, NTFS automatically compresses the file.

The compression technology built into NTFS 5 is more sophisticated than that available in earlier Windows operating systems. With NTFS compression, you can specify a drive, a folder, or a file within a folder. With Windows 98 and DoubleSpace compression, you had to specify an entire drive to be compressed.

Setting compression on files or folders

Compressing a file or folder is simple, as shown by Lab 3-3. The lab assumes that your system drive is formatted with the NTFS file system.

Lab 3-3 Compressing a Folder

1. **Log on as an administrator to the local PC.**

   You must have Write permission for any file or folder that you want to compress.

2. **Right-click the My Computer icon on the desktop and choose Explore.**

3. **Expand the tree in the left window pane to display the** `C:\Program Files\Accessories` **folder.**

   If your Windows 2000 system uses a different drive letter, substitute it for C.

4. **Right-click the Accessories folder in the left window pane and choose Properties.**

5. **Click the Advanced button in the Accessories Properties dialog box.**

   You should see the Advanced Attributes dialog box, as shown in Figure 3-1.

6. **Click the box labeled Compress Contents to Save Disk Space.**

   This check box should really be a radio button, because you can't check it simultaneously with the check box that says Encrypt Contents to Secure Data. (Go ahead and try.)

7. **Click OK, then click OK again, to close two dialog boxes.**

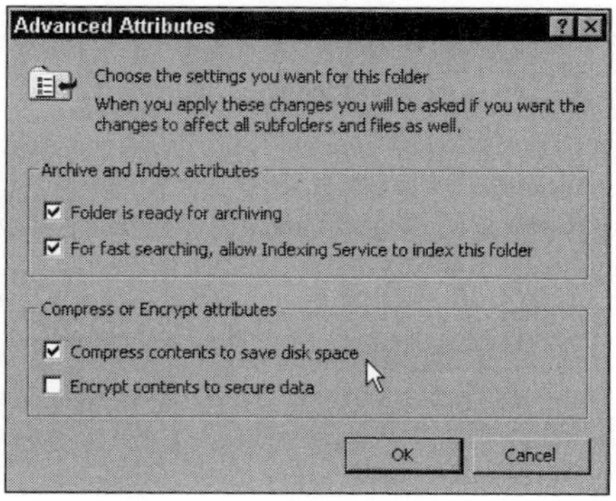

Figure 3-1: Set compression or encryption by using this dialog box.

8. **In the Confirm Attribute Changes dialog box (see Figure 3-2), check the box labeled Apply Changes to This Folder, Subfolders, and Files.**

   This action means that Windows 2000 will compress everything inside the Accessories folder. If you check the other box, then you designate the folder as being compressed without designating any of its contents as being compressed. That's perfectly legal, and if you did so, from that point forward, any file that you copy into the Accessories folder is automatically compressed.

   Note also that you get this same option when you "uncompress" a folder.

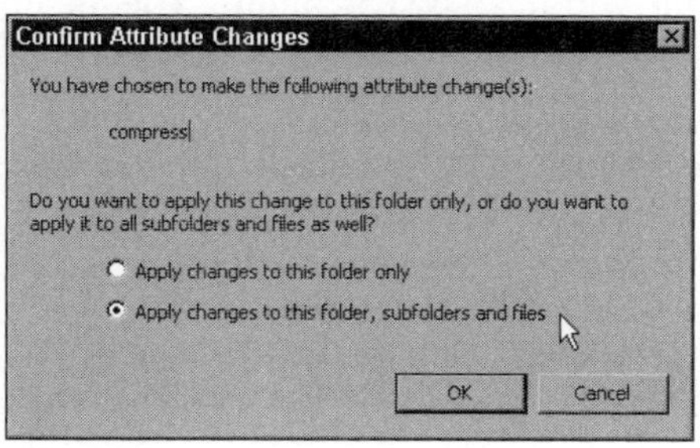

Figure 3-2: This dialog box controls the extent of the change you want to make.

9. **Click OK.**

   The Accessories folder and its contents are now compressed.

Viewing compressed files and folders

Most of us find it handy to have a visual cue to indicate whether a given file or folder is compressed. Windows 2000 gives you the option to specify that you'd like the user interface to show compressed files and folders in a different color than uncompressed ones. Lab 3-4 takes you through the simple procedure, again assuming that your C drive uses NTFS.

Lab 3-4 Seeing the Difference between Compressed and Uncompressed Files

1. **Choose Start⇨Settings⇨Control Panel⇨Folder Options.**
2. **Click the View tab.**
3. **Check the box that says Display Compressed Files and Folders with Alternate Color.**
4. **Click OK.**

   You can now glance at `C:\WINNT\SYSTEM32\DLLCACHE`. It should appear in an alternate color, indicating that the folder's contents are compressed.

Copying and moving

What happens to a compressed file when you copy or move it? The rules aren't intuitively obvious, and they make perfect fodder for exam designers. So here we go, easier rules first:

- *Copying* or *moving* a compressed file to a FAT disk or to a diskette: The file is uncompressed in its new location.

  This makes sense when you remember that compression is an NTFS-only feature.
- *Copying* or *moving* a compressed file from one NTFS volume to another: The file inherits the compression status of the destination folder.
- *Copying* a compressed file within an NTFS volume: The file inherits the compression status of the destination folder.
- *Moving* a compressed file or folder within an NTFS volume: The file or folder keeps its compression status, regardless of the status of the destination folder.

Compression tips

Here are a few tips to remember:

- Don't compress if you don't need it. Even if you need it, consider alternatives (such as adding a hard drive). Compression may be transparent after you've set it up, but it does incur some system overhead.
- Don't compress files with formats that tend to be space-efficient to begin with, such as JPG, GIF, ZIP, DLL, and EXE files.
- Don't compress volatile files that change often (again, due to system overhead). For example, compression is generally a bad idea for active database files.

Encryption

Windows 2000's NTFS 5 brings encryption to the file system for the first time. (The acronym — you *knew* there had to be an acronym, didn't you? — is EFS, for Encrypted File System.) *Encryption* simply means "scrambling" data in such a way that only someone with a software key can unscramble it.

EFS is a *public key encryption* method, meaning that a public key is used to encrypt a file, and a private key is used to decrypt it. Windows 2000 handles the public and private keys automatically, behind the scenes; the encryption keys actually reside on disk as part of the encrypted file's header.

Without logging on with the correct user name and password, you can't access encrypted files, even if you yank out the hard drive and put it into a different computer.

How to do it

The procedure for encrypting a folder is very similar to the procedure for compressing a folder (refer to Lab 3-3). The only difference is Step 6, wherein you should check the Encrypt Contents to Secure Data box. After you encrypt a folder, you can only have access to that folder and its contents when you log on with the same user account and password that you used when you encrypted the folder originally.

Decrypting a file or folder is a piece o' cake. Log on with the correct user account, view the file or folder's property sheet, click Advanced, and clear the Encrypt Contents to Secure Data check box.

You can even encrypt a folder that resides on a remote computer.

INSTANT ANSWER

Core facts

Here are some core facts about encryption that you must know for the test:

- It's only available with the NTFS file system.
- It doesn't work with system files. You can't encrypt PAGEFILE.SYS, for example.
- It's incompatible with compression.

  A file or folder may be either compressed or encrypted, but not both at the same time.
- Standard EFS uses 56-bit encryption; you can get stronger, 128-bit encryption from Microsoft via the "Enhanced CryptoPak."

- When you encrypt a folder, you encrypt all the files in that folder; the folder itself isn't really encrypted.
- A file stays encrypted if you rename it, move it, copy it, or back it up, as long as the file stays on an NTFS disk.
- Someone other than an encrypted file's owner gets an "access denied" error when attempting to open the file.
- You can't share an encrypted folder. (That falls into the "painfully obvious" category, but we have to be thorough here.)
- Encryption, like compression, is transparent. That is, you don't have to explicitly descramble a file before you edit it and rescramble it when you're done.

Secure security

As long as applications create temporary or backup files within the same folder as the original data file, you're protected, because encryption works on a folder basis. That is, if you open up LOVELETTER.DOC in `C:\Personal\Letters`, which is an encrypted folder, and your word processor creates an "autosave" temporary file named ~LOVELETTER.DOC in the same folder, then the temporary file is encrypted, just like the original file.

To go one better, Microsoft makes sure that the encryption keys never show up in the pagefile. You wouldn't want someone sifting through PAGEFILE.SYS in the middle of the night and discovering how to decrypt your encrypted files.

In a network environment, administrators can use Windows 2000 *policies* to control the use of encryption. For example, an administrator could disable EFS for a domain, or for an organizational unit within a domain. Chapter 11 explores the concept of policies in painful detail.

The safety net

If a user forgets his or her account password, and you just know that's going to happen at some point, the *recovery agent* has a private key that will unlock an encrypted file.

INSTANT ANSWER

By default, the recovery agent is the administrator of the local PC, or (if the PC is on a network) the domain administrator.

The recommended practice is to copy the encrypted file to the recovery agent's PC, where the recovery agent can decrypt the file simply by clearing the Encrypt Contents to Secure Data checkbox on the file's property sheet.

Basic versus dynamic disks

Windows 2000 supports two kinds of disk organization:

- *Basic disks*, which use partitions in much the same way as Windows NT Workstation 4.0 or Windows 98/95.
- *Dynamic disks*, which are unique to Windows 2000. The default behavior is for Windows 2000 to set up your disks as basic disks, unless you're upgrading a Windows NT Workstation 4.0 machine that uses advanced disk management features. Chapter 7 goes into the details.

  You need to use a dynamic disk if you want to create

  - *Striped volumes* (a single drive letter with multiple physical disks running a high-speed configuration)
  - *Spanned volumes* (a single drive letter with multiple physical disks running a normal-speed configuration)

For now, just know that you can use dynamic disks with any of the three Windows 2000 file systems, but certain features (such as extending a volume) are only available if you use NTFS.

Converting from One File System to Another

So you chose file system A, and now you realize you should have chosen file system B. What can you do?

- If you're installing Windows 2000, the setup program asks you if you'd like to convert an existing FAT16 or FAT32 drive to NTFS. The default answer is "no" on Windows 2000 Professional (but "yes" on Windows 2000 Server).
- If you're past the installation phase, you can use a supplied program to convert from FAT or FAT32 to NTFS, but not in the reverse direction.

From FAT or FAT32 to NTFS

The conversion utility typically lives in `C:\WINNT\SYSTEM32` and is named CONVERT.EXE. This tool converts your disk while keeping all the files on the disk intact, unlike a format operation. (Still, you're well advised to make a backup of the drive before conversion, anyway, just in case.) The syntax is

```
CONVERT.EXE <driveletter>: /fs:ntfs [/v]
```

where *<driveletter>* is the letter of the drive you want to convert. The */v* qualifier is optional (hence the square brackets, which you would not actually type) and means "run the utility in verbose mode," that is, with status messages.

Note that you can't convert the current drive. If you have only a C drive on a given PC, CONVERT.EXE will advise you that it will perform the conversion at the next restart.

From NTFS to FAT or FAT32

You can go through the looking glass, but not back again. The CONVERT.EXE utility doesn't let you change an NTFS disk back to FAT16 or FAT32. If you need to perform this operation, you must perform a backup, reformat, and restore cycle. (Or go out and get a copy of PowerQuest's Partition Magic, which won't be on the test but which I highly recommend for real life.)

Prep Test

1 **You're setting up a PC to dual-boot between Windows 98 and Windows 2000 Professional. You want the most efficient possible use of disk space. You also want to see all partitions from each operating system. Which file system is best for the system partition?**

A ❍ NTFS
B ❍ FAT
C ❍ FAT16
D ❍ FAT32
E ❍ FAT64

2 **You've encrypted a file SECRETS.DOC on your Windows 2000 Professional PC's C drive, which uses NTFS. The D drive on your system uses FAT32. You need to call the file something less obvious, so you rename it MISCINFO.DOC. To back it up for safekeeping, you copy MISCINFO.DOC with your other data files from drive C to drive D. One day, your C drive is corrupt, so you reformat it and reinstall the operating system. You then copy all the data files from D back to C, including MISCINFO.DOC. Which of the following statements is true? (Choose all that apply.)**

A ❑ MISCINFO.DOC is still encrypted, because you restored it to an NTFS disk.
B ❑ MISCINFO.DOC is no longer encrypted, because you lose encryption the moment you rename a file.
C ❑ MISCINFO.DOC is no longer encrypted, because you lose encryption the moment you copy a file to a FAT32 disk.
D ❑ MISCINFO.DOC is still encrypted, because FAT32 supports the encryption attribute.

3 **You've encrypted a file MCSE.TXT on your Windows 2000 Professional PC's C drive, which uses NTFS. A different user (named Friedrich) logs onto your PC. Which of the following statements is true? (Choose all that apply.)**

A ❑ Friedrich can see the encrypted file in Windows Explorer, but can't open it.
B ❑ Friedrich can see the encrypted file in Windows Explorer, but can't edit it.
C ❑ Friedrich can see the encrypted file in Windows Explorer, but can't delete it.
D ❑ Friedrich can see the encrypted file in Windows Explorer, but can't rename it.
E ❑ Friedrich can't see the encrypted file in Windows Explorer.

4 **Mary, an employee at the corporation whose Windows 2000 workstations you manage, comes to you with a special request. She needs to maximize the performance of her Windows 2000 Professional computer for playing back digital video. She has the fastest video card available, as well as the fastest processor, 256MB of RAM, and two fast hard drives. What step could you suggest to Mary to improve file I/O performance? (Choose the best answer.)**

- **A** ❍ Convert her hard drives to basic disks and combine them into a spanned volume.
- **B** ❍ Convert her hard drives to basic disks and combine them into a striped volume.
- **C** ❍ Convert her hard drives to dynamic disks and combine them into a spanned volume.
- **D** ❍ Convert her hard drives to dynamic disks and combine them into a striped volume.

5 **You compress a file named HUGE.XLS that resides on your Windows 2000 Professional system in the folder C:\DATA. You move the file to the uncompressed folder D:\WORKFILS. Both C and D are formatted to use the NTFS file system. Which of the following statements is correct? (Choose all that apply.)**

- **A** ❑ The file D:\WORKFILS\HUGE.XLS is uncompressed.
- **B** ❑ The file D:\WORKFILS\HUGE.XLS is compressed.
- **C** ❑ When you move the file, Windows 2000 asks you whether it should be compressed in its new location.
- **D** ❑ You can't move compressed files between disks without uncompressing them first.

6 **You're asked to set up a Windows NT 4.0 Workstation PC running NTFS for dual-booting with Windows 2000. Which NT Service Pack level is the minimum required for such a system?**

- **A** ❍ 3
- **B** ❍ 4
- **C** ❍ 5
- **D** ❍ 6

7 **Gia wants to install Windows 2000 Professional. She deals with large data files as large as 3GB per file, but will never exceed that value. Which file systems could you advise under Windows 2000?**

- **A** ❑ FAT
- **B** ❑ FAT32
- **C** ❑ NTFS Version 4
- **D** ❑ NTFS Version 5

8 **You've set up a dual-boot PC that runs both Windows NT Workstation 4.0 and Windows 2000. You set up disk quotas under Windows 2000, but you notice that users can exceed those quotas when working under NT. Why? (Choose the best answer.)**

A ❍ Windows NT and Windows 2000 use a different Registry.

B ❍ Windows NT can't use features specific to NTFS Version 5.

C ❍ Windows NT can't use features specific to NTFS Version 4.

D ❍ A default policy setting in Windows 2000 limits quotas to users with Windows 2000 accounts.

9 **You want to convert a FAT32 disk (presently drive C) to NTFS. What is the correct syntax for the CONVERT command?**

A ❍ CONVERT.EXE C: /FS:NTFS

B ❍ CONVERT.EXE C: /FS:FAT32

C ❍ CONVERT.EXE C: FAT32

D ❍ CONVERT.EXE C: NTFS

Answers

1 **D.** Both FAT and FAT32 are supported by both operating systems, but FAT32 uses less disk space and is therefore the better choice here. NTFS is out because Windows 98 can't see NTFS partitions, and FAT64 doesn't exist. See the "FAT32" section.

2 **C.** Renaming a file doesn't change its encryption status, but the file must remain on an NTFS disk. The copy made onto drive D therefore is unencrypted, and it is this copy that is later restored to drive C. See "Encryption."

3 **A, B, C,** and **D.** Users can see files that other users have encrypted, but that's it — they can't open, edit, delete, or rename them. If you think about it, it has to be this way: A Recovery Agent can't recover a file if he can't even find it in Windows Explorer. See "Encryption."

4 **D.** Striping is the fastest disk setup in Windows 2000 Professional. You have to have dynamic disks in order to support striping, so A and B are out. Spanned volumes don't do a thing for speed. See "Basic versus dynamic disks."

5 **A.** When you copy or move a compressed file to a folder on another NTFS volume, the file inherits the compression status of the destination folder. Memorize this and other compression rules in "Copying and moving."

6 **B.** Service Pack 4 is the minimum level necessary to ensure that you can boot to Windows NT 4.0 and still see NTFS disks after Windows 2000 automatically upgrades them to NTFS Version 5. See "New NTFS perks."

7 **B** and **D.** The maximum size of a file on a FAT disk is 2GB; on a FAT32 disk, 4GB; and on an NTFS disk, file size is limited only by the size of the disk. Windows 2000 uses NTFS Version 5; Windows NT 4.0 uses NTFS Version 4. See "NTFS basics."

8 **B.** Just because an NT system can "see" an NTFS Version 5 disk doesn't mean that NT 4.0 can use the features that NTFS Version 5 and Windows 2000 make possible. See "New NTFS perks."

9 **A.** The CONVERT program doesn't need to be told whether the present disk is FAT or FAT32; it can figure that out on its own. See "From FAT or FAT32 to NTFS."

Chapter 4

Installing Windows 2000 Professional

Exam Objectives

- Performing an attended installation of Windows 2000 Professional
- Installing Windows 2000 Professional by using Windows 2000 Server Remote Installation Services (RIS)
- Installing Windows 2000 Professional by using the System Preparation Tool
- Creating unattended answer files by using Setup Manager to automate the installation of Windows 2000 Professional
- Applying update packs to installed software applications
- Preparing a computer to meet upgrade requirements
- Deploying service packs

Installing Windows NT Workstation was never a piece of cake, and Microsoft knew that it had to do significantly better on the installation procedure if it wanted to make the NT platform less user-hostile. Fortunately, you'll have much more hair left on your head after installing Windows 2000 than after installing NT.

In addition to installing Windows 2000 Professional interactively, Microsoft provides three separate methods for installing the software in an automated fashion. This chapter covers what you must know about all the various methods, starting with the one-user, one-machine, interactive install.

Quick Assessment

Attended installation of Windows 2000 Professional

1 To install Windows 2000 onto a Windows 3.1 PC, run the program ______.

2 To ensure networking components install correctly in a domain environment, verify that a ______ and a ______ are available at install time.

Using Windows 2000 Server Remote Installation Services (RIS)

3 Two server operating systems that can run RIS are ______ and ______.

4 The network services that must be available in a RIS environment are ______, ______, and ______.

Using the System Preparation Tool

5 When a user starts a PC for the first time after it has been configured using SysPrep, the ______ executes one time only.

Using Setup Manager to automate the installation

6 The default name for an answer file is ______.

7 The batch file that Setup Manager creates to run setup with an answer file is named ______.

Applying update packs

8 Update packs usually consist of ______ files.

Preparing a computer to meet upgrade requirements

9 To perform a quick software and hardware compatibility check, run WINNT32.EXE with the ______ qualifier.

Deploying service packs

10 (True/False) Windows 2000 is just like Windows NT 4.0 in that you must reapply service packs after making major configuration changes.

Answers

1 *WINNT.EXE.* Use WINNT32.EXE for Windows 9*x* or NT, as the "Which setup?" section explains.

2 *Domain controller, DNS server.* See the "Network choices" section for more.

3 *Windows 2000 Server, Windows 2000 Advanced Server.* See "Method three: RIS" in this chapter.

4 *DNS, DHCP, Active Directory.* See "Method three: RIS" for more on this remote installation method.

5 *Mini-setup wizard.* The "Using SysPrep" section explains.

6 *UNATTEND.TXT.* However, you can use other names. The "Scripting basics" section goes into detail.

7 *UNATTEND.BAT.* If you missed 6, you probably missed this one too. "Implementing the scripted setup" contains more info.

8 *DLL.* See "Upgrade packs" for more.

9 */CHECKUPGRADEONLY.* If you didn't know this one, read "Prepping for installation" in this chapter.

10 *False.* Praise be! See "Installing Service Packs and Upgrade Packs."

Installing Windows 2000 Interactively

This section deals with the one-on-one installation scenario: one person sitting in front of one PC installing one copy of Windows 2000 Professional.

I realize that you may not have a machine available, but if you do, use it. The fastest way to understand the Windows 2000 installation process is to run through it two or three times on a test PC.

Minimum hardware requirements

Microsoft's published minimum hardware requirements for its operating systems are always an entertaining subject for debate.

For the exam, know the company line about hardware requirements:

- **CPU:** Pentium 133 MHz
- **RAM:** 64MB
- **Disk:** 1GB partition, 650MB required after setup (2GB partition recommended)
- **CD:** Optional, 12X or faster recommended
- **Display:** VGA
- **Input:** Keyboard, mouse, or other pointing device

For real life, double just about everything, and realize that the minimum practical requirements for CPU, RAM, and disk depend greatly on the particular services and applications you intend to run.

In every situation, Windows 2000 requires substantially more hardware horsepower than Windows 9*x*, and moderately more horsepower than Windows NT 4.0.

Prepping for installation

Here are a few pre-installation checks that you should perform:

- Verify that you're running the most recent functional BIOS. Windows 2000 decides which Hardware Abstraction Layer (HAL) to install partly on the basis of the BIOS type and version that it detects at install time.

- Verify that all hardware is on Microsoft's Hardware Compatibility List (HCL). You can check the HCL.TXT file on the CD in the SUPPORT folder, or consult Microsoft's Web site (`www.microsoft.com/hwtest/hcl` among other places). In general, hardware that works in NT 4 should work with Windows 2000 but will likely need new drivers.
- If you're upgrading a Windows NT 4.0 machine or a Windows 98 machine, you can run WINNT32.EXE with the **/CHECKUPGRADEONLY** qualifier to see a report of potential upgrade problems (see Figure 4-1). This action is identical to running the separately downloadable utility CHKUPGRD.EXE.

You can perform a compatibility check without performing an actual upgrade when running a scripted installation over Windows 95 or 98. Include the line **ReportOnly=Yes** in the [Win9xUpg] section of UNATTEND.TXT. Windows writes the compatibility report as a text file to the root of the system drive by default, but you can change the location with the **SaveReportTo** option. That's handy if you want to specify a network location where you can collect all the reports for review. Use a parameter such as *%computername%* in the filename that you specify with SaveReportTo in order to save each file under a different name. See "Method one: Scripting" later in this chapter.

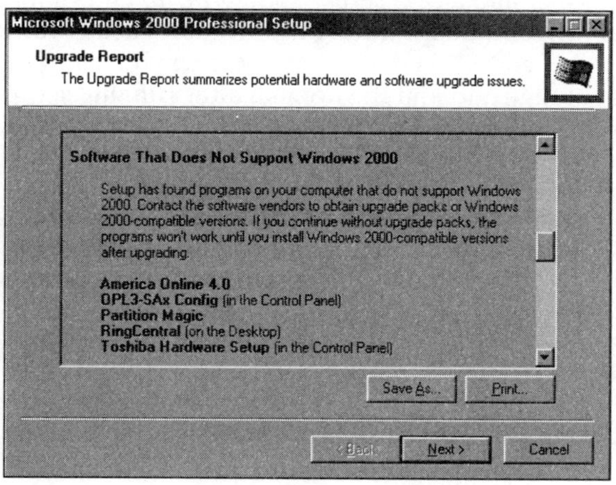

Figure 4-1: The upgrade check looks at software and hardware.

- Run a virus scanner on your system and correct any reported problems.

  If your system has a BIOS-based virus scanner, disable it for the installation, or be prepared to click Continue when the scanner asks you if it's okay to modify the boot record.
- If you're upgrading a Windows 9*x* machine, check Device Manager for any conflicts (red X's) or alerts (yellow !'s). Correct these if possible.
- If you're upgrading a Windows NT 4.0 machine, check the System, Application, and Security event logs for errors or warnings. Deal with these before proceeding.

- In an upgrade scenario, record system resource assignments (IRQs, DMA channels, base I/O addresses, upper-memory addresses). You can use a tool such as MSINFO to print or save such data to disk.
- If you're upgrading from NT 3.1 or 3.5, Microsoft wants you to upgrade first to NT 3.51 or 4.0, then upgrade to Windows 2000 Pro. (Yecch.)

Network choices

You should also figure out some network choices ahead of time.

If a Microsoft *network domain* (the usual choice in the corporate environment) is the environment, bear in mind the following:

- You must know the *domain name*, such as `corphq.i-sw.com` (the domain for the test network I built to write this book).
- You must provide for a *computer account* in the domain.

  Do so by either defining it ahead of time (domain administrators can do this) or specifying an account at setup time that has administrative rights on the domain and can therefore create the computer account as part of the setup process.
- A *domain controller* and a *DNS server* should be up and running and connected to the workstation PC during the Windows 2000 Professional installation. If this condition doesn't apply, then you can specify "workgroup" at install time and join the domain after running setup; it's just more convenient to get it all done at once.

If you're joining a *workgroup* environment, you need the workgroup name, which can be the name of an existing workgroup or the name of a new one.

Which setup?

In addition, you should determine which version of the setup program you should run, as follows:

- Run **WINNT.EXE** if you're performing a clean installation on a PC running DOS or Windows 3.*x*.
- Run **WINNT32.EXE** if you're performing either a clean installation or an upgrade on a PC running Windows 95, 98, or NT.

Clean or dirty?

Finally, resolve whether to perform an upgrade or a "clean install" (Microspeak).

A "clean" installation doesn't necessarily mean that the existing hard drive is wiped clean; it means, at minimum, that Windows 2000 installs into a fresh folder or partition. These are your options:

- Choose a clean installation if you have an existing operating system with which you'd like to dual boot; you want to make sure you have removed all traces of a previous operating system; or you'd like to reformat a partition with NTFS 5.

  This route entails reinstalling applications and making any customizations that differ from a "stock" operating system installation.

- Choose an upgrade installation if you have an existing operating system with which you don't want to dual-boot, and you want to retain the Registry settings that allow you to run existing applications.

If you decide to perform a clean upgrade and wipe the disk, you must provide for Windows 2000's setup program to start somehow. That is, you must provide a path to display a command prompt from which to run WINNT.EXE or WINNT32.EXE. Choose one of these methods:

- Create a DOS or Windows 9*x* boot diskette with the appropriate device drivers for your CD-ROM or network share.
- Boot from the setup CD-ROM, but only if the PC supports the "El Torito" bootable CD standard. (You may have to enable CD-based booting in the BIOS.)
- Create a set of boot diskettes using the MAKEBOOT program in the BOOTDISK folder of the Windows 2000 CD.
- Install a network card with remote-boot capability.

Installation phases

The typical installation procedure has four distinct stages: (1) basic setup — text mode; (2) basic setup — graphical mode; (3) network setup; and (4) final configuration. The following sections take a closer look.

Stage 1: Basic setup — text mode

You can start the installation several ways. For example, you can boot from the CD-ROM (if your PC supports the El Torito specification), you can boot from the set of four setup diskettes, or you can run WINNT or WINNT32 from a network distribution point.

If you're performing an upgrade and you let the Windows 2000 CD start the process via the Autorun facility (say, from Windows 98), then you answer a few questions before you even get to Stage 1. These include: clean install or upgrade; partition to install to; product key; language options; and accessibility options.

However you start the process, here are the key steps in Stage 1:

1. Setup loads a bare-bones version of Windows 2000 into memory.
2. You review and accept the licensing agreement.
3. You either create an installation partition or specify an existing partition for the installation.

   You can delete partitions here, too. No more FDISK!
4. If you create a new partition, you must pick a file system so that Windows 2000 can format it.
5. Windows 2000 copies some files to the hard disk, creates an embryonic Registry from the HIVE*.INF files, and restarts.

Stage 2: Basic setup — graphical mode

After Windows 2000 reboots, you enter the graphical part of the basic setup program, which Microsoft sometimes calls the setup wizard. Here's what happens in Stage 2:

1. The "Installing Devices" screen shows the progress of hardware detection for both Plug and Play and legacy devices.
2. If you're not upgrading from a previous version of Windows, you must supply
   - Language information
   - Locale
   - Keyboard layout
   - Name
   - Organization
   - Product key
   - Computer name

   If you are upgrading, the setup program asks you for this stuff before Stage 1.

   The computer name (also known as NetBIOS name) must contain no more than 15 characters. It must also be unique among other computer names, domain names, and workgroup names! Also note that on a Windows 2000 network, the computer name appears in Active Directory as an object; unlike Windows 9*x*, computers in Windows 2000 have their own security accounts.
3. You supply a password for the Administrator account.

4. You specify dialing information (area code, how to get an outside line, tone versus pulse dialing) if your PC has a modem.
5. You set the date and time and time zone.

Stage 3: Network setup

Yes, you're still running the setup wizard here, but Microsoft considers network detection a separate stage. Ours is not to reason why, ours is but to do or die. Here's what happens in Stage 3:

1. Windows 2000 tries to autodetect your network card.
2. Windows 2000 copies a bunch of network-related files to your PC.
3. You must tell Windows 2000 whether you want typical network settings (defined as: Client for Microsoft Networks + File and Printer Sharing + TCP/IP) or custom settings. FYI, I always recommend going with the typical settings and customizing things after setup completes.
4. If you're not upgrading, Windows 2000 asks you to join a workgroup or join a domain. (If you are upgrading, Windows 2000 uses your existing settings for these options.) You may have to provide a password for an account with domain administration rights in order to create a computer account if one doesn't already exist for you. Also, you see errors if a domain controller and DNS server aren't available at this time.
5. Windows 2000 configures your network setup amidst much clicking and whirring.

Stage 4: Final configuration

Stage 4 is pretty much automatic unless something goes wrong, so this is a good time to go have lunch, or at least a nutritious snack such as a doughnut. Here's what happens:

1. The Installing Components window shows the progress of various file copy and installation steps, typically including COM+, Fax Service, games, accessories, and Indexing Service, among others.
2. The Performing Final Tasks window shows the progress of Start menu initialization, component registration, saving settings, and removing any temporary files used.
3. The PC restarts.
4. Your final actions are to proceed through the Network Identification wizard, which lets you choose whether to use the autologon feature, and then to log on to Windows 2000, at which point you receive an "out of memory" error message. (Kidding.)

Notes on dual-boot systems

Microsoft has generally not supported dual-boot systems in the past. The company has changed its position regarding dual-booting Windows 2000, however. You can bet that the exam has a couple of dual-boot questions on it, so here's the lowdown.

Dual-boot pros and cons

Advantages of dual-boot systems include:

- Reduced costs for research and test-bench environments
- Handy for support technicians who must support multiple operating systems
- Excellent teaching tool
- Ability to compare performance on identical hardware

Disadvantages include:

- Far more complex software setup
- More complex maintenance and troubleshooting
- Potential file system incompatibilities
- Potential application incompatibilities
- Larger hard drive space requirements

Operating systems

In the absence of third-party partitioning and multi-boot software, Windows 2000 can dual-boot with any of the following operating systems:

- Windows NT 4.0 (preferably with Service Pack 4 or higher for NTFS 5 compatibility)
- Windows NT 3.51
- Windows 95 (all versions)
- Windows 98 (all versions)
- Windows for Workgroups 3.11
- Windows 3.1
- DOS
- OS/2

If you use Microsoft software without any additional utilities, the general rule is to install operating systems in order from oldest to newest. That is, if you want to create a triple-boot machine with Windows 3.1, Windows 95, and Windows 2000, install the operating systems in that order. In that scenario, you would specify a different folder for Windows 95, and you would preferably dedicate a separate disk partition to Windows 2000.

When installing Windows 2000 to dual-boot with Windows 98, you can install either operating system first.

When installing Windows 2000 to multi-boot with a system that was previously set up to dual-boot DOS and OS/2, Windows 2000 will dual-boot with whichever of DOS or OS/2 was run most recently before the Windows 2000 installation.

Partitioning considerations

Here are Microsoft's rules for creating partitions:

- The best approach is to install each operating system on its own partition (whether that partition is on the same physical drive, or a different one). Doing so makes it highly unlikely that one operating system will ever overwrite another operating system's boot files.
- If you can't install each operating system onto its own partition, the next best thing is to install Windows 2000 on its own partition, while leaving other operating systems (Windows 9*x*, 3.*x*, DOS) on their own partition.
- Problems have been reported with the partitioning code that runs as part of the Windows 2000 setup program. Therefore, only use the Windows 2000 setup program to partition the volume onto which Windows 2000 is to be installed. Use Windows 2000's disk management console to create or format other partitions, or use a third-party partitioning tool such as Partition Magic.
- Each partition must be large enough to meet the minimum hardware requirements published for that particular operating system.

File system considerations

Here are the rules for deciding on file systems on a multi-boot machine:

- If you want to dual-boot with DOS, Windows 3.*x*, or Windows 95 (original version through OSR1), and you want those operating systems to be able to see the Windows 2000 partition, use the FAT file system for Windows 2000 and for the primary partition.
- If you want to dual-boot with Windows 95 (OSR2 and higher) or Windows 98, and you want those operating systems to be able to see the Windows 2000 partition, use the FAT or FAT32 file system for Windows 2000 and for the primary partition. (FAT32 uses less disk space but is incompatible with DOS and Windows 3.*x*.)

- On a dual-boot machine with Windows 9*x*, you may configure a Windows 2000 partition as NTFS, but the primary (boot) partition must be either FAT or (in the case of Windows 95 OSR2+ and Windows 98) FAT32.

Procedural notes

A few points to bear in mind when setting up a dual-boot system:

- During the installation, say "no" to the question "Do you want to upgrade your version of Windows?" and choose a clean install instead.
- At the Select Special Options screen, click the Advanced Options button. In the Advanced Options dialog box, check the box that reads "I want to choose the installation partition during Setup." If you don't, Windows 2000 installs itself onto the system's first partition.
- At each boot after the installation finishes, you can select "Windows 2000 Professional" or "Windows." (The exact wording resides in BOOT.INI.) The second option runs your earlier version of Windows.
- If you need to correct drive letter mismatches, for example a CD-ROM drive that is E: under Windows 98 but F: under Windows 2000, then boot to Windows 2000, right-click the My Computer icon, and choose Manage. Then use the Disk Management snap-in to change the drive letter so that it matches the other operating system.

Automating the Windows 2000 Installation

Up to this point, this chapter has dealt with an interactive installation, but that type isn't the norm in most organizations — users have too many opportunities to take a wrong turn! This section looks at the three primary methods that Microsoft provides for automating the Windows 2000 installation: scripting, cloning, and Remote Installation Service (RIS).

A fourth method, using System Management Server or SMS, is available for rolling out Windows 2000, but only to PCs that are already connected to the network and running an existing operating system. This method provides centralized control and scheduling flexibility. You're unlikely to see SMS questions on the test, so don't worry about learning more than the contents of this paragraph.

Method one: Scripting

This method involves running the setup program from a central network server (or, alternatively, from a custom-built CD) under control of a script.

When to use scripting

This method works well in situations where you have a hodgepodge of PC makes, models, and components. The setup program can still autodetect PC hardware and make adjustments for the fact (for example) that Carina has a 3Com network card while Cecily has a Madge network card.

The customized script that you create to guide the setup program doesn't mandate that everyone's initial Registry look identical — that doesn't work, for example, with the two different network cards. The script mandates only that certain settings such as the time zone and standard networking language are identical on each PC.

Scripting basics

With any version of Windows, the setup program asks you a number of questions. The *answer file* in Windows 2000 is a text-format script that behaves like a virtual user, automatically answering each of the setup program's questions as they come up. Because the answers come from a file instead of an interactive user, the installation is termed *unattended*, hence the typical name of the answer file: UNATTEND.TXT. Figure 4-2 shows an example.

Figure 4-2: A fairly brief and simple answer file.

Typical answer file parameters include the following items:

- Product (Windows 2000 Professional, Windows 2000 Server)
- Automation level (from "Fully Automated" to "Provide Defaults")
- Default user data and computer names (may use UDF file to feed)
- Network settings (workgroup, domain, etc.)
- Custom wallpaper
- Run Once commands
- CMDLINES.TXT
- Code pages
- Regional options
- Time zone
- Telephony details

Microsoft provides a loooong document (UNATTEND.DOC, located in the DEPLOY.CAB file on the Windows 2000 CD's `\SUPPORT\TOOLS` folder) explaining all the details of creating an answer file. I recommend you read this file if you have access to it; the exam is likely to include one or two very nitpicky questions covering possible UNATTEND.TXT settings. Happily, the company also provides a friendly, graphical utility called *Setup Manager* (SETUPMGR.EXE) that does a pretty good job of building an answer file for you, along with a batch file demonstrating how to run setup with the answer file (see Figure 4-3). The UNATTEND.DOC file is handy to know about in case you want to fine-tune your answer file by hand.

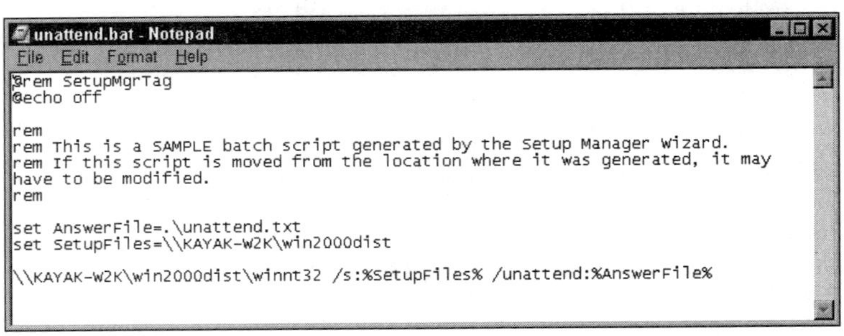

Figure 4-3: An auto-generated batch file to run setup with the answer file.

Installing Setup Manager

Windows 2000 doesn't automatically install Setup Manager, so you have to install it yourself. The tool lives in a "cabinet" file named DEPLOY.CAB on the Windows 2000 CD in the `\SUPPORT\TOOLS` folder. Follow these steps to install Setup Manager:

1. **Put the Windows 2000 CD-ROM into the drive.**

   You can use either the Professional or Server versions.

2. **Open Windows Explorer.**

3. **Create a new folder for the Setup Manager program.**

4. **Double-click the CD file** `\SUPPORT\TOOLS\DEPLOY.CAB`.

   Windows 2000 automatically opens up compressed CAB, or *cabinet*, files within the Explorer window. You don't have to extract the files one by one, as you do with some other Windows versions.

5. **Drag and drop all the contents of DEPLOY.CAB into the folder you created in Step 3.**

6. **Right-click and drag SETUPMGR.EXE onto the desktop and choose Create Shortcut Here. Alternatively or additionally, you can drag and drop this file to a position on your Start menu.**

After you install Setup Manager, running it is a matter of double-clicking the icon you created, or selecting the Start menu option you made. You then see the manager's main screen.

Setting script options via Run Once

As you go through the various screens in Setup Manager, you provide the answers to as many setup questions as you want. These screens are mostly self-explanatory until you come to the name Run Once screen. (To see the Run Once screen, you must click "yes" when asked if you want to specify additional settings after you've created the basic answer file.)

The commands that you enter here run automatically the first time a user logs onto Windows 2000 after setup has finished. You can include here, for example, a command such as **REGEDIT CUSTOM.REG** if you want to merge the contents of CUSTOM.REG into the user's Registry. (The commands that you enter in Setup Manager's Run Once screen appear in the [GUIRunOnce] section of UNATTEND.TXT.)

Because the Run Once commands execute after the first user logon, any user-related settings affect the current user rather than the default user. Also, the Run Once commands are subject to any permissions restrictions that may apply to the logged-on user. If you want to perform actions that are not restricted by any potential permissions issues, you should use the CMDLINES.TXT file instead, as discussed later in this section.

Creating the distribution point

An essential step in creating a network-based setup procedure is to install a complete copy of the Windows 2000 source files onto a server, called a *distribution server,* from which a new user can install Windows 2000 across the network onto the workstation. (The server "distributes" Windows 2000 to the network users.)

Setup Manager offers to create a distribution point for you as its final act, saving you the trouble of manually copying the necessary files to your network server. Creating a distribution point is also necessary if you want to run a CMDLINES.TXT file (see next section), which won't run from a CD-ROM even if you burn your own.

If you want to include your own custom help files, application files, drivers, utilities, or any other sort of files in the Windows 2000 distribution folder, Setup Manager lets you do that in the Additional Files or Folders window toward the end of the procedure. Those additional files go into the folder named OEM in recognition of the fact that Original Equipment Manufacturers (*OEMs*) make heavy use of this feature; see Figure 4-4. (The OEM folder is also used for custom *HALs*, or *Hardware Abstraction Layers*, and for hardware-specific SCSI drivers.)

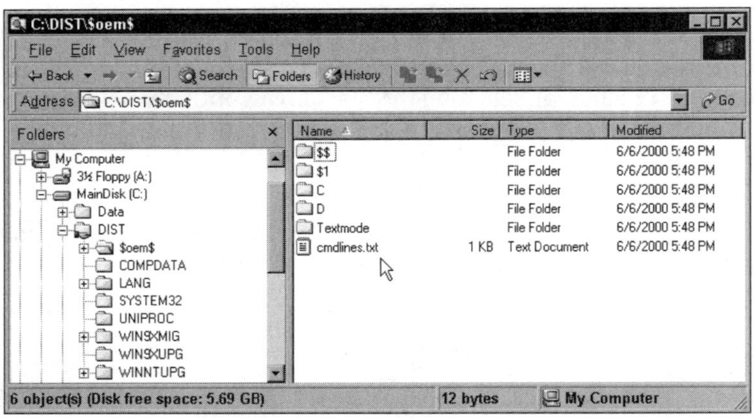

Figure 4-4: A typical distribution point created by Setup Manager.

INSTANT ANSWER

You can use Setup Manager to create an answer file that you can use *without* a distribution point. For example, you can distribute the answer file on diskette and have users install Windows 2000 from the Microsoft-supplied CD. If you take this approach, the answer file must have the name WINNT.SIF, the PC must support booting from the CD via the "El Torito" specification, and you must include in the answer file a [Data] section with options set up as described in UNATTEND.DOC.

Creating CMDLINES.TXT

After you tell Setup Manager where you want your distribution point to be, and after you answer a few more questions, you get to the Additional Commands screen. Any additional commands that you type into this window ultimately go into the text file CMDLINES.TXT, which Setup Manager places into the OEM folder of your distribution point.

The simple CMDLINES.TXT file has a section labeled *[Commands]* under which appear the commands you created in the Additional Commands screen. As with the Run Once section, these commands can include instructions to load REG files of your own devising. And if you want to get fancy, they can also include VBScript or JavaScript programs that you create.

Unlike the Run Once commands, commands in CMDLINES.TXT execute at the end of the setup procedure but *before* the user logs on to Windows 2000 for the first time. These commands basically run with system privileges, so they aren't subject to any user-specific access control restrictions. Furthermore, CMDLINES.TXT runs whether the user is performing an upgrade from a previous version of Windows, or from a fresh install. However, because no user is logged on, no access to protected network resources is available.

Implementing the scripted setup

Your final step is to include the setup command file (typically UNATTEND.BAT) in a network logon script. Here's a typical procedure:

1. **Set up a special user account (for example, UPGRADE) for the user who wants to install Windows 2000 to log on to.**
2. **Define appropriate security for the UPGRADE account (no changing passwords, rights to the server with Windows 2000 on it, and so on).**
3. **Create a logon script and associate it with the UPGRADE user.**

When a user wants to install Windows 2000, she can log on to the UPGRADE account and answer only the questions that you left for users to decide on their own (if any).

Method two: Cloning

If you're lucky enough to work in a network where everyone has pretty much the same hardware, you may want to consider disk cloning as an alternative to a scripted, network-based setup. Microsoft provides the *SysPrep* utility for this situation. (This utility actually made its debut late in the life cycle of Windows NT 4.0 Workstation.)

You use SysPrep in conjunction with a third-party image replication tool, such as a hard drive duplicating machine or a program such as Ghost or Drive Image.

Cloning basics

Disk cloning normally means that you crank out carbon-copy hard drives that include not only Windows 2000 but also any desired Windows 2000 applications.

This technique works only if all the PCs have the same basic hardware (Hardware Abstraction Layer, power management, hard disk controller, and number of processors); other hardware can vary, because of Windows 2000's new Plug and Play detection capabilities. That is, Windows 2000 can autodetect devices such as network cards and display adapters after the main installation is finished.

If your network PCs are all very similar, disk cloning may be faster and easier than setting up a network-based setup with a custom script. Cloning a hard drive over a network can take as little as ten minutes.

Using SysPrep

To clone Windows 2000 by using SysPrep, follow these steps:

1. **Create a test PC with Windows 2000 installed just the way you want it.**

   Don't specify a domain or an administrative password.

2. **Install whatever applications you need and customize them, too.**
3. **Clean up the event logs and any other application install log files that you don't need to duplicate.**
4. **Put the files SYSPREP.EXE, SETUPCL.EXE (which generates new security IDs), and (optionally) the answer file SYSPREP.INF (which has the same structure as UNATTEND.TXT) into the folder** `%SystemDrive%\SYSPREP`.

   (%SystemDrive% is shorthand for the drive letter of the system drive, usually C but not always.) The files reside in DEPLOY.CAB on the Windows 2000 CD's `\SUPPORT\TOOLS` folder. Windows 2000 deletes the SYSPREP folder after the "Mini-Setup Wizard" runs on the user's cloned machine. The SYSPREP.INF file provides predefined answers to the "Mini-Setup Wizard."

5. **Add a CMDLINES.TXT file, if desired, to the SYSPREP folder to run post-Setup commands, for example, to install software applications after Windows 2000 has already been installed.**
6. **Run SYSPREP.EXE with the** -reboot **qualifier to make sure it runs as desired.**
7. **Run SYSPREP.EXE again, this time without the** -reboot **qualifier, and shut down the machine.**
8. **Image the disk with a hardware or software duplicator (such as Ghost) and (depending on your choice) install cloned disks into the target PCs or run the image copying program across the network.**

When a cloned PC is first started, the disk runs the "Mini-Setup Wizard." Depending on whether you used SYSPREP.INF, and on the options included in that answer file, the wizard asks the user to specify the following:

- Agreement with the license (as if you have a choice!)
- Regional options
- User and company name
- Computer name and administrator password
- Network settings
- Time zone

Although the more typical use for SysPrep is to clone identical hard drives, you can also use it to create a custom installation CD-ROM.

Method three: RIS

You can set up a Windows 2000 Server with Remote Installation Service (RIS), which enables you to install Windows 2000 onto PCs that don't even have an existing operating system on their hard drives. Such PCs can boot to a special diskette that the network administrator provides, or the PCs may have a network card with remote-boot capabilities (compatibility with the *Pre-Boot eXecution Environment*, or *PXE*, remote boot standard is presumed). The network card uses DHCP to find a RIS server from which to download the operating system files.

Using RIS places a fair amount of traffic onto the network and requires a server optimized for file-intensive tasks.

RIS requirements

Here's what you must know about requirements for a RIS installation:

- RIS does *not* ship with Windows 2000 Professional.

  The software comes with all server versions of Windows 2000 and requires that operating system. (This rules out RIS for sites that don't run Windows 2000 Server.)
- Clients must have either a PXE-capable BIOS (version .99c or greater), a PXE-capable network card, or a regular PCI-bus network card that's on the list of those supported by the Remote Boot Disk Generator program, RBFG.
- The user account you intend to use for installation must have the right to log on as a batch job.

  Assign this via Active Directory utilities on the server.
- The server running RIS can be either a member server or a domain.
- DNS must be running on some network server for Windows 2000 to find Active Directory and workstation computer accounts.

- DHCP must be running on some network server so that PCs with bootable network cards can receive an IP address.

  If you're using RIS with routers that don't support the relaying of DHCP/BOOTP messages, then you must have *either* a DHCP server or a DHCP *relay agent* (which can be a Windows NT 4.0 server or a Windows 2000 server) running on the same subnet as the client PC.
- The RIS software must reside on a shared NTFS volume on a drive other than the drive from which Windows 2000 Server runs.

Installing and configuring RIS

The procedure for installing RIS onto a Windows 2000 Server machine probably won't be on Exam #70-210, so I'll keep this brief. On the server, open the Control Panel, run Add/Remove Programs, click Add/Remove Windows Components, and select Remote Installation Services.

After your server reboots, follow the prompts to configure RIS. You specify (among other things) a folder on an NTFS volume where the Windows 2000 Professional installation files should reside. Make sure at least 300MB is available at this location. The wizard copies all the files for you.

On the client side, you can set up computers to boot from the network if the BIOS or network adapters support PXE. Set the BIOS to use the network card as the primary boot device.

If neither the BIOS nor the network card supports PXE, create a boot diskette using the *Windows 2000 Remote Boot Disk Generator* (RBFG.EXE, and yes, the F is for Floppy and it should be D for Disk). RBFG comes with the RIS software. The exam is likely to test your knowledge of this program's name.

If you want to get fancy, you can use RIS to set up a client PC, modify that client PC so that it looks exactly the way you want all other PCs to look (for example, by installing user applications), then run RIPREP.EXE (the *Remote Installation Preparation Wizard*) to copy the files from the client up to the RIS server. As with SysPrep, the client PC that you set up to be the master image must use the same HAL as the PCs onto which you intend to install Windows 2000. Another caution: Once you copy the files to the RIS server, you can't change the installation image.

Installing Service Packs and Upgrade Packs

Service packs upgrade the operating system; upgrade packs upgrade applications. Here are a few words of wisdom on each subject.

Upgrade packs

Upgrade packs are collections of files (usually one or more DLLs) that update applications for better compatibility with Windows 2000. For example, an upgrade pack DLL may contain information about moving configuration settings from one part of the Registry to another. You normally use an upgrade pack when upgrading an earlier version of Windows to Windows 2000, as opposed to performing a clean install.

Upgrade packs are available from the application vendor rather than from Microsoft, although Microsoft provides information for designing them via the Software Development Kit (SDK). Follow the vendor's guidelines for installation; Windows 2000 processes the upgrade packs during the graphical mode of setup. You can see examples on the Windows 2000 CD under `\I386\WIN9XUPG`.

Service packs

One of the welcome changes from Windows NT 4.0 is the *slipstreaming* of service packs. This term means that you can apply a Windows 2000 service pack to your network-based distribution server, and all future installations from that server incorporate the service pack updates and changes. That is, installers or users don't need to install Windows 2000 Professional first and then apply the service pack in a separate step.

The command for applying a service pack to a master image is **UPDATE.EXE/SLIP**.

Another nice improvement is that you no longer have to reinstall Windows components (such as network protocols) after applying a service pack, a requirement that often reared its ugly head in NT 4.

The command for applying a service pack to an individual Windows 2000 Professional workstation is **UPDATE.EXE**.

Third and last, in the "old days" with NT 4, you had to reapply service packs after changing the configuration of operating system services. For example, if you added the file and printer sharing service, you'd have to reapply the service pack. Windows 2000 is smart enough to ask for the proper files when you make a configuration change, removing the need to perform a service pack reinstall. Three cheers for these three changes.

Prep Test

1 **What are ways of checking a PC's hardware and software compatibility before upgrading to Windows 2000 Professional? (Choose all that apply.)**

A ❑ Run WINNT32.EXE /CHECKUPGRADE.

B ❑ Run WINNT32.EXE /CHECKUPGRADEONLY.

C ❑ Download and run CHKUPGRD.EXE from Microsoft's Web site.

D ❑ Download and run UPGRDCHK.EXE from Microsoft's Web site.

E ❑ For Windows 95 and 98 systems, add the line ReportOnly=Yes to the [Win9xUpg] section of UNATTEND.TXT.

2 **You decide to automate your Windows 2000 deployment by using SysPrep. Which file do you need to create in order to avoid users having to answer questions during the "Mini-Setup Wizard"?**

A ❍ UNATTEND.TXT

B ❍ ANSWER.TXT

C ❍ SYSPREP.INF

D ❍ SYSPREP.TXT

3 **You use Remote Installation Service (RIS) to deploy Windows 2000 Professional. However, many of the PCs aren't PXE compliant at the BIOS level or the network adapter card level. What program do you use to create a boot diskette for these PCs?**

A ❍ MAKEBOOT.EXE

B ❍ RIPREP.EXE

C ❍ RBFG.EXE

D ❍ RBDG.EXE

4 **You create an unattended installation script with Setup Manager. Users will install Windows 2000 Professional from their CD-ROM drives, using the Microsoft-supplied Windows 2000 CD. You will distribute the answer file on diskette as UNATTEND.TXT. All the user PCs support booting from the CD using the El Torito specification. During a test, the setup program doesn't seem to use the UNATTEND.TXT file on the diskette, and the program asks the user for answers to all the setup questions interactively. What must you do to fix this problem? (Choose all that apply.)**

A ❑ Rename the file WINNT.INF.

B ❑ Rename the file WINNT.SIF.

C ❑ Create a folder named OEM on the hard drive and create a batch file on the diskette that copies UNATTEND.TXT to that folder.

D ❑ Make sure the answer file contains a [Data] section containing the required keys.

5 **You have set up a Windows 2000 Server as a RIS server for automating the deployment of Windows 2000. However, when you boot a PXE-enabled PC, it can't seem to find the RIS server. What are the possible reasons for this problem? (Choose all that apply.)**

- **A** ❑ No DHCP server exists on the subnet, and the router is not configured to forward DHCP or BOOTP packets.
- **B** ❑ A DHCP server exists on the subnet, but is down.
- **C** ❑ You must boot PXE-enabled PCs from a diskette created by RBFG.EXE.
- **D** ❑ The PXE BIOS is too old.

6 **This file automatically generates security IDs on cloned machines.**

- **A** ❍ SETUPCL.EXE
- **B** ❍ SYSPREP.EXE
- **C** ❍ SID.EXE
- **D** ❍ SYSPREP.DLL

7 **Which of the following commands runs before the user logs on to Windows 2000 Professional for the first time after a fresh installation? (Choose all that apply.)**

- **A** ❑ Run Once
- **B** ❑ Run Twice
- **C** ❑ CMDLINES.BAT
- **D** ❑ CMDLINES.TXT
- **E** ❑ CMDLINE.TXT

8 **You are creating a dual-boot PC. Microsoft recommends that you install Windows 2000 Professional into its own:**

- **A** ❍ Folder
- **B** ❍ Partition
- **C** ❍ Physical drive
- **D** ❍ Directory

9 **What is the minimum amount of RAM specified by Microsoft for a successful Windows 2000 Professional installation?**

- **A** ❍ 16MB
- **B** ❍ 32MB
- **C** ❍ 64MB
- **D** ❍ 128MB

Answers

1 **B, C,** and **E.** Memorize the syntax, as this is a likely candidate for an exam question. See "Prepping for Installation."

2 **C.** This file is optional. If you use it, put it in the folder %SystemDrive%\SYSPREP. See "Using SysPrep."

3 **C.** It stands for Remote Boot Floppy Generator — if you can remember that, you're in good shape. See "Installing and configuring RIS."

4 **B** and **D.** If you meet these requirements, the setup program automatically uses the answer file on the diskette. You might use this method, for example, to upgrade a bunch of notebook computers not connected to any network. See "Creating the distribution point."

5 **A, B,** and **D.** PXE uses DHCP to obtain an IP address for itself and for the RIS server. Choice C is wrong because a PXE-enabled PC does not require a boot diskette to locate the RIS server. See "RIS requirements."

6 **A.** This file also activates the Mini-Setup Wizard. See "Using SysPrep."

7 **D.** The Run Once commands execute after the user logs on and within the user's security context. No "Run Twice" commands exist, and choices C and E are misspelled. See "Creating CMDLINES.TXT."

8 **B.** To be more specific, Microsoft recommends installing every operating system on a multiple-boot machine into its own partition; failing that, install Windows 2000 onto its own partition, and all other operating systems into a second partition. See "Partitioning considerations."

9 **B.** It'll run with 32MB, but "walk" would be a better word. A far cry from Windows 95's minimum requirement of 4MB! See "Minimum hardware requirements."

Chapter 5

Configuring the User Environment

Exam Objectives

- ▶ Enable multiple language support
- ▶ Configure multiple language support for users
- ▶ Configure local settings
- ▶ Configure Windows 2000 Professional for multiple locations
- ▶ Configure and troubleshoot desktop settings
- ▶ Configure and troubleshoot accessibility services

Windows 2000 Professional supports multiple languages, multiple locations, and a wide variety of user-specific and machine-specific desktop settings. You control these settings through the old, familiar "Control Panel" and through the new (and possibly unfamiliar) Microsoft Management Consoles. This chapter looks at language, locale, and accessibility settings in detail, and presents some general points on control panel and management console technology.

Quick Assessment

Enable multiple language support

1 Adding language support to Windows 2000 requires access to ______.

2 The two technologies for displaying foreign-language documents are ______ and ______.

Configure multiple language support for users

3 You configure additional language groups by using the ______ control panel.

4 The "system locale" defines the code page that Windows 2000 will use for ______ applications.

Configure local settings

5 The four tabs that define a given PC's local language-related settings are ______, ______, ______, and ______.

Configure Windows 2000 Professional for multiple locations

6 If you want to change the default locale, use the ______ tab of the Regional Options control panel.

7 If you want to keep the default locale but add a new, alternate locale, use the ______ tab of the Regional Options control panel.

Configure and troubleshoot desktop settings

8 The two types of tools that you normally use to change desktop settings are ______ and ______.

Configure and troubleshoot accessibility services

9 The control panel that lets you set up accessibility options is called the ______ control panel.

10 The accessibility feature that would let you type Ctrl, Alt, and Del in succession, instead of simultaneously, is called ______.

Answers

1 The Windows 2000 CD or the network installation point. Didn't know this one? See "Implementing multiple language support" in this chapter.

2 Code pages and Unicode. See the sections "What's a code page?" and "What's Unicode?" for more.

3 Regional Options. The "Implementing multiple language support" section goes into details.

4 Non-Unicode. Again, see the "Implementing multiple language support" section.

5 Numbers, Currency, Date, and Time. The "Locales" section explains.

6 General. For more, see "Locales" in this chapter.

7 Input Locales. Ditto.

8 Control panels and management consoles. Miss this one? Check out the section titled (appropriately) "Control Panels and Management Consoles."

9 Accessibility Options. Okay, you deserve a "gimme" from time to time.

10 StickyKeys. The "Accessibility" section has more on this.

Language Support

Windows 2000 Professional can support multiple languages via the Control Panel's Regional Options icon. With multiple language support installed, you can create documents in a foreign language, such as "French" or "rap music," as well as read documents created in that language.

What's a code page?

You have to understand code pages before you can grasp the mechanics of multiple language support. A *code page* is typically a table of characters in which each character corresponds to a single byte. Because a byte has a minimum value of 0 and a maximum value of 255, a code page can contain a maximum of 256 characters. That's not enough to contain all the possible characters in all possible languages, so computer systems use different code pages for different languages.

Some code pages support only a single language; others can support multiple languages. Furthermore, for some languages, such as Chinese and Japanese, 256 characters isn't enough, hence the existence of *double-byte code pages* to handle those special situations.

In a system based on code pages, a program needs to know two pieces of information to properly display and print a character: the byte value of the character within the code page, and which code page to use (expressed as a number — for example, "Latin 1" is code page 1252). You can see the potential problem when a user running a PC with a specific code page creates a document and sends it to a user running a different code page: The document is likely to look like gibberish.

What's Unicode?

Unicode is an international-standard character set that has extra characters above and beyond those that appear in the ASCII (American Standard Code for Information Interchange) character set. Unlike ASCII, which uses a single-byte code, Unicode uses a double-byte character code, which makes code pages irrelevant. Every character in every language can be defined by a single double-byte value. Therefore, all a program needs to know to properly display a Unicode character is the double-byte value of that character.

Windows 2000 supports Unicode Version 2.0, which permits roughly 40,000 unique characters. Windows NT 4.0 also supports Unicode, but Windows 98 and 95 do not. (Office 97, Internet Explorer 4.0 and above, and SQL Server 7.0

and above support Unicode although they don't require a Unicode operating system.) Over time, Unicode will continue to phase in and code pages will continue to phase out.

Implementing multiple language support

So, how do you add multiple language support in Windows 2000? The procedure centers on the Regional Options control panel (see Figure 5-1). (If you aren't familiar with code pages or Unicode, please read the preceding sections before you read this one.)

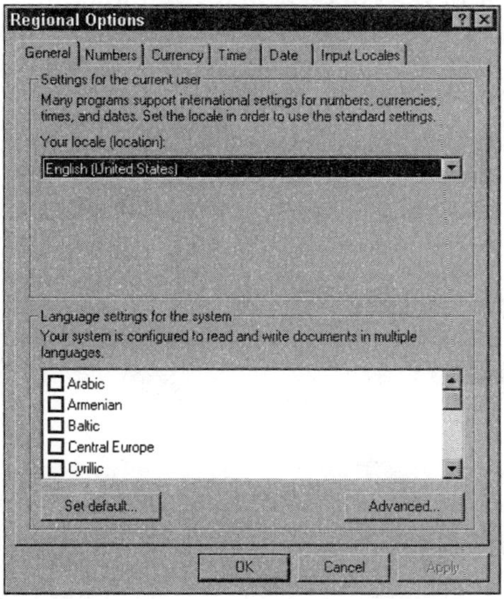

Figure 5-1: Add multiple language support in the Regional Options control panel.

The Regional Options control panel is a serious contender for the worst-designed control panel in the entire operating system. For one thing, the General tab is upside down! Normally, you would first select the language(s) you want to use, and then choose the most appropriate locale(s), because your choice of languages affects the locales from which you can choose. However, this control panel puts the locale choice at the top and the language choice at the bottom. I'll mention another anomaly a little later. For now, Lab 5-1 shows you how to add support for a new language.

Lab 5-1 Adding a New Language

1. **Log on as the local PC's Administrator.**

   You must have administrative rights to add language support. Also note that the ability to add language support may be restricted by group policies; this lab assumes that it is not.

2. **Choose Start⇨Settings⇨Control Panel.**
3. **Double-click the Regional Options icon.**

   The General tab of the Regional Options property sheet appears.
4. **Look at the lower part of the screen, the area labeled Language Settings for the System.**

   Scroll around until you see the default language choice. For most readers in North America and in the United Kingdom, this is "Western Europe and United States."
5. **Click a check box next to a language you'd like to add.**

   For example, "Arabic." You would choose a language in which you need to compose documents, or read documents. If you want to specify the precise code page or pages to install, click the Advanced button and make the appropriate choices from the Advanced Regional Options dialog box (see Figure 5-2).

   TIP: If you compose a document that depends on a language group that you've added, anyone else to whom you send that document must have the same language group support installed on his or her computer.

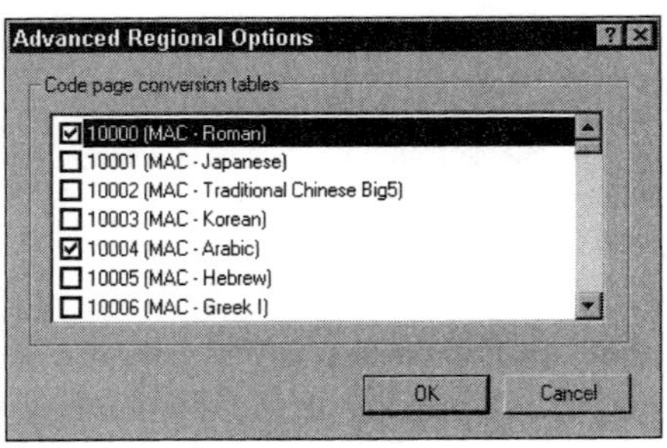

Figure 5-2: Here's where you can specify precise code page tables to load.

6. **Click the OK button and insert the Windows 2000 CD-ROM when prompted (or choose a network installation point if available).**
7. **Restart the computer when prompted to do so.**

So what actually happens when you choose to add support for an alternative language? Basically, three things.

- The operating system loads the necessary *code page translation tables* from the Windows 2000 CD-ROM or from the network installation point.
- Windows 2000 sets a default *keyboard layout* for that language. (Many languages have alternative keyboard layouts, which you can set later if you prefer.)
- Windows 2000 modifies the list of allowable locales.

Now, what's that "Set default..." button inside the language settings box on the General tab? That lets you specify the *system locale.*

This is an especially annoying misnomer, because the system locale isn't a locale, it's a *language*. (I *told* you this control panel was awful.) Here's the definition to remember:

The *system locale* is the language support (that is, the code page and associated font sets) that Windows 2000 uses by default for any applications that don't include Unicode support.

Locales

Windows NT 4.0 and Windows 2000 support the concept of a *locale*, while Windows 98 and 95 do not. What does the locale setting do?

In a nutshell, it's a convenient way to set the other Regional Options control panel choices all at one time (that is, the ones on the Number, Currency, Time, and Date tabs). These tabbed property sheets define how Windows 2000 displays (and, for example in spreadsheet or database applications, sorts) numbers, currency, time values, and date values. Sure, you could change each of these individually. But chances are that in a given locale, you're going to want the most common settings for users in that locale. After you set the locale, you probably don't need to fiddle with the Number, Currency, Time, and Date tabs because they'll be set as you would want them.

Some Windows 2000 and Windows NT 4.0 applications check the locale setting to determine the behavior of specific features (such as a spell-checker, for example). Windows 98 and 95 applications typically don't do this.

The locales that are available on any given machine are determined by which languages are installed on that machine. After you've chosen the languages for which you want operating system support, and restarted the computer (refer to Lab 5-1), you can go back to the Regional Options control panel and select a preferred default locale. For example, if you chose to add support for the "Arabic" language group in Lab 5-1, you would notice the appearance of a whole slew of new locales, such as "Arabic (Morocco)" or "Arabic (Qatar)," on the General tab's drop-down list box titled Your Locale (Location).

The General tab of the Regional Options control panel lets you change the default locale. If you want to add *non-default* locales that you can switch to by using a special hotkey combination (or the locale icon that appears automatically in the System Tray part of your taskbar), you must use the Input Locales tab of the Regional Options control panel (see Figure 5-3). The Installed Input Locales list shows the locales and keyboard layouts currently installed.

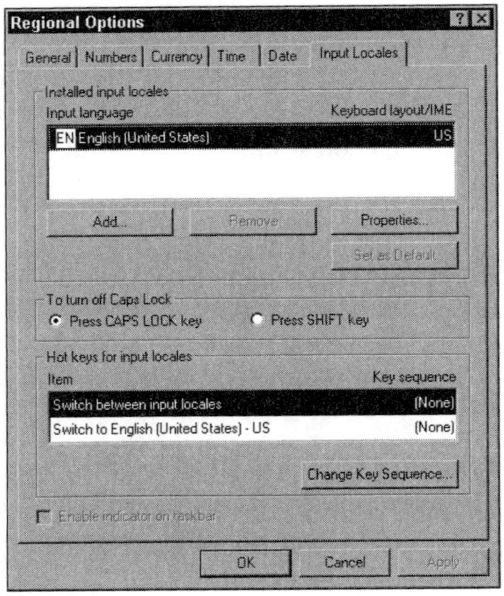

Figure 5-3: Add a locale (as opposed to setting the default locale) in this dialog box.

When you add a locale via the Input Locales tab, you can use the same dialog box to perform several other actions:

- Specify the keyboard layout you want for that locale (click the locale in the list and then click the Properties button).
- Define "hotkeys" to switch from one locale to another (click the Change Key Sequence button).
- Have Windows put an icon on the taskbar to make changing locales easier (check the Enable Indicator On Taskbar box).
- Make the Caps Lock key turn off when you hit the Shift key, like a typewriter (this is a global setting that applies to all locales).

Number formats

The Numbers tab of the Regional Options control panel gives you fine control over how Windows 2000 displays and sorts numbers. Some of the options you can control include:

- Decimal point character
- Number of digits to display after decimal point
- "Digit grouping" character (for example, the comma in 1,000)
- Negative number indicator
- Displaying a leading zero in decimal numbers

Currency formats

The big news here, and the point to remember for the test, is that Windows 2000 supports the *Euro*, the new European currency standard.

The Currency tab of the Regional Options control panel also lets you change the decimal point character and the digital grouping character, as in the Numbers tab.

Time and date formats

The Time dialog box lets you set the time format, the time separator symbol, and the AM and PM symbols. The Date dialog box lets you set the date format (short and long versions) and date separator. The Date dialog box also lets you change how Windows 2000 interprets two-digit dates; the default is to assume a year between 1930 and 2029, that is, "30" would mean "1930" and "29" would mean "2029."

While we're on the subject of time and date, make a note that if you use the new "offline files" feature of Windows 2000 — in which Windows makes a copy of a network file on your hard disk, so you can work with it away from the network — the computer time and date are critical! Windows uses the time and date stamp when synchronizing offline files, for example after you've been away on a trip. If your PC's time and date (which you set in the Date/Time control panel) don't match up with your network servers' settings, synchronization isn't reliable.

Troubleshooting Languages and Locales

If you're having problems with a PC that has multiple languages and/or locales installed, here are a few troubleshooting tips.

- If you're having trouble with a single application, check to see if it supports Unicode. If it doesn't, you may need to change the "system locale" (the default language that Windows 2000 uses for non-Unicode applications).
- If you're moving documents between two PCs, make sure both have the same language groups added via the Regional Options control panel.
- Try removing language groups one at a time and see if the problem goes away.
- Try learning the language in which the document you're reading was written. (Windows 2000 can't help you there! Maybe Windows 2020 . . .)

Accessibility

Windows 2000 includes some accessibility features that make it friendlier to a wider variety of users. The Accessibility Options control panel has five tabs: Keyboard, Sound, Display, Mouse, and General. However, unlike most control panels, the General tab does not appear first; the Keyboard tab does.

Keyboard

Here are the various accessibility settings you can control on the Keyboard tab:

- **StickyKeys:** Lets you type a multikey combination (the most famous example being Ctrl+Alt+Del, the "three finger salute") one key at a time, instead of all keys simultaneously.

  The keys that become sticky are Ctrl, Alt, Shift, and the Windows logo key. By default, you can toggle StickyKeys on or off by tapping the Shift key five times in succession; the Settings button offers various other customizations.

- **FilterKeys:** Lets you customize how Windows 2000 deals with quick keystrokes and repeated keystrokes.

  Some users may tap keys involuntarily and unintentionally; the Settings button lets you specify a minimum time that a user holds a key down before Windows recognizes it as a bona fide keystroke. You can also specify key repeat delay and repeat rate settings that override those on the Keyboard control panel.

- **ToggleKeys:** Lets you instruct Windows 2000 to make sounds when the user types the CapsLock, NumLock, and ScrollLock keys.

  A high tone sounds when one of these keys turns on, and a low tone sounds when it turns off.

Sound

The Sound tab lets you instruct Windows 2000 to provide some visual cues for those who cannot hear system sounds easily or at all:

- **SoundSentry:** An on/off check box that lets you tell Windows 2000 to "flash" a part of the screen (which you can select via the Settings button) whenever Windows or a Windows program plays a sound.
- **ShowSounds:** Another on/off check box that signals applications to display captions for any sounds they may generate. Application developers must write their programs to support this feature for it to work.

Display

The Display tab lets you instruct Windows 2000 to override the color scheme on the Display control panel and use a high-contrast color scheme, which is more easily viewable by those with vision limitations. The Settings button gives you a few options for customizing the display's appearance (white-on-black, black-on-white, or a custom color scheme).

Mouse

The MouseKeys feature lets the user operate the mouse with the numeric keypad. The Settings button lets you control speed and whether to use the Ctrl and Shift keys to modify acceleration.

General

Here are the features that you control via the General tab:

- **Automatic reset.** Deactivates accessibility features automatically after a specified number of minutes ranging from 5 to 30.
- **Feature switch notification.** This helps ensure against accidental feature deactivation or activation.
- **SerialKey.** This setting lets Windows 2000 use a serial port for an alternative keyboard device.
- **Administrative options.** You can set the accessibility options so that they apply only to the currently-logged-on user, or to all users of the machine, automatically at logon time.

Accessibility Accessories

If you think that the only Windows 2000 accessibility options are in the Accessibility control panel, well, that would be reasonable (I assumed it myself!) but wrong. Microsoft put some new tools on the Accessories branch of the Programs menu, including the following:

- **Magnifier**. This utility helps people with poor vision see the screen by placing a magnified view of the present cursor location at the top of the display (or wherever you want it to appear). You can set the zoom level, window size (drag the border), window placement, tracking options (cursor, keyboard, or both), and color scheme.

- **Narrator**. This program provides voice feedback for vision-impaired users. You can control whether Narrator relates typed keystrokes; announces screen events (new windows and menus); and moves the mouse pointer to follow the active screen item. You can also control the Narrator's voice (speed, volume, and pitch). Don't rely on Narrator to work in programs other than Windows 2000's desktop and control panels, Wordpad, Notepad, and Internet Explorer. I was also unable to get it to sound like Angelina Jolie, but maybe in Service Pack 1 . . .
- **On Screen Keyboard**. This utility displays a keyboard image on your screen and lets you "type" using a mouse, joystick, or other device. You can enable a click sound on the Settings menu, where you can also select a typing mode: *click* (in which you click keys on the virtual keyboard), *scan* (in which the keyboard display cycles through rows and keys until you select the key you want with a joystick or other device), and *hover* (in which Windows selects a key after you hover the cursor over it for a preset duration).
- **Accessibility Wizard**. This wizard steps you through a series of windows that help you select accessibility options. It's handy in that you don't have to slog through the control panel and every individual accessibility accessory.
- **Utility Manager**. An administrator can run this utility to specify which accessibility accessories should start automatically with Windows. (How this differs from simply putting programs into the Startup group, I'm not sure.) You can also see which accessibility accessories are running; again, the Taskbar works fine for that purpose, so the added value of Utility Manager is hard to discern. Know about it anyway.

Control Panels and Management Consoles

Well beyond language, locale, and accessibility settings, you can use *control panels* and *management consoles* to tailor many other aspects of the user environment.

Although I examine specific control panel and management console settings throughout the book as appropriate, a few words are in order here to introduce these two technologies.

Control panels

The control panels that appear when you choose Start⇨Settings⇨Control Panel look and work much like their predecessors in earlier versions of

Windows. These icons, and the underlying software code that determines their appearance and actions, live in files with the extension *.CPL. The files typically reside in the `C:\WINNT\SYSTEM32` folder.

Control panels provide a relatively safe, user-friendly way to modify Windows 2000 settings and preferences. Most control panels offer context-sensitive and field-level help via the "?" button on the title bar. Many include data entry filters to help prevent users from keying in inappropriate or badly formatted data.

Some control panels modify settings that apply to all users of the machine, while others modify settings that apply only to the currently logged-on user.

Note especially the new and modified control panels:

- "Folder Options" lets you modify the behavior of specific file types and is also accessible from Windows Explorer via the Tools⇨Folder Options command.
- "Users and Passwords" lets you manage local user accounts and profiles.
- "Scanners and Cameras" controls those digital devices.
- "Display" now has a Web tab that enables you to view the desktop as a Web page and add Web elements (graphics, applets, whole Web pages) to the desktop.

  This capability comes over from the Windows 9*x* product line.
- "Network and Dial-Up Connections" is redesigned, combining local network settings and dial-up connection settings.
- "Sounds and Multimedia" likewise combines settings that formerly occupied separate control panels.

While nearly all the control panels in Windows 2000 Professional modify the Registry, that is, the computer's central database of configuration data, the boot options that appear on the System control panel's Advanced tab (click the Startup and Recovery button) modify the BOOT.INI file at the root of the system partition (usually C) rather than the Registry. Furthermore, on Windows 2000 Server, some control panels and management consoles (as shown in Figure 5-5) modify the Active Directory database rather than the Registry. And on Windows 2000 machines running Internet Information Server (IIS), management consoles can also modify an IIS-only configuration database that Microsoft calls the *metabase*.

You can control which control panels users can and cannot see by using *policies* (see Chapter 11 for details). You can also exercise such control (although less elegantly) by moving, deleting, or renaming the various *.CPL files.

Microsoft Management Console (MMC)

A new kind of control panel, the *Microsoft Management Console (MMC),* appears in Windows 2000. You can reach most of the management consoles on your computer by choosing Start⇨Settings⇨Control Panel and selecting the Administrative Tools folder (see Figure 5-4). The preconfigured MMC consoles that appear are easily distinguishable from traditional control panel files by the presence of a shortcut arrow on the icon. These shortcuts point to *.MSC files on disk, which run the MMC host program MMC.EXE.

Figure 5-4: This folder contains lots of management console icons.

All these preconfigured consoles share the same basic window layout and certain menus. In fact, the idea behind MMC is to provide a somewhat standardized structure for hosting administrative tools. Microsoft supplies a number of such tools, but third parties can write their own, too. In other words, MMC.EXE provides the frame, and the tool designer (be it Microsoft or someone else) provides the painting.

If you select one of the Administrative Tools shortcuts (for example, "Computer Management"), you see a typical management console layout (see Figure 5-5). (You can also see this console by right-clicking the desktop's My Computer icon and selecting Manage.)

The left window is a hierarchical, Explorer-like "console tree" showing the individual *snap-ins* (which are programs that actually do useful work within that particular console). Examples of snap-ins are Device Manager and Event Viewer. (And no, they don't actually make a sound when you add them to a console. Would have been funny if they did, though.)

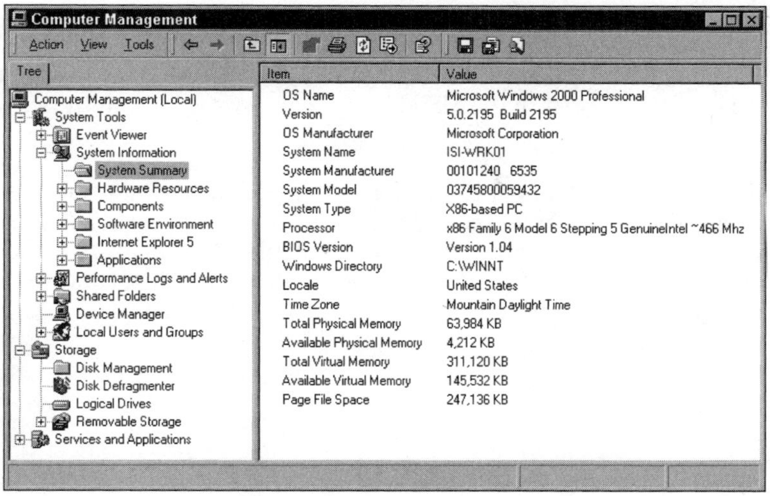

Figure 5-5: A typical MMC console.

Microsoft distinguishes between "stand-alone" snap-ins and "extension" snap-ins. The latter work only as helpers in the context of one or more stand-alone snap-ins. Some snap-ins can function either way.

The right window is the "details pane" showing the contents of the active snap-in that's highlighted in the console tree. The menu bar of every console contains the Action and View menus, but the choices beneath these menus can and do vary widely. In most MMC consoles, you can generally avoid menus completely by right-clicking the object on which you wish to perform an action. Consoles are highly object-oriented.

The level of standardization that MMC provides is minimal, and MMC windows are inherently no more user-friendly than tabbed property sheets. However, one significant benefit for technical folks is that you can put together your own MMC consoles with any combination of snap-ins. That's something you can't do with the traditional control panel files, and it's sure to come in handy for those who have to spend a lot of time configuring or managing Windows 2000 systems.

If you want to experiment with making your own "mission control" MMC consoles, choose Start⇨Run, type **MMC,** and press Enter. When the Microsoft Management Console is up and running, choose Console⇨Add/Remove Snap-In, click Add, and select the snap-ins you want. When you're done, save your custom console. Practice this; you're likely to be quizzed on it.

Some important snap-ins don't appear in any supplied consoles — you have to build a custom console in order to use them! These include the Group Policy editor, the Security Template tool, and the Security Configuration and Analysis tool. Most of the MSC files on your system live in the `C:\WINNT\SYSTEM32` folder.

If you use the Administrative Tools often, you may want to put them on your Programs menu. To do so, choose Start⇨Settings⇨Taskbar & Start Menu, click the Advanced tab, and check the Display Administrative Tools box. And while you're there, check the Expand Control Panel box as well; this lets you navigate to a specific control panel from the Start menu.

Prep Test

1 **A user in your office has a disability that makes it hard for him to make the "three finger salute" by holding down Ctrl, Alt, and Del at the same time. How could you ease his computing sessions? (Choose the best answer.)**

A ○ Choose Start⇨Settings⇨Control Panel⇨Keyboard. Click the Accessibility tab and check StickyKeys.

B ○ Choose Start⇨Settings⇨Control Panel⇨Keyboard. Set the repeat rate to the lowest value.

C ○ Choose Start⇨Settings⇨Control Panel⇨Keyboard. Set the delay period to the lowest value.

D ○ Choose Start⇨Settings⇨Control Panel⇨Accessibility Options. Click the Use StickyKeys check box.

E ○ Choose Start⇨Settings⇨Control Panel⇨Accessibility Options. Click the Use FilterKeys check box.

2 **You're teaching some PC troubleshooters at your organization how to get familiar with Windows 2000 Professional. One of them asks you how you can tell an MMC console icon from an old-style Control Panel icon. Which of the following answers are correct? (Choose all that apply.)**

A ❑ MMC icons all have a shortcut arrow on them; old-style Control Panel icons don't.

B ❑ The property sheet for old-style Control Panel icons points to CPL files, while for MMC icons it points to MSC files.

C ❑ The only way you can tell is to run the icon. All MMC consoles have a dual-pane window and an Action and View menu.

D ❑ Look at the location. The Control Panel folder itself only contains control panels; the Administrative Tools folder only contains MMC consoles.

3 **As your company's Windows support guru, you get a call from an employee who's working in your Kuwait office. He received a PC shipped from the U.S. with all U.S. settings. What steps would you advise that he take to configure his PC for Kuwait? (Choose all that apply.)**

A ❑ Add Arabic language support by clicking the Arabic check box on the General tab of the Regional Options control panel.

B ❑ Add Arabic language support by clicking the Arabic check box on the Language tab of the Regional Options control panel.

C ❑ Specify Kuwait as a locale via the Input Locales tab of the Regional Options control panel.

D ❑ Set the proper choices for Kuwait by modifying the Currency, Date, Time, and Numbers tabs of the Regional Options control panel.

4 **What entities can Windows 2000 control panels and management consoles modify? (Choose all that apply.)**

A ❑ The Registry
B ❑ INI files
C ❑ The Master Boot Record
D ❑ Active Directory

5 **What's the name that Microsoft uses to describe console snap-ins that only function as subsidiary nodes to one other specific snap-in, as opposed to "stand-alone" snap-ins that can function without any other snap-in present? (Choose the best answer.)**

A ❍ Ancillary
B ❍ Auxiliary
C ❍ Extension
D ❍ Subordinate

6 **A code page can contain a maximum of how many characters?**

A ❍ 64
B ❍ 128
C ❍ 256
D ❍ 512

7 **Name one Microsoft Management Console snap-in that you must add yourself to a custom console, because it doesn't come with any pre-built consoles in Windows 2000 Professional.**

A ❍ System Configuration and Analysis
B ❍ Security Analysis
C ❍ Security Configuration and Analysis
D ❍ Security Configuration
E ❍ System Template Security Policy Configuration Analysis

8 **Where do most console files make their home?**

A ❑ C:\WINNT\SYSTEM32
B ❑ %systemroot%\SYSTEM32
C ❑ C:\WINNT
D ❑ C:\WINNT\CONSOLE

Answers

1 **D.** The StickyKeys feature in the Accessibility Options control panel enables the user to press Ctrl, Alt, and Del in sequence instead of all at once. *See the "Keyboard" section.*

2 **A** and **D.** Choice B sounds good, until you realize that Control Panel icons don't have property sheets. Choice C's second sentence is true, but its first sentence isn't. Remember also for the exam that MMC.EXE is the executable file for consoles, but each console has the extension MSC (not MMC). *See the "Microsoft Management Console" section.*

3 **A** and **C.** Choice A by itself isn't enough; you need to add a language, then specify a locale. Remember that locales include settings for currency, number, date, and time formats, so you don't have to set those individually. *See the "Locales" section.*

4 **A, B,** and **D.** The System control panel can modify BOOT.INI, which contains (among other things) details about the operating system boot menu. Most control panels on the Professional product modify the Registry; many consoles on the Server product modify the Active Directory database. *See the "Control Panels" section.*

5 **C.** Just another term you should memorize. *See the "Microsoft Management Console" section.*

6 **C.** Code pages use one byte, or eight bits, per character. Two raised to the eighth power is 256. Unicode uses two bytes per character. *See the section "What's a code page?."*

7 **C.** The exam expects you to know this one, as well as the Security Templates console; Chapter 11 takes a closer look at these two. *See the section "Microsoft Management Console."*

8 **A** and **B.** This is a bit of a trick question, for two reasons. The question doesn't tell you how many choices to select, so you must pay attention to whether the answers use circles or squares. Second, the question expects you to know that the variable %systemroot% normally is the same as C:\WINNT. You should also know the variable %systemdrive%, which is normally C. *See the "Microsoft Management Console" section.*

Chapter 6

Configuring Network Components and Protocols

Exam Objectives

- Installing, configuring, and troubleshooting network adapters
- Configuring and troubleshooting the TCP/IP protocol

One of the best things any test prep book can do is clue you in to which areas carry greater weight on the exam than others. Therefore, verily I say unto you, networking is a *huge* topic on the Windows 2000 Professional exam. This chapter deals with two network-related objectives, and although few in number, they're much more important than many other objectives on Microsoft's list.

This chapter takes a look at getting Windows 2000 Professional ready for network participation, from installing a network card driver to configuring the protocols necessary to run Microsoft and Novell networks. Think of this material as "network plumbing." Other chapters (10 and 13) deal with other, higher-level aspects of networking. The dishwasher doesn't work if the pipes are misrouted, so it makes sense to look at the plumbing issues first.

Quick Assessment

Installing, configuring, and troubleshooting network adapters

1 Plug and Play network adapters automatically show up in the ______ folder.

2 Settings that are specific to a particular make and model of network adapter appear on the ______ tab of the adapter's configuration sheet.

3 The Microsoft adapter driver standard that permits multiple network protocols to work with a single network adapter is called ______.

4 Network adapters bind to ______.

Configuring and troubleshooting the TCP/IP protocol

5 The network feature that automatically assigns Windows 2000 IP addresses without a DHCP server present is called ______.

6 The subnet mask divides out the ______ ID part of the IP address from the ______ ID part.

7 If you can see local computers but not remote ones, you have probably misconfigured the ______.

8 You can use WINIPCFG in Windows 98 to examine IP settings. In Windows 2000, you use ______.

9 The part of TCP/IP that guarantees delivery is ______.

10 The name of Microsoft's implementation of Novell's IPX/SPX protocol is ______.

Answers

1 Network and Dial-Up Connections. See "Installing a network adapter" if you missed this question.

2 Advanced. "Configuring and troubleshooting a network adapter" has more.

3 NDIS. No points if you said "Network Device Interface Specification" because nobody likes a show-off. See "Installing a network adapter" for this tidbit.

4 Protocols. The "Bound for Glory" section explains what "binding" means.

5 Automatic Private IP Addressing. The "DHCP" section holds forth on this new-to-the-NT-platform feature.

6 Network, host. See "The IP address and subnet mask" if this is Greek to you (and you're not Greek).

7 Default gateway. See "The default gateway" in this chapter for details.

8 IPCONFIG. Windows 2000 doesn't get the pretty user interface of the Windows 98 tool, but the information is the same. See "Troubleshooting TCP/IP."

9 TCP. The IP part assembles and delivers packets. See "TCP/IP."

10 NWLink. No, this isn't really a TCP/IP question, but the exam does deal with NetWare protocols, even though Microsoft's objective list doesn't. See "NWLink, or should I say 'IPX/SPX/NetBIOS-compatible protocol.'"

Network Layers

Years ago, when vendors other than IBM got into the computer networking act, the industry realized the importance of defining a standard interface between different layers of the network "stack" (the software levels through which data travels, on both sending and receiving machines). Thus was born the famous seven-layer OSI (Open Systems Interconnect) model.

The OSI model

In case you see a question on the OSI model on the exam, the layers from top to bottom are the following:

- Application
- Presentation
- Session
- Transport
- Network
- Datalink
- Physical

The interfaces between each layer are published and standardized, so that you can use, say, a transport protocol from one vendor with a network card driver from another vendor, if both vendors follow the model.

TIME SHAVER

For the exam, you probably won't need to know exactly what each layer does, but I suggest that you remember the layer order. Use a memory aid. The phrases "**P**lease **D**o **N**ot **T**hrow **S**ausage **P**izza **A**way" (bottom to top) or "**A**ll **P**eople **S**eem **T**o **N**eed **D**ata **P**rocessing" (top to bottom) can jog your memory by providing the first letter of each layer.

Microsoft modules

Microsoft designed Windows 2000 in a modular fashion, including the networking bits, which correlate fairly closely to the OSI model. Some of the OSI layers are fixed in Windows 2000, such as the Win32 network API (Application Program Interface) that programmers use when writing applications. Some other OSI layers combine to form a single software component that you can add, replace, or delete in Windows 2000. The end result is that in Windows 2000, user-installable networking modules fall into the following four categories:

- **Adapter:** The network interface card (NIC) adapter requires a software device driver so that the upper layers of network software can communicate across the physical medium (copper cable, fiberoptic cable, and so on). You must have at least one adapter to participate in a network.
- **Protocol:** The "network language," or transport protocol, defines how Windows 2000 packages information. Two computers must speak the same protocol to communicate across a network. You must have at least one protocol to participate in a network.
- **Client:** The network client allows Windows 2000 to communicate with specific network operating systems, such as Windows 2000 Server and Novell NetWare. You must have at least one client to participate in a network.
- **Service:** Network services provide specialized capabilities, such as resource sharing (File and Printer Sharing for Microsoft Networks). You don't necessarily have to have any services loaded to participate in a network, but services are necessary to perform certain network functions.

You can see evidence of this four-level structure when you right-click a local area connection in the Network and Dial-Up Connections folder and choose Properties, displaying a screen such as Figure 6-1.

- The adapter for the specific LAN connection appears at the top in its own little area.
- Clients, protocols, and services are in the main components list.

This layout differs from that in Windows 9*x*, where all adapter drivers appear in the same list with all the other components, in the Network control panel.

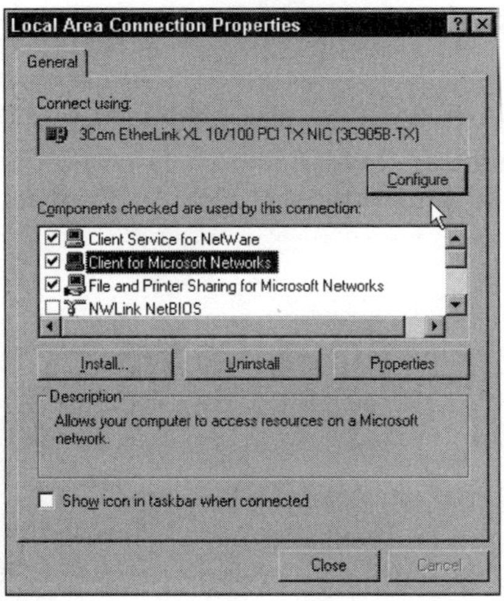

Figure 6-1: The LAN link's property sheet.

The fact that these four modular pieces are separately installable means that you can mix and match pieces to some extent. For example, a single adapter can support two protocols; you can run two or more clients over a single protocol; you can run a specific client over one protocol, or over a different one; and so on. You can also get modules from manufacturers other than Microsoft. The freedom to mix and match components provides flexibility, but it also begets a certain amount of complexity for the system designer.

Network Adapters

Network adapters, also known as network interface cards or NICs, typically plug into a bus slot of the PC on one end and into a network cable on the other end. Windows 2000 comes with a wide variety of network adapter *drivers,* the software components that allow Windows to communicate with the devices.

Installing a network adapter

You can install a network adapter driver two ways:

- If it's Plug and Play compatible, pop it into a bus slot and start the computer. Windows 2000 may ask for the installation CD-ROM or for a third-party diskette. And as the French say, wallah — an icon automatically appears for the network card in the Network and Dial-Up Connections folder.
- If it's not Plug and Play, run the Add New Hardware wizard from the control panel and follow the prompts to select the adapter's make and model.

NDIS (*Network Device Interface Specification*) Version 5.0 is Microsoft's preferred adapter driver type. It permits several different protocols and networks to run on a single adapter and it supports Plug and Play hardware detection.

Configuring and troubleshooting a network adapter

You can configure network adapter properties in two places:

- Device Manager tab of the System control panel
- Configure button in the network connection's property sheet

You generally won't need to change the resource settings that Windows 2000 assigns automatically (see Figure 6-2), and indeed you may not be *able* to change them depending on your PC and network card. But check the Resources tab for any reports of a conflict with another device's interrupt or memory requirements.

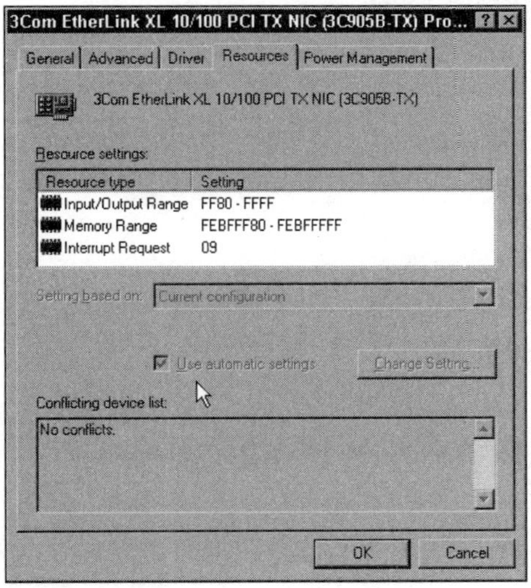

Figure 6-2: The resources this NIC uses can't be changed here.

The Advanced tab's appearance varies from one network adapter to the next (see Figure 6-3). You may find settings to:

- Use a twisted-pair connection (possibly abbreviated *TPE*, for Twisted-Pair Ethernet) or a coaxial cable connection (possibly appearing as *BNC*, for British Naval Connector) on a combo card. These connection choices sometimes go by the name "transceiver type" in the dialog box.
- Select a regular Ethernet plug or a Fast Ethernet plug.
- Choose full- or half-duplex communications.
- Offload error-checking calculations to the network card (usually a good idea as it frees up the main CPU for other chores).

Installing and configuring a network adapter is usually no big deal. The next section looks at the next higher network layer, the transport protocol, which (unfortunately) can get a *lot* more complicated.

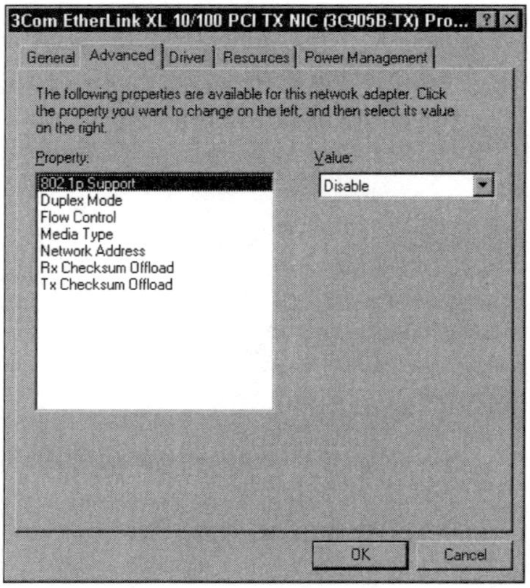

Figure 6-3: Settings on this tab depend on the NIC's make and model.

Network Protocols

The *protocol*, or, more properly, *transport protocol*, describes how network clients and servers package information for delivery and unpackage it upon receipt. The protocol communicates downward with the adapter driver, and upward with both client and service software. Protocol setup ranges from pleasingly simple (NetBEUI) to pretty darned complicated (TCP/IP).

INSTANT ANSWER

Two computers must "speak" the same protocol to communicate across a network.

Windows 2000 supports three main protocols, which are in common use for general purpose networking:

- NetBEUI
- IPX/SPX
- TCP/IP

The operating system also supports several secondary protocols, which are less common or provide a specialized networking function:

- DLC
- AppleTalk
- Network Monitor Driver (a pseudo-protocol)

You can install all of them via the local area network connection's property sheet by clicking the Install button and choosing Protocol, as shown in Figure 6-4. Note that when you install a protocol for one network adapter, that protocol becomes available for all other network adapters, too.

Although the published objective list only mentions TCP/IP, I'll bet a deep-dish pizza that the exam you take has at least one question on one other protocol.

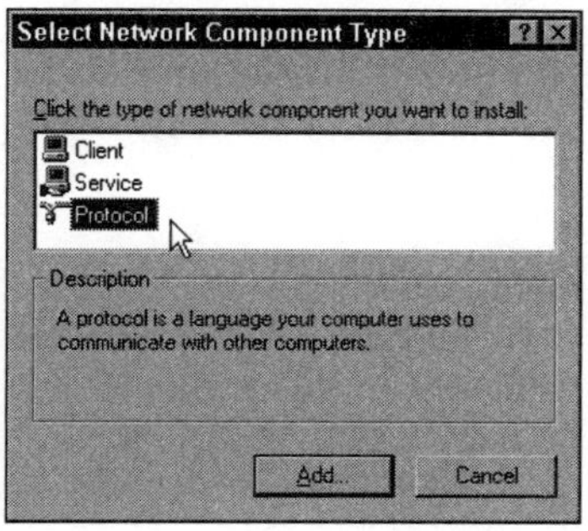

Figure 6-4: Installing a network protocol.

REMEMBER

Old hands at Windows should note that in Windows 2000, you activate network protocols on a *per-connection basis*, by opening the Network and Dial-Up Connections folder, right-clicking the connection of interest, and choosing Properties. For example, if you have two network cards in one PC, you can run TCP/IP on one card and NetBEUI on the other. In previous versions of Windows, you configured all connections in one big catch-all control panel window that could get pretty confusing.

NetBEUI

NetBIOS Extended User Interface, or NetBEUI for short (pronounced Net-BOOie), is great for a small local area network (Microsoft says 20 to 200 computers) that doesn't need to connect to the Internet and isn't likely to grow beyond a single physical location. Remember the following points about NetBEUI:

- NetBEUI works with a wide variety of operating systems, including Windows 9*x*, NT, Windows for Workgroups, and (now we're *really* going back in time) LAN Manager and MS-DOS.
- The NetBEUI addressing scheme is very simple: NetBEUI uses the computer name that you specify on the property sheet of the System control panel's Network Identification tab (see Figure 6-5).

- Managing a NetBEUI network is a piece of cake. All you have to do is make sure all computer names are unique. This protocol may be the only object in the entire Windows 2000 Professional operating system without a property sheet.

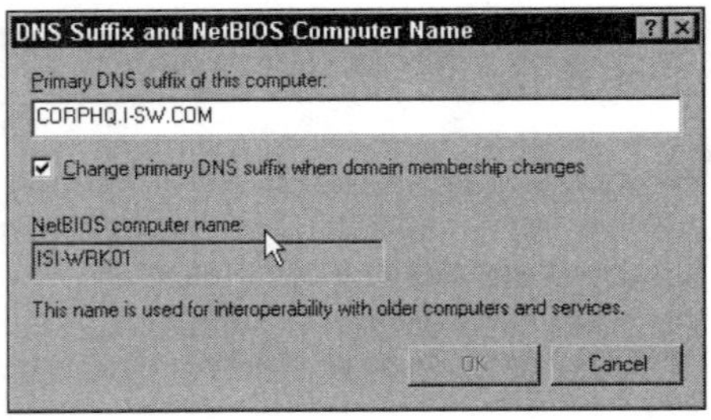

Figure 6-5: Viewing the old-style NetBIOS computer name.

Large networks don't use this protocol for two reasons:

- The main reason is that, unlike IPX/SPX and TCP/IP, NetBEUI isn't *routable*. That is, it can't communicate across routers, the traffic management devices that link subnetworks together.
- A secondary reason is that NetBEUI puts more "broadcast" traffic onto the network than other protocols.

Use NetBEUI for troubleshooting network connections. It's so simple and bulletproof that it's a great tool for verifying that you have a continuous physical connection between two PCs. Just add the protocol to the two PCs that you're troubleshooting, and see if the machines can see each other in My Network Places.

NWLink, or should I say "IPX/SPX/NetBIOS-compatible protocol"

Novell developed the IPX/SPX protocol (Internet Packet eXchange/Sequenced Packet eXchange) for its popular NetWare network.

You can use this network protocol in two ways:

- Microsoft workstations communicating with NetWare servers
- Microsoft-only environment

  In a Microsoft-only environment, you give up the benefits of Active Directory, which requires TCP/IP.

NWLink basics

Microsoft's version of IPX/SPX now goes by the name "IPX/SPX/NetBIOS-compatible protocol" or *NWLink* for short. NWLink is a workalike for Novell's network protocol in all key respects:

- NWLink is routable, so you can use it in large networks.
- NWLink runs programs that use *Winsock* or *NetBIOS-over-IPX* to communicate with the network. (Just memorize this point.)
- For computer addressing purposes, this protocol uses a unique identifier (the "MAC address" where MAC = Media Access Layer) that is burned into a chip on the network interface card.
- This protocol is relatively easy to manage, because NIC manufacturers worry about ensuring unique MAC addresses on every adapter.
- IPX/SPX grew out of the PC DOS environment, which means support for other platforms (notably, UNIX) isn't strong.

NWLink and related components

On the exam, NWLink appears most often with reference to NetWare servers. In fact, if you install the *Client Service for NetWare* (which lets you access NetWare 2.*x*, 3.*x*, or 4.*x* servers), Windows 2000 installs NWLink automatically. However, you can use NWLink in all-Microsoft networks, too, so don't be fooled.

Client Service for NetWare doesn't support NetWare 5.*x* servers running IP.

The Client Service for NetWare supports NDS (NetWare Directory Services) without additional components. NDS is software for NetWare versions 4.*x* and above that organizes network resources into a single, hierarchical structure. This method is an advance over the bindery method in NetWare 3.*x*, because the bindery is a server-centric database of users and groups. In other words, if you want to use a resource on a bindery-based server other than the bindery-based server you're logged onto already, you must log on to the other server. When a user logs on to an NDS "tree," however, all the network resources that that user has rights to access are available, regardless of where those resources live. Microsoft's Active Directory is a direct response to the success of NDS in large organizations.

When you configure Client Service for NetWare (and, oddly, you must do that via the CSN control panel; the client's Properties button in the Network and Dial-Up Connections folder doesn't work), you can set either a *preferred server* (for bindery-based networks) or a *preferred tree and context* (for NDS-based networks). But you shouldn't set both. The "context" is the tree location of the user's NetWare user object. And that's about all you need to know about that; you shouldn't have to know any details about the NDS structure or about Novell's NDS object naming conventions for the Windows 2000 Professional exam.

If you only need to connect to client/server applications (such as SQL Server) running on a NetWare server, NWLink is all you need. You don't have to have the Client Service for NetWare, unless you also need connectivity to NetWare file and print services.

If the exam refers to a network component named File and Print Services for NetWare (FPSN), that animal only works with Windows 2000 Server. It lets NetWare clients access file and print services on a Windows 2000 Server machine. I mention this because many test-takers confuse FPSN with the Client Service for NetWare, which runs on Windows 2000 Professional.

Configuring NWLink

Configuring NWLink is pretty simple. This section covers the three variables you can set: *frame type*, *network number*, and *internal network number*. Set these via the property sheet for the protocol, as listed on the Networking tab of the connection's property sheet (see Figure 6-6).

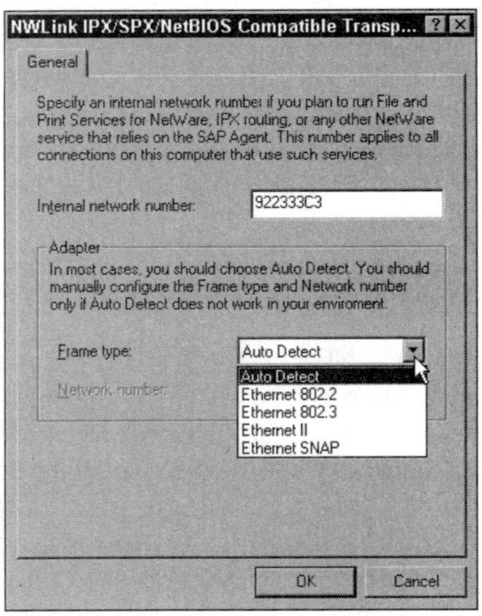

Figure 6-6: NWLink properties for a specific LAN connection.

Frame type

One of the more common reasons for a failure to connect in an NWLink network is a frame type mismatch.

Don't worry about the details of what a frame type is. Just know that it

- Affects how Windows packages network data
- Must match the frame type that your server uses for you to connect to that server

The default setting of "Auto Detect" means that Windows 2000 tries to sense the correct frame type at the time you install NWLink. However, if it can't, then on an Ethernet network, it defaults to 802.2, the frame type used by NetWare 3.12 and above. (The 802.3 frame type is an older version in less common use today, despite the newer number.) You can manually set the frame type and not worry about whether Windows 2000's autodetection will work properly or not.

Network number

Computers on an NWLink network segment must all have the same network number to see each other. Usually, Windows 2000's autodetection capability works fine and you don't need to modify this value. (Good thing, because to change it, you must use a Registry editor.) In fact, if you enable autodetection for the frame type, you can't manually enter a network number — the field appears "grayed out" in the dialog box.

Internal network number

This eight-digit number is for internal routing. You normally don't need to use it unless you're running Windows 2000 Server and either File and Print Service for NetWare or IPX routing. The default value is 00000000.

TCP/IP

Configuring TCP/IP is simple, fun, and I lie like a rug. The subject receives its own major section (following this one) because TCP/IP can be complex to configure and because Exam #70-210 (to say nothing of the other exams) focuses on it. But first, a brief introduction is in order.

TCP/IP is the protocol of choice in organizations large and small. Why, if it's so complicated?

- PCs can connect to the Internet without adding another protocol, because TCP/IP is the native protocol of the Net.
- TCP/IP is routable and works well over wide-area networks.
- TCP/IP runs on lots of operating systems: Mac, UNIX, and so on.
- TCP/IP isn't a proprietary, closed standard, but rather, a set of standards developed with public funds and not controlled by any single computer company.

TCP/IP is actually two network protocols: TCP, or Transmission Control Protocol, guarantees delivery and handles errors, while IP, or Internet Protocol, packages and delivers data packets.

Focus on TCP/IP

Of the primary network protocols, the exam hits TCP/IP the hardest, so this rather long section presents the details you should know.

If this is new territory for you, don't expect to absorb this stuff in a single read; it may take two or three.

The IP address and subnet mask

In the TCP/IP scheme of things, computers find each other by means of *IP addresses:* unique numbers having four numeric parts (called *octets*) separated by periods (like 127.0.0.1). Actually, it's more correct to say "*network cards* find each other," because two or more network cards in the same computer may have their own IP addresses, subnet masks, and default gateways.

You can assign a specific, *static* IP address to a network card via the TCP/IP property sheet's Use The Following IP Address radio button and related fields (see Figure 6-7). You might do that, for example, if other computers on the network need to know your computer's IP address ahead of time. Such might be the case when you're playing a multiuser Internet game in which other players need to know your PC's IP address. Another time you'd use a static IP address is when you're configuring a Windows 2000 Server machine that workstations may be configured to find at a specific, constant IP address — for example, a server running either the DNS or WINS service. (This chapter discusses DNS and WINS a bit later.)

The more normal situation (and the default setup) for Windows 2000 Professional is to have Windows go fetch an IP address from another computer on the network whose job is to provide such dynamic addresses on demand. Such a computer is called a *DHCP server* (see "DHCP, WINS, and DNS" later in this section).

The *subnet mask* is another four-number number, but it has a very specific function. Wrapped up in the four octets of an IP address are actually two addresses: the network ID and the computer or "host" ID. (Kind of like a street name and a house number in a physical mail address.) However, the dividing line between where the network ID ends and where the host ID begins is a flexible one; that is, it can change from one network to the next.

In order to figure out what exact part of any given IP address is the network ID and what part is the host ID, it's necessary to look at a second number that defines where the dividing line is for this particular IP address. That second number is — you guessed it — the subnet mask. TCP/IP uses the subnet mask to figure out, for example, whether a particular IP address is on the local network or on a remote network.

An example of a subnet mask is 255.255.255.0.

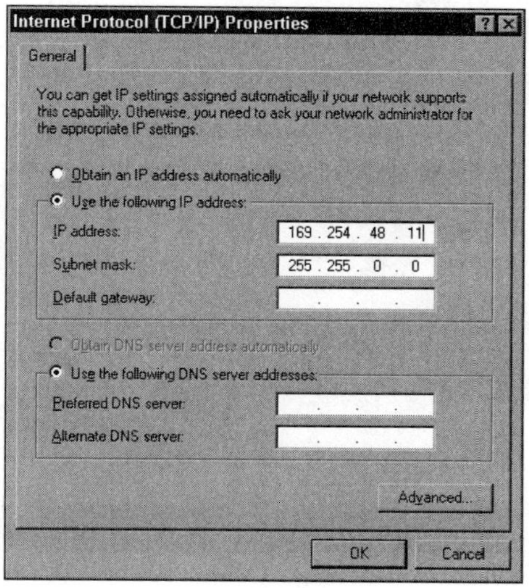

Figure 6-7: Windows 2000 can have a static IP address or a dynamic, automatic address.

INSTANT ANSWER

The bare minimum configuration information that a Windows 2000 Pro PC must have to participate in a TCP/IP network are

- IP address
- Subnet mask

INSTANT ANSWER

If a PC's IP address and subnet mask are correctly configured, then the PC should be able to connect to a server on the local network.

TIME SHAVER

You probably won't have to know the details of different classes of IP addresses, or how to interpret a particular subnet mask, for the Windows 2000 exam.

The default gateway

If you want to connect to other networks, then you must configure TCP/IP to look for a *gateway* — a computer that links your network with another one (such as the public Internet). In this context, a gateway is simply a *router,* if you're already familiar with that term.

You can specify a default gateway on the General tab of the TCP/IP protocol's property sheet, and you can specify additional gateways by clicking that property sheet's Advanced button and entering the gateway IP addresses on the IP Settings tab (see Figure 6-8). The default gateway is the one your computer will use to connect to other networks unless the default gateway isn't available, in which case Windows 2000 tries to use a gateway that appears on the supplemental list.

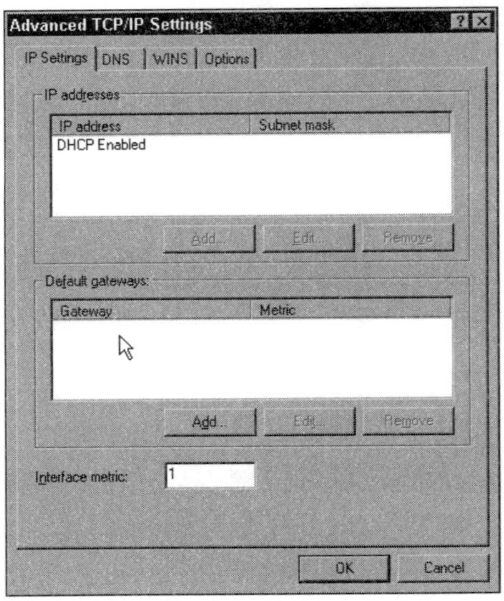

Figure 6-8: You can enter one or more extra gateway addresses here.

You're likely to see more than one exam question expecting you to know that on a routed network, the proper default gateway for a client workstation is the IP address of the router's network port nearest that workstation — that is, on the same subnet as the workstation.

If you have a DHCP server on your network and you choose the Obtain An IP Address Automatically radio button in Figure 6-7, then the DHCP server assigns your Windows 2000 PC a default gateway upon logon. If you specify a static IP address for your computer and for the default gateway, the static address for the gateway takes precedence over the address that the DHCP server would assign.

DHCP, WINS, and DNS

Get out your bowl because here comes the alphabet soup. The programs in this section all have one overarching goal: to make managing IP addresses more automatic.

DHCP

DHCP (Dynamic Host Configuration Protocol) is a service that assigns, or "leases," a computer an IP address from a range of IP addresses when that computer logs on to the network. Actually, DHCP also typically assigns a subnet mask, a default gateway address, and a DNS server address. DHCP can run on a Windows 2000 Server, but it can also run on an NT server, a NetWare 4.11 or 5.0+ server, or a UNIX computer. The DHCP service does *not* run on Windows 2000 Professional, although Windows 2000 Professional machines can be DHCP clients.

DHCP sure beats running around from machine to machine keying in fixed, or "static," IP addresses and subnet masks in the TCP/IP control panel. Activate a Windows 2000 Professional machine as a DHCP client by clicking the Obtain An IP Address Automatically option on the General tab of the TCP/IP property sheet. That's it!

TIP: You can see the currently assigned IP address for your computer, and lease details for that address, by running the command-line program IPCONFIG. You can also use IPCONFIG to terminate or renew an address lease.

If you've set the automatic option, but no DHCP server is available, Windows 2000 uses a new feature called *Automatic Private IP Addressing (APIPA)*. This feature makes the PC assign itself an IP address with a predefined format (169.254.x.x and a subnet mask of 255.255.0.0, but don't memorize that for the exam unless you feel the need to get an "A" instead of a mere passing grade).

TIME SHAVER: The only way to turn APIPA off is to hack the Registry, but you don't need to know the specific key for the exam.

INSTANT ANSWER: Windows 2000 PCs that have assigned themselves an IP address via Automatic Private IP Addressing can usually only communicate with other Windows 2000 or Windows 98 PCs on the same subnet that have done the same.

INSTANT ANSWER: If no DHCP server exists on a subnet, Windows 2000 Professional machines can still use DHCP in two cases: If a router on the subnet supports DHCP forwarding (also called *DHCP/BOOTP forwarding*), or if a server (Windows 2000 or NT 4) on the subnet runs a service called *DHCP Relay Agent*. A machine running DHCP Relay Agent knows the IP address of the remote DHCP server, and can shuttle DHCP messages back and forth from subnet to subnet. You may see this tidbit crop up in exam questions having to do with Windows 2000 Remote Installation Service (RIS), which only works if clients can "see" a DHCP server in one fashion or another.

WINS

Before Windows 2000, every Windows computer has a *NetBIOS name,* or "computer name," which identifies it on a Microsoft-based network. In order for a network user to find your PC anywhere on a TCP/IP network by specifying your PC's NetBIOS name, the TCP/IP protocol must consult a lookup directory somewhere that correlates the NetBIOS name with an IP address.

That lookup is exactly what a *WINS (Windows Internet Naming Service)* server does. You set it up on the WINS tab of the TCP/IP advanced property sheet (see Figure 6-9). WINS is another program that can run on a Windows 2000 or NT Server in a TCP/IP network.

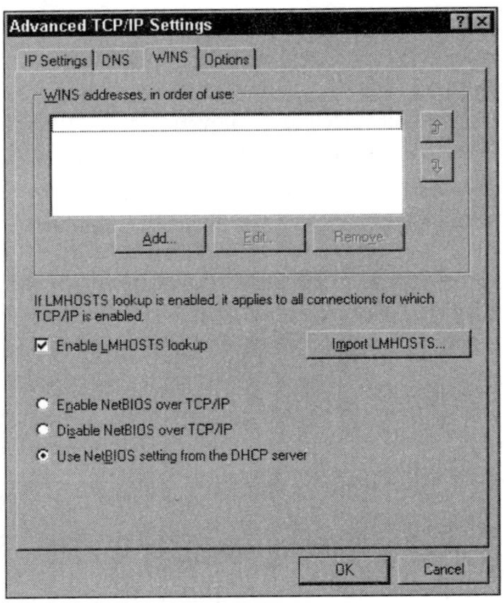

Figure 6-9: You can let DHCP provide WINS information, or specify it yourself.

There are two ways to set the address of a WINS server:

- Click the radio button "Use NetBIOS Setting From The DHCP Server."

  Windows 2000 gets the address of a WINS server from the DHCP server.

- Click the "Enable NetBIOS Over TCP/IP" radio button and enter the WINS server's IP address(es) yourself.

Without WINS, you can still browse the local subnetwork using NetBIOS names, but you can't connect to Windows PCs on a remote subnetwork. The exam may include a question describing a situation where a user can see other PCs on the local subnet but can't find PCs on other subnets using their NetBIOS names. The answer will probably reflect the likelihood that the user's WINS configuration isn't correct, or the WINS server is down.

It's possible that the exam will ask you about LMHOSTS (see the related check box in Figure 6-9). This text file lives on the local PC and correlates NetBIOS names with IP addresses. Because administrators must maintain LMHOSTS manually every time an IP address change or a computer name change occurs on the network, LMHOSTS is an awful pain. Just remember that with WINS, you don't need LMHOSTS anymore. In fact, with DNS, one day you won't need WINS anymore, either, as the following section explains.

DNS

Yet another way of accessing computers on a TCP/IP network is by domain name (also called *host name*). You're already familiar with domain names such as `www.dummies.com`. A TCP/IP network doesn't have to use domain names, but doing so is often very convenient; for example, in a company-wide intranet. Here again, some facility must exist for domain names to be matched up with IP addresses. The typical facility is a DNS server, where DNS is short for Domain Naming Service (or, sometimes, Domain Naming System). Windows 2000 networks rely heavily on DNS, not least for the new Active Directory service.

The DNS service itself only runs on Windows 2000 Server, but you must know how to configure a Windows 2000 Professional machine to locate a DNS server on the network. The usual approach is to leave the Obtain DNS Server Address Automatically radio button selected on the TCP/IP property sheet for the connection of interest. (This method uses DHCP to get the DNS server address or addresses — see earlier in this chapter.) Otherwise, you can click Use The Following DNS Server Addresses and type in a main and alternate IP address for the DNS server(s) on your network.

Troubleshooting TCP/IP

The more settings that exist for a given computer feature, the greater the likelihood that something won't work. Client configuration problems are nonexistent under NetBEUI, rare under NWLink, and as common as Bill Gates haircut jokes under TCP/IP. Following is my four-step program for troubleshooting TCP/IP connections which illustrates the use of two utilities you may well see on the exam: *ipconfig* and *ping*.

1. **Make sure that the TCP/IP protocol has initialized itself on your computer. Open a command prompt with Start⇨Run⇨CMD, then type** IPCONFIG /ALL | MORE.

   You should see a display something like Figure 6-10 if the protocol is running, including your IP address, subnet mask, and other details. If the subnet mask is 0.0.0.0, then your computer has a duplicate IP address!

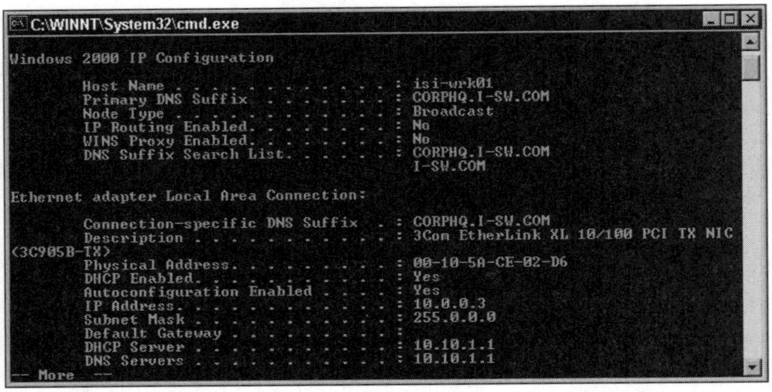

Figure 6-10: Windows 2000 offers IPCONFIG as a text command.

2. **While still at the command prompt, type** PING 127.0.0.1 **to confirm that TCP/IP is bound to your network adapter.**

   The IP address 127.0.0.1 is known as the *loopback address*. A successful result is a "reply from" message repeated four times.

3. **Ping the default gateway.**

   If you get a successful result here (again, four happy reply messages), then your computer can "see" other computers on the same subnet and (specifically) the gateway computer or router that is your link to computers on other subnets.

4. **Ping a computer on a remote subnet, to ensure that your computer can see computers on the other side of the router.**

Secondary Network Protocols

The exam may quiz you on one of the secondary network protocols that Windows 2000 Professional supports. Thankfully, you don't need to remember a lot of details about these protocols.

Microsoft DLC

The *Data Link Control* (*DLC*) protocol is handy for connecting a Windows 2000 PC to certain types of networked printers, particularly Hewlett-Packard models with JetDirect network adapters. You would also use DLC to communicate with some IBM minicomputers and mainframes.

Know the following material for the exam:

- DLC has a "continuous mode" that locks up a networked printer until a print job transmission is complete.
- DLC needs only be installed on the computer that acts as print server, not on every workstation that can submit a print job.
- You don't use this protocol as your main protocol for communicating with Windows NT Server or Novell NetWare networks.

AppleTalk

AppleTalk lets Windows 2000 machines interoperate with Apple Macintosh computers. You can install it on a Windows 2000 Professional machine, but I'm not sure why, as it's intended mainly for use on Windows 2000 Server. Microsoft's massive *Windows 2000 Professional Resource Kit* doesn't even list AppleTalk in the index, so I think it's safe to assume that the exam won't annoy you about the subject.

Network Monitor Driver

The Network Monitor Driver isn't a network protocol in the traditional sense. Installing it enables Windows 2000 to collect statistics about your computer's network card activity, for reporting to a Windows 2000 Server machine running either Network Monitor or Systems Management Server.

Bound for Glory

A *binding* is simply a rather unusual word for an active connection between network layers. View bindings by opening the Network and Dial-Up Connections folder and choosing Advanced⇨Advanced Settings (see Figure 6-11). As usual, you've got to be an Administrator to make any changes here.

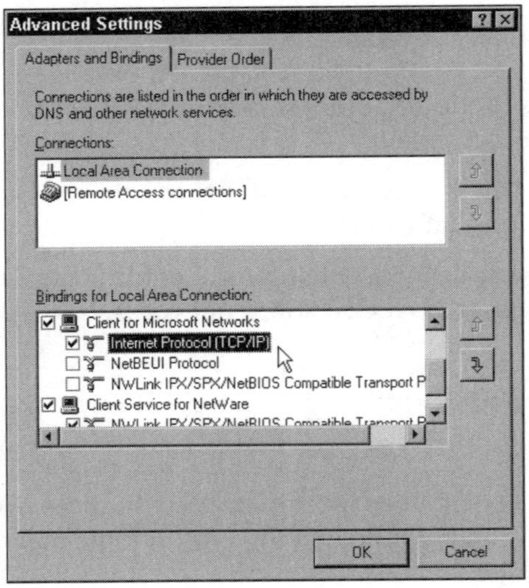

Figure 6-11: Control active network bindings here.

The check boxes indicate which network protocols, services, and clients you can use at this moment on the selected connection. You may very well want to modify these settings. For example, if you use your adapter solely for communicating on a NetWare network running NWLink, you would clear the TCP/IP check box. (You may have TCP/IP installed for use with a modem, but you configure that connection using a different icon in the Network and Dial-Up Connections folder.)

REMEMBER

Remember these two rules of the Bindings and Adapters tab:

- Disable unused adapter bindings for better speed and security and for a somewhat smaller memory footprint.

  Perform this task by clearing the related check boxes.

- Position protocols in the order that you're likely to use them, using the up and down arrows to the right of the dialog box.

  This improves performance over the long run, as Windows doesn't waste as much time trying to establish connections with inappropriate protocols.

Prep Test

1 **James can't access computers at a remote office, although he can access computers in the local office just fine. When you go to James' computer and ping the default gateway as specified in James' Network and Dial-Up Connections folder, you get an error message instead of the normal "reply from" messages.**

Which of the following explanations are possible? (Choose all that apply.)

A ❑ The router whose address appears in the default gateway field on James's machine has a problem.

B ❑ The router address specified in the default gateway field on James' machine is incorrect.

C ❑ James has an invalid subnet mask setting.

D ❑ James has an invalid DHCP setting.

E ❑ The primary domain controller for the network is down.

2 **You're setting up a small, 10-computer workgroup network that will not need Internet connectivity or a connection to your corporate WAN. The workgroup is to be managed by the users and therefore should be as simple and easy to configure and maintain as possible. Which network protocol would be a good choice for this situation? (Choose the best answer.)**

A ❍ DNS

B ❍ NetBIOS

C ❍ NetBEUI

D ❍ IPX/SPX

E ❍ TCP/IP

3 **In order for computers on the same physical TCP/IP network (subnet) to communicate with each other, they must have the same what? (Choose all that apply.)**

A ❑ Network ID

B ❑ Host ID

C ❑ Subnet mask

D ❑ Workgroup name

4 **You set up a subnet of 20 computers running TCP/IP and Windows 2000 Professional, and 1 computer running Windows 2000 Server. A router connects the subnet to other subnets in your company. However, the router does not support DHCP/BOOTP forwarding, and you have no DHCP server on your subnet, although two DHCP servers exist on the other side of the router. How could you configure the network so that the Windows 2000 Professional machines can use DHCP? (Choose all that apply.)**

A ❑ Load and activate the DHCP service on the Windows 2000 Server machine on your local subnet.

B ❑ Load and activate the DHCP service on a relatively lightly used Windows 2000 Professional machine on your local subnet.

C ❑ Load and activate the DHCP Relay Agent on the Windows 2000 Server machine on your local subnet.

D ❑ Load and activate the DHCP Relay Agent on a relatively lightly used Windows 2000 Professional machine on your local subnet.

5 **NWLink is required by which of the following network services? (Choose all that apply.)**

A ❑ Client Service for NetWare

B ❑ Novell Client for Windows 2000

C ❑ Gateway Service for NetWare

D ❑ IPX/SPX

6 **Which IP address is known as the "loopback address?"**

A ❍ 10.0.0.1

B ❍ 10.1.1.1

C ❍ 169.254.0.1

D ❍ 127.0.0.1

7 **What does PING stand for?**

A ❍ Pretty Important Network Gizmo

B ❍ Packet InterNet Groper

C ❍ Packet Internet Notification Genie

D ❍ It's not an acronym, it's the sound a submarine's radar makes.

8 **A Windows 2000 Professional machine has the "Obtain DNS Server Address Automatically" radio button selected. What service does this workstation actually use to obtain one or more DNS server addresses? (Choose the best answer.)**

A ❍ APIPA

B ❍ Broadcast

C ❍ WINS

D ❍ DHCP

9 **You are a local PC tech support person for a large company. A user in your office named Vicky complains of poor performance when accessing network resources. You call the corporate guru, who tells you to install the Network Monitor Driver on Vicky's machine. How do you do this? (Choose the best answer.)**

A ❍ On Vicky's computer, open Network and Dial-Up Connections, right-click the Local Area Connection icon, choose Properties, click the Install button, and choose Protocol.

B ❍ On Vicky's computer, open Network and Dial-Up Connections, right-click the Local Area Connection icon, choose Properties, click the Install button, and choose Service.

C ❍ On Vicky's computer, open Network and Dial-Up Connections, right-click the Local Area Connection icon, choose Properties, and check the box labeled "Network Monitor Driver."

D ❍ Run the Add/Remove Programs wizard and choose Windows Components.

10 **James (from Question #1) calls back. You fixed his system so that he can communicate with remote computers as long as he specifies their IP address. However, he can't communicate with them by specifying their NetBIOS names. What should you do? (Choose the best answer.)**

A ❍ Tell James to go away, he's being a pest.

B ❍ Check out the address setting for James's DNS server.

C ❍ Check out the address setting for James's WINS server.

D ❍ Check out the address setting for James's default gateway.

Answers

1 **A** and **B**. If James had an invalid subnet mask, or an invalid DHCP setting, he couldn't see local computers. If the domain controller were down, James wouldn't be able to log on to the network.

2 **C**. NetBEUI isn't routable, but that's not needed in this situation, and the protocol is trivial to set up and maintain. Choices A and B aren't protocols in the sense that the question implies. Choice D would be a close second to NetBEUI, but the latter is still simpler and faster. Choice E would not make sense here, despite the advance that Automatic Private IP Addressing makes in terms of ease of use for small TCP/IP networks.

3 **A** and **C**. Because the same network ID is required, the same subnet mask is also required; two computers cannot have the same network ID without also having the same subnet mask, for the subnet mask determines how many bits are in the network ID. The workgroup name answer is wrong because the computers may not even be in a workgroup — they may be in a Windows 2000 domain, in which case the computers would not have workgroup names configured.

4 **A** and **C**. The exam expects you to know that you can use either the DHCP service or the DHCP Relay Agent service on a subnet to permit Windows 2000 Professional machines to access DHCP. The exam also expects you to know that these services require a member of the Windows 2000 Server family. No, these are not strictly workstation topics, so be aware that the exam expects a fair knowledge of server technology!

5 **A** and **C**. Novell's client software comes with Novell's own implementation of IPX/SPX and also supports TCP/IP access to NetWare 5 servers. Choice D is wrong because NWLink is a lookalike replacement for IPX/SPX. Remember for the exam that CSNW runs on Windows 2000 Professional, while GSNW runs on Windows 2000 Server.

6 **D**. You would use this address (memorize it) with the PING command in order to verify that TCP/IP is properly installed and bound to your network adapter.

7 **B**. Yes, this is the gag question, but the answer is correct. My favorite computer industry acronym of all time, however, remains APL, which stands for A Programming Language. I swear.

8 **D.** The DHCP service can provide DNS server addresses in addition to IP addresses, subnet masks, and default gateway addresses.

9 **A.** The Network Monitor Driver allows a Windows 2000 Server machine running Network Monitor to gather performance data about Vicky's network connection.

10 **C.** WINS, or Windows Internet Name Service, is responsible for matching up NetBIOS names with IP addresses on a routed network.

Part III

Installing and Configuring Hardware

The 5th Wave By Rich Tennant

"Look, I've told you the story of `OSI and the Seven Layers' twice this week already."

In this part . . .

A huge part of any operating system's day-to-day responsibilities is acting as intermediary between user and hardware. This part breaks out hardware into three groups. Chapter 7 deals with disks, tapes, and printers. Chapter 8 covers displays and other input/output devices. Chapter 9 concentrates on portable computing hardware, including important discussions on Plug and Play and power management — two features that set Windows 2000 apart from Windows NT.

Chapter 7

Installing and Configuring Disks, Tapes, and Printers

Exam Objectives

- Monitoring and configuring disks
- Monitoring, configuring, and troubleshooting volumes
- Installing, configuring, and managing DVD and CD-ROM devices
- Monitoring and configuring removable media, such as tape devices
- Managing printers and print jobs
- Connecting to a local print device
- Connecting to an Internet printer

If you have a CPU, some RAM, a keyboard, and a display, you can do some computing. However, if you want to *keep* your work from one session to another, or share it with others, then disks, tapes, and printers come in mighty handy. Ergo, almost all PCs have some form of magnetic storage and printout capability.

This chapter discusses how Windows 2000 Professional deals with storage devices of the magnetic and paper variety. As usual, the chapter covers all bases, but you would be smart to focus especially closely on the "new and cool" topics — such as dynamic disks and Internet printing. Hint, hint, nudge, nudge. Chapter 8 looks at how Windows 2000 supports other, less universal hardware, such as multiple displays and USB devices.

Quick Assessment

Monitoring and configuring disks

1 Nearly all of your disk configuration activity can be performed with the _____ console snap-in.

2 If you want to monitor disk usage by user, activate the _____ feature.

Monitoring, configuring, and troubleshooting volumes

3 How many partitions can you create on a dynamic disk? _____

4 For the best possible disk performance, create a _____ volume.

Installing, configuring, and managing DVD and CD-ROM devices

5 If Windows 2000 doesn't work with a given CD-ROM drive, you should _____.

Monitoring and configuring removable media

6 A removable cartridge disk can contain a maximum of _____ partition(s).

Managing printers and print jobs

7 In Microspeak, the software interface between the operating system and a physical print device is called a _____.

8 You can create a printer _____ so that a single logical printer connects to multiple physical print devices.

Connecting to a local print device

9 You can tell that a specific printer is the default printer because its icon features a _____.

Connecting to an Internet printer

10 You can connect to a TCP/IP network printer by using the printer's _____ or its _____.

Answers

1 *Disk Management*. "Hard Drives, Partitions, and Volumes" refers to this utility, which supersedes the NT 4.0 Disk Administrator tool.

2 *Quota*. See "Setting quotas" for the details.

3 *None*. Dynamic disks use volumes instead of partitions. See "Hard Drives, Partitions, and Volumes" for this and other wisdom.

4 *Striped*. No points if you said "fast." The "Creating volumes" section has the lowdown.

5 *Replace it*. There are no settings to adjust. The "Optical Disks" section elaborates.

6 *One*. The "Removable Media" section has more.

7 *Printer*. If you missed this one (and most do), "A bit of terminology" is the section to read.

8 *Pool*. See "Pooling" in this chapter for how to set this up.

9 *Check mark*. See "Installing a new printer" for more.

10 *IP address, DNS name*. The "Finding a printer" section explains.

Hard Drives, Partitions, and Volumes

Organizing disk drives is a central function of any operating system and a sure subject for exam questions. Windows 2000 supports two kinds of disk organization:

- *Basic disks*, which use *partitions* to organize the disk into storage units in much the same way that Windows NT Workstation 4.0, Windows 98/95, and MS-DOS do.
- *Dynamic disks*, which use *volumes* to organize the disk and which are unique to Windows 2000.

Use partitions with basic disks. Use volumes with dynamic disks.

Dynamic disks use a special database, called the *Logical Disk Manager* (LDM) database, that lives on the disk's last megabyte of space. Windows replicates the LDM database onto each disk in a dynamic disk group. Because only Windows 2000 knows how to access and interpret the LDM, dynamic disks work only with Windows 2000.

A single physical disk must be either basic or dynamic. On a PC with multiple disks, however, basic disks can cohabitate with dynamic disks.

Windows 2000 sets up disks as basic disks by default, unless you're upgrading a Windows NT Workstation 4.0 machine that uses advanced disk management features such as stripe sets or volume sets. You can upgrade a basic disk to a dynamic disk with the Disk Management utility (see Lab 7-1 later in this chapter). You might perform such an upgrade if you want to create a *striped volume* (for better speed) or a *spanned volume* (for better use of space).

You can use dynamic disks with any of the three Windows 2000 file systems, but certain features, such as extending a volume, are available only if you use NTFS. (If you don't know what the heck NTFS is, please read Chapter 3.)

No matter whether you use basic or dynamic disks, Windows 2000 Professional does *not* provide any form of fault tolerance for disks in any configuration. You don't get mirroring, duplexing, or RAID unless you use Windows 2000 Server, or unless you buy a third-party hardware solution that provides such features independently from the operating system. (If I may subtly editorialize: "Boooo!")

Configuring hard drives

Here are the actions that you can take to configure hard drives:

- Partition a basic disk.
- Promote a basic disk to a dynamic disk.
- Create volumes.
- Extend volumes.
- Set quotas.
- Set mount points.

The following sections examine each action in turn.

Partitioning a basic disk

Those of you who are familiar with partitioning disks in earlier versions of Windows will see no earth-shattering differences with Windows 2000 Professional, but do take note that you use either Windows 2000 setup (during installation) or the Disk Management "snap-in" (after installation) to partition disks. (You can forget about FDISK, praise be.)

Creating a partition in Disk Management is simplicity itself:

- On a primary partition, right-click an area of unallocated space in the graphical display and choose Create Partition.
- On an extended partition, right-click an area of free space and choose Create Logical Drive.

Know the following two key terms for the exam. These may be the same, but they don't have to be; the boot partition could live on a second primary partition, for example, or on a logical drive on an extended partition.

- The *system partition* is the partition containing hardware-specific files and the one from which Windows 2000 starts the boot process.
- The *boot partition* is the partition containing the operating system files themselves (usually, the WINNT folder).

The terminology is perverse:

- The computer *boots* from the *system* partition.
- The operating *system* is on the *boot* partition.

Here are the basic rules of partitioning:

- Any basic disk must have at least one partition.
- Partitions come in two types:
  - **Primary:** You can set this as the active *system partition.*
  - **Extended:** Cannot be the active system partition, but can contain multiple logical drives, each of which you format separately.
- A hard disk may have no more than one extended partition.
- A hard disk may have no more than four partitions total. These can be three primary plus one extended, or four primary.
- Microsoft recommends using a separate partition for each operating system in a multiple-boot setup.
- You must create a primary partition first, then (if desired) an extended partition, then any logical drives on the extended partition.

Promoting a basic disk to a dynamic disk

Windows 2000 sets up your disks as basic disks by default. So, usually, when you want to set up a dynamic disk, you'll be upgrading, or *promoting,* a basic disk. You can promote a basic disk to a dynamic disk without losing data, but watch out: Going in the reverse direction (*reverting* to a basic disk) wipes out all the data on the disk!

Promoting a basic disk to a dynamic disk is simple, as Lab 7-1 explains.

Lab 7-1 Promoting a Basic Disk to a Dynamic Disk

1. **Back up the disk that you want to promote.**

   You may not need this backup, but better safe than sorry.

2. **Log on as Administrator.**
3. **Right-click My Computer and choose Manage.**

   The Computer Management console appears.

4. **Click the Disk Management icon in the tree pane (on the left; see Figure 7-1).**
5. **In the lower-right window frame, right-click the box containing the disk icon and the words "Disk 0" or "Disk 1" or whatever number it may be.**

   Don't right-click any of the partition boxes that appear to the right.

6. **Select the Upgrade To Dynamic Disk menu option.**

   You won't see this option on removable disk devices because such devices can only be basic disks in Windows 2000 Professional.

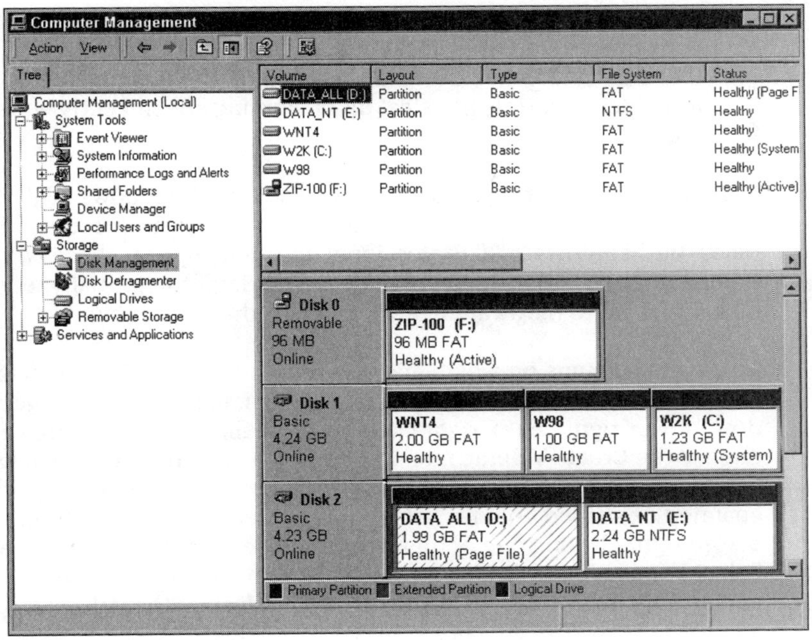

Figure 7-1: The Disk Management snap-in offers a tree view (upper right) or graphical view (lower right).

7. **Confirm your choice of which disk to promote by checking the correct box next to the disk name.**

   Windows then displays various warning messages that you should read but (if you're like me) probably won't.

8. **Finish with the upgrade wizard and reboot.**

WARNING!

The option to upgrade a basic disk to a dynamic disk may appear on a portable PC, but Microsoft doesn't support Windows 2000 dynamic disks on portable computers. Dynamic disks only convey benefits when you have more than one hard drive in a computer, and most notebook PCs have only one hard drive. Also, if a notebook PC uses one hard drive internally, and a second hard drive in a docking station, the two drives' LDM databases could easily get out of sync.

Creating volumes

Windows 2000 Professional supports three kinds of volumes on dynamic disks:

- **Simple:** One disk, one volume.
- **Spanned:** Multiple (2 to 32) disks, one volume. Windows fills the first disk completely before moving to the second, and so on. Efficient use of space (no "slack" at the end of a disk).

- **Striped:** Multiple (2 to 32) disks, one volume. Windows fills each disk at the same rate, in 64K blocks, so, for example, a 2-disk striped volume that's half full consists of 2 disks, each of which is half full. Fastest performance (multiple physical disks working concurrently equals better speed).

WARNING!

Don't let the exam trip you up if it asks you about Windows 2000 Professional and fault tolerance: Windows 2000 Server supports mirrored and RAID-5 volumes, but Windows 2000 Professional does not support these two additional types. Spanned and striped volumes are not fault-tolerant: If you lose one disk in the set to hardware failure, you lose the whole volume.

To create a volume on a dynamic disk, first make sure that the disk is dynamic (see the previous section if necessary). Then, in the Disk Management window (lower-right pane), right-click in the unallocated space area and then choose the Create Volume menu option. (If you choose only a single unallocated space area, you will create a simple volume. If you want to create a spanned or striped volume, select unallocated areas from multiple disks before right-clicking one of them, and choose "spanned" or "striped" in the Select Volume Type window.) Give the volume a size, assign it a drive letter, and specify how you want Windows 2000 to format the volume.

REMEMBER

Microsoft suggests that you use the Logical Disk Management snap-in (see Figure 7-2) to manage volumes on dynamic disks.

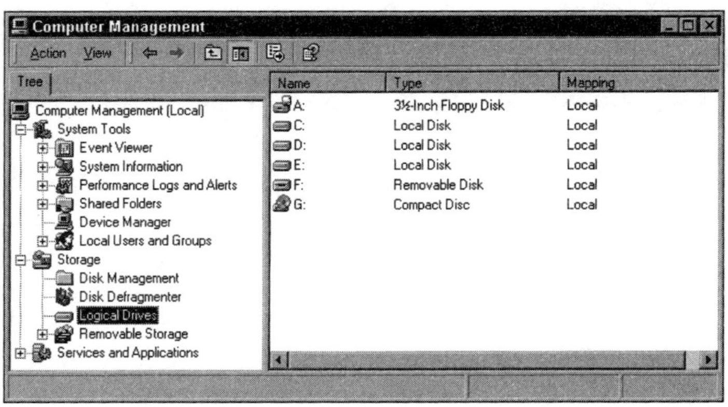

Figure 7-2: The Logical Disk Management snap-in of the Computer Management console.

Extending volumes

You can extend a simple volume to include unallocated space on the same physical disk without restarting the PC, if the simple volume uses NTFS. The result is a larger simple volume.

You can extend a simple volume to include unallocated space on *another* physical disk, thereby creating a *spanned volume*. You can do this with a FAT volume as well as with an NTFS volume, but after you create a spanned FAT volume, you can't extend it further.

You can't extend a striped volume, the system volume, or the boot volume.

Follow this procedure to extend a volume:

1. **Right-click the volume that you want to extend.**
2. **Choose the Extend Volume menu option.**
3. **Follow the wizard prompts.**

Setting quotas

Disk *quotas* are a new feature of NTFS 5 (you can't use quotas on non-NTFS disks). This feature lets you limit the amount of disk space that any user on the system can use on a given volume. (Windows determines usage based on *ownership;* when a user saves a new file or copies a file, the user takes ownership of that file.) You can set different limits for specific users, and you can set different limits for different drive letters or volumes. So this feature is fairly flexible.

Although the disk quotas feature is (as you'd expect) more important on the Server product than on Windows 2000 Professional, you may see it crop up on Exam #70-210 anyway, so here are the basics in a nutshell:

- Disk quotas are off by default.

  Turn them on by right-clicking a drive icon in My Computer or Explorer, choosing Properties, clicking the Quota tab, and checking the box labeled Enable Quota Management (see Figure 7-3). You must do this separately for each logical drive or volume on the system.
- You must be an Administrator to set up and configure quotas.
- To use quotas for enforcement rather than mere usage monitoring, check the Deny Disk Space to Users Exceeding Quota Limit box, as shown in Figure 7-3. A user who is about to create or take ownership of a file that would put her over the limit receives an "out of disk space" error message from Windows 2000.
- Quotas permit two threshold settings:
  - *Warning* level, at which point Windows creates an entry in the system even log.
  - Higher *limit* level, at which point Windows denies disk space to the user if the second check box on the Quota sheet is checked.

  Decimal values are okay for both.

- When you activate quotas, the values you specify for warning and limit levels apply to new users only. To set quotas for existing users, click the Quota Entries button and choose New Quota Entry from the Quota menu. Choose a local or domain user account and set the warning and limit values.
- To limit the event logging that the quota system performs, clear one or both of the check boxes that say "Log event when a user exceeds their quota limit" and "Log event when a user exceeds their warning level." (Yes, it's bad grammar, but most programmers no write can.)

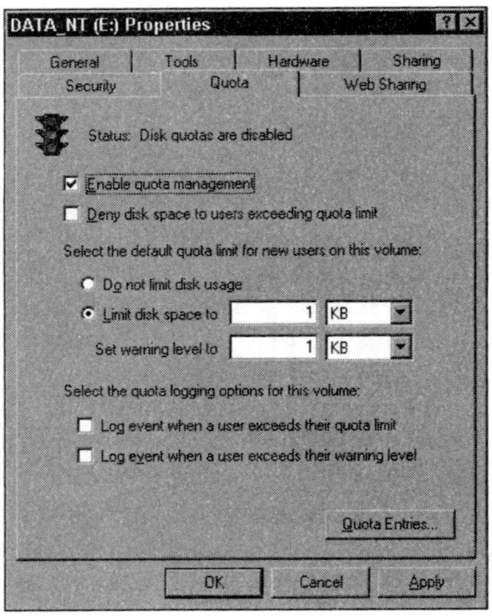

Figure 7-3: The traffic light icon is red if quotas are off, green if on, and yellow if Windows is rebuilding the data.

The initial values for the warning and limit levels are 1KB! Don't forget to change KB to MB in a real-world situation.

Quotas don't look at the compressed value of files, they look at the uncompressed value. So it's possible for a user to own 40MB of actual space but still trigger a 50MB quota limit. (This is quotas Version 1.0, remember!)

Setting mount points

When you're going through the wizard screens in order to create a new volume, you have the option to click a check box (on the Assign Drive Letter or Path window) that says Mount This Volume At An Empty Folder That Supports Drive Paths. What this means is that you can create a new volume that maps to an existing folder on an NTFS disk. That is, you can add a 4GB hard drive that the user sees as a very large 4GB folder living under an existing drive letter.

If a user is running out of room on drive C, you can add a second physical drive but map it in its entirety to a folder on drive C. This way, the user doesn't have to worry about keeping track of a second drive letter. ("D colon? What's that? Part of D intestine?") Magically, drive C has a new folder with 4GB of free space. You've just discovered the wonder of *mount points,* a type of "reparse point" that's new to NTFS Version 5.

If the exam asks you how to add disk capacity when you're already maxed out on drive letters, "mount points" should figure into the correct answer.

Monitoring hard drives

You can check various details of a local hard drive by using the Disk Management snap-in to the Computer Management console.

1. **In the lower-right window frame, right-click the box containing the disk icon and the words "Disk 0" or "Disk 1" or whatever number it may be.**

   Don't right-click any of the partition boxes that appear to the right.

2. **Choose Properties, and you see a window such as Figure 7-4.**

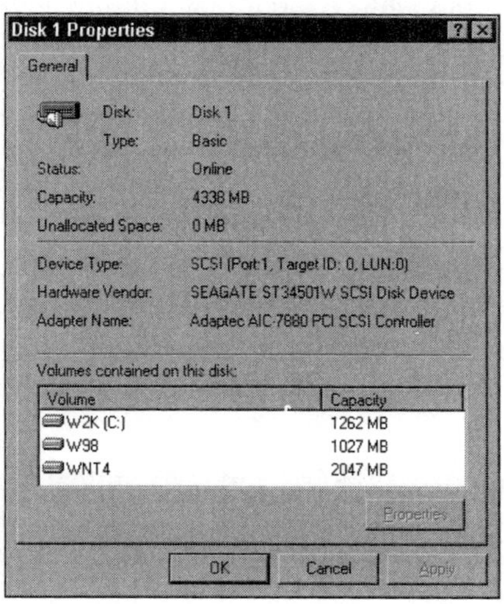

Figure 7-4: Monitoring drive details.

Again in Disk Management, if you right-click a *partition* on a basic disk (as opposed to the disk itself) and choose Properties, you see some or all of the following tabs:

- General
- Tools
- Hardware
- Sharing
- Web Sharing
- Security (on an NTFS partition)
- Quota (on an NTFS partition)

Right-click a volume on a dynamic disk and you see the same tabs as when you right-click a partition on a basic disk.

If you want to check on a remote disk, you can do so by creating a custom Microsoft Management Console containing the Disk Management snap-in and pointing to the remote computer.

INSTANT ANSWER

Finally, you can monitor disk space use on a user-by-user basis by *enabling* disk quotas but not *enforcing* them. That is, on the Quota tab of the disk property sheet, check the Enable Quota Management box, but uncheck the Deny Disk Space to Users Exceeding Quota Limit box. This way, when you click the Quota Entries button, you can view space usage by user name without having any impact on users' ability to create new files. For convenience, you can set warning and limit levels that trigger system event logging and that affect the icons that display in the Quota Entries list, but these settings don't have any effect on users. (For more information, see the "Setting Quotas" section earlier in this chapter.)

Optical Disks

Windows 2000 Professional supports CD-ROM and DVD optical storage devices. Some (but not all) writeable optical devices, such as CD-R/W drives, can also work with Windows 2000 Professional depending on the availability of Windows 2000 device drivers.

CD-ROM

Windows 2000 either works with a given make and model CD-ROM drive, or it doesn't. The famous Microsoft Hardware Compatibility List (HCL) is the guide here.

If you need to install Windows 2000 Professional and your PC's CD-ROM drive isn't on the HCL and doesn't work, Microsoft recommends that you choose an alternative method of installation (such as using a network distribution server) or install a different model CD-ROM drive.

If the exam mentions "El Torito," it's not referring to a brand of tortilla chip. It's referring to a specification that lets a computer boot from the CD-ROM drive. You may have to set the option in the PC's BIOS setup. Booting from the Windows 2000 Professional CD is handy for installation and system recovery purposes (beats the heck out of using those four diskettes to start the computer).

If audio CDs aren't working, check the CD-ROM drive's property sheet via Device Manager (in the System control panel). You may need to clear the Enable Digital CD Audio For This CD-ROM Device check box to ensure analog playback of audio content.

DVD

So what does DVD stand for? No one seems to know, and the exam doesn't ask. These devices can store 133 minutes of digital video/audio data in the MPEG-2 format. DVD drives also let you play regular CD-ROMs. You need a *DVD decoder* (which can be hardware- or software-based) to play DVD movies. Windows 2000 Professional includes a DVD Player applet for playing DVD movies.

Windows 2000 Professional "out of the box" supports DVD in read-only mode for both multimedia and data, but does not support this medium in read-write mode as of this writing.

Removable Media

Although Microsoft lists configuring and monitoring removable media as a test objective, the exam isn't likely to cover this material in any depth. Tape backup is much more relevant in connection with Windows 2000 Server, and very few Windows 2000 Professional PCs have tape drives, much less robotic tape library devices.

Having said that, here are a few basics you may need to know about Windows 2000 "removable media:"

- Removable storage disks, such as Zip or Jaz disks, are basic disks containing one primary partition only.
- You can manage removable media to some extent via the Remote Storage snap-in from the Computer Management console. However, most

of your interaction with tape drives will be through an application such as Microsoft Backup. Most Windows 2000 Professional users will never work with the Remote Storage snap-in, and I have yet to see it appear on the exam.

- Windows 2000 doesn't directly support write-once media, such as CD-R or DVD-R. Such hardware requires third-party software support.
- A removable storage *library* is a device, such as a robotic tape changer or a stand-alone tape drive unit.
- A *media pool* is a group of removable media that Windows 2000 or a Windows application manages the same way. For example, a backup program could create one media pool for incremental backups and another (using a higher-capacity media type) for full backups.

Chapter 8 discusses the Microsoft Backup program in more detail.

Configuring Printing

Printing in Windows 2000 isn't radically different from printing in Windows NT 4.0, so if you feel very comfortable with how printing works in that older operating system, skim this section lightly. It provides the basics that the exam expects you to know.

This section looks at configuring printing. The section that follows looks at using a preconfigured printer. You have to know how to do both!

A bit of terminology

You should have some understanding of Microspeak when it comes to answering printer questions on the exam. Here are the terms to know:

- A **printer** isn't a printer, it's a software construct representing the interface between the operating system and the physical print device.
- A **print device** is what you'd refer to as a "printer" in normal speech: a physical printing machine. It can be connected locally, via a parallel, serial, infrared, or USB port, or remotely, across a network cable (in the case of *net-direct* printers having their own network interface card).
- A **printer port** is the software interface to such a hardware port, not a hardware port to which a print device is attached.

  This distinction is a bit fine, but it may clarify things if you consider that some computers permit printing via an infrared link that appears to the operating system as a COM port. In that case, the COM port is the "printer port" even though the actual hardware isn't a typical serial interface at all.

- A **print server** is a computer that manages print requests for a shared printer.

  A print server may manage a locally connected print device or a network-connected print device; the physical location doesn't matter. What does matter is that the print server receives print requests from clients, queues such requests, converts documents into printer-specific code via the printer driver, and transmits the code to the physical print device.

- A **printer pool** is a single "printer" that can send documents to multiple ports and multiple identical print devices. The ports can be local or networked. Windows 2000 finds the first available print device for any given document.

- A **printer driver** is the software that describes to Windows 2000 the features and commands of a particular model of print device.

Installing a new printer

Installing a printer follows a very similar sequence of steps, whether the printer connects directly to your PC or to the network. The procedure centers around the Add Printer wizard in the Printers control panel. (Windows 98 users, take note: The Printers virtual folder in My Computer doesn't appear in Windows 2000.)

REMEMBER

You must be logged on as Administrator to install a printer.

When you launch the Add Printer wizard, the general procedure is as detailed in Lab 7-2.

Lab 7-2 Installing a Printer with the Add Printer Wizard

1. **Specify whether the printer is directly attached to your PC, or connected to the network.**

   If the printer is directly attached, you can let Windows 2000 try to autodetect it, or you can skip autodetection and provide the manufacturer and model information yourself. Most modern print devices support the Plug and Play standard, and Windows 2000 typically recognizes them automatically and prompts to install the necessary driver. Plug and Play doesn't work over the network wire, however, so autodetection isn't an option in this case.

You have to click the Local Printer radio button even if you're setting up your PC to be a print server for a network-attached printer. Seems counterintuitive, but if you click Network Printer, you can only *search* for printers that already have print servers created for them, you can't *create* a new print server on the local PC.

2. **Specify the printer port (see Figure 7-5).**

   A direct-attached printer typically connects to a serial (COM:) or parallel (LPT:) port, although FILE: is an option if you want to create print files that you will send out (for example, to a printing service bureau) for hardcopy output. A network-attached printer generally requires you to click the Create a New Port radio button and specify a port type. For example, "Standard TCP/IP Port" would be your choice for a TCP/IP printer, and you would then be prompted to specify an IP address or DNS name for the printer.

   Hewlett-Packard net-direct printers often use the DLC (Data Link Control) protocol for communications. Windows 2000 doesn't normally install this protocol, so you have to add it yourself via the Network and Dial-Up Connections control panel. Also, be aware that DLC has a "continuous mode" that may tie up the printer until the current job finishes printing.

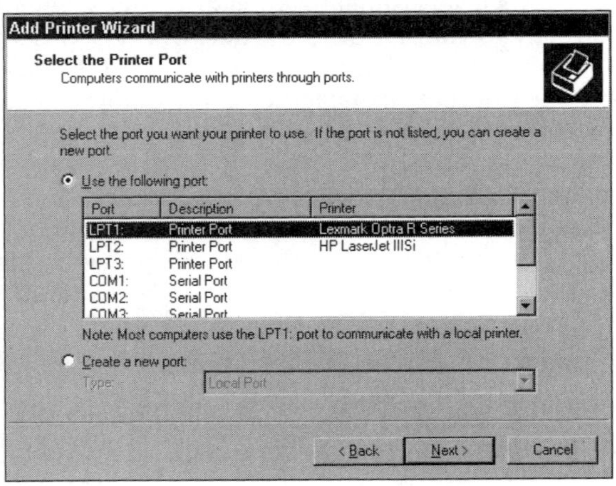

Figure 7-5: Specifying a local or network port for your new printer.

3. **Specify manufacturer and model.**

   Skip this step if Windows 2000 correctly autodetects your printer.

4. **Give the printer a name.**

   You can use a name that's different from (and more descriptive than) the device driver name. Just remember that 31 characters is a safe maximum length. The name you assign here appears with the printer's icon in the Printers folder.

5. **Choose whether the printer should be the default printer for Windows applications.**

   You see this choice only if you have at least one printer already defined. The default printer appears in the user interface with a black check mark on its icon.

6. **Give the printer a share name, if you plan to share it.**

   The "share name" defaults to the printer name you assigned in Step 4, chopped off to the old DOS-style 8.3 name format. That's because other people on your network may be using DOS or early versions of Windows that get confused with longer resource names. When network users browse a list of shared printers, the share name is what they see.

7. **If you gave the printer a share name in Step 6, you can enter optional Location and Comment information.**

   This information appears in an Active Directory network when users perform printer searches. So it can help users find the right printer if the share name isn't descriptive enough.

8. **View and confirm a summary of your choices.**

   If everything's correct, click the Finish button, and Windows 2000 installs the required files (it may prompt you for the installation CD-ROM or the location of the installation files on the network). The wizard will also share the printer for you. If any of the information on the summary screen is wrong, you can go back and make changes until it's all correct.

As the Add Printer wizard enables you to share a printer with others, a word is in order here about using Windows 2000 Professional as a print server. This operating system makes a rather limited print server (although it does support Unix clients).

REMEMBER

You would use Windows 2000 Server instead if any of the following conditions apply:

- The print server must support more than ten simultaneous clients.
- The print server must support Macintosh computers. (The Server product includes Services for Macintosh.)
- The print server must support NetWare users.

Configuring a new printer

After you install the printer, you can configure it by setting options in the printer's property sheet. This section looks at a few of the common ones.

Copy printer icons from the Printers folder onto the desktop. Users can then quickly print files by dragging and dropping them onto the printer icons.

If you share a printer with the Add Printer wizard, Windows 2000 installs printer drivers for Windows NT and Windows 98/95 clients, so that those operating systems can automatically download the necessary driver when the user first prints to the shared printer. Windows 3.1 users must install the correct printer driver on their systems manually, however.

Bidirectional local printing

Windows 2000 supports *bidirectional* parallel printing (U.S. standard *IEEE-1284*) because of its faster speed and because the printer can "tell" the computer about configuration details and operating conditions (such as "toner low"). For the exam, know these requirements for bidirectional printing:

- **An IEEE-1284-compatible parallel port on the printer.** These usually go by the name ECP (Extended Capabilities Port) or EPP (Enhanced Parallel Port).
- **An IEEE-1284-compatible parallel port on the PC, activated in the BIOS setup.** Some BIOS models still default to the old, slow "compatible" mode for the parallel port.
- **An IEEE-1284-compatible parallel cable.** These aren't the same as the older, Centronics-standard parallel cables.
- **Bidirectional printing enabled on the printer driver's property sheet.** The Enable Bidirectional Printing check box is on the Ports tab.

Spooling

By default, Windows 2000 *spools* print jobs to disk (normally, to the folder `C:\WINNT\SYSTEM32\SPOOL\PRINTERS`) before submitting them to the physical local printer. Spooling brings several benefits:

- The ability to create a print queue of documents that can be managed
- The ability to resubmit a job that doesn't print without restarting the application that created it
- Deferred printing — for example, with an undocked notebook PC
- A quicker return-to-application time for the user

Windows 2000 gives you some control over spooling options in the printer's Advanced property sheet, shown in Figure 7-6. Get there by right-clicking the printer icon in the Printers folder, choosing Properties, and clicking the Advanced tab.

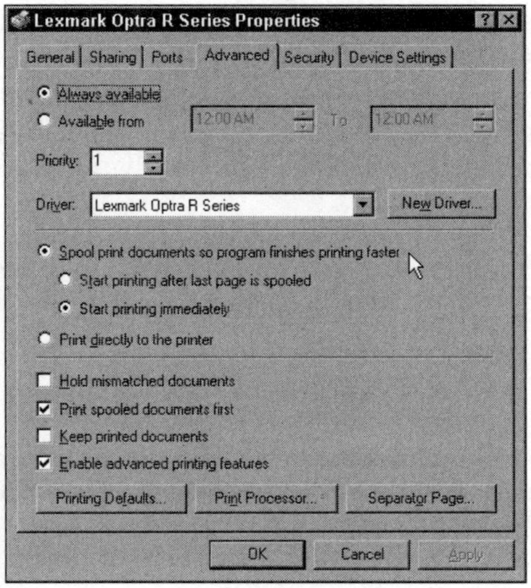

Figure 7-6: You can configure spool settings for each printer individually.

You can bet that you'll see a question on these spool options on the exam, so here are the salient facts about each option:

- Spool Print Jobs So Program Finishes Printing Faster is the same as saying "turn on spooling."
- Start Printing After Last Page Is Spooled provides the quickest return-to-application time, but requires enough disk space to hold the entire print job and doesn't necessarily get you your physical printout in the shortest time.
- Start Printing Immediately provides a slower return-to-application time, but requires less disk space.
- Print Directly To The Printer is the same as saying "turn off spooling." For a local printer, you can use this option for troubleshooting. For example, I've found that, in rare cases, documents don't print correctly using spooling. Further, disabling spooling removes one variable (the disk drive) from the printing equation.

Spooling carries an implicit hardware requirement for adequate disk space. Windows 2000 must be able to create a disk image of a print document before it can actually send that document to the print device. Without lots of megabytes at the ready, spooling may fail, and print jobs can stop before they start.

Pooling

You can create a *pool* of printers wherein two or more identical physical printers correspond to a single logical printer in the operating system. (Actually, the physical print devices don't need to be identical, but they must use the same printer driver.) Windows 2000 automatically routes documents to the first available device in the pool.

Simply check the Enable Printer Pooling box on the Ports tab of the printers' property sheets, then (in the same dialog box) check each of the ports that connects to a printer that you want to be in the pool.

Redirecting

If you find that you need to redirect documents to a different printer — for example, due to a printer hardware glitch — Windows 2000 provides a method, described in Lab 7-3.

Lab 7-3 Redirecting Documents from a Stuck Printer

1. **Choose Start⇨Settings⇨Printers to open the Printers folder.**
2. **Right-click the stuck printer and choose Properties.**
3. **Click the Ports tab.**
4. **If a working printer of the same type exists on a different local port on the *same* print server, click the port's check box and click OK. Otherwise, if a working printer of the same type exists on a *different* print server, proceed to Step #5.**
5. **Click the Add Port button.**
6. **Click Local Port in the Printer Ports dialog box.**
7. **Click the New Port button in the Printer Ports dialog box.**
8. **In the Port Name dialog box, specify the working printer with UNC notation.**

   That is, use the form *printservername**printersharename*.

INSTANT ANSWER

If a printer fails, you don't want to lose queued documents, and another print server has a compatible printer, add a local port on the stuck print server.

Adding drivers

If you share a printer that already exists on a Windows 2000 PC, as opposed to sharing the printer when you create it (see "Installing a new printer," earlier in this chapter), you have to add drivers to your PC for any non-Windows 2000 operating system that may print to the printer. The procedure is mercifully easy: Click the Sharing tab of the printer's property sheet and click the Additional Drivers button.

Windows NT and 2000 clients check the print server for driver updates before they print each document. That's handy, because when you update a driver on the PC that acts as print server, you don't have to run around updating all the client PCs as well. Note, however, that Windows 9*x* clients do not perform this check and therefore do require manual driver updates.

Playing with priorities

Unlike Windows 9*x*, the NT platform (including Windows 2000) lets you assign a priority to a printer. Just right-click the printer icon, choose Properties, click the Advanced tab, and pick a number from 1 (low) to 99 (high).

Priority 1 is the lowest priority, 99 is the highest. I used to have a terrible time keeping this rule straight. "Ninety-nine high" is an easy, rhyming jingle to remember.

You can use printer priorities in a tricky way to make sure that one user or group's print jobs always receive preferential treatment. (This bit of wizardry always seems to be on the MCSE tests.) Suppose, for example, that you have a single physical print device but two users who print to it. In order to give user A's print jobs priority over user B's, you can create two Windows 2000 printers with different names, each of which points to the same physical print device. Give one printer a high priority, the other a low one. Then configure user A's computer to print to "Serf" and user B's computer to print to "Lord." (You can enforce these settings using access permissions on the printer objects.) Their documents go to the same device, but Windows 2000 prioritizes them differently. You could also use the same trick to differentiate different kinds of documents, instead of different users or groups.

Using a Printer

This last section deals with some common actions that users perform in the course of printing documents: finding a printer, managing print jobs, and printing offline.

Finding a printer

First things first: You must find a printer before you can print to it. Finding locally-attached printers is easy — they appear by default in the drop-down list box in the Print dialog box of most Windows applications. Finding network printers is almost as easy in Windows 2000. Simply run the Add Printer wizard, click the Network Printer radio button in the Local or Network Printer dialog box, click Next, and you see a dialog box like that in Figure 7-7. (If you're not running an Active Directory network with Windows 2000 Server, you won't see the option to Find a Printer In the Directory.)

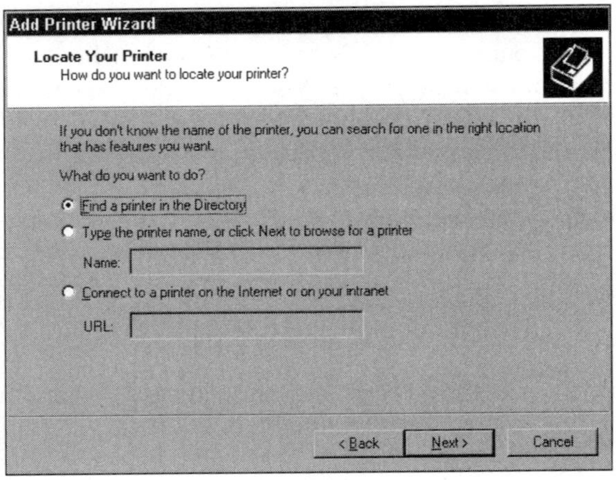

Figure 7-7: You can find a network printer three main ways.

Here are your options:

- On an Active Directory network, you can click Find a Printer in the Directory. Clicking Next takes you to a dialog box where you can search based on printer name, location, comment, or printer capability (such as color).
- You can specify a printer name (such as the UNC, or Universal Naming Convention, name — format *printserver**printername*), or leave the name field blank and click Next to browse the network (Active Directory or otherwise) to view all printer names.
- You can click the Connect to a Printer on the Internet or Your Intranet button to find a TCP/IP printer by URL (Uniform Resource Locator).

Managing print jobs

Some of the routine chores associated with managing your print jobs are as follows:

- To pause printing, right-click the printer icon in the Printers folder and select Pause Printing.
- Resume printing with the same procedure, which "toggles" the Pause Printing setting off.
- To cancel all documents, right-click the printer icon and select Cancel All Documents.
- To pause one or more specific documents, double-click the printer icon, right-click the document(s) you want to pause (you can use the Shift or Ctrl keys to choose multiple documents), and choose Pause.

- To resume one or more specific documents, double-click the printer icon, right-click the document(s) you want to resume, and choose Resume. (Note that this procedure doesn't work like the pause/resume procedure for the entire printer, which is a "toggle" setting. Hey, if the user interface were consistent, it wouldn't be Windows.)
- To cancel one or more specific documents, select them as in the previous item, right-click, and choose Cancel.
- If you want to start a document print job over from the beginning, select one or more documents, right-click, and choose Restart.
- To schedule a document to print at a later time (as, for example, when the printer isn't busy), right-click the document in the printer's window and choose Properties. You can then set the "Only From" time to the earliest time you want the job to start printing (see Figure 7-8).
- To change the priority of a document, right-click the document, choose Properties, and change the priority setting by using the graphical slider control. Priority 1 is the lowest, and 99 is the highest, just as with printers.

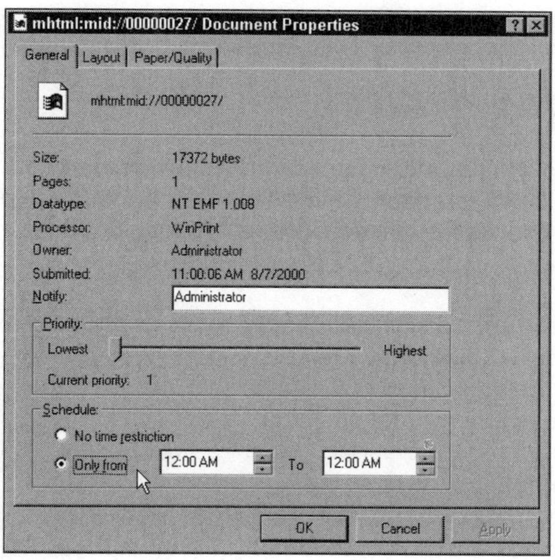

Figure 7-8: Setting a print job's time slot.

Generally, you can print, pause, resume, cancel, and restart document print jobs that you own (that is, that you submitted with a Print command); another way to put this is that the Everyone group has the *Print* permission. To modify jobs submitted by other users, you need the *Manage Documents* permission for that printer. To have full administrative control of the printer — pause it, stop it, start it, share it, change its properties — you need the *Manage Printers* permission for that printer. By default, Administrators and

Power Users have all three printer permissions: Print, Manage Documents, and Manage Printers. They can change printer permissions via the printer's property sheet, Security tab.

Printing offline

Users can *defer* printing in Windows 2000, meaning that they create the spool file from their application program, but physically print the document later — for example, when they return to the office and dock their notebooks. Windows 2000 handles deferred printing automatically with notebook PCs, but a user can set it manually with the Printers folder command File⇨Use Printer Offline.

Another way to defer printing is by selecting File as the port, instead of a parallel or serial port, on the printer's property sheet. If you do this, Windows 2000 creates print files with the suffix *.PRN. You can then print the document on your printer, or on someone else's printer (as long as it's the same model), by copying the PRN file to the printer port.

Printing to fax devices

Normally, you print to a fax modem just as you would print to a physical print device. If Windows 2000 doesn't autodetect the fax capability of your modem, open the Fax control panel's Advanced Options tab, click Add A Fax Printer, and follow the wizard.

The Advanced Options tab is also where you gain access to the Fax Service Management Console (FAXSERV.MSC).

INSTANT ANSWER

In the Fax Service Management Console, click Devices in the tree pane, then right-click your fax modem in the details pane. Choose Receive to enable fax reception (which is off by default). Or, choose Properties if you also want to specify the fax receive folder (`C:\Documents and Settings\All Users\Documents\My Faxes\Received Faxes` is the default setting).

Set up fax cover pages using the Fax control panel's User Information and Cover Pages tabs. The Status Monitor tab controls the automatic opening of the Fax Monitor window when a fax arrives; the display of a taskbar icon; notification by sound; and whether Windows automatically answers incoming calls to the fax modem.

Prep Test

1 **You're a PC tech support analyst for a large cookie manufacturer. You get a call from Dino, who suddenly is unable to save new documents to his My Documents folder. You have used folder redirection to point My Documents to `\\SRV01\USERDOCS\%username%`. No one else in Dino's office is experiencing the same problem, and Dino was able to save new files to his My Documents folder yesterday without difficulty. What would be a likely course of action to fix Dino's complaint? (Choose the best answer.)**

A ❍ Replace Dino's local hard disk with a larger one.

B ❍ Add a hard disk and mount it to an empty folder on Dino's main hard disk.

C ❍ Add disk space to \\SRV01.

D ❍ Increase the quota limit for Dino.

2 **You need to give different priorities to different users who share the same printer on a Windows 2000 network. You create two different logical printers, A and B, that point to the same physical port. Then, you modify the access control list for each printer. Finally, you change each printer's priority settings.**

What number would you specify in order to make Printer A the highest possible priority?

A ❍ 1

B ❍ 9

C ❍ 99

D ❍ 999

3 **You're in charge of capacity planning for your network PCs. As part of your responsibilities, you decide to track disk space usage as a function of time. You enable Windows 2000 disk quotas for this purpose.**

How should you configure the quota feature so that you can see, via Event Viewer, when users exceed 50MB *and* when users exceed 100MB? (Choose all that apply.)

A ❑ Check the Enable Quota Management box for each drive you want to track.

B ❑ Clear the Deny Disk Space to Users Exceeding Quota Limit check box.

C ❑ Click the Do Not Limit Disk Usage radio button.

D ❑ Click the Limit Disk Space To: radio button.

E ❑ Click the Quota Entries button to activate quotas on existing user accounts.

4 **A Windows 2000 Professional computer shares a printer connected to the PC's parallel port. Users of that printer are running Windows 2000 Professional and Windows 98. You receive a driver update and you want to make sure that every computer on the network gets the new driver. What steps should you take? (Choose all that apply.)**

A ❑ Update the driver on the computer sharing the printer.

B ❑ Update the driver on all network clients that use the printer.

C ❑ Update the driver on all Windows 2000 network clients that use the printer.

D ❑ Update the driver on all Windows 98 network clients that use the printer.

5 **You receive a brand new printer preconfigured for TCP/IP networking. Which of the following statements is true in order to use this printer with Windows 2000 Professional? (Choose all that apply.)**

A ❑ TCP/IP printers have an icon in the Printers folder for queue management, but no property sheets for configuration. You configure all printer options from the Web browser interface.

B ❑ You can use the printer's DNS name when identifying it in the Add Printer Wizard.

C ❑ You can use the printer's IP address when identifying it in the Add Printer Wizard.

D ❑ You should use DHCP to assign IP configuration details to the printer.

6 **Wilma calls you with a Windows 2000 Professional question. Should she update her notebook PC to a dynamic disk? She has heard that dynamic disks offer cool new features. Wilma never uses DOS and her machine is not configured for dual-booting. How should you answer her? (Choose the best answer.)**

A ❍ Yes. Dynamic disks have the greatest feature set and the most flexibility.

B ❍ Yes. Dynamic disks are more flexible, and Wilma can easily reverse the setting later if she desires.

C ❍ Yes. Dynamic disks offer the best possible performance.

D ❍ No. Dynamic disks generally offer no benefit for notebook PCs.

7 **Betty, your boss, has asked you to configure a network printer for the Windows 2000 network that you manage for your department. The network consists of 14 PCs running Windows 2000 Professional and one PC running Windows 2000 Server. The network contains no Macintosh computers, nor does it contain any NetWare servers.**

You must decide whether to share the network printer from a Windows 2000 Professional machine or from the Windows 2000 Server machine. What factors should you consider when making that decision? (Choose all that apply.)

A ❑ Performance

B ❑ Expected print volume

C ❑ Windows licenses

D ❑ Potential future growth

8 **Which of the following disk fault tolerance features work with Windows 2000 Professional? (Choose all that apply.)**

A ❑ RAID 0

B ❑ RAID 5

C ❑ Mirroring

D ❑ Duplexing

E ❑ Power backup

9 **Fred is trying to receive a fax on his standalone Windows 2000 Professional computer, but is unable to do so. He's tested his modem via the Phone and Modem Options control panel, and it passes diagnostics. You advise him to check the Advanced Options tab of his Fax control panel, but he reports that no such tab exists. What should you do? (Choose all that apply.)**

A ❑ Tell Fred to log off and back on as an Administrator.

B ❑ Tell Fred to open the Fax Service Management console to enable the receive toggle for his device.

C ❑ Tell Fred to reinstall the modem driver in Add/Remove Hardware.

D ❑ Tell Fred to open the Phone and Modem Options control panel instead of the Fax control panel. The Advanced Options tab appears. He should click it and then enable the receive toggle for his device.

Answers

1 **D**. The folder redirection means that Dino's My Documents folder actually lives on the SRV01 server machine. Adding local disk space isn't likely to help. Adding disk space to SRV01 isn't likely to solve the problem; apparently, SRV01 has space available, given that other users are able to save their files. *See* "Setting quotas."

2 **C**. Microsoft loves printer priorities. *See* "Playing with priorities."

3 **A, B, D,** and **E**. Choice D is the one that is most likely to trip you up, but if you don't set a limit, you can't enter a threshold value to trigger a logged event. The question suggests that merely logging warning events is insufficient, because two threshold values must be logged — namely, warnings and limit violations. As long as the Deny Disk Space to Users Exceeding Quota Limit check box is clear, the quota feature cannot prevent a user from exceeding a quota. *See* "Setting quotas."

4 **A** and **D**. Windows 2000 clients automatically check the print server for an updated driver before printing. Windows 98 clients do not. You must install the new driver manually on the Windows 98 clients. *See* "Adding drivers."

5 **B** and **C**. Typically, TCP/IP printers permit configuration both by property sheets and by the browser interface, so A is wrong. Also, the recommended practice is to give network printers fixed, or static, IP addresses. These devices need to be available at all times and therefore do not benefit by leasing an IP address; also, printer configuration and troubleshooting is easier if the IP address is fixed. *See* "Installing a new printer."

6 **D**. Notebook computers typically have only one hard drive, and the benefits of dynamic disks apply to systems with two or more hard drives. Note that choice B's comment about easy reversibility is incorrect. Choice C may be correct in a multiple-drive system with striping configured. *See* "Promoting a basic disk to a dynamic disk."

7 **C**. This question is a bit sly, as all of the choices are normally worth considering. However, in this situation, only one criterion matters: the fact that a Windows 2000 Professional machine is only licensed to support ten simultaneous users at a time of any shared resource, be it a printer or a folder. *See* "Installing a new printer."

8 **E**. If you want any of the other four features, you must use Windows 2000 Server. *See* "Creating volumes."

9 **A** and **B**. In general, when you know an option exists but a user can't access it, chances are good that the user needs administrative privileges. The default behavior of Windows 2000's fax service is to enable sending but not receiving. *See* "Printing to fax devices."

Chapter 8

Installing and Configuring Displays and I/O Devices

Exam Objectives

- Configuring multiple-display support
- Installing, configuring, and troubleshooting a video adapter
- Monitoring, configuring, and troubleshooting I/O devices, such as printers, scanners, multimedia devices, mice, keyboards, and smart card readers
- Monitoring, configuring, and troubleshooting multimedia hardware, such as cameras
- Installing, configuring, and managing modems
- Installing, configuring, and managing USB devices

This chapter focuses on hardware that moves data around without necessarily storing it. (Hardware for portable computers gets its due in Chapter 9.) For example, you may display, type, and download many megabytes whose final resting place is your brain (or that of someone else), rather than a magnetic disk or printed page. Windows 2000 offers generally improved support for *input/output* (I/O) devices, such as keyboards, displays, and modems, that facilitate getting information into or out of the PC. (When people use the term *I/O devices,* they typically aren't referring to disks or printers.)

The exam tends to focus on goodies that are new to the NT platform, such as multiple displays, the Universal Serial Bus (USB), DVD, multilink connections, and the like. However, you can expect a question or two on "traditional" topics, such as how to configure a single video adapter, just to keep you honest.

Quick Assessment

Configuring multiple-display support

1 Adapters for multiple displays must use either the ______ bus or the ______ bus.

2 You have to enable a secondary video adapter using the Display control panel's ______ tab.

Video adapter

3 If a game isn't working, you can test DirectX for your display driver using the program ______.

4 If your new video adapter makes the mouse cursor disappear, try changing the ______ setting.

I/O devices

5 If Device Manager shows a red "stop" icon by a device name, the device was ______.

6 I/O devices are allowed to share the same interrupt on the ______ bus.

Multimedia hardware

7 You can change a camera's or scanner's color profile using the ______ control panel.

Modems

8 The name of the log file that Windows 2000 uses to record modem activity is ______.

USB devices

9 No USB device can be farther than ______ meters from a USB hub.

10 The maximum permitted current draw on the USB bus is ______ milliamps.

Answers

1 *PCI, AGP*. See "Multiple display requirements and limitations" if this was news to you.

2 *Settings*. The "Troubleshooting multiple monitors" section has more.

3 *DXDIAG.EXE*. You get half a point if you said "DirectX Diagnostic Tool." See the "DirectX marks the spot" section for details.

4 *Acceleration slider*. See "Configuring single displays" if you missed this one.

5 *Disabled*. Check for a resource conflict. The section "Device Manager errors" has more.

6 *PCI*. The "IRQ sharing" section elaborates. If you said "USB," you get full credit as well, because the USB bus uses a single interrupt for all connected devices.

7 *Scanners and Cameras*. No points if you said "cameras and scanners." See the "Scanners and cameras" section.

8 *<ModemName>LOG.TXT*. This is sort of a trick question, because <ModemName> depends on the specific modem.

9 *Five*. You get full credit if you said "5." See "Getting on the Universal Serial Bus" if you missed this detail.

10 *It depends*. The property sheet for the root hub shows this information for a specific PC. "Getting on the Universal Serial Bus" has more.

Displays, Single and Multiple

Windows 2000 Professional configures single displays much as Windows NT 4.0 and Windows 98 do, although DirectX support is new to the NT platform. The first two parts of this section cover the essentials, which may crop up on the exam. Things get a bit more interesting when discussing multiple displays, covered in the third part of this section.

Single display technology

Notable improvements in Windows 2000's core display capabilities include support for DirectX, OpenGL 1.2, and better support for Advanced Graphics Port (AGP) adapters.

DirectX marks the spot

The biggest advance that Windows 2000 Professional brings to single display technology on the NT technology platform is support for *DirectX*, specifically, DirectX 7. DirectX is a set of APIs (Application Program Interfaces) that Microsoft designed to provide multimedia and graphics software developers a degree of consistency across different Windows versions.

TIME SHAVER

The list of specific APIs is a long one: DirectSound, DirectInput (for joysticks), Direct3D, DirectDraw, DirectAnimation (for vector graphics mainly), DirectShow (formerly ActiveMovie), and so forth. Don't memorize the functions of each API — just be generally aware of their existence.

INSTANT ANSWER

Test your version of DirectX (it's upgradable) and various DirectX features and functions using the handy DXDIAG.EXE program in `C:\WINNT\SYSTEM32` (see Figure 8-1). The utility offers specific tests for the video-related DirectDraw and Direct3D interfaces.

OpenGL

Silicon Graphics developed the OpenGL language for use with its high performance workstation chips, and Windows 2000 supports version 1.2 of this language. To see it at work, preview any of the 3D screen savers on the Display control panel's Screen Saver tab.

AGP

Touted as a technological advance, in one sense AGP (Advanced Graphics Port, supported by Windows 2000 Professional) is a step backward in computer design to the days of single-purpose expansion slots. You can put anything you want into an AGP slot as long as it's an AGP video adapter. Also, you can't put an AGP video adapter onto a motherboard that doesn't have an AGP port built in.

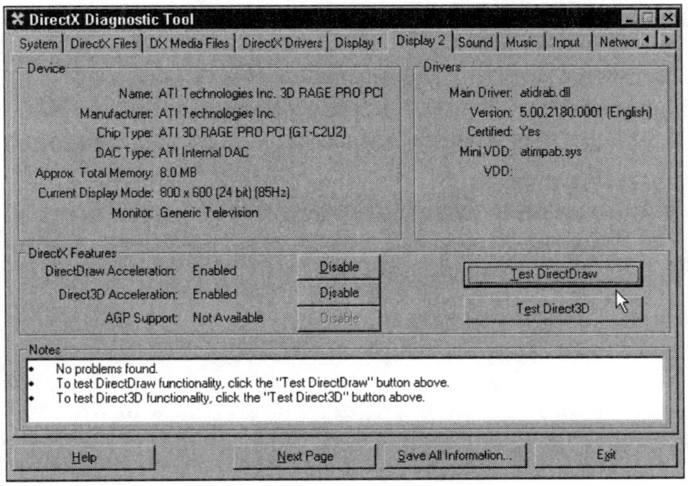

Figure 8-1: Testing DirectX with the DirectX Diagnostic Tool.

Theoretically, AGP cards are faster than PCI cards, for at least two reasons: They don't have to deal with traffic on the shared PCI bus, and peak data rates are higher. As a practical matter, I've seen some awfully slow AGP systems, so I suspect that here, as in certain other aspects of life that I can't mention explicitly, the execution is more important than the theory.

Configuring single displays

Not much is new compared to earlier versions of Windows when it comes to configuring a single display system. You still set the resolution, color depth, refresh rate (important for eye fatigue), background, colors-and-fonts scheme, and (optionally) temperature or color profile in the Display control panel. The quick way to get there: Right-click any empty space on the desktop and choose Properties.

A handy quick way to set an adapter's color depth and pixel resolution at once, along with the refresh rate, is as follows:

1. Choose the Display control panel.
2. Click the Settings tab.
3. Click the Advanced button.
4. Click the Adapter tab.
5. Click the List All Modes button to display a dialog box that looks like the one in Figure 8-2.

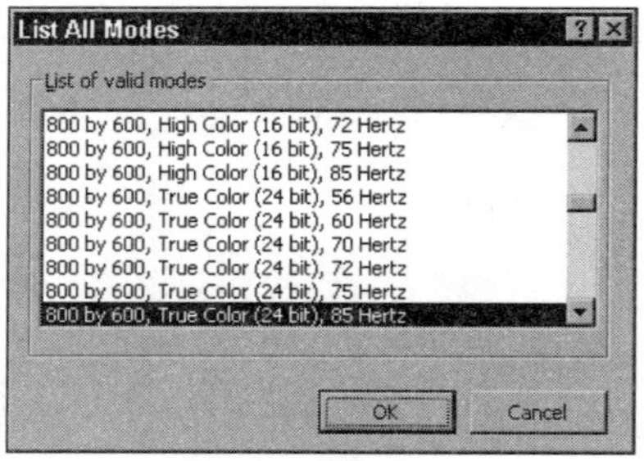

Figure 8-2: Set three display settings in one fell swoop.

The Web tab (new since NT, included in Windows 98) allows you to control whether or not your desktop appears as a Web page, and if so, which Web elements you wish to be there. The desktop Web view in Windows 2000 doesn't seem to slow your system down as much as it does in Windows 98, but it still seems to be an answer to a question no one was asking.

You can change the video resolution on the fly (that is, without restarting), but you see a message that doing so can create problems for some programs, so some testing on your part can confirm or deny whether you must, in fact, restart after changing pixel resolution or color depth. Set the default behavior in the General tab of the Advanced Settings property sheet, in the box marked Compatibility.

You may need to know that the *acceleration slider* (which by the way isn't a baseball pitch) can be found on the Display control panel by clicking Settings, Advanced, and Troubleshooting. Back off from full acceleration if you have mouse pointer problems or problems with images getting corrupted (see Figure 8-3).

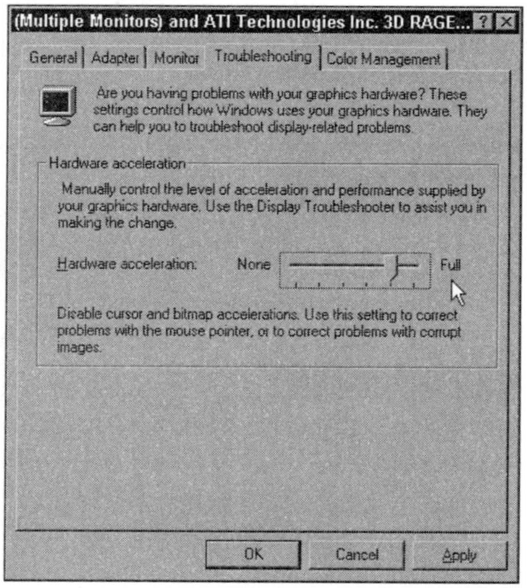

Figure 8-3: The acceleration slider is handy for troubleshooting display problems.

TIP

If you're having video problems, one time-honored technique is to boot with the plain old VGA driver and then check your configuration in Device Manager. Windows 2000 Professional automatically uses the plain VGA driver if it detects a video problem, but who's to say its detection is perfect? You can manually force basic VGA by pressing F8 at the text mode "Starting Windows..." prompt, then selecting Enable VGA Mode. Once you get Windows running, change or update the video driver and reboot.

You can also fire up the Windows 2000 display troubleshooter (part of the help system) by clicking the Troubleshoot button on the Settings tab.

TIP

JPG backgrounds require the Web view of the desktop to be active.

Configuring multiple displays

Microsoft introduced multiple monitor support in Windows 98, and the feature finds its way onto the NT platform in Windows 2000. You can have up to ten monitors running simultaneously (a mere two appear in Figure 8-4). A number of prerequisites and caveats apply, however.

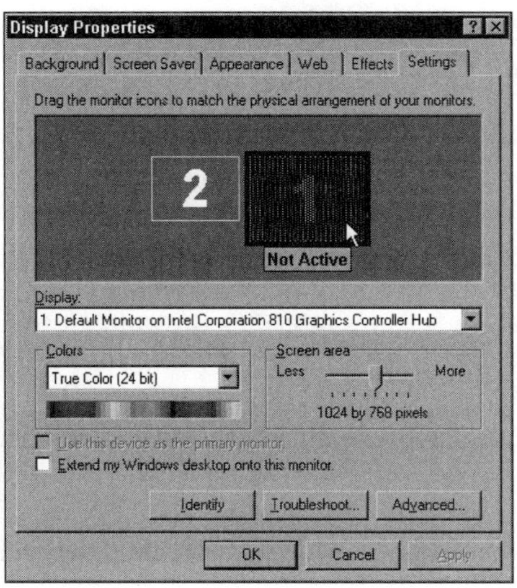

Figure 8-4: In this display, the primary monitor isn't yet active.

Multiple display requirements and limitations

First, a terminology note. The *primary display adapter* is where the PC's boot process sends video signals, where Windows 2000 displays the startup screens and logon dialog box, and where applications typically display their main window at startup. A *secondary display adapter* is any adapter above and beyond the primary one.

Here are the rules and regs for multiple monitor support in Windows 2000:

- Both display adapters must connect via a PCI (Peripheral Component Interconnect) or AGP (Accelerated Graphics Port) slot.
- For a device to work as a secondary display adapter, it must be on Microsoft's list of acceptable secondary display adapters (see the HCL, or Hardware Compatibility List). Many video cards work as primary adapters, but not as secondary adapters.
- If one of the display adapters is integrated onto the motherboard, that adapter must always be a secondary adapter.
- The BIOS in some PCs automatically disables an on-board video adapter if it detects a plug-in video adapter. You may be able to turn this "feature" off in the BIOS setup, but you may not.
- If one of the display adapters is integrated onto the motherboard, you must install Windows 2000 before you install the secondary adapter. Setup isn't smart enough to know about multiple displays, and if it sees an on-board display adapter and a plug-in display adapter, it disables the on-board one. Install the secondary adapter by using the Add/Remove Hardware wizard if Windows 2000 doesn't detect the adapter automatically.

Troubleshooting multiple monitors

A few tips for shooting multiple-monitor trouble follow:

- If you can't easily tell which monitor is connected to the primary display and which to the secondary display, reboot the PC. The BIOS startup and POST (Power-On Self-Test) appear on the primary monitor.
- If a secondary monitor doesn't seem to be coming up, you probably haven't activated it. (I know, this should be automatic, but it isn't.) Go to the Display control panel's Settings tab, click the number two monitor (or three or four or whatever), and check the box that says "Extend my Windows desktop onto this monitor."
- A docked laptop typically can't use the internal display for multiple display capability; you'd have to put two (or more) adapters in the docking station.
- You can set the color depth and resolution separately for each monitor.
- You can set the relative positioning of the two (or more) monitors by dragging and dropping the monitor images in the Display control panel's Settings tab.
- If your primary monitor isn't the one you want it to be, and both video adapters are plug-in cards, swap their positions in the PCI bus. The PC BIOS activates these cards in order according to their slot number. The BIOS on some PCs lets you override this automatic assignment.
- If an application doesn't extend its window to a secondary display, try maximizing it.

Modems, Single Link and Multilink

Modem connectivity in Windows 2000 Professional is considered part of the networking architecture, and therefore to set up and configure modem connections, you use the command Start⇨Settings⇨Network and Dial-Up Connections.

In this chapter, I focus on getting the hardware installed and configured. Chapter 13 contains a lot more information about configuring specific connections.

Analog modems

Installing and configuring good old digital-to-analog-to-digital modems (called *analog modems* now for short, as opposed to all-digital devices such as ISDN adapters, which aren't really modems at all) may be the subject of an exam question or two.

Modem driver installation

Windows 2000 Professional just isn't very good at automatically detecting modems. If the operating system fails to detect a new modem (and in my experience it *always* fails if the modem connects via an external COM port), then you must initiate the driver installation process yourself. Do so by double-clicking the Phone and Modem Options icon in Control Panel and clicking the Modems tab followed by the Add button. Go ahead and let Windows try to autodetect the modem first; if that fails, specify the manufacturer and model yourself.

INSTANT ANSWER

If Windows 2000 Professional can't seem to find your modem to install its driver, you may need to perform a separate step to install a COM port serial driver associated with that modem.

TIP

The redesigned Phone and Modem Options control panel replaces two control panels found in Windows NT 4.0, Modems and Telephony.

Connection logging

Modem logging is on by default in Windows 2000 Professional. You can't turn it off; all you can do is control whether a new log gets created every time a DUN (Dial-up network) connection occurs, or the logging info appends to the existing DUN log. Set this via the Telephone and Modem Options control panel, on the Diagnostics tab of the modem's property sheet (see Figure 8-5).

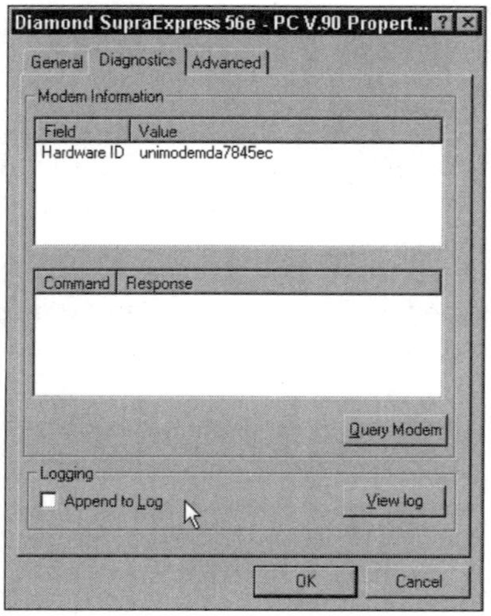

Figure 8-5: Here, you can control logging and view the current log file.

The log file is typically in `C:\WINNT` and has a name that begins with MODEMLOG and ends in .TXT. The precise filename depends on the make and model of your modem.

Modem testing

You can click the Query Modem button on the property sheet's Diagnostics tab to perform a routine communications check. If this check fails, then Windows and your modem aren't on speaking terms, and you may want to check whether you have the correct driver. Also look for a problem icon in Device Manager indicating a resource conflict.

ISDN

Integrated Services Digital Network (ISDN) lines are digital lines, installed by the phone company, that provide better speed than analog modems. An ISDN connection sports two "B" channels for data and voice, each of which can handle 64 kilobits per second, and one 16Kbps "D" channel for control.

Windows 2000 generally autodetects newly installed ISDN adapters automatically upon restart. Failing that, run the Add/Remove Hardware wizard and specify the device category as Network Adapter. (ISDN devices don't have their own separate category.)

You can configure in Device Manager the type of switch the line connects to. Create ISDN connections using the Make New Connection wizard in the Network and Dial-Up Connections folder.

TIP

Internal ISDN adapters show up in Device Manager under the Network Adapters category.

Multilink setups

Multilink dialing means that you can combine two communications devices to act as a single "virtual" channel. Windows 2000 Professional supports multilink setups with ISDN and analog modem lines, with the caveat that the server side of the connection must support them, too. That is, if you're connecting to the Internet, for example, your ISP (Internet Service Provider) must support multilink access, and some don't.

You set up multilink connections in the Networking and Dial-Up Connections folder, on a connection-by-connection basis. Chapter 13 provides the details. It's not necessary to do anything special in Device Manager other than make sure both devices (ISDN adapter, two modems, whatever) are properly installed.

I/O Hardware Configuration Tips

This section contains small bits of wisdom on Device Manager, interrupt sharing, a Plug and Play wrinkle, and mouse configuration.

Device Mangler

Microsoft uses Device Mangler (oops, that's "Manager") for all those hardware configuration details that don't appear in any control panel. The Device Manager display (see Figure 8-6) has been around for a long time in the Windows 9*x* environment but it's a new (and welcome) addition to the NT platform.

Get to the Device Manager in a variety of ways, including:

- Choose Start⇨Settings⇨Control Panel, choose the System control panel, click the Hardware tab, and click the Device Manager button.
- Right-click My Computer, choose Properties, click the Hardware tab, and click the Device Manager button.
- Right-click My Computer, choose Manage, and click the Device Manager icon in the left window.

Figure 8-6: The Device Manager window goes beyond Control Panel.

The general procedure is to expand the tree by clicking the + sign next to the device category of interest. Then, right-click the device you want to configure and choose Properties. What you see at that point varies from device to device.

Device Manager errors

Device Manager communicates errors three ways:

- A yellow exclamation point icon next to a device name means the device's driver is wrong, configured improperly, or missing.
- A red "stop" icon next to a device name means either you or Windows 2000 has disabled the device.
- A yellow question mark means Windows 2000 knows that something is there, but doesn't know what it is or which driver to assign it.

In any of these three cases, the device doesn't work right, and you must give its property sheet some attention. For example, the Resources tab of the device's property sheet should list the interrupts, base memory addresses, upper-memory addresses, and (if applicable) Direct Memory Access (DMA) channels that the device is using. You may need to clear the Use Automatic Configuration check box and set one or more of these values manually if you find a conflict reported at the bottom of the Resources tab.

Another place where you can view actual or potential conflicts is the System Information snap-in of the Computer Management console (see Figure 8-7).

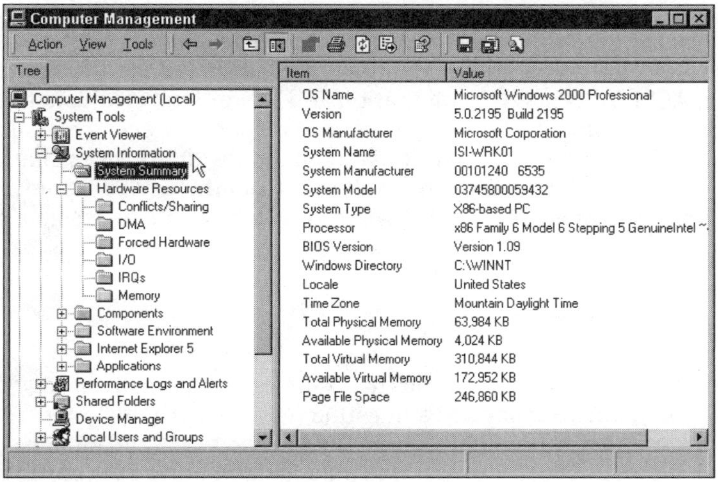

Figure 8-7: The System Information snap-in contains a wealth of detail.

- The **Conflicts/Sharing** subfolder lists any conflicting resource assignments (however, see the next section, "IRQ sharing," before concluding that a shared interrupt is actually a problem).
- The **Forced Hardware** subfolder lists any resource settings that you have made manually via Device Manager, and that therefore Plug and Play may not reconfigure in the future.

The System Information snap-in can generate reports in custom or text formats — and you can run it remotely by right-clicking the topmost node in the left window pane ("Computer Management") and choosing Connect To Another Computer.

Administrators and Plug and Play

An interesting quirk of Plug and Play is that the procedure for automatically installing a device driver doesn't normally require you to be logged on as an administrator — unless Windows asks you to provide a location for the driver file. It seems that if Windows can't find the driver itself, it asks you to find it, but you must have administrative rights on the system to do so. I guess the theory is that you could point to a location containing an untrusted and buggy driver if you didn't have administrative experience. Anyway, you may well see an exam question covering this quirk.

IRQ sharing

In the "olden days" of the ISA (Industry Standard Architecture) bus, sharing interrupts (IRQs) was *verboten*. The PCI bus, however, permits multiple devices to share the same interrupt without any major problems. Generally, Windows 2000 configures such interrupt sharing behind the scenes. In fact, on an ACPI (Advanced Configuration and Power Interface) machine, you can't modify interrupt sharing using Device Manager. However, you can have a performance problem if two very busy, high-bandwidth devices share the same IRQ. You may need to use setup software from the device manufacturer to manually assign an unused IRQ when Windows wants to assign a shared IRQ.

A mouse tip

Mice generally don't appear on the exam, except in really grungy test facilities (joke), but you may see a question pertaining to the "Snap To Default" feature. Set this via a check box on the Motion tab of the Mouse control panel; it moves the mouse cursor to the default button of (most) dialog boxes, saving wrist wear and tear. The behavior is odd at first but you may grow to like it (I do). Too bad it doesn't work in all dialog boxes.

Keyboard kontrol

Sometimes, when my editors are after me to turn in material that's a little late, I tell them I'm busy keyboarding. (What I mean by that phrase is that I'm in Keystone, snowboarding.) Bad jokes aside, here are a few quick tips on keyboard configuration:

- Use the Input Locales tab on the Keyboard control panel or the Regional Options control panel (the tab is the same in both places) to change the keyboard layout for different languages and locales; see Chapter 5.
- If you want a keystroke to "wake up" your computer after it's gone into sleep mode, check the Allow This Device To Bring The Computer Out Of Standby box.
- If you enable keyboard sound effects and they repeat uncontrollably, try changing the interrupt for your sound card.
- If you have a keyboard with special keys (such as mine, which has keys for Internet, Search, Help, and Mute), you may need a third-party driver from the keyboard or PC manufacturer. Test it carefully.

Getting carded

Smart cards are authentication devices that can provide a higher degree of authentication security than simple username and password schemes. You must have the card and your personal identification number (PIN) to authenticate yourself to the network. The reader devices typically connect via the PC Card bus (what we used to call PCMCIA) or a serial port.

Microsoft makes the following recommendations about smart card readers:

- If they're not Plug and Play compatible, don't use 'em.
- If they don't carry the Windows Hardware Quality Labs logo, don't use 'em.
- Let Windows 2000 autodetect the reader at startup; supply any third-party device drivers at that time if necessary.

Multimedia Hardware

A few notes are in order here about multimedia hardware, specifically, the Windows Driver Model, DVD, and the new Scanners and Cameras control panel. (See "DirectX marks the spot" earlier in this chapter for display-related multimedia issues.)

Windows Driver Model

Windows Driver Model (WDM) is a 32-bit driver model in which Windows NT and 2000 drivers work with Windows 98 and vice versa. It is supported for USB and FireWire devices, but not all other types of hardware. The idea of WDM is to make life a bit easier on device manufacturers by not making them write a separate device driver for each Windows version.

Multimedia devices in Windows 2000 Professional typically use the WDM *streaming class driver* for audio and video. This driver permits more than one application to play sound at the same time, and it allows sound output to travel to any relevant device on any system bus. It also lets the operating system handle audio mixing instead of hardware, which is why you now sometimes hear a beep five seconds after you see its related dialog box, for example.

WARNING!

You should generally not expect Windows NT 4.0 drivers to work under Windows 2000. The only ones in my experience that do seem to work are the SCSI miniport drivers and a few printer drivers. Display drivers, network card drivers, mouse drivers, and so forth seem to require specific Windows 2000 support to work right with the new operating system.

DVD

At least in the reasonably standardized read-only flavor, *DVD* (short for *Digital Video Disc* or *Digital Versatile Disc*) devices now receive Windows support in the form of a DVD-ROM driver and a DVD-Video player. DVDs can hold video, audio, and computer data content on the same disc, and their capacity can go as high as 17GB. Windows 2000 supports writable DVD in the future, according to Microsoft.

DVD devices use the *Universal Disk Format (UDF)* file system. A UDF disk can be a boot device. UDF also supports Unicode filenames and file-and-folder level access control, much as NTFS does. Remember, though, that Windows 2000 can't write to a UDF disk without extra software.

DVD drives use the *streaming class* WDM driver (see previous section), which supports both of the compression types found on DVD disks, MPEG-2 and AC-3 (Dolby Digital). In addition to the WDM driver, you typically need a minidriver from the manufacturer to support features specific to the drive make and model.

Scanners and cameras

Windows 2000 Professional sports a new control panel, *Scanners and Cameras*. (I chuckle at the name, because a total of two, count 'em *two,* scanner models are supported — 99 percent of the devices you can add or configure here are digital cameras.)

- Click this control panel's Add button to install drivers for a camera or scanner that Plug and Play doesn't find on its own.
- To modify the color profile that a scanner or camera uses, select the device, click Properties, click the Color Management tab.
- To make a just-scanned document load into a specified application program automatically: Select the device, click Properties, click the Events tab, choose the application, and click Send to This Application.

Scanners and cameras make up a hardware class that Microsoft calls *still image* devices. The Windows Driver Model supports still image devices that use the USB, FireWire, or SCSI bus; therefore, Windows 2000 doesn't directly support parallel-port still image devices or those on a network. That's not to say that those devices don't work, but you'll probably need third-party drivers for them.

Getting on the Universal Serial Bus

The *Universal Serial Bus*, or *USB*, is a popular choice for adding low- to medium-speed peripherals to a Windows 2000 PC. (Windows 95 OSR2 supported USB to a limited extent, Windows 98 supports USB natively, and Windows NT 4 never successfully supported USB.)

The data transfer speed of the USB depends on whether it's operating in *isochronous* or *asynchronous* mode. Both modes can't be active simultaneously.

- In isochronous mode, data transfers occur at a fixed, guaranteed level of 12 Mbps (megabits per second).

  Speakers, modems, and monitors typically use this mode.
- In asynchronous mode, data transfers occur at 1.5 Mbps.

  Keyboards and mice typically use this mode.

REMEMBER

Remember these basic facts about USB for the test, which is highly likely to ask you at least one USB-related question:

- USB is an external bus.

  You can use a single port (and interrupt) to daisy-chain up to 127 devices, such as mice, keyboards, speakers, and monitors.
- You may not exceed five tiers on the USB bus.
- USB is a Plug and Play bus that supports *hot swapping* (nothing to do with experimental marriages), so you can add and remove devices without powering down the computer.
- Unlike devices on other buses, USB devices typically don't have resource settings that can cause device failure.
- You may have to enable your USB controller in the PC's BIOS for USB devices to work. Windows 2000 doesn't even show the controller in Device Manager if the BIOS doesn't enable it.
- Bus-powered hubs (as opposed to self-powered hubs with their own power supply) can support a maximum of four downstream ports.
- The bus fails if devices on a bus-powered hub draw too much power. "Too much" is determined by checking the milliamp rating on the root hub's property sheet in Device Manager; look at the Power tab.
- You can suppress USB error messages on the USB controller's property sheet in the Advanced tab (see Figure 8-8), but as a general rule, you shouldn't.

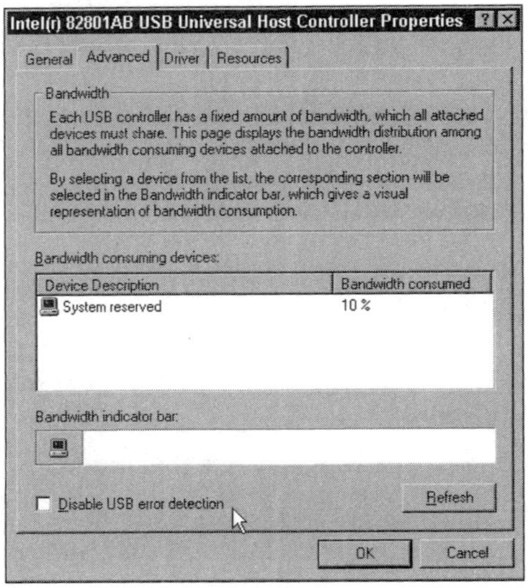

Figure 8-8: The check box should normally be clear, as is the default.

- Hubs provide device connection points, power management, and device detection services. USB devices can be no more than five meters from a hub. The USB host (usually a circuit on the PC's motherboard but may be an add-in adapter) is also called the *root hub*.
- Don't connect a bus-powered hub to another bus-powered hub.

TIP

Older PCs that support USB 1.0 generally don't work well with modern USB peripherals.

INSTANT ANSWER

If the PC's BIOS enables the USB bus but Windows 2000 still has problems finding devices on the bus, try removing the bus host controller in Device Manager, and rebooting. That lets Windows redetect the controller and every USB device connected to it.

FireWire: USB Plus Caffeine

FireWire, or *IEEE 1394* (which isn't nearly as much fun to say but which you should memorize anyway), is yet another new hardware bus that Windows 2000 supports. This bus is suitable for high-bandwidth devices, such as digital camcorders and VCRs, video teleconferencing equipment, and so on. FireWire hardware support may be built in to a given PC's system board, or added via an adapter. Windows 2000 Professional provides the system-level support.

FireWire is a lot like the Universal Serial Bus (Plug and Play, external bus, daisy-chain design, asynchronous and isochronous modes, and so on), but bigger and faster.

- FireWire supports up to 63 devices on a single bus, and you can connect up to 1023 buses together, for a total number of devices that is . . . well, let's just say a *lot*.
- FireWire supports data transfer rates of 100, 200, and even 400 Mbps (megabits per second), compared to the 12 Mbps maximum for USB. Although you can put devices having different speeds on the same bus, the maximum bus speed is limited by the slowest device.
- FireWire components come in four flavors: *devices, splitters, bridges,* and *repeaters*. Don't learn any more detail than this for the exam. Learn a lot more detail if you plan to set up a large net of FireWire components.

Prep Test

1 **Thurston comes to you with a PC question. He has just installed Windows 2000 Professional and he is excited about using the new peripherals and buses that it supports. However, after removing and reinstalling new USB speakers, keyboard, and mouse several times, none of the devices are working properly, even though the USB host controller appears in Device Manager without an exclamation point or a red "X." What would you advise Thurston to try? (Choose two answers.)**

A ❑ Disable the USB host controller in Device Manager, and reboot.

B ❑ Consult the PC documentation to find out if the USB hardware version is 1.0.

C ❑ Uninstall the USB host controller in Device Manager, and reboot.

D ❑ Enable the USB host controller in the BIOS.

2 **Ginger adds an ISDN adapter to her Windows 2000 Professional machine. Windows doesn't detect it automatically at the next restart, so she runs the Add/Remove Hardware wizard. However, she does not see a separate category for ISDN adapters. Which category contains this class of device? (Choose one.)**

A ❍ Network adapters

B ❍ Modems

C ❍ Multi-Port serial adapters

D ❍ System devices

E ❍ Other devices

3 **What file system do DVD devices use under Windows 2000?**

A ❍ CDFS

B ❍ VFAT

C ❍ NTFS

D ❍ UDF

E ❍ UDP

4 **Mary Ann reports a device failure on her Windows 2000 Professional PC. Her sound system stopped working when she installed a video capture card. You suspect a device resource conflict.**

Where could you look to confirm or refute this suspicion? (Choose all that apply.)

A ❑ The Computer Management console, System Information snap-in, Conflicts/Sharing folder.

B ❑ The Computer Management console, Device Manager snap-in, Resources property sheet for the sound card.

C ❑ The Computer Management console, Device Manager snap-in, Resources property sheet for the video capture card.

D ❑ The System control panel, Hardware tab, Device Manager button, Resources property sheet for the sound card.

E ❑ The System control panel, Hardware tab, Device Manager button, Resources property sheet for the video capture card.

5 **As PC technical liaison for your department, you get a call from an employee named Skip who is having problems with intermittent dial-up modem connections. Sometimes he's able to connect to a remote server, other times he's not. You check Skip's connection icon settings and they appear to be in order. So, you decide to take a look at modem log activity. Where do you look? (Choose the best answer.)**

A ❍ The Event Viewer

B ❍ The file C:\WINNT\MODEMLOG.TXT

C ❍ The file C:\MODEMLOG.TXT

D ❍ The file C:\WINNT\MODEM*<modelname>*LOG.TXT

6 **You install a new PCI modem into your Windows 2000 Professional computer. Upon restart, Plug and Play doesn't detect the modem. When you run the Add/Remove Hardware wizard, Windows 2000 doesn't detect the modem then, either. What is a likely guess about what you must do first in order to get Windows 2000 to detect the modem? (Choose the best answer.)**

A ❍ Disable IRQ conflict checking.

B ❍ Disable IRQ sharing on the PCI bus.

C ❍ Add a driver for the integrated serial port.

D ❍ Activate the modem in the BIOS.

7 **Your Windows 2000 Professional PC has an internal SCSI adapter for your hard drive, but the adapter also has an external connection for I/O devices. You connect a scanner to the external connection and add a scanner driver via the Add/Remove Hardware wizard. When you restart the computer, Windows 2000 crashes with a STOP screen before you even see the logon dialog box. How can you fix this problem most quickly so that you can again boot to Windows 2000 Professional? (Choose the best answer.)**

A ❍ Reboot holding down the CTRL key, and choose Safe Mode at the text-mode boot menu. Then remove the driver using Device Manager.

B ❍ Reboot holding down the CTRL key, and choose Last Known Good Configuration. Then remove the driver using Device Manager.

C ❍ Reboot holding down the CTRL key, and choose Last Known Good Configuration.

D ❍ Reboot from the Windows 2000 CD and enter the Recovery Console. Disable the SCSI service with the DISABLE command. Reboot normally.

8 **Windows 2000 supports the AGP bus for what types of devices? (Choose all that apply.)**

A ❑ Video adapters

B ❑ Network adapters

C ❑ Multiport serial adapters

D ❑ SCSI host controllers

9 **When installing a Plug and Play device, Windows 2000 Professional prompts you for the location of the device driver. You provide the drive letter of your CD-ROM drive (the device manufacturer provided the CD). However, the installation fails. What is the likely cause?**

A ❍ Your computer supports APM but not ACPI.

B ❍ The CD is corrupt.

C ❍ You are not logged on as an Administrator.

D ❍ Plug and Play has been disabled by a group policy.

10 **Approximately how many times faster can a FireWire device be than a USB device, in terms of data transfer?**

A ❍ 5

B ❍ 10

C ❍ 33

D ❍ 67

Answers

1 **B** and **C.** Merely disabling the controller won't work. Uninstalling it forces Windows 2000 to redetect the controller, and all connected peripherals, at the next restart. Choice D is wrong because the controller wouldn't appear in Device Manager if it were disabled at the BIOS level.

2 **A.** Just one of those facts to memorize, I'm afraid. The answer does make sense in the sense that ISDN adapters are typically used to connect to networks.

3 **D.** UDF stands for Universal Data Format. UDF has some of the features of NTFS, but it isn't the same animal. UDP stands for User Datagram Protocol, a transport-level network protocol used in TCP/IP networks. CDFS is the CD-ROM File System. For the exam, you should also remember that DVD under Windows 2000 is a read-only medium, at least as of the initial publicly available version of the operating system.

4 **A, B, C, D,** and **E.** The Windows operating system is becoming well known for providing several different paths to the same utility. Sometimes that's handy, sometimes it's confusing, but you never know which method the exam expects you to know. So know them all.

5 **D.** Examples are *MODEMLOG_56K Data Fax Modem PnP.TXT* and *MODEMLOG_Conexant SoftK56 PCI Modem(M).TXT*. One could make a strong argument that this information really should be in the Event Viewer, so that answer is logical but wrong. The modem logging feature works just like in Windows 98, which doesn't have Event Viewer, so that may explain why Windows 2000 logs these activities this way.

6 **C.** Once you add the port driver, Windows 2000 can probably access the port and detect the modem's presence. Choices A and B are not options that Windows 2000 allows you to perform, and choice D is not necessary.

7 **C.** Now, let me say right away that this question presupposes some knowledge from Chapter 15, so if you haven't read that one yet, do *not* feel bad about missing this one. The main point here is that if you add a device that messes up your system, but you do not log on after a restart, then you can use the Last Known Good Configuration boot option to restore your system to its state before you added the evil driver. Note also that SCSI support is provided via device drivers, not via an operating system service.

8 **A.** AGP is for video adapters only.

9 **C.** Only an administrator can install a Plug and Play device for which Windows 2000 can't automatically find the driver.

10 **B.** 400 divided by 12 is 33.33. This is one of those questions where it's handy to be able to use the Windows calculator.

Chapter 9

Mobile Computers and Power Management

Exam Objectives

- Configuring Advanced Power Management (APM)
- Configuring and managing card services
- Installing, configuring, and managing Infrared Data Association (IrDA) devices
- Installing, configuring, and managing wireless devices
- Managing hardware profiles

Windows NT Workstation 4.0 was notorious for being less than completely convenient on portable computers. With the world getting more mobile every day, Microsoft wisely added two Windows 9*x* features to the NT platform in Windows 2000: power management and Plug and Play. This chapter looks at these two technologies as well as a couple other issues of interest to notebook users: wireless devices and hardware profiles. (The topic of offline files and folders, also of interest to mobile computer users, gets its due in Chapter 12, as it's considered part of IntelliMirror.)

Quick Assessment

Configuring Advanced Power Management (APM)

1 You're on an airplane and asked to power down your notebook computer. Would you choose Hibernate or Standby?

2 The power management standard that Windows 2000 prefers is ______.

3 A group of settings for powering down disks and displays is known as a ______ in Windows 2000.

4 You typically connect a UPS to a PC with a ______ cable.

Configuring and managing card services

5 Before removing a PC Card, you should tell Windows 2000 about your intention via the ______ control panel.

Installing, configuring, and managing Infrared Data Association (IrDA) devices

6 If two infrared devices aren't communicating reliably, consider reducing the ______ setting.

Installing, configuring, and managing wireless devices

7 Most infrared devices need to be within ______ of each other in order to communicate.

8 If you want to use a wireless device to connect a computer to a network, use the ______ control panel.

Managing hardware profiles

9 Portable computers typically have two hardware profiles, ______ and ______.

10 To create a new hardware profile, use the ______ control panel's Hardware tab.

Answers

1 *Hibernate.* Didn't know this one? See "Power Management."

2 *ACPI.* See the "ACPI" section for more information.

3 *Power scheme.* The "Power Management" section explains.

4 *Serial.* See "Uninterruptible Power Supplies" for details.

5 *Add/Remove Hardware.* The "PC Cards" section includes this and other tips.

6 *Maximum connection speed.* The "Infrared and Wireless Devices" section has more.

7 *One meter.* They also typically need to be pointing at each other. See "Infrared and Wireless Devices" for details.

8 *Network and Dial-Up Connections.* Again, the "Infrared and Wireless Devices" section elaborates.

9 *Docked, undocked.* See "Docking stations" and "Hardware Profiles" for more.

10 *System.* The "Hardware Profiles" section explains.

Power Management

The basic idea behind power management is that the operating system, in cooperation with the BIOS, can power down your display and hard drive after a predefined period of inactivity. The goal is to save battery juice on your mobile computer, extending your work time — or to reduce the part of your electric bill that's attributable to your desktop computer, which by the way can be significant!

All power management functions in Windows 2000 Professional appear in the Power Options control panel, whose contents can vary depending on the power-saving features of the specific computer. You typically see four or five tabs on this control panel, as follows:

- **Power Schemes** (see Figure 9-1) lets you select from a predefined group of schemes for when to turn off your monitor and hard disk, and when (or whether) to put the computer into standby mode. (Standby mode is a low-power mode suitable for stretches when you're not using the PC but you expect to resume doing so in a few minutes.) If you enable Hibernate support (see two bullets down), you can also specify how long a period of inactivity must occur before the PC hibernates. You can change an existing scheme and save it under a new name, as Lab 9-1 explains.

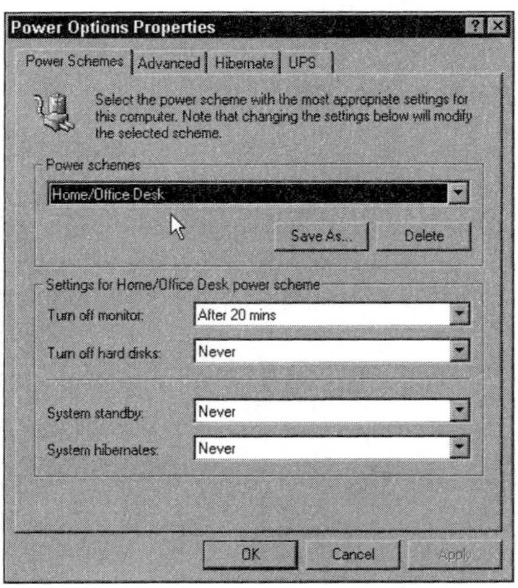

Figure 9-1: You can use predefined power schemes or define your own.

- **Advanced** (see Figure 9-2) lets you specify whether the power management icon appears in your system tray (the "sunken" area on the taskbar opposite the Start button). If you chose a standby mode option on the Power Schemes tab, the Advanced tab also lets you specify whether Windows should prompt you for your password when you bring your PC out of standby mode. On some computers, you also get to choose whether pushing your PC's power switch truly powers it down or instead puts it into standby mode.

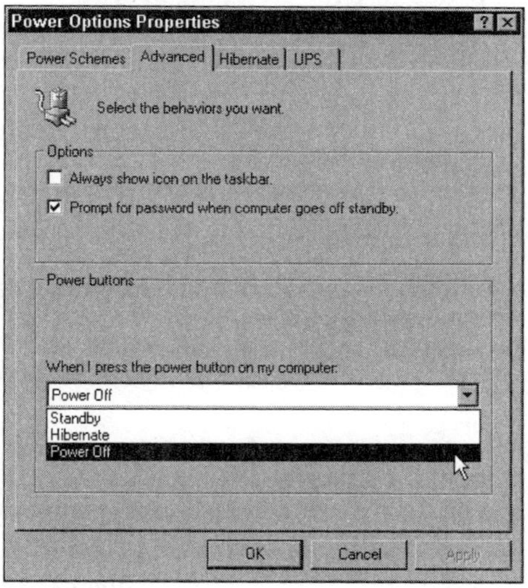

Figure 9-2: You may not see all these options on any given PC.

- **Hibernate** lets you turn hibernation on or off via the Enable Hibernate Support check box. Hibernation is different from standby. When your PC hibernates, Windows writes the contents of memory to a disk file and then powers off. When you power back on later, Windows retrieves the contents of memory from the disk file, which is usually a lot quicker than a normal boot process. Your programs and even LAN connections come back to life.

  Standby = low power but still on; hibernate = off, but ready to restart fast.

- **APM** only appears if your PC supports it. See the "APM" section for details.

- **UPS** lets you configure a battery backup device. See the "Uninterruptible Power Supplies" section for details.

You can manually put your computer into hibernation mode by choosing Start⇨Shut Down and choosing Hibernate in the Shut Down Windows dialog box. If your computer supports hibernation fully, you can also specify when to hibernate automatically with the Power Schemes tab of the Power Options control panel. The same holds true for manually and automatically entering Standby mode. Some portable computers let you choose a Power Options setting to force Standby mode when you close the computer's lid.

You're responsible for saving your work to disk before initiating Standby mode. If your battery dies while your computer is on Standby, and you haven't saved your data files, you could lose some work.

On any given PC, some power management features may require activation in the BIOS setup program. The procedure for changing BIOS settings varies, but you usually have to press a function key, or combination of keys, during power-up. The startup text sequence usually clues you in on the details.

Lab 9-1 presents the steps for modifying an existing scheme and saving it under a new name.

Lab 9-1 Changing a Power Management Scheme

1. **Open the Power Management control panel by choosing Start⇨Settings⇨Control Panel⇨Power Options.**
2. **Choose the scheme Always On using the drop-down list box on the Power Schemes tab.**
3. **Change the setting for Turn Off Hard Disks to read After 4 Hours.**
4. **Click the Save As button and provide a name for the new power scheme.**

   If you simply click OK instead of Save As, Windows 2000 saves the revised settings with the same scheme name.

Windows 2000 Professional supports two different power management standards: APM (Advanced Power Management) and ACPI (Advanced Configuration and Power Interface). The next two sections explore the differences.

APM

Advanced Power Management, or APM, is a pseudo-standard common on pre-1999 machines but getting less common every day. I say "pseudo-standard" because APM doesn't nail down a lot of details, leaving the computer manufacturer to interpret some of its guidelines. That's one of the reasons APM isn't completely satisfactory, but it may be the only power management capability a given PC has to offer. APM must be supported by a given computer's hardware and BIOS for Windows 2000 Professional to be able to use it.

You can tell whether Windows 2000 thinks your PC fully supports APM by choosing the Power Options control panel and looking for the APM tab. If it's there, you can enable APM if it isn't already enabled (and it's not by default) by checking the box labeled Enable Advanced Power Management Support. If the APM tab isn't there, Windows 2000 doesn't perceive your PC as APM-capable.

If your APM machine isn't powering down at shutdown, and it used to do so with a previous version of Windows, go to the APM tab of the Power Options control panel, enable APM, and restart.

Three quick facts you may need:

- Windows 2000 Professional supports APM version 1.2.
- You have to be logged on as an Administrator in order to turn APM on or off.
- Windows 2000 Server doesn't support APM at all. (This just might appear, even though the exam technically doesn't cover the Server product.)

ACPI

Advanced Configuration and Power Interface (ACPI) is a newer and more rigorous standard than APM, and the designers of Windows 2000 Professional wrote the operating system with ACPI in mind. ACPI makes power management (and, incidentally, Plug and Play) work better.

As with APM, the PC must support ACPI in the hardware and the BIOS for Windows 2000 to use this standard. You can tell whether Windows 2000 thinks your PC fully supports ACPI by choosing Start⇨Settings⇨Control Panel⇨System⇨Hardware, clicking the Device Manager tab, and expanding the Computer icon. If the computer's label says:

- Advanced Configuration and Power Interface (ACPI) PC
- ACPI Uniprocessor PC
- ACPI Multiprocessor PC

you have ACPI support. If it says

- Standard PC
- MPS Uniprocessor PC
- MPS Multiprocessor PC

you don't.

If your BIOS setup program lets you switch between these two power management standards, don't try doing so after Windows 2000 is already installed (unless you want to reinstall the operating system!). Windows 2000 installs a *Hardware Abstraction Layer,* or *HAL,* based on what power management standard Windows "sees" in the BIOS at installation time. You can't change the HAL to support a different power management standard without reinstalling Windows!

Uninterruptible Power Supplies

You probably don't typically carry an *Uninterruptible Power Supply (UPS)* with your notebook computer as you travel around. However, we're on the subject of power management, so here's a brief look at UPS support in Windows 2000.

A UPS is a battery backup device that can supply power to your plugged-in notebook or (more likely) desktop computer if AC power fails. For example, I'm writing this in the foothills of the Rocky Mountains, where power glitches occur so frequently that no VCR in the county displays the correct time. Many UPS devices can communicate with your PC via a serial cable. That way, the UPS can let your PC know when AC power has been lost or when the UPS battery is low.

Setup

To set up your UPS, click the Select button on the UPS tab of the Power Options control panel. You must specify the vendor, model, and which serial port the UPS attaches to (you may need to use a special cable supplied by the UPS manufacturer).

Configuration

To configure your UPS, click the Configure button on the UPS tab of the Power Options control panel. You should see a dialog box similar to Figure 9-3. The options you can set here include:

- Enabling notification messages of power failure, power restoration, low battery condition, and UPS-to-computer communication.
- If you enable notification messages, setting a time after a power failure that Windows 2000 waits to display a message the first time and how long it waits to display subsequent messages.
- Specifying when Windows issues a *critical alarm* if the UPS didn't issue one automatically because of a low battery. Enter the number of minutes you feel confident the UPS can run your PC. This is a belt-and-suspenders setting just in case the low-battery-sensing feature of the UPS fails.

- Running a program (if any) when a critical alarm occurs. The UPS vendor typically provides such a program.
- Shutting down or (if hibernation is enabled) hibernating after the vendor-supplied program runs.

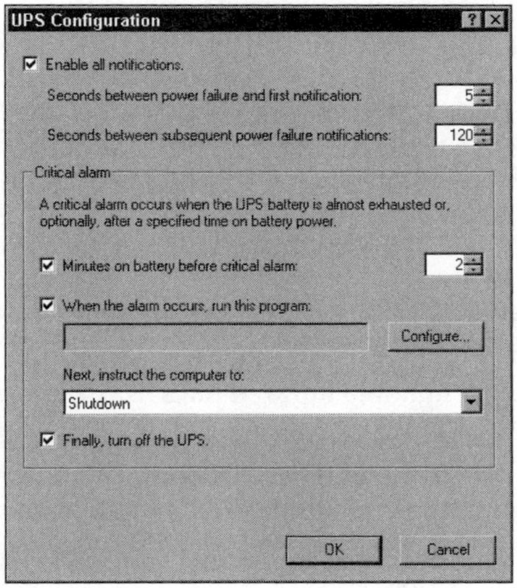

Figure 9-3: Configuring a UPS.

Infrared and Wireless Devices

Windows 2000 provides infrared and wireless device support equivalent to that of Windows 98 and superior to that of Windows NT Workstation 4.0. With a wireless link, you can transfer files between two computers, or print a document from a computer to a printer, without an interconnecting cable. (Better have a good clear line of sight, though.)

Heck, you can even create a network link, which you accomplish via the Make New Connection icon in the Network and Dial-Up Connections control panel. The procedure is very similar to creating a Direct Cable Connection link: You specify one machine to be the "host" and the other to be the "guest."

The most common wireless device is the *infrared* link. Infrared light has a wavelength longer than visible red light (and a frequency less than red light). In the personal computer world, nearly all infrared devices adhere to the *IrDA (Infrared Data Association)* standards, which specify speeds of 115Kbps for older devices (the standard name is IrDA-SIR) and 4Mbps for newer ones (IrDA-FIR). IrDA-equipped computers and printers have a little red window somewhere on the device that acts as the line-of-sight communications port.

Both IrDA-SIR and IrDA-FIR are *half-duplex* systems. That is, communication only occurs in one direction at a time.

Windows 2000 normally autodetects built-in infrared devices such as often come with notebook computers, but you may have to run the Add/Remove Hardware wizard if you're retrofitting an infrared device to a serial port. On some computers, enabling the built-in infrared port requires that a COM port be disabled in the BIOS setup program. After you do that, Windows 2000 probably detects the infrared port at the next reboot via Plug and Play. After you install an infrared or other wireless device and Windows 2000 recognizes it, a new icon (*Wireless Link*) appears in the Control Panel. Also, if you run the Add Printer wizard, a new port (IrLPT) appears in the list of available device ports.

TIME SHAVER

Relevant facts about infrared communications include the following:

- Windows 2000 can support multiple sessions (programs communicating with each other) over a single link.
- Windows 2000 can support multiple infrared links, too, but each infrared port can only communicate with one other infrared port at a time.
- Most infrared devices need to be within one meter of each other, and with each red window pointing at the other, to communicate.
- When two infrared devices are within range and properly positioned, an infrared port icon appears on the taskbar, and a wireless link icon appears on the desktop.
- You can copy files from one infrared device to another by dragging-and-dropping files to the Wireless Link icon, or by running IRFTP.EXE from the Run dialog box (see Figure 9-4), selecting the files, and clicking the Send button.
- Lowering the maximum connection rate on the infrared device's property sheet may correct some communication problems.

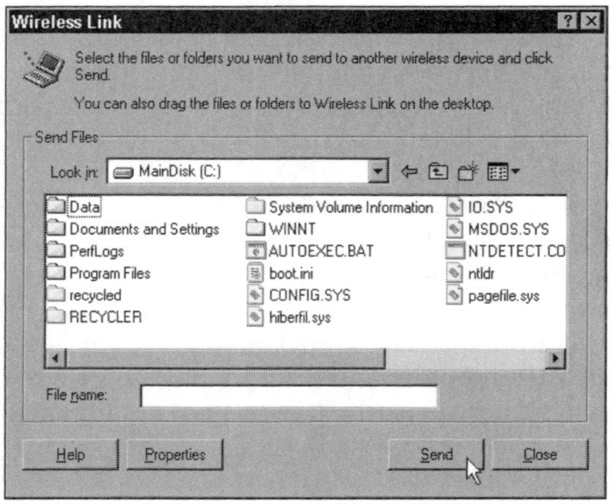

Figure 9-4: Sending files via IRFTP.EXE.

Plug and Play and Mobile Computers

Plug and Play is a systemwide specification that makes adding, configuring, and removing devices easier and more automatic. (At least when it works. In fairness, it seems to work better in Windows 2000 than in any previous version of Windows.) This technology is especially important to portable computer users who often disconnect and reconnect different devices to their notebook PCs. Plug and Play's goal is to let such users plug and unplug devices as they need to without having to worry about installing or uninstalling device drivers; manually resetting resource assignments (interrupts, memory addresses, and so on); or restarting their computers.

For Plug and Play to work, the specification requires support at all levels: computer hardware, BIOS, bus, operating system (ta-daa), device driver, and device. Windows 2000 looks at the first two items at setup time and installs the appropriate HAL, or Hardware Abstraction Layer.

REMEMBER

As with power management, Windows 2000 Plug and Play works best with PCs that support the ACPI standard (see the "ACPI" section).

TIP

If you need to remove and reinstall a Plug and Play driver, for example because you chose the wrong driver file when you originally installed the device, here's how. Uninstall the driver using Device Manager, then restart the system, and let Windows 2000 Professional autodetect the device again. At that time, you can provide the proper driver files, for example on a CD from the device's manufacturer.

REMEMBER

Plug and Play can normally install devices even if you're not logged on as an Administrator, as long as the computer doesn't have to ask you for the location of a device driver. In that case, you must be an Administrator. You must always log on as Administrator to install devices with the Add/Remove Hardware wizard.

PC Cards

Plug and Play doesn't work equally well for all different computer buses, but it works quite well on mobile computers that use the *PC Card* bus (what we formerly called PCMCIA, an acronym that you still see occasionally). PC Card devices also go by the name "credit-card devices." Typically, PC Cards are modems, disk drives, and network adapters.

The system level software that controls PC Cards is *card services*.

ACPI machines support dynamic reconfiguration of PC Card devices, meaning that you can plug in and unplug these devices without having to reboot. However, if you're removing an Ethernet PC Card, you may need to "stop" the card before removing it, by using the PC Card icon on the System Tray. And Microsoft wants you to run the "Add/Remove Hardware" wizard to remove a PC Card device before you actually unplug it. In either case, Windows 2000 tells you when it's okay to remove the device.

I should add that APM machines can sometimes offer the same capability; my old APM notebook automatically detects my plugging in a PC Card Ethernet adapter just fine.

PC Card modems (as well as internal PCI modems) often require you to install a COM port driver first, before you can install the modem driver itself.

Docking stations

Many mobile computer users plug their computers into a *docking station* when they're dropping by the office to collect a paycheck, submit an expense report, or flirt with the boss's [son, daughter] (choose the best answer). The docking station may have a different keyboard, display, network adapter, and so on.

Plug and Play support in Windows 2000 makes it more likely that the operating system can detect all that different hardware automatically. It also enables the user to connect or disconnect the computer to or from the docking station without powering everything down ("hot docking"). Microsoft recommends that you use the Start⇨Eject PC command, if it's present, before undocking your notebook PC.

However, redetecting a bunch of devices is a time-consuming chore, and therefore a better way should exist for the mobile computer user who must occasionally dock into port. Thankfully, it does, and I explain it in the next section.

Hardware Profiles

You probably know that you can log on to Windows 2000 Professional with different user names and you can see different desktop settings, programs, menus, and so forth. These different sets of preferences go by the name "user profiles."

Similarly, you can set up the operating system so that the computer hardware itself changes, depending on which *hardware profile* you activate at boot time.

Normally, desktop computers don't change hardware configurations frequently (if ever), but many mobile computers often do. For example, your notebook computer may have a drive bay that can hold either a diskette drive or a CD-ROM drive. Or, you may want to use your notebook computer on an airplane or train sometimes, and in the office connected to a docking station at other times.

Although you could rely on Plug and Play to redetect all the hardware changes at boot time, that can add precious minutes to the startup process. Furthermore, some of your hardware may not be Plug and Play compliant. Finally, if Windows 2000 tries to detect hardware that Windows expects to see but that *isn't* present, the boot process slows to a crawl while Windows waits the maximum prescribed time for the device to respond before concluding that it's missing.

Windows 2000's hardware profiles feature lets you predefine two, three, or any number of discrete hardware configurations to avoid these potential problems. Lab 9-2 presents the technique for creating a new hardware profile.

Lab 9-2 Creating a New Hardware Profile

1. **Choose Start⇨Settings⇨Control Panel.**
2. **Double-click the System icon.**
3. **Click the Hardware tab of the System control panel.**
4. **Click the Hardware Profiles button to display the dialog box shown in Figure 9-5.**

   Windows 2000 creates the "Profile 1 (Current)" profile automatically during setup.
5. **Highlight a profile in the Available Hardware Profiles list.**
6. **Click the Copy button for a new profile based on the existing one.**
7. **Name the new profile in the Copy Profile dialog box and click OK.**
8. **Click OK twice to close all open dialog boxes.**

How does Windows 2000 choose a hardware configuration at startup? You set the options in the Hardware Profiles dialog box: Either you make Windows wait for you to choose from the list, or you let Windows pick the top profile in the list after a fixed delay period. Change the relative position of any listed profile by selecting it and moving it with the arrow keys.

After you boot to a hardware profile, the System control panel's Device Manager tab navigates through the *hardware tree* on a device-by-device basis, and specifies hardware configurations for devices should belong to (see Figure 9-6). The Registry stores all hardware profile information.

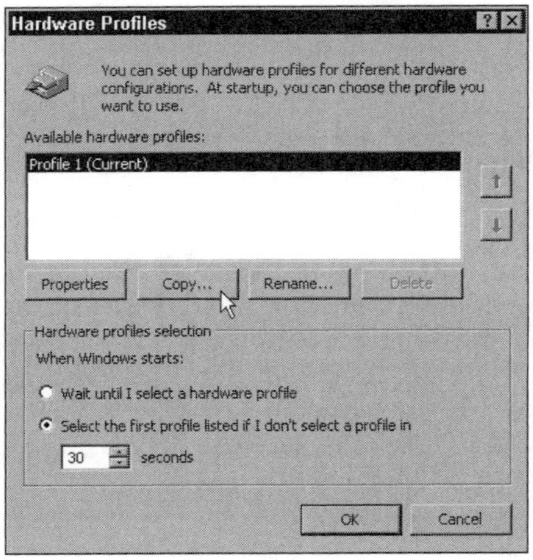

Figure 9-5: Create a new hardware profile here.

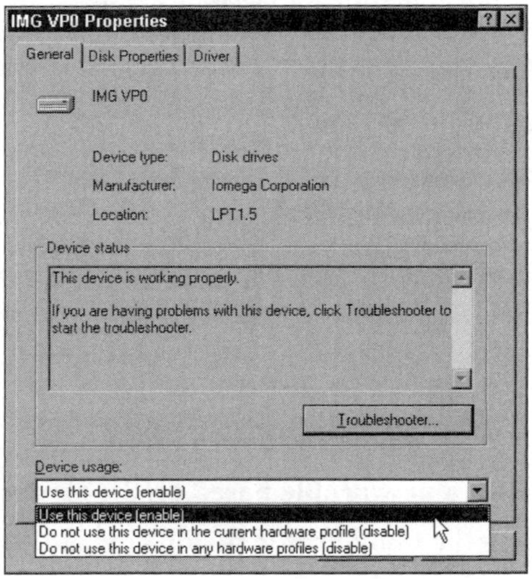

Figure 9-6: Disable a device in the current profile or in all profiles.

If you *disable* a device using Device Manager, the driver remains on the local hard disk and is available for use in other hardware profiles. Disabling a device renders it inactive, prevents the Registry from loading the driver at startup, and frees the resources (interrupt, memory, and so on) that the device was using. However, if you *uninstall* a device, Windows 2000 deletes the driver files and the device is not available for use in other hardware profiles.

Prep Test

1 **You have a portable computer that you have upgraded to Windows 2000 from Windows 98. You notice that the computer no longer powers down when you execute the Shutdown command. What must you enable with the Power Options control panel in order to fix this problem? (Choose the best answer.)**

A ❍ APM
B ❍ ACPI
C ❍ A power scheme
D ❍ MPS
E ❍ SMP

2 **You have a portable computer that runs Windows 2000. You spend about half your time at the office and half your time on the road, so your manager authorizes a docking station, which you get a good deal on because it's been discontinued by the manufacturer. You set up a second hardware profile so that Windows 2000 can take advantage of the docking station's network card and high-res display adapter.**

You reboot the computer, go for a cup of coffee, and come back to find that your docked computer does not seem to be using the network card. You check the maximum resolution of the display, and the computer isn't using the high-res video card, either. What setting should you change in order to fix this problem? (Choose the best answer.)

A ❍ Wait until I select a hardware profile, on the Hardware Profiles property sheet
B ❍ Select the first hardware profile listed, on the Hardware Profiles property sheet
C ❍ Profile= , in the BOOT.INI file
D ❍ StartupProfile, in the Registry

3 **You're traveling on a transatlantic flight and need to conserve battery power for your ACPI Windows 2000 Professional notebook computer. When you get ready to take a nap after the delectable airline meal, what state should you put your notebook computer into? (Choose the best answer.)**

A ❍ Perform a normal shutdown that powers your PC off
B ❍ Initiate Standby mode
C ❍ Initiate Hibernate mode
D ❍ Initiate ACPI mode

4 **You're a traveling salesperson with a Windows 2000 Professional notebook computer. While on the road, it's very important for you to be in touch with the home office. So, you travel with two modems, just in case one breaks. Both use the PC Card bus. You install the first one with Plug and Play and it tests out fine; the installation script puts the modem on COM1. Then you install the second modem into your second PC Card slot. It seems to install fine, but when you try to use it, you get an error message that says "Unable to open port."**

Clearly, the two devices are not happily coexisting on this computer, probably because both are wanting to use COM1. What should you do to correct the problem? (Choose all that apply.)

A ❑ Create two hardware profiles. Uninstall one modem in each profile.
B ❑ Create two hardware profiles. Disable one modem in each profile.
C ❑ Use Device Manager to disable one of the modems.
D ❑ Use Device Manager to uninstall one of the modems.
E ❑ Use Phone and Modem Options to disable one of the modems.
F ❑ Use Phone and Modem Options to uninstall one of the modems.

5 **Jim is a member of the Power Users group. He gets a new PC Card network adapter for his notebook computer. During the installation, Plug and Play asks Jim for the location of the appropriate driver for the network adapter. He provides that information, but the driver installation fails. What should Jim do? (Choose the best answer.)**

A ❍ Run the Add/Remove Hardware wizard instead of using Plug and Play.
B ❍ Run the Scan New Hardware command in Device Manager.
C ❍ Log on as Administrator and try again.
D ❍ Obtain another copy of the driver media.

6 **You want to retrofit an infrared data port to your Windows 2000 Professional computer. You evaluate various models and review their spec sheets. Which of the following is the most attractive specification? (Choose the best answer.)**

A ❍ IrLPT
B ❍ IrDA-SIR
C ❍ IrDA-FIR
D ❍ IrDA-XIR

7 **You're installing a PC Card modem into a Windows 2000 notebook and you can't get the modem driver to install. What should you try? (Choose the best answer.)**

A ❍ Boot to Safe Mode.
B ❍ Install a COM port.
C ❍ Install the generic PC Card minidriver.
D ❍ Disable Plug and Play.
E ❍ Log on as a Power User.

Answers

1 **A.** APM is supported for Windows 2000 Professional running on older computers, but it is not enabled by default. Activate it on the APM tab of the Power Options control panel. You can't enable or disable ACPI; if Windows 2000 detects that a machine is ACPI-capable, Windows uses ACPI features automatically. See "APM."

2 **A.** What happened, most likely, is that when you rebooted the PC and left for a caffeine infusion, Windows waited the default number of seconds and chose the first hardware profile in the list, which specifies the undocked configuration. In that case, Windows may not autodetect the hardware in the docking station, especially considering that the station is a bit outdated. Your best bet would be to tell Windows to always wait and let you decide which profile you want, at boot time. Choice B isn't flagrantly wrong, but if you spend half your time at the office (docked) and half on the road (undocked), you don't have a clear choice. See "Hardware Profiles."

3 **C.** On most machines, hibernation is the best choice. Performing a normal shutdown takes more time, both to shutdown and to restart, thereby expending more battery power. Regarding choice B, Standby mode is a low-power mode, but Hibernate is a no-power mode, and therefore better for conserving precious battery juice. There's no such thing as ACPI mode (D). See "Power Management."

4 **B** and **C.** You want to disable one of the modems, not uninstall it. If you uninstall a modem, then you'd have to reinstall the driver from CD or diskette if you ever needed it later. You couldn't get the device driver from the Internet, because your modem is broken! Either go the hardware profile route, or simply use Device Manager. To switch between the two modems on a regular basis, the profile method is the preferable one. See "Hardware Profiles."

5 **C.** If Plug and Play can't find the right driver, you must log on as an Administrator to install. See "Plug and Play and Mobile Computers."

6 **C.** IrDA-FIR supports much faster data transfers than IrDA-SIR, although 4MBPS is noticeably slower than a regular Ethernet connection (10MBPS). IrLPT is the protocol for an infrared printer port. IrDA-XIR does not exist. See "Infrared and Wireless Devices."

7 **B.** This method also works often for non-PC-Card modems. Installing the COM (serial) port allows Windows 2000 to autodetect the modem at the next restart. Make sure that the new COM port doesn't conflict with any built-in devices, such as an external COM1 port or an infrared port. See "PC Cards."

Part IV

Configuring and Managing Resource Access

The 5th Wave — By Rich Tennant

In this part . . .

Network designers work hard to make important resources shareable, and then they turn right around and work equally hard to make sure only the right people can gain access to those resources. (It's a bit like fertilizing your lawn and then mowing it.) Part IV deals with providing (and restricting) access to files, printers, and other resources for both local and networked users. Microsoft was clearly very focused on this area when building Windows 2000, and the company has extended Windows NT's strengths in several key ways.

Chapter 10

Managing Local Users and Groups

Exam Objectives

- Creating and managing local users and groups
- Configuring and troubleshooting local user accounts
- Configuring and troubleshooting domain user accounts
- Implementing, configuring, managing, and troubleshooting account settings
- Implementing, configuring, managing, and troubleshooting user rights
- Implementing, configuring, managing, and troubleshooting auditing
- Implementing, configuring, managing, and troubleshooting account policy

Microsoft exam-writers' jobs mainly consist of making exams difficult enough that certification continues to mean something. When these anonymous test architects run across a topic as complex and confusing as Windows 2000 security, you can imagine their cold gray eyes sparkling with malicious glee in the dim half-light of their grim cubicles. You can beat them at their own game, but it's no walk in the park. For example, you may have to read this chapter twice (and Chapter 11 three times).

You can categorize Windows 2000 security features into pre-logon security (computer accounts), logon security, user and group rights, object permissions (access control), encryption for stored data, encryption for transmitted data, auditing, and policies.

Sometimes you can implement security in these areas with multiple techniques and tools, and sometimes the areas overlap. For example, group membership can determine user rights ("User" versus "Power User"), domain-level policies, or both.

This chapter takes a user-and-group focus and deals with four of the eight features: logon security, rights, auditing, and a subset of policies called account policies. Chapter 11 targets access-control and covers permissions, computer accounts, and group policies. Finally, file system encryption gets its due in Chapter 3, and transmission encryption in Chapter 13.

Quick Assessment

Local users and groups

1 Windows 2000 automatically creates a local user account that is, however, not enabled. Its name is ______.

Local user accounts

2 A local user account name has a maximum of ______ meaningful characters.

Domain user accounts

3 Create a domain user account in Windows 2000 Professional with the ______ control panel.

4 Your domain user account information is maintained on a Windows 2000 ______.

Account settings

5 For proper security, always ______ the local Administrator account.

User rights

6 The Windows 2000 built-in group that corresponds most closely to the Users group in Windows NT 4.0 is ______.

7 You can view current user rights assignments by using the ______ administrative tool.

Auditing

8 To track logon events on a domain, choose the ______ auditing policy.

Account policy

9 Setting the password history policy is a way of limiting how often users can ______ old passwords.

10 To help foil unauthorized access through repeated logon attempts, set the account ______ policies.

Answers

1 *Guest.* See "Built-in user accounts" for more.

2 *20.* "Creating local user accounts" offers additional details.

3 *Active Directory Users and Computers.* You will have to install the server's Administration Tools onto the workstation in order to see this utility. See "Domain User Accounts" for more.

4 *Domain controller.* The "Domains" section explains further.

5 *Rename.* See "Built-in user accounts" for more.

6 *Power users.* "User rights and built-in local groups" has details.

7 *Local security policy.* See "User rights and built-in local groups" for this and related tidbits.

8 *Audit account logon events.* The "Auditing User Activities" section provides this nugget.

9 *Reuse.* See "Sorry, it's company policy" for other password policy settings.

10 *Lockout.* "Sorry, it's company policy" has the details on lockout options.

Windows 2000 Networking Models

Windows 2000 supports two basic networking models: workgroups and domains. The exam focuses on domains, but you need to understand the difference between these two models.

Workgroups

In the workgroup, or *peer-to-peer,* networking model, no central database of users, groups, and access permissions exists. (Another way to say this is that no central logon authority exists.) Instead, each PC user has the option to share resources (printers, disks, folders — not individual files) and to control access to those resources by user or group name. In a workgroup, you typically have no "dedicated" server: Any PC can act both as client and as server.

Workgroup networking in Windows 2000 is different from workgroup networking in Windows 9*x*. With 9*x* systems, you assign passwords to shared resources (Microsoft calls this *share-level security*), and you have no database of users and groups. With Windows 2000 systems, you use the local database of users and groups on each PC to assign access permissions.

Some small organizations may have only a single workgroup; larger organizations may have several, broken out by department, office, or project. Workgroup names (set on the Network Identification tab of the System control panel) should not exceed 15 characters, contain no spaces, and not duplicate any existing computer names. (Workgroup names, like computer names, are NetBIOS names and so they have the same format.)

If you use a workgroup, the Computers Near Me folder inside the My Network Places folder shows other computers in the same workgroup.

The workgroup networking model is appropriate for up to ten users, according to Microsoft. Administrative chores, such as making backups, are decentralized (shared resources exist on several PCs instead of just one) and therefore unwieldy beyond a small number of computers. However, you don't need to buy a separate license for Windows 2000 Server to set up a Windows 2000 workgroup. You have all the software you need:

- A network adapter driver
- A transport protocol
- A network client (Client for Microsoft Networks)
- A sharing service (File and Printer Sharing for Microsoft Networks, which appears simply as "Server" in the Services console of the Administrative Tools folder)

Domains

Domain-based networks are more common than workgroups in the business environment, and they have a number of advantages: better security, centralized administration, and better expandability. In a simple domain-based network, a central server maintains a database of users, groups, and access permissions, and handles network logons. In Windows 2000, that database is called *Active Directory*.

One of the cool features of a domain is that Windows may *replicate* the security database if more than one server is present on the network. In this situation, you can have several servers acting as *domain controllers*, sharing the same database and updating each other automatically when the database changes on one of the machines. Unlike Windows NT 4.0 Server, Windows 2000 Server doesn't distinguish between primary and backup domain controllers; all domain controllers have equal standing.

In addition to handling the security database, central servers can also host shared programs, data files, and hardware for use by the client workstations. In fact, a server doesn't have to be a domain controller. If a server is simply sharing one or more resources, but doesn't participate in user authentication, it's called a *member server*.

Windows 2000 contains all the software elements necessary for accessing a domain-type network:

- A network adapter driver
- A transport protocol
- A network client (Client for Microsoft Networks)

You don't need the sharing service if the Windows 2000 PC won't be sharing any of its own local resources. However, it's optional, and you can therefore make a Windows 2000 Professional "client PC" into a "mini-server" by sharing a folder with other domain users. Sometimes a network like this, which uses the domain model but which lets client machines as well as servers share resources, goes by the title of *hybrid* network.

In order to host an Active Directory-based domain-type network — that is, in order to be a domain controller or member server — you must have Windows 2000 Server.

Creating Local Users

Unlike Windows 98 or 95, Windows 2000 Professional maintains its own *local* database of users and groups. This database lives in the SAM and SECURITY

Registry hives of the local computer, and it's entirely separate and distinct from the domain-based Active Directory database (NTDS.DIT) that lives on a Windows 2000 Server domain controller. Windows 2000 Professional uses the local user and group database to help determine who can access resources on the local PC.

In a workgroup environment, no domain-based database exists, meaning that each user must have a local user account on at least one Windows 2000 Professional machine. Each workgroup user must log on to a local PC. In a domain environment, however, you can log on to Windows 2000 Pro in one of two ways: you can log on to the local machine (through a local user account), or to the domain (through a domain account). On a PC configured as a domain client, you can choose which entity you want to log onto at the logon dialog box.

INSTANT ANSWER

When you create a user account in Windows 2000 Professional through the Users and Passwords control panel, it's a *local* user account. (You'd create a domain account on a Windows 2000 Server machine with the Active Directory Users and Computers console.) Microsoft recommends not creating local user accounts on PCs that participate in a domain, for two reasons: Local users can't gain access to domain resources, and domain administrators can't manage local user accounts.

Built-in user accounts

To get you started, Microsoft sets up Windows 2000 Professional with two built-in local user accounts, which you can view with the Users and Passwords control panel: Administrator and Guest (see Figure 10-1). You may never need more than that if you're configuring a domain PC because you'd use the domain account for everyday use and the built-in Administrator account to manage or configure the local PC.

Here's what you must know about these accounts:

- The Administrator account is all-powerful. You should log on as Administrator when you need to configure or manage the computer.
- Always rename the Administrator account.
- You can't delete the Administrator account.
- Don't use the Administrator account for everyday work. The risk of unintentionally damaging your system (or of giving a virus unfettered access to it) is too great.
- The Guest account is weak and is disabled by default. Microsoft recommends using it for occasional, temporary purposes.

- You should probably rename the Guest account if you use it, but at least assign a password to it.
- You can't delete the Guest account, either.

TIP

When you install software, configure desktop icons, modify the Start menu, and so on while logged on as a particular user, you don't see those changes when you log on as a different user. Chapter 12 explores the issue of *user profiles* in greater detail.

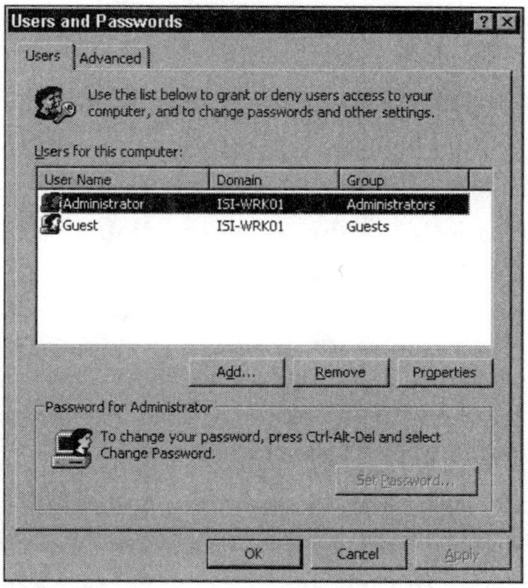

Figure 10-1: The two "built-in" local accounts.

Creating local user accounts

The built-in Administrator and Guest accounts may not meet all of your needs for local user accounts. For example, if you're setting up a workgroup PC, you probably want an account for that PC's regular user — an account that won't have the unlimited power of the Administrator account, but that has more power than the measly Guest account. (If you're setting up a domain PC, you're probably better off creating domain accounts on a Windows 2000 Server machine than creating local user accounts.)

You can create additional local user accounts two ways: by running the Users and Passwords control panel (Start⇨Settings⇨Control Panel and double-click Users and Passwords) on a non-domain PC, and by running the computer's management console (right-click My Computer and choose Manage) on a domain or non-domain PC.

WARNING!

Method #1 doesn't work if you have a domain PC; when you click the Add button on the Users tab of the Users and Passwords control panel, Windows 2000 prompts you to add a preexisting domain user. I *told* you Microsoft doesn't want you adding local accounts to a domain PC!

Lab 10-1 goes through the steps for using Method #2.

Lab 10-1 Creating a Local User Account

1. **Right-click My Computer and choose Manage.**
2. **Expand the Local Users and Groups node in the tree pane (to the left) by clicking the + sign next to it.**
3. **Click the Users icon in the tree pane.**
4. **Right-click any blank space in the details pane (to the right) and choose New User (see Figure 10-2).**
5. **Fill in the requested data fields in the New User dialog box (see Figure 10-3).**

   You can specify that the user must change the password at the next logon, placing the user in charge of his or her own password. If you don't specify this, then you can tell Windows that the user may never change the password, and/or that the password never expires.

   Finally, you can disable the account for the time being — for example, if you're setting it up in advance of hiring a new employee, or if you're about to delete an account and you want to verify first that no ill effects will occur.

Windows NT 4.0 users, note that the Local Users and Groups snap-in is the successor to NT's User Manager utility.

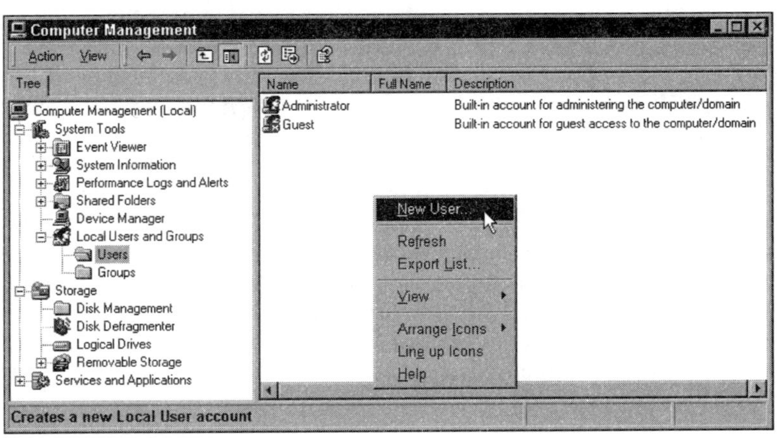

Figure 10-2: The management console's Local Users and Groups snap-in.

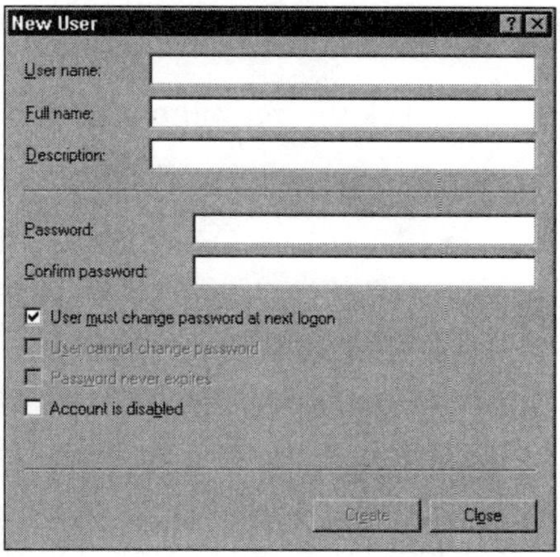

Figure 10-3: Creating a new local user is easy.

Here are some tips on creating new local user accounts:

- User names must be unique among other user names on the machine and among other user names on the domain (if the PC belongs to a domain) or on the workgroup (if the PC belongs to a workgroup).
- Windows only cares about the first 20 characters of the user name.
- You can't use the special characters = + [ ] \ | / ; : < > or ?.
- The full name and description fields are optional.
- Passwords can't be longer than 128 characters, and Microsoft recommends they not be shorter than 8.
- Passwords can't use the special characters that are forbidden for user names (see above).

Deleting user accounts

Lab 10-2 goes through the simple procedure for deleting a user account through the Users and Groups management console snap-in.

Lab 10-2 Deleting a Local User Account

1. **Right-click My Computer and choose Manage.**
2. **Expand the Local Users and Groups node in the tree pane (to the left) by clicking the + sign next to it.**
3. **Click the Users icon in the tree pane.**

4. **Right-click the user's icon in the details pane (to the right) and choose Delete.**
5. **Read the warning message and click the Yes button.**

   The warning message you see reminds you that if you delete a user account, you permanently and irretrievably delete the Security ID (SID) associated with that account, as well as all its various access tokens conveying permissions to shared files, folders, printers, and so on. Which point leads me to an Instant Answer, as follows.

If an employee leaves your organization and you replace him with someone new, and you want the new person to have the same access privileges as the old person, don't delete the old employee's account. Right-click its icon in the Local Users and Groups snap-in and choose Rename to give the account a new name. Then, right-click it again and choose Set Password to give it a new password.

Configuring user accounts

Two aspects of configuring user accounts are likely to receive mention on the test: account policy, and group membership.

Sorry, it's company policy

If you ask most Microsoft network administrators to identify the most complex and confusing security feature of Windows operating systems, I'll bet a nickel that most of them respond with a single word: *policies*. From "system policies" in Windows NT 4.0 and Windows 9*x* to "group policy," "account policy," "security policy," and so on *ad nauseam* in Windows 2000, it takes a combination of dogged determination and hundreds of hours playing around with real live networks to fully grasp how Windows policies really work. (I've been working on this for years and I'm still not quite there. My only consolation is that there aren't many people even inside Microsoft who fully "get" all this stuff.)

Thankfully, you don't have to achieve total policy enlightenment. Partial enlightenment serves you just fine. This section aims to illuminate a small subset of the entire policy population: *account policies*. As you may have guessed, account policies apply to user accounts, which is why I'm talking about them in this chapter.

Account policies can do two things for you:

- They can enforce requirements that can increase the security of passwords.
- They can help prevent crackers from getting into a system by guessing account names and passwords.

View account policies in the Local Security Policy console (it's in the Administrative Tools control panel folder); see Figure 10-4. Change an account policy by double-clicking it and modifying its value. (If the same policy exists at the domain level, the domain policy overrides the local policy.)

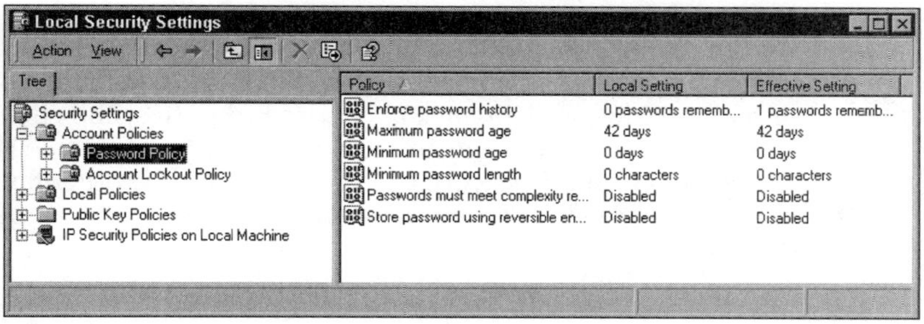

Figure 10-4: Password policies are one of two types of account policy.

Here's what the password policies mean, in brief:

- **Enforce password history.** How many new passwords the user must specify before he or she is allowed to reuse an old one.
- **Maximum password age.** This value is in days and the default is 42; a value of 0 means the password doesn't expire.
- **Minimum password age.** How many days a user must keep a password before changing it. Zero means you can change a password at any time, which sort of defeats "Enforce password history" if you think about it.
- **Minimum password length.** The range is 0 to 14 characters; 0 means no password is required for the account (bad idea).
- **Passwords must meet complexity requirements.** This option makes the user include numbers or punctuation marks in the password and forbids including the user's account name or full name (if present).

Note that these policies apply to all local user accounts on the computer. You can't set 'em on an individual-by-individual basis.

The account lockout policies, which help foil evil people who repeatedly try to log on to your PC, are described below:

- **Account lockout duration.** How many minutes Windows 2000 locks out a user after the user makes X number of invalid logon attempts. A value of zero means "until an Administrator clears the account."
- **Account lockout threshold.** How many invalid logon attempts trigger the lockout, at which point Windows won't let the user try anymore until the account lockout duration period has passed. The range is 0 to 999.

- **Reset account lockout counter after.** How many minutes to wait after an account lockout before giving the user a "clean slate" to try logging on again. The range is 1 to 99,999 minutes.

Members only

If you use the Computer Management console to create a local user account (Method #2 in the section "Creating local user accounts" earlier in this chapter), you can't assign the new local user account to any local groups until you created it and it appears as a new entry in the Local Users and Groups snap-in. After it does, you can right-click it, choose Properties, and click the Member Of tab to assign the account to one or more groups (see Figure 10-5). If you use the Users and Passwords control panel, on the other hand (Method #1), the wizard asks you to join the new account to a group during the creation process.

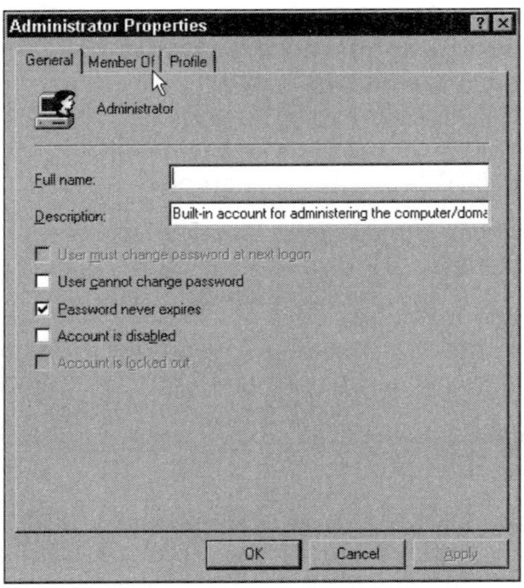

Figure 10-5: Joining a new local user to a predefined group.

Why would you want the local account to belong to a group? And, going back a step, what *is* a group, anyway? The next section walks you through some group therapy, Windows 2000 style.

Groups in Windows 2000

A Windows 2000 group is just a defined group of user accounts who share certain security-related settings. So why do you need groups? Why not treat every individual as a unique and special being? The short answer: You work in a corporation, which consists not of unique and special beings, but of replaceable cogs in a giant machine!

Seriously (although for some of you, the previous answer *may* be serious!), the real reason is simply ease of administration. In most organizations, configuring every employee with a unique set of rights and access permissions just isn't necessary. Chances are pretty good that everybody in Bookkeeping does more or less the same thing and needs more or less the same rights and permissions on the network. (And because I'm discussing the network situation here, you can correctly infer that groups are far less useful when you have a stand-alone PC.) If I'm a network manager, configuring one batch of settings for the Bookkeeping group is a heckuva lot faster (and more secure) than configuring every Tom, Dick, and Harriet individually.

Local and global groups

Just as with user accounts, Windows 2000 offers two sorts of groups: *local* and *global*. A local group consists of local user accounts. A global group consists of domain user accounts. Here's what you must know about local and global groups:

REMEMBER

- Users can belong to more than one group at a time.
- Groups can belong to other groups.
- Local groups live on the local PC's security database and are for assigning permissions to resources on the local PC.
- Global groups live on the domain's security database (Active Directory) and are for assigning permissions to resources on the domain.
- You can't create local groups on Windows 2000 Server domain controllers.
- Global groups can belong to local groups, allowing domain users to have rights and permissions at a local PC.
- Windows 2000 Professional can't create or manage global groups; that's a job for Server.
- As is the case with local user accounts, and for the same reasons, Microsoft discourages you from creating local groups on a domain PC.

User rights and built-in local groups

As with local users, where Microsoft provides built-in accounts, so it is with local groups, with the exception that there are more of 'em. You see these built-in local groups on Windows 2000 Professional machines and on Windows 2000 servers that aren't domain controllers. These built-in local groups convey sets of rights, or privileges, on the local PC.

What's a *right*? It's an action that a user or group is allowed to do. Changing the desktop, installing a program, backing up the local hard drive, sharing a folder, are all examples of user rights. (For an example of how user rights can affect seemingly unrelated chores, see the sidebar, "User rights and Task Scheduler.") So you can think of built-in local groups as offering convenient groupings of user rights that often correspond to different roles of users on the PC.

TIP

If you want to see which rights Microsoft has associated with which built-in local groups, open the Local Security Policy console (it's in the Administrative Tools control panel folder) and look under *Local Policies\User Rights Assignment* (see Figure 10-6).

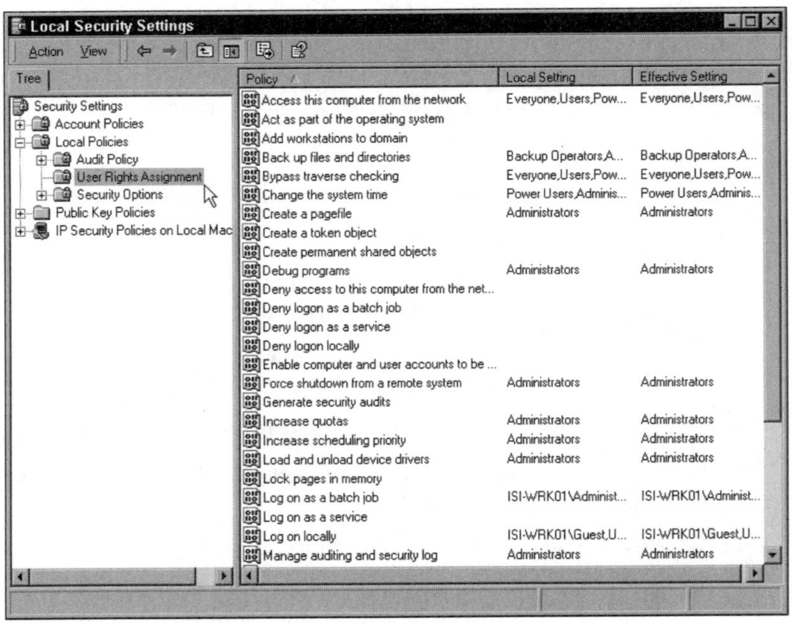

Figure 10-6: A fine-grained look at user rights.

INSTANT ANSWER

Users and groups have *rights*. Objects (such as NTFS files and folders, Registry keys, and so on) have *permissions*. Chapter 11 deals with object permissions in excruciating detail.

TIP

You can change the default rights that accrue to users in different groups by applying security templates (see Chapter 11) with the Security Analysis and Configuration snap-in, or the SECEDIT command-line utility.

Here's a list of the built-in local groups and their usual functions:

- **Administrators.** Includes the built-in local user account, Administrator. Belonging to this group means you can do anything on the computer.

- **Guests.** Includes the built-in local user account, Guest. Members of Guests can't change their desktop setup, and you normally must grant them explicit rights to do just about anything productive.
- **Users.** Windows 2000 also (inconsistently) calls these "Restricted Users" in certain dialog boxes. When you add a local user account, it automatically receives membership in this group.
  - Membership in this group entitles the user to run "certified" Windows 2000 applications, but may not provide sufficient rights and access permissions to run some "legacy" Windows NT 4.0 applications.
  - Users can't share folders (that is, designate them to be shared).
  - Users can't install programs for use by other Users.
  - Users can't modify systemwide settings, whether in the operating system, the Registry, or applications.
  - Users can't create local printers.

The COMPATWS.INF security template (see Chapter 11) relaxes some of the restrictions on the Users group to improve compatibility with Windows NT 4.0 applications. Other options for letting members of Users run older applications include moving Users to the Power Users group, and upgrading the applications to Windows 2000–compliant versions if available.

- **Power Users.** This group corresponds roughly with the Windows NT 4.0 group "Users" and sometimes appears in the Windows 2000 user interface as "Standard Users."
  - Members can create local user accounts and offer resources for sharing across the network.
  - They can install applications, as long as the applications don't install operating system services or modify operating system files.
  - They can stop and start system services as long as the services didn't start automatically.
  - They can't modify or delete user accounts that they did not create.
  - They can remove users from the Guests, Users, and Power Users groups.
  - They can't modify membership in the Administrators or Backup Operators groups.
  - They can't take ownership of files.
- **Backup Operators.** Members of this group can back up and restore files on the system, irrespective of file access permissions, which a regular member of the Users group can't do.

All Windows 2000 systems, Professional and Server, also sport a number of built-in *system groups* whose memberships you cannot change but which reflect how a user achieved access to the PC or network. (The list of system groups increases in a domain environment, to include Domain Administrators and Domain Users.) You shouldn't be quizzed heavily on these for the Professional exam, so just be familiar with their fairly self-explanatory names:

- *Everyone* (which includes the Guest account)
- *Authenticated Users* (that is, authenticated either on the local PC or on the domain; the same as the Everyone group, minus anonymous users)
- *Creator/Owner* (such as the user who creates a folder)
- *Network* (someone who gains access to the computer via a network)
- *Interactive* (someone who gains access to the computer by logging on to it interactively)
- *Anonymous Logon* (that is, unauthenticated)
- *Dialup* (someone who gains access to the computer via a dial-up connection)

User rights and Task Scheduler

The Task Scheduler has come a long way since its early incarnation as System Agent in the Plus! add-on product for Windows 95. In Windows 2000, the scheduler service appears as the Scheduled Tasks folder (odd grammar that!) in the Control Panel. You can define a task, such as backing up your C drive, and schedule it for recurring automatic operation, say at 2 a.m. nightly. You might not suppose so, but using this tool successfully requires an awareness of user and group rights!

When you define a task using the Add Scheduled Task wizard, Windows asks you for the name of the user account under whose security context the task should run. That is, you must decide whether you want the task to run as though initiated by the user account named Bob, or Sue, or Administrator. (That user doesn't have to be logged on when time comes for the task to run, by the way.) If you choose a user who doesn't have sufficient rights to run the scheduled task, the task doesn't run. Whether you're notified of the problem depends on whether you've activated the Notify Me of Missed Tasks toggle on the Task Scheduler's Advanced menu. (If not, then the log file `C:\WINNT\SCHEDLOG.TXT` may give you some clues; you can read it with the View Log command on the Advanced menu.)

Insufficient rights may not be the only reason a scheduled task fails. Someone may have stopped the service by choosing Stop Using Task Scheduler on the Advanced menu; the service doesn't automatically restart. That's probably the cause of a problem in which *no* tasks are running, even ones that don't normally require special rights or permissions. Chapter 14 offers more details on Task Scheduler.

Creating and deleting local groups

Should you find that the built-in local groups don't meet all your needs, you can create new ones. (Remember that Microsoft suggests you *not* do this on PCs that participate in a domain-based network.) The procedure is exactly analogous to creating new local user accounts (see Lab 10-3).

Lab 10-3 Creating a Local Group

1. **Right-click My Computer and choose Manage.**

   The Computer Management console opens.

2. **Expand the Local Users and Groups node.**
3. **Click the Groups icon in the tree pane.**
4. **Right-click in any blank area of the details pane and choose New Group.**
5. **Give your new group a name (up to 256 characters).**
6. **Add users via the Add button (see Figure 10-7).**

   You can also add users to the group later, either through the user's Member Of property sheet or through the group's property sheet in the Local Users and Groups console.

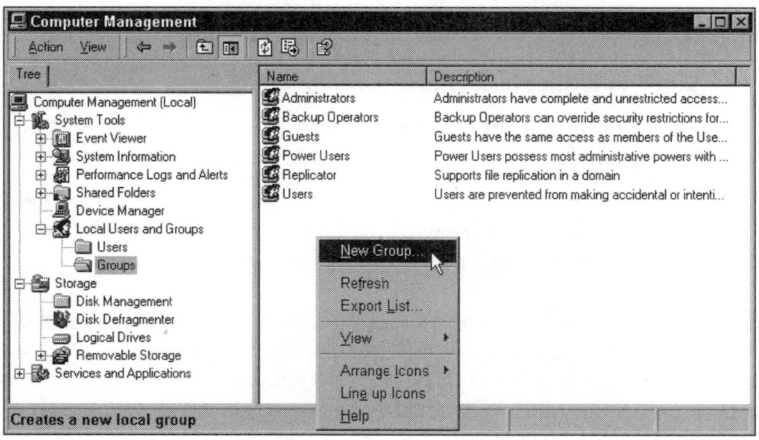

Figure 10-7: Creating a new local group.

Deleting local groups is a matter of right-clicking and choosing Delete. Note that you don't blow away any user accounts by deleting groups to which those users may belong.

Domain User Accounts

The bulk of this chapter (and the exam) deals with local user accounts, but you also need to know a few facts about domain user accounts. Create these accounts using the Active Directory Users and Computers console, which is present by default on a domain controller, and which you can install onto a Windows 2000 Professional machine by double-clicking ADMINPAK.MSI on the Server CD. Configure domain accounts by clicking the Users node in the console's tree pane, right-clicking the user account icon in the details pane, and choosing Properties.

Configuring domain accounts

Although the Windows 2000 Server exam covers this material in much greater detail, the more common domain user configuration chores include the following:

- **User profile.** As I discuss in more detail in Chapter 12, you can specify the location of a server-based roaming user profile for a domain account, so that the user's documents and settings follow them from PC to PC. Use the Profile tab of the property sheet for this setting.
- **Logon hours.** You can set a schedule for permitted domain logons; use the Account tab of the property sheet.
- **Idle disconnect.** You can kick a user off the network after a predetermined amount of idle time; set this on the Sessions tab.
- **Group membership.** Change the groups to which the domain user belongs in the Member Of tab.
- **Dial-in permission.** Control whether the user has permission to call up remote access servers with the Dial-In tab. You can also set a callback option here for better security; see Chapter 13.

You can also disable accounts, copy them (creating a new user based on an existing user's account), change passwords, move an account to a different organizational unit, delete, and rename accounts — all from the user's property sheet in the Active Directory Users and Computers console.

Troubleshooting domain accounts

Know the following tips for troubleshooting access problems with domain accounts:

- A new domain account takes time to propagate to all the domain controllers in an organization. If you've just created a new account on one server, other domain controllers can't immediately authenticate the user and permit logon.
- If a user can't log on to a domain account, ensure that the user has chosen the correct domain from the list box at the logon window, and is not trying to log on to the local PC or a different domain. Also check the log on hours restriction and any security constraints that appear on the Account tab, such as "Smart Card Is Required For Interactive Logon."
- Remote dial-in access is denied by default for a new account. If a domain user can't connect to a remote access server, change the access setting on the Dial-In tab of the account property sheet from Deny to Allow.
- Domain group policies override local group policies. In Active Directory Users and Computers, right-click the domain, choose Properties, and click the Group Policy tab to inspect policy settings for the domain that may be countermanding locally set policies. (More on policies in Chapter 11.)

Auditing User Activities

If you're reading this chapter end to end, and you're not confused yet, either your mind is seriously warped or you've been doing this sort of thing for a while in the real world. Windows 2000 users and groups aren't radically different from Windows NT 4.0 users and groups, after all. Not that this tidbit is much help to those of you who never had the pleasure of wrestling with NT.

In either case, whether you're warped or simply experienced, I have to throw one more iron into the fire before we can be legitimately done with Windows 2000 users and groups: auditing. The good news is that unlike relatively abstract concepts such as user rights, auditing is pretty easy to understand. Chapter 11 explains how to use auditing to monitor user access to files, folders, and the Registry. All I want to do here is mention logon event auditing.

Logon event auditing (see Lab 10-4) means that Windows 2000 can monitor logons, both successful and unsuccessful, and record them in the Security event log (which you can view with the Event Viewer snap-in to the Computer Management console). This could help you find out if and when Snidely Whiplash is trying to crack his way into a PC by guessing account names and passwords. It may also lead you to inquire why Bertram the bookkeeper is logging on to his system at 3 a.m. when the workday is over at 5 p.m.

Lab 10-4 Activating Logon Event Auditing

1. **Choose Start⇨Settings⇨Control Panel.**
2. **Double-click Administrative Tools.**
3. **Double-click Local Security Policy.**
4. **In the tree pane to the left, expand Local Policies.**
5. **In the tree pane, click Audit Policy.**

   All the various quantities that you can audit now appear in the details pane to the right.
6. **In the details pane, double-click Audit Logon Events.**

   You see the dialog box in Figure 10-8. If you're interested in Snidely (see paragraph just before this lab), click Failure; if you're interested in Bertram, click Success; and if you're interested in both, click both.
7. **Click OK and close the Local Security Policy console.**
8. **Restart the machine to make your changes take effect.**

   From this point forward, watch the Security log. Bertram can't see it, because he's not an Administrator — at least, he'd better not be!

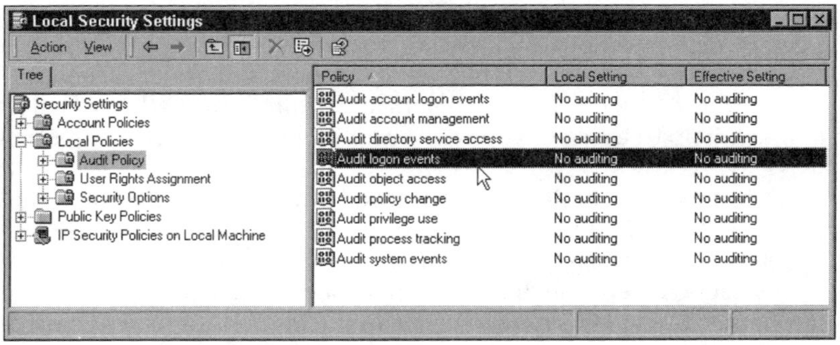

Figure 10-8: Setting up auditing on logon events.

If you double-click Audit Account Logon Events instead of Audit Logon Events in Step 6 of Lab 10-4, Windows 2000 tracks *domain* logon events (that is, successful or failed attempts to log on to a domain controller). Yeah, I know, you'd never guess that from the names, but that's why an MCSE is such a treasured certification: It demonstrates your ability to memorize all kinds of stuff that should be obvious in the user interface, but isn't.

Prep Test

1 **In a pure Windows 2000 network, what sort of machine authenticates domain users when they log on? (Choose all that apply.)**

A ❑ Domain controller
B ❑ Primary domain controller
C ❑ Backup domain controller
D ❑ Primary or backup domain controller, whichever is closer to the user
E ❑ Member server
F ❑ Workstation

2 **You receive an anonymous tip that someone who's not an employee but who has a key to your office is trying to log on to your Windows 2000 domain from your workstation in the middle of the night. You decide to enable auditing so that you can check domain logon attempts in the Security event log (SECEVENT.EVT). Which item and logging option do you choose in the Local Security Policy tool? (Choose the best answer.)**

A ❍ Audit Account Logon Events. Click Failure.
B ❍ Audit Account Logon Events. Click Success.
C ❍ Audit Account Logon Events. Do not click Failure or Success.
D ❍ Audit Logon Events. Click Failure.
E ❍ Audit Logon Events. Click Success.
F ❍ Audit Logon Events. Do not click Failure or Success.

3 **Vendela is a new employee at Acme Cognac, where you enjoy gainful employment as a PC coordinator. One of your jobs is to set up new user accounts. In Vendela's job, she needs to run three applications, all of which have Microsoft logo certification to run on Windows 2000. She needs the ability to modify user-specific application settings for her own account; to shut down her own computer; and to print to shared network printers. Which predefined group should you select for Vendela's new user account? (Choose the best answer.)**

A ❍ Users
B ❍ Power Users
C ❍ Guests
D ❍ Administrators
E ❍ New Users

4 **Rebecca is a new employee at Acme Cognac, and you're still a PC coordinator there, by virtue of having successfully answered Question 3 above. Rebecca needs a domain user account. What Windows 2000 tool would you use to create such an account? (Choose the best answer.)**

A ❍ Users and Passwords
B ❍ Local Users and Groups
C ❍ Active Directory Users and Computers
D ❍ Local Users and Passwords
E ❍ Domain Users and Groups
F ❍ User Manager for Domains

5 **You receive a promotion after answering Question 4 above, and you're now a network administrator at Acme Cognac (motto: "The Spirits with Spirit"). Tyra comes to you complaining that her Windows 2000 Professional computer isn't allowing her to set the following account password: TORA!TORA!TYRA!. However, she tried using a different password, 1234PASS, and the system permitted that setting. You advise her that this is a security precaution that you have implemented with a local account policy. Which one? (Choose the best answer.)**

A ❍ Passwords must not contain user name
B ❍ Passwords must contain alpha and numeric characters
C ❍ Require alphanumeric passwords
D ❍ Passwords must meet complexity requirements
E ❍ Maximum password length
F ❍ Passwords must not contain special symbols

6 **Cindy, an Acme Cognac employee, quits her job as a brandy taster to become a restaurateur. You have no plans to replace her in the next six months as Famke, her boss, assumes Cindy's brandy-tasting responsibilities. Therefore, you delete Cindy's account in the Local Users and Groups utility.**

What else do you delete when you delete Cindy's account? (Choose all that apply.)

A ❑ Cindy's SID
B ❑ Cindy's ACLs
C ❑ Cindy's access tokens
D ❑ Cindy's user profile

7 **Which of the following statements is true about Power Users? (Choose all that apply.)**

A ❑ They cannot delete user accounts that they did not originally create.

B ❑ They cannot install applications.

C ❑ They cannot remove users from the Backup Operators group.

D ❑ They can take ownership of files.

E ❑ They can make folders and printers available for sharing.

8 **You set Heather's account lockout threshold to 3, and her account lockout duration to 0. Heather is a terrible typist and one day she misspells her password three times in a row. What must she do next? (Choose the best answer.)**

A ❍ Try again. The account lockout duration of 0 means that she can retype her password immediately.

B ❍ Wait five minutes and try again. The account lockout duration of 0 means that Windows uses the default value of five minutes.

C ❍ Find an administrator. The account lockout duration of 0 means that Heather can't attempt additional logons until her account is cleared.

D ❍ Quit Acme Cognac and go to work in TV.

Answers

1 **A.** Windows 2000 doesn't implement primary and backup domain controllers; all domain controllers are peers. See "Windows 2000 Networking Models."

2 **A.** Because you suspect someone of trying to access a domain account, you should specify "account logon events" as plain old "logon events" audits logons to the local PC's security database only. You must choose either Success or Failure or both. Typically, if you suspect that someone doesn't already have a valid username, or password and is trying to guess one or the other or both, you audit failed logon attempts. See "Auditing User Activities."

3 **A.** The Users group conveys all the necessary rights. If Jaimie needed to run applications written for NT Workstation 4.0, you would consider making her a Power User. As for choice E, no predefined group named New Users exists. See "User rights and built-in local groups."

4 **C.** The Users and Passwords control panel is intended for adding local user accounts, so choice A is out. Ditto for choice B, hence the word "local" in the program's name. Choices D and E don't exist, and choice F harks back to Windows NT Server 4.0. See "Creating Local Users."

5 **D.** Choices A, B, and C don't exist, nor does choice E (although a policy does exist to enforce a minimum password length). Choice F is not a valid policy, and furthermore, the use of special characters such as the exclamation point is encouraged as it makes passwords harder to guess. The complexity requirement means that Tyra can't include her user name or any part of her full name in her password. See "Sorry, it's company policy."

6 **A** and **C.** You delete Cindy's Security ID, and with it, all of her access tokens for accessing shared resources. Access Control Lists, or ACLs, are associated with objects rather than users. As for choice D, deleting an account does not automatically delete a user profile, so you may want to run Windows Explorer to remove C:\Documents and Settings\Cindy. See "Deleting user accounts."

7 **A, C,** and **E.** Power Users can install applications, as long as the applications don't install system services or modify operating system files. Power Users cannot take ownership of files; only Administrators can do that. See "User rights and built-in local groups."

8 **C.** Maybe Heather could also trim her fingernails a bit. "See Sorry, it's company policy."

Chapter 11

Access Permissions

Exam Objectives

- Controlling access to files and folders by using permissions
- Optimizing access to files and folders
- Creating and removing shared folders
- Controlling access to shared folders by using permissions
- Connecting to shared resources on a Microsoft network
- Managing and troubleshooting Web server resources
- Implementing, configuring, managing, and troubleshooting a security configuration
- Implementing, configuring, managing, and troubleshooting Local Group Policy

Following on the discussion of users and groups in Chapter 10 (which I strongly suggest you read before this one), this chapter looks at securing Windows 2000 systems by posting virtual "Authorized Personnel Only" signs all around the operating system. Share permissions, file-and-folder (NTFS) permissions, computer accounts, Web server permissions, and Local Group Policy are the topics of the day here. This chapter also looks briefly at auditing object access in the file system and the Registry.

You can expect three or more exam questions on the material in this chapter, as access permissions are always a prime concern of corporate network managers (and, therefore, exam question authors).

Quick Assessment

Controlling access to files and folders by using permissions

1 You can control local or network access to specific files on a Windows 2000 Professional machine by using _____.

2 On an NTFS disk, the one permission that a folder can have, but a file cannot, is _____.

Optimizing access to files and folders

3 When using either shared folder permissions or NTFS permissions, ease administrative chores by assigning permissions to _____ rather than to _____.

Creating and removing shared folders

4 The fastest way to share a folder is to right-click it and choose _____.

Controlling access to shared folders by using permissions

5 To share a file on a Windows 2000 Professional machine with other users over a local area network connection, you must copy the file to a _____.

6 The three shared folder permissions are _____, _____, and _____.

Connecting to shared resources on a Microsoft network

7 For UNC names to work properly across routers, a network needs a functioning _____ server.

Managing and troubleshooting Web server resources

8 Internet Information Server allows you to control user access by IP address as well as by _____.

Implementing, configuring, managing, and troubleshooting Local Group Policy

9 To view or change all possible Local Group Policy settings, you must create a custom console using _____.

10 The pecking order for Group Policy settings, from weakest to strongest, is _____, _____, _____, and _____.

Answers

1 *NTFS permissions.* See the "NTFS Permissions" section if you missed this one.

2 *List folder contents.* The "NTFS Permissions" section has more.

3 *Groups, users.* See "Who can have access" in this chapter.

4 *Sharing.* The section "Sharing a folder" expands on this subject.

5 *Shared folder.* See "Sharing a folder."

6 *Read, change, full control.* The section "Assigning shared folder permissions" has more.

7 *WINS.* See the section entitled "Connecting to Shared Resources."

8 *DNS address.* The "Web Server Access Control" section fills in this and other gaps.

9 *MMC.EXE.* See "Policies and the Local Group Policy console" for details on building this console.

10 *Local, site, domain, organizational unit.* "Policies and the Local Security Policy console" contains this invaluable nugget.

Access Permissions Overview

Access. The ability to see, read, touch, change, explore, append, copy, destroy. Too little access and you can't do your work; too much, and you can (accidentally or intentionally) prevent other people from doing theirs. As organizations transfuse more and more of their lifeblood information into computer systems, controlling access becomes a hugely important task — one that Windows 2000 addresses through many features and facilities.

The subject is so large that it can seem overwhelming. So, I begin by breaking it down into more manageable chunks. First, consider access control over network links as opposed to access control on the local PC. Second, consider the main steps in configuring access permissions: which, who, and what. The following sections elaborate.

Network access control versus local access control

One way to make access control more understandable is to divide it out into two major categories: access control over a network connection, and access control for users who log on at the local PC. Here are some facts about controlling access:

- On a FAT, FAT32, or NTFS disk, you can control access over a network by using *shared folder permissions* or *share permissions*. This control extends to identifying who may use a shared folder and, in a limited way, what they can do with it. This is folder-level access control only.
- On an NTFS disk, you can also control access over a network by using *NTFS permissions*, also known as *file-and-folder permissions*. This control extends to identifying who may use a file or folder and, in a detailed way, what they can do with it. You can control access at the folder level or at the file level.

  NTFS permissions apply access control for network users and for local users, and for unshared as well as shared folders.
- You can control network access to an Internet or intranet server by using the Internet Information Service (IIS) snap-in to the Computer Management console. This control gives you lots of options for restricting access (see the "Web Server Access Control" section later in this chapter).

- On a local PC, you can control access by using NTFS permissions (see previous bullet). Shared folder permissions don't work in this case; they only work over a network connection.
- On both networked and local PCs, you can control access by using *policies*. See the "Local Group Policy" section later in this chapter.

Configuring access control

Three considerations exist when you configure access permissions for any given resource on a Windows 2000 PC. Remember them easily by the key words *which, who,* and *what.*

Which resources users can access

The first step in configuring access permissions is to specify which resources users can access. *Resources* typically means files, folders, printers, Registry keys, and Web servers (which you can create in Windows 2000 Professional through the optional IIS component).

- To share a resource across a network link, you typically right-click the resource and click a command like "Sharing." The main requirement is that you have the File and Printer Sharing for Microsoft Networks service (which appears as simply "Server" in the Services administrative tool) installed for the network connection. Open the Network and Dial-Up Connections folder from the Settings menu, right-click the icon for your network adapter, and see whether this service appears in the list and is checked as active (see Figure 11-1). If it doesn't appear, install it by clicking the Install button.
- You can control access at the folder level only when using the shared folders method on a non-NTFS disk. If you want to share a file, put it into a shared folder. If you want to control access to a file, set access privileges for the folder in which it resides.
- In the absence of a policy setting to the contrary, you can share folders on removable disc devices, such as CD-ROM drives, as well as hard drives.
- In the case of local resources, the default behavior is for all files, folders, and printers to be accessible to all users. In the case of network resources, the default behavior is just the opposite, and you must explicitly share resources.

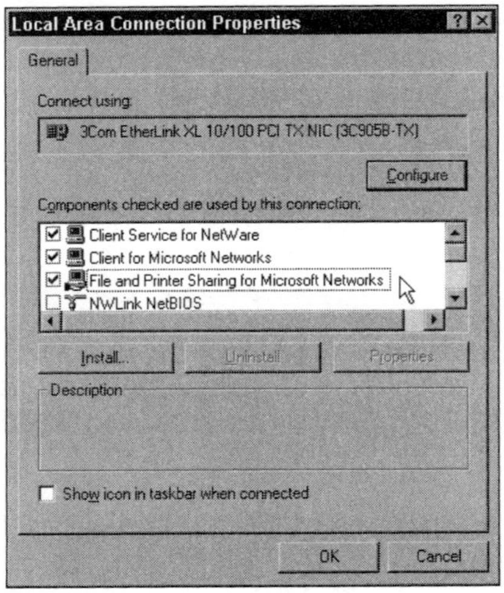

Figure 11-1: This network connection has the sharing service installed and activated.

Who can have access

Step 2 in configuring access permissions is to specify who you want to have access to the resource. You may want to share a folder and make it available to certain departments but not others.

- If you're using shared folder permissions and/or NTFS permissions, you can grant access based on user names and group memberships.
- Generally, using groups is preferable, because it takes less time and effort to administer group-based security.
- Certain special groups make granting access permission more convenient.

What users can do with the resource

You can control which resources become shared, and who gets to use those resources. Even that may be insufficient control, however. In many cases, you want to control *what* those users can do with those resources. The third and (usually) final step is to specify what users can do with the resources that you share.

- The specific actions vary depending upon the type of resource. For example, the action "query a Registry key" doesn't really mean anything when you're talking about accessing a printer.
- You define which actions are allowed and which aren't by checking and unchecking boxes in an *ACL editor* window where ACL means *Access Control List*. The three types of ACL editors you see are for Registry keys, files/folders, and printers.

Shared Folder Permissions

Use *shared folders* to give network users access to folders on your PC. Use *shared folder permissions* to control access to folders on your PC.

Shared folders don't restrict what locally logged-on users can do on your PC.

Shared folder permissions are the *only* means available for restricting network user access to a FAT or FAT32 disk. One more reason Microsoft suggests you use NTFS instead.

Sharing a folder

The procedure for sharing a folder is simple. You must be a member of the Administrators or Power Users groups to share folders.

To share folders, you need to install the File and Print Sharing for Microsoft Networks service for at least one network connection in your Network and Dial-Up Connections folder.

Open Windows Explorer, right-click the folder you want to share, and choose Sharing... from the context menu. In the dialog box shown in Figure 11-2, give the shared folder a share name and (optionally) a comment. You can also reduce the maximum number of simultaneous users from the default maximum of 10. (If you want to share a resource with more than 10 simultaneous users, Microsoft wants you to get Windows 2000 Server.)

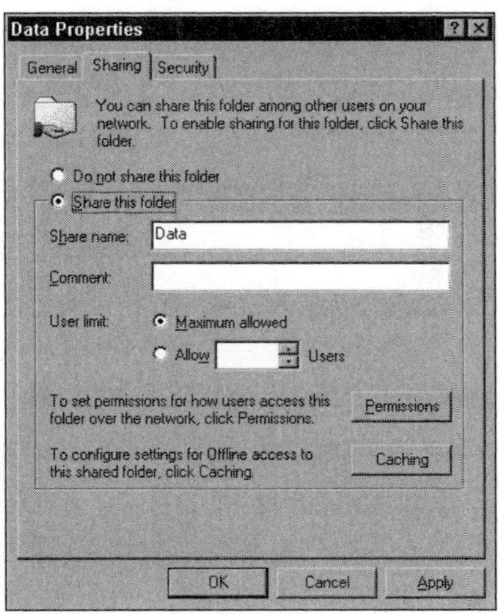

Figure 11-2: Sharing a folder.

When you look at the folder in Windows Explorer next time, it will appear with a small hand below it, indicating that it has become a "served" folder.

TIP

Shorter share names ensure visibility by downlevel clients. For example, using a maximum of eight characters guarantees that Windows 3.*x* and DOS users can see the share.

Assigning shared folder permissions

Clicking the Permissions button on the Sharing tab brings up the dialog box shown in Figure 11-3, from which you can add and remove groups or users from the permissions list, and change which permissions each group or user has. (You can also add, remove, and change permissions by computer name.)

The three sorts of permissions that you can assign for a shared folder are as follows:

- **Read:** Users can open and read files and file attributes, but not modify them. Users can run programs.
- **Change:** Users can do everything granted by the Read permission, plus change files and file attributes and delete files and folders.
- **Full Control:** Users can do everything granted by the Change permission, plus take ownership of files and change permissions.

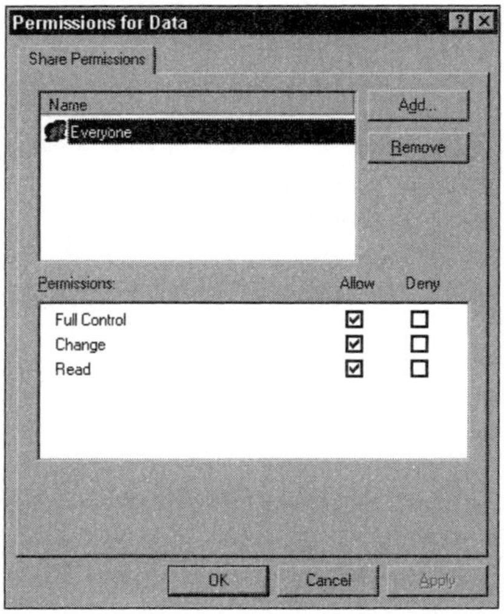

Figure 11-3: Applying shared folder permissions.

The default for a newly-shared folder is Full Control assigned to the *Everyone* group. "Everyone" is a predefined group that includes any network user, whether authenticated or not. You cannot use the built-in Authenticated Users group to assign permissions.

Normally, you'd remove Full Control from the Everyone group, then add back the specific groups or users that you want to have access. After you add groups or users, you can modify which of the three permissions each of those groups or users has, by using the Permissions For *<foldername>* dialog box. For example, in a shared folder that holds programs that users can run, you may want to assign Full Control to the Administrators group only, and Read to the Users group. In a shared folder that contains data, give the Users group the Change permission.

If you plan to combine shared folder permissions with NTFS permissions (see next section), one common practice is to use the default "Full control for Everyone" shared folder permissions and then use the finer-grained NTFS permissions to control access.

NTFS Permissions

NTFS permissions only work on NTFS disks (duh). Further, you can use these permissions to control network access, but also to control access by local users logged on to the PC hosting the resources. Unlike shared folder permissions, NTFS permissions do not require the presence of the File and Printer Sharing for Microsoft Networks service.

The technique for assigning NTFS permissions is pretty similar to that for assigning shared folder permissions (see previous section), with the exception that you don't have to "share" a folder first. Simply right-click the file or folder you wish to apply permissions to, choose Properties, and click the Security tab. You should see something like Figure 11-4.

The various sorts of NTFS permissions that you can allow or deny for a file or folder are as follows, roughly in order from least powerful to most powerful:

- **Read:** Users can open and read files, file attributes, subfolders, and permissions, but not modify them.
- **Read and Execute:** Read permissions, plus the ability to "traverse" folders you don't have permissions to in order to get to files or folders you do have permissions to.
- **List Folder Contents:** (Folders only) Pretty self-explanatory.

- **Write:** Users can modify files and subfolders.
- **Modify:** The sum of the Read and Execute and Write permissions, plus the ability to delete stuff.
- **Full Control:** Everything the other permissions allow, plus the ability to change permissions and take ownership of resources.

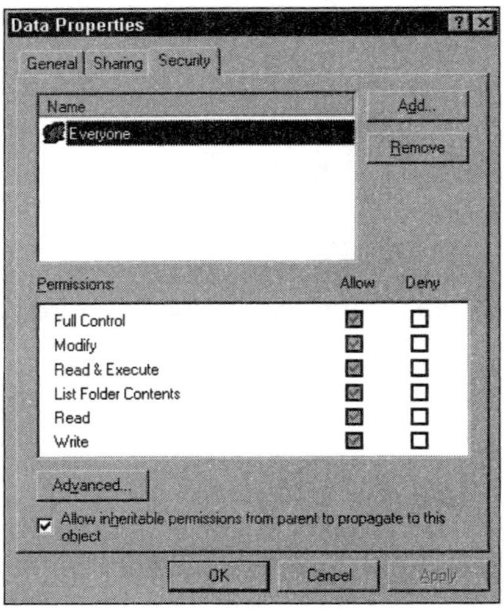

Figure 11-4: Applying NTFS permissions.

Permission Conflicts and Inheritance

This section discusses two important nuances of access permissions: conflict resolution and inheritance. (If you haven't read the two previous sections on shared folder permissions and NTFS permissions, please do so first.)

Conflict resolution

Sometimes, permissions that you assign can potentially conflict with each other. For example, you may assign an access permission to one group, but deny it in another group. What about Mary, who belongs to both groups?

Here are the rules for conflict resolution.

- If Mary belongs to two groups, one of which grants an access permission and the other of which denies it, Mary is denied. *Denials override everything else.* (That's why you should use denials sparingly.) This is true of shared folder permissions and NTFS permissions.

- If Jill belongs to two groups, one of which grants a shared access permission (such as Read) and the other of which grants an even broader access permission (such as Change), Mary gets the broader permission, which incorporates the narrower permission. In other words, the effective permission is the sum of all the individual permissions. This is true of shared folder permissions and NTFS permissions.
- If Tom has an NTFS permission to a file, but has been denied an NTFS permission to the containing folder, then Tom can still access the file, but he has to find it using a complete path name — he can't browse Explorer to find it.
- If Jim accesses a file that lives in a folder having shared folder permissions, and furthermore the file lives on an NTFS disk and has NTFS permissions, then Jim needs both the shared folder permission *and* the NTFS permission to access the file. Put another way, when both NTFS and shared folder permissions apply, the effective overall permission is the more restrictive of the two.

Inheritance

When you share a folder that contains other folders, and you assign permissions to the upper-level folder in order to prescribe what users can and can't do with that folder, what permissions does Windows 2000 associate with the subfolders? Or, with NTFS permissions, when you assign a permission for a folder, does it automatically apply to subfolders?

Here are the rules for permissions inheritance.

- The default behavior is for permissions you assign to folders to "propagate downwards" to all contained files and subfolders, including new ones you create later on. This applies for both shared folder permissions and NTFS permissions.
- To change the shared folder permissions of a subfolder to be different than its parent, you have to create a separate share name for the subfolder to which you want to grant different access rights. Any such explicit change overrides the inherited rights, in either direction (more rights or fewer rights).
- To change the NTFS permissions of a subfolder to be different than its parent, click the Security tab for the subfolder and clear the checkbox that says Allow Inheritable Permissions From Parent To Propagate To This Object. At that point, you can assign different NTFS permissions, which by default will then flow downward to sub-subfolders and files.

Connecting to Shared Resources

You can connect to shared resources on a Microsoft network in several ways, including the following:

- **Mapped drives.** These are network shares that associate with a drive letter. (Create drive mappings by right-clicking a network folder and choosing Map Network Drive. See Figure 11-5.) Creating mapped drives is not the best practice anymore, largely because there are only so many letters in the alphabet. However, many users are accustomed to accessing the network this way — largely because it was the *only* way available in years past.
- **Universal Naming Convention (UNC) paths.** These are path names of the format *server**folder**file*, where the *server* part of the name is the computer's legacy (NetBIOS) name.
- **My Network Places.** Formerly "Network Neighborhood" (why does Microsoft change these names?), this virtual folder lives on the desktop and lets users connect to any servers on the LAN or WAN — subject to server availability and access restrictions.

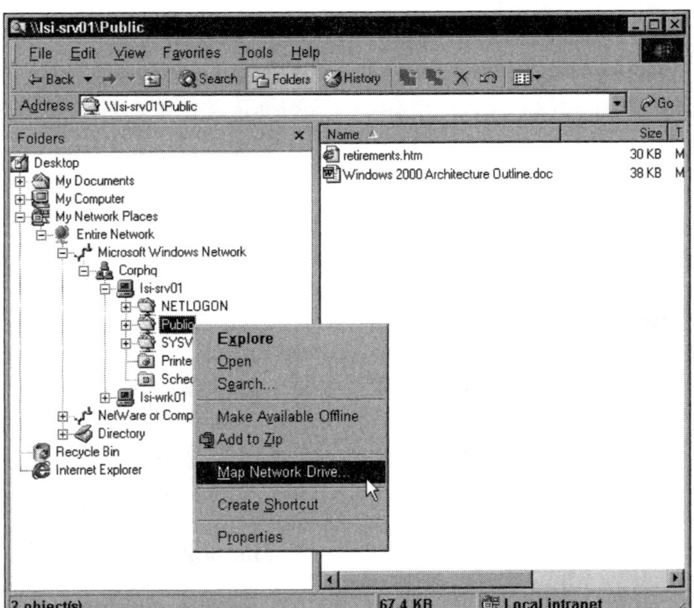

Figure 11-5: Mapping a network drive.

If you can't connect to a shared folder on a remote computer by using a UNC name, your connection's TCP/IP property sheet may not be properly configured to find a WINS server, or no WINS server may be available on the network at that moment. WINS servers let you find a computer on a TCP/IP network by using the NetBIOS computer name.

Web Server Access Control

Windows 2000 Professional comes with *Internet Information Server (IIS)* Version 5.0, although the software doesn't install with the operating system unless you're upgrading a system with an earlier version of Microsoft's Web server software (such as Personal Web Server or PWS). IIS lets you share resources on your computer with users running Web browsers or FTP utilities.

The exam doesn't spend a lot of time on installing and configuring IIS, so don't worry about these topics. What you *are* likely to see is one or two questions on controlling *access* to resources that you've shared with IIS.

You can restrict access to IIS servers by one or more of the following methods, many of which are reached via the Internet Information Services snap-in to the Computer Management console:

- Don't start all the services. For example, if you don't want FTP, make sure the service is disabled.
- Change the service's TCP/IP port. The default port for a Web server is 80, while the default port for an FTP server is 21. Changing these port numbers forces users to append the port number (preceded by a colon) to the URL in order to access the server.

Speaking of ports, you can also restrict access to an IIS server by setting *TCP/IP filtering* via the advanced TCP/IP property sheet for the Local Area Connection. You can set filters so that only specific TCP or UDP ports, or specific IP protocols, are allowed for incoming traffic.

- Limit the maximum number of simultaneous connections.
- Limit the number of users with operator privileges for the Web server.
- Control access to the service's home directory (read, write, browse, and so on). The WWW and FTP services each have their own.
- Modify rights associated with the user account that Windows uses for anonymous users, or disable anonymous access entirely.
- Grant or deny access for specific IP addresses or address ranges, or for specific DNS addresses.
- Enable client certificates for secure authentication.

A new feature of IIS 5.0 is *Web folders,* which permits users to connect to shared folders on a Web server in the same way that users can connect to shared folders on a traditional file server. The subject receives no discussion in the 1,600-page Microsoft Windows 2000 Professional Resource Kit, and very little mention in the help file, which suggests that you can probably skip learning any details.

Local Group Policy

The Group Policy feature in Windows 2000 is, shall we say, a tad bit confusing. However, you have to know about it for the exam — although not in as much detail as for other Windows 2000 track MCSE tests.

Policies and the Local Security Policy console

If you took my advice and read Chapter 10 before reading this chapter, you've already been introduced to one galaxy of the Group Policy universe, namely, *account policies*. These appear in the Local Security Policy console (in the Administrative Tools control panel folder) and apply to users and groups, which is why Chapter 10 deals with them.

Another galaxy of settings is in the *local policies* branch of the security settings tree. The general idea is that local policies apply to the machine, rather than to users, although between you and me, this distinction doesn't stand up under critical scrutiny. Local policies consist of *audit policies* (discussed later in the "Auditing Object Access" section), *user rights assignment* (mentioned in Chapter 10), and *security options,* a mishmash of access- and security-related settings. Figure 11-6 shows a flock of policies in the security options node.

After you set them, these policies apply to the local computer *assuming it's not participating in an Active Directory network*. If the computer is part of an AD network, any local policies you set through the Local Security Policy console may be overridden by higher-level policies set by a network administrator. The order of precedence, from weakest to strongest, is local; site; domain; and organizational unit. Put differently, if you set a local policy, it goes into effect as long as no contradictory setting for that policy has been made on a Windows 2000 Server at a site, domain, or organizational unit level.

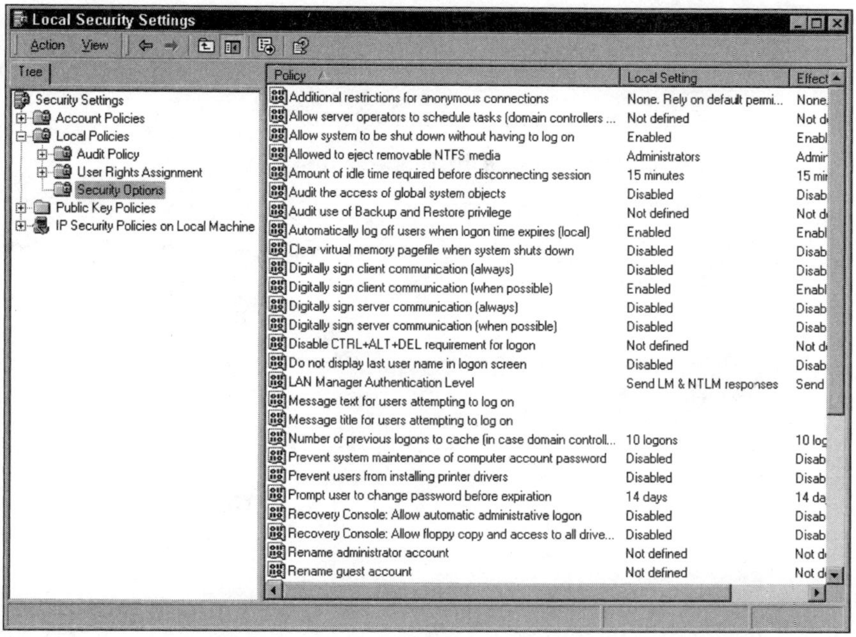

Figure 11-6: Set security options through the Local Security Policy console.

A few of the access-related policies of interest in the security options node are as follows:

- Disable CTRL-ALT-DEL Requirement for Logon
- Prevent Users from Installing Printer Drivers
- Recovery Console: Allow Automatic Administrative Logon
- Restrict CD-ROM Access to Locally Logged-On User Only

INSTANT ANSWER

If a policy setting conflicts with a *user right* that you would normally have, for example, by virtue of belonging to a group such as Power Users, the policy setting wins. (See Chapter 10 for more on user rights.)

Policies and the Local Group Policy console

If you were hoping that the Local Security Policy console contained all the policy settings you may need to understand for the exam, you may be right, but you probably aren't. The Local Security Policy console only shows a fairly small subset of the entire policy cornucopia. In order to see the whole banana, you need to create your own custom Microsoft Management Console. Lab 11-1 shows you how.

Lab 11-1 Creating a Group Policy Console

1. **Choose Start⇨Run, type** MMC **in the dialog box, and click OK.**

   This runs the Microsoft Management Console "host" program, MMC.EXE.

2. **Choose Console⇨Add/Remove Snap-In.**

3. **Click the Add button.**

   You should see a list of snap-ins available on your PC, as shown in Figure 11-7.

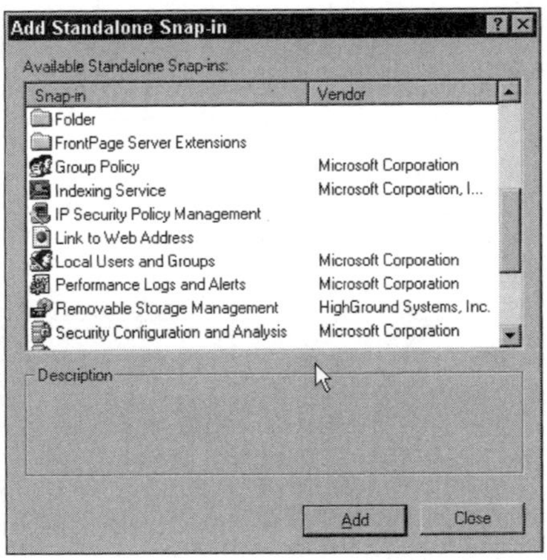

Figure 11-7: Build your own custom management console.

4. **Click Group Policy and then click Add.**

5. **In the Select Group Policy Object dialog box, click Finish.**

   For the purposes of viewing and editing policies on the local PC, the local group policy object (default) is the one you want.

6. **Click Close and OK to close the two dialog boxes.**

7. **Choose Console⇨Save and give your new custom console a name ("Local Group Policy" is a good choice).**

   The default save location is the Administrative Tools folder.

To run the new console, choose Start⇨Programs⇨Administrative Tools⇨ Local Group Policy. (I suggest creating a shortcut to the MSC file in the Administrative Tools folder in the Control Panel, too. Windows doesn't automatically synchronize these two locations.) You should see something like Figure 11-8.

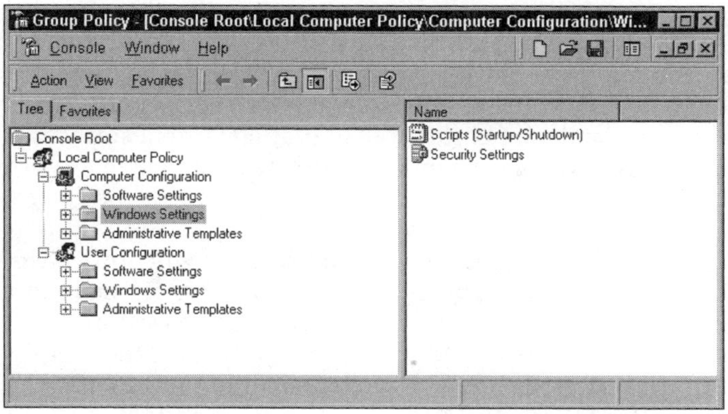

Figure 11-8: Build your own custom management console.

As you expand the nodes in the left windowpane, notice that the top-level categories pertain to the machine and to the user, respectively. Windows 2000 applies machine-specific policies before the network user even logs on; the user-specific policies apply after logon. This setup is a primary reason that computers in a Windows 2000 network have their own unique account IDs — Windows must have some way of assigning machine-specific policies to each computer as it connects to the network. This requirement for each computer to have a unique computer account ID is the rationale behind utilities like SysPrep (see Chapter 4).

Note that in each of the two main categories exists a subcategory called "Administrative Templates." These are settings contained in *.ADM files that modify the local Registry. You find a variety of miscellaneous settings under Administrative Templates, and more nodes appear here as you add applications that come with their own *.ADM files.

Just for fun, expand the node *Local Computer Policy\Computer Configuration\Windows Settings\Security Settings*. Look familiar? If not, open up the Local Security Policy console in your Administrative Tools folder.

Working with Security Templates

Policies aren't the only way to apply security settings in a Windows 2000 environment. Consider, for example, a small organization with a dozen or so standalone PCs. You don't have a domain-based network, so the advantage that the Group Policy tools confer in terms of easing administration chores doesn't apply to your situation. You need to apply security to the workstations, but you don't look forward to going around from one computer to the next, firing up the Local Group Policy or Local Security Policy consoles, and making a lot of settings one by one.

Security templates are convenient just for such a situation. They're files with the suffix INF that contain a whole slew of security settings which you can apply to a computer in one fell swoop. These settings include account policies, local policies, group membership, registry key security, file system access controls, and configuration of operating system services. Microsoft supplies a number of pre-assembled templates that live in `C:\WINNT\SECURITY\TEMPLATES`.

Although security templates come in handy when you don't have a domain-based network, you can certainly use them in a network environment, too. For example, you can apply a security template to a Group Policy object, thereby applying all the individual security settings in the template to a domain or organizational unit. (The command is Import Policy on the context menu of the policy object's Security Settings node.)

Security template snap-ins

Microsoft figures that most Windows 2000 Professional users won't need to muck around with security templates, so if you want to use them, you have a bit of customizing to do. Lab 11-2 takes you through the process of creating a custom management console containing the two snap-ins that are relevant to security templates: *Security Templates* and *Security Configuration and Analysis*.

Lab 11-2 Building a Security Templates Console

1. **Choose Start⇨Run, type** MMC **in the dialog box, and click OK.**
2. **Choose Console⇨Add/Remove Snap-In.**
3. **Click the Add button.**
4. **Click Security Templates and then click Add.**
5. **Click Security Configuration and Analysis and then click Add.**
6. **In the Select Group Policy Object dialog box, click Finish.**
7. **Click Close and OK to close the two dialog boxes.**
8. **Choose Console⇨Save and give your new custom console a name ("Security Templates" is a good choice).**

   The default save location is the Administrative Tools folder.

The Security Templates snap-in

The job of the Security Templates snap-in is to add and edit INF security templates (see Figure 11-9). This is a great place to view the settings in an organized, hierarchical structure.

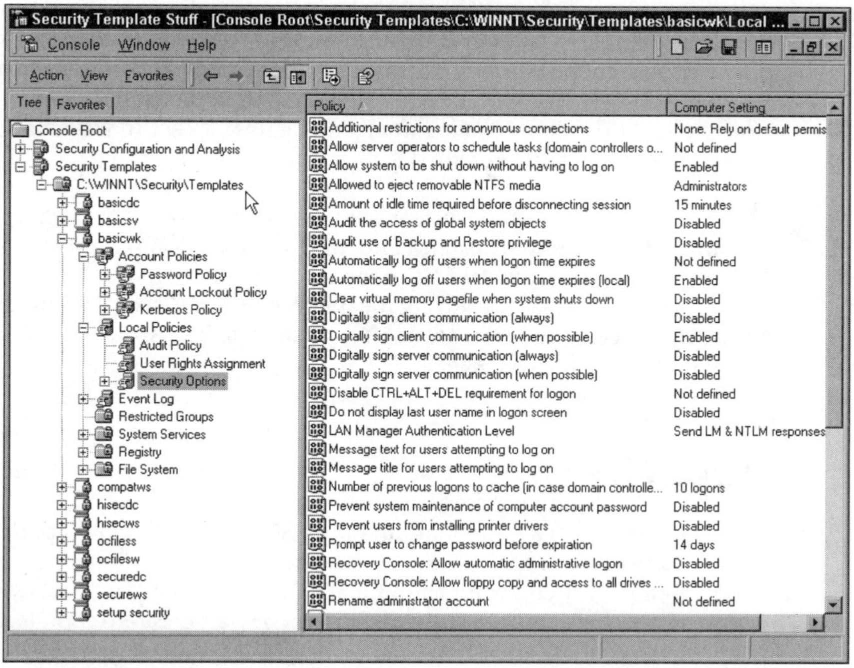

Figure 11-9: Divine the meaning of inscrutable INF files here.

You should memorize the meaning of the various predefined templates:

- **BASICDC** is the default template for a domain controller.
- **BASICSV** is the default template for a regular server.
- **BASICWK** is the default template for a workstation.
- **COMPATWS** relaxes access controls for the Users group and is therefore well suited for workstations that need compatibility with older applications.
- **HISECDC** is for a maximum-security domain controller.
- **HISECWS** is for a maximum-security workstation. Power Users have more restrictions than usual.
- **SECUREDC** is for a high-security domain controller.
- **SECUREWS** is for a high-security workstation.

The Security Configuration and Analysis snap-in

The Security Configuration and Analysis snap-in has two jobs: first, to compare the PC's current configuration against a security template, and second, to apply a template to a local PC (or Group Policy object, in a networked environment).

To compare the PC's current configuration against a security template, right-click the Security Configuration and Analysis node in the console's tree pane and choose Open Database. If this is a new database, Windows prompts you to specify a security template to load into the database. For example, if you want to see how your system stacks up against a secure workstation configuration, you'd choose SECUREWS.

After you open the database, perform the analysis by right-clicking Security Configuration and Analysis and choosing Analyze Computer Now. When the utility finishes its evaluation, it presents a display such as that in Figure 11-10. A green check mark by a setting means that your PC's setting matches the one in the database; a red "X" means that your PC is less secure than the setting in the database would make it.

SECEDIT

Microsoft supplies a command-line tool, SECEDIT.EXE, which performs most of the same tasks that the console snap-ins perform, but from a batch file or script — handy if you want to put a SECEDIT command into a systemwide logon script, for example. With SECEDIT, you can create templates, apply templates, and analyze security.

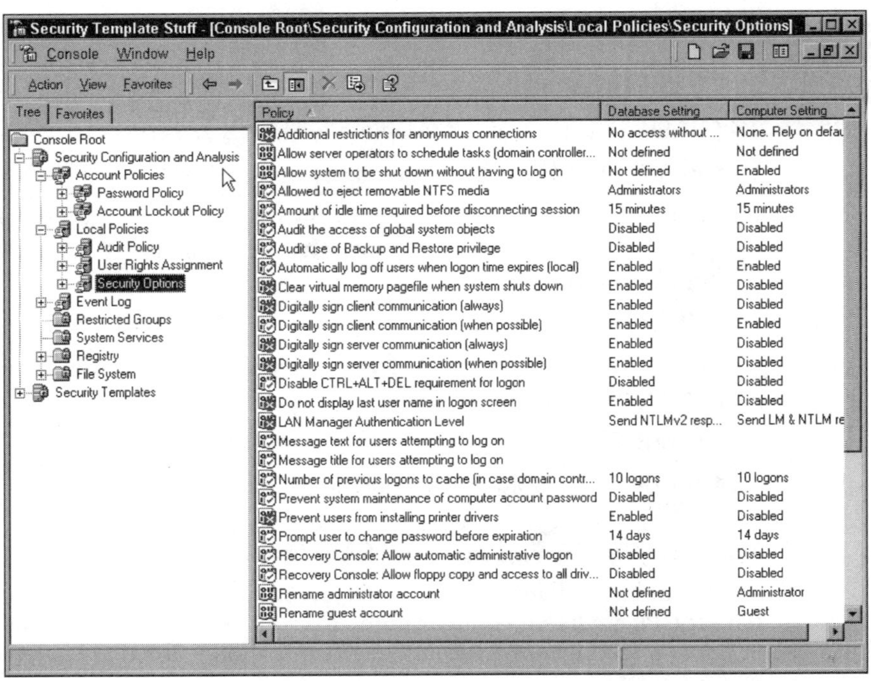

Figure 11-10: See how your PC stacks up against a template.

The exam is likely to quiz your knowledge of SECEDIT's various command qualifiers, which include the following:

- **/analyze** analyzes the current system's security, and uses the /DB and /CFG parameters.
- **/configure** configures the current system's security, and uses the /DB and /CFG parameters.
- **/export** exports a template from a security database to an INF template file, and uses the /DB and /CFG parameters.
- **/DB <*filename*>** specifies the database containing a stored configuration against which the analysis will be made (with the /analyze option) or into which a template will be imported (with the /configure option).
- **/CFG <*filename*>** specifies the path to the security template that SECEDIT will use to analyze or configure the database specified in /DB.
- **/refreshpolicy** reapplies security settings for the local computer and logged-on user; handy if you don't want to wait for a policy change to propagate on its own.
- **/validate <*filename*>** checks the syntax of a security template.

Auditing Object Access

Object access auditing means that Windows 2000 can monitor accesses (both successful and unsuccessful) to files, folders, the Registry, and printers, and record those accesses in the Security event log (which you can view with the Event Viewer snap-in to the Computer Management console). The details that Windows 2000 records include the action performed, who performed it, when it occurred, and whether it succeeded or failed.

If you're having some trouble with file corruption, file system performance, Registry errors, or potential cybervandalism, object access auditing may help you figure out who's trying to gain access to what. (For logon auditing, please see Chapter 10's section entitled "Auditing User Activities.")

Activating object access auditing

Auditing is always off by default because of its system overhead. To activate object access auditing on your PC, open the Local Security Policy console (it's in the Administrative Tools folder of Control Panel). In the left pane, under Local Policies, click Audit Policy. All the various quantities that you can audit appear in the right pane. Double-click Audit Object Access (or, alternatively, single-click it and choose Action⇨Security) and choose whether you want to track successful events, unsuccessful ones, or both. (Careful here — file system reads occur frequently, and can easily swamp the event log, creating both disk space and performance problems for your system.) Restart the machine to make your changes take effect.

Auditing *successful* actions is a good way to do some capacity planning and performance analysis. Auditing *failed* actions is a good way to zero in on potential security problems.

Choosing what to audit

Activating object auditing simply turns the feature "on" — you must tell Windows 2000 which specific objects you want it to audit.

Use Windows Explorer to identify files and folders to audit. Use REGEDT32 to identify Registry keys to audit.

File and folder auditing

On an NTFS volume, Windows 2000 can audit access to files and folders. To tell Windows 2000 which ones to track, simply open Windows Explorer (for example, by right-clicking My Computer and choosing Explore), right-click the file or folder to audit, and choose Properties. Then, click the Security tab and the Advanced button. Finally, click the Auditing tab to display a dialog box that looks like the one in Figure 11-11.

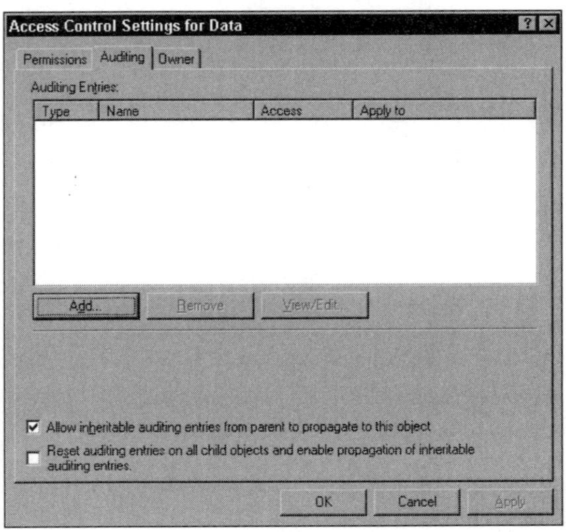

Figure 11-11: Set auditing on an NTFS folder.

Note the two check boxes at the bottom of the Auditing dialog box:

- **Allow inheritable auditing entries from parent to propagate to this object.** The default behavior is for auditing settings to propagate downward in the file structure; that is, if you enable auditing for a folder, you automatically enable auditing for all subfolders contained therein. Clearing this check box defeats this inherited behavior for the selected folder.
- **Reset auditing entries on all child objects and enable propagation of inheritable auditing entries.** This clears any pre-existing auditing settings on any subfolders of the current folder and sets them to inherit the settings you make on the folder.

From the Auditing tab, simply click the Add button and specify whose actions you want to audit. You can choose from local users, local groups, domain users, and domain groups. After you choose who, Windows prompts you to choose what, by displaying the ACL editor ("Auditing Entry") in Figure 11-12. Pick the relevant checkboxes and click OK, OK, OK.

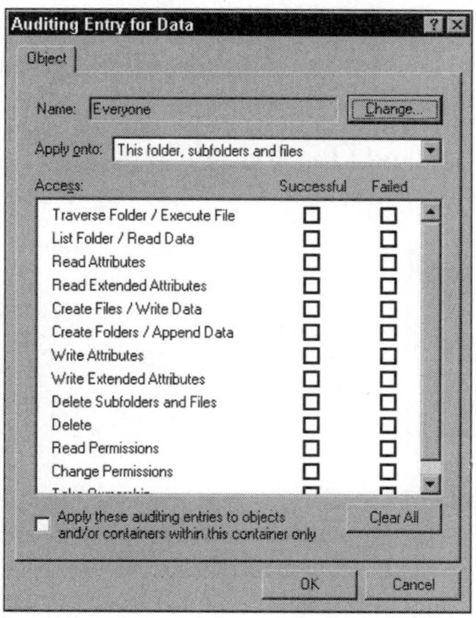

Figure 11-12: Tell Windows what file system actions to track.

Registry auditing

Registry auditing is really similar to file-and-folder auditing. Run the NT-style Registry Editor, REGEDT32.EXE, and navigate to the Registry key of interest. Click it, and then choose Security⇨Permissions. Choose the Advanced button and click the Auditing tab, just as in the preceding section. The "who" part works just the same, the "what" part looks a bit different, because Registry accesses don't work exactly like file and folder accesses (see Figure 11-13).

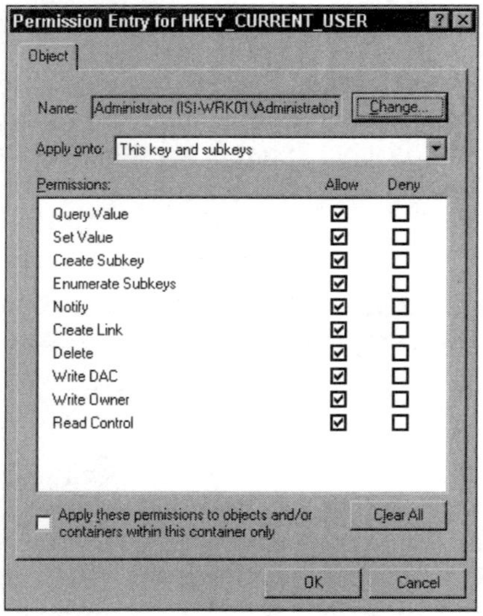

Figure 11-13: Registry key auditing uses some different access types.

Printer auditing

I'm tempted to simply say "ditto" here. Hey, why not: "ditto." The only difference is that the starting point is the printer's property sheet (Start⇨Settings⇨Printers gets you to the printer icons). See Figure 11-14 for the types of access Windows 2000 can audit for printers.

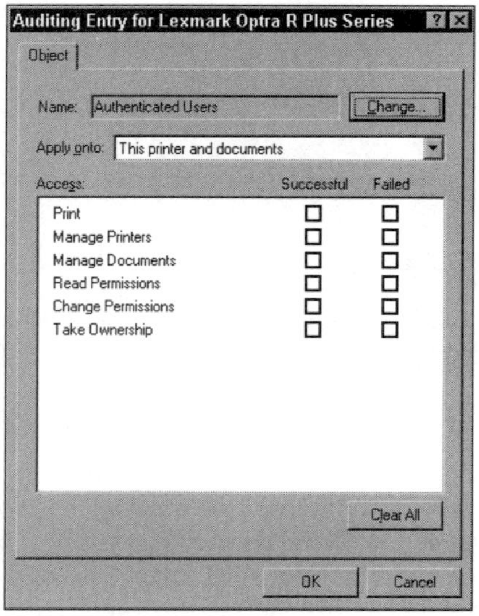

Figure 11-14: Tell Windows what printer actions to audit.

Prep Test

1 **Which of the following types of permissions can you assign to file system directories for local users of a Windows 2000 Professional computer? The local hard disk is formatted with the FAT32 file system as a basic disk.**

- **A** ❍ Shared folder permissions
- **B** ❍ Shared printer permissions
- **C** ❍ File-and-folder permissions
- **D** ❍ Access Control Lists
- **E** ❍ None of the above

2 **Alicia comes to you with a suspicion that someone is using her files and damaging them in the process. You decide to enable auditing so that you can confirm or dismiss her suspicion. What tool would you use to designate specific folders for auditing? (Choose the best answer.)**

- **A** ❍ Local Group Policy
- **B** ❍ REGEDT32
- **C** ❍ Local Security Policy
- **D** ❍ Windows Explorer
- **E** ❍ Disk Management

3 **Robin is an employee at your software company. She has happily run a particular application for a couple of years now as a Windows NT Workstation 4.0 user. You upgrade her system to Windows 2000 Professional, and her application no longer works. Which of the following security templates might solve Robin's problem? (Choose the best answer.)**

- **A** ❍ COMPATWS.INF
- **B** ❍ BASICWS.INF
- **C** ❍ BASICWK.INF
- **D** ❍ SECUREDC.INF

4 **You're running Windows 2000 Professional. You try connecting to a shared folder on another Windows 2000 Professional computer by creating a desktop shortcut pointing to the shared folder. You use the Universal Naming Convention. You verify that the computer name and folder name you're using are correct, and you also verify that the remote computer is powered on. However, you still can't get the shortcut icon to work. You can successfully PING the remote computer using its IP address. What setting on your system should you check?**

A ❍ Capitalization of the UNC path.

B ❍ Your PC's DNS server address setting.

C ❍ Your PC's WINS server address setting.

D ❍ Your PC's NetBIOS name.

5 **Someone has disabled the Ctrl+Alt+Del requirement for logon on a stand-alone Windows 2000 Professional computer. You want to restore that requirement. How would you do so? (Choose all that apply.)**

A ❑ Right-click My Computer, choose Manage, click the Local Security Policy node, navigate to Security Settings, and clear the policy named Disable Ctrl+Alt+Del Requirement for Logon.

B ❑ Right-click My Computer, choose Manage, click the Local Security Policy node, navigate to Account Settings, and check the policy named Disable Ctrl+Alt+Del Requirement for Logon.

C ❑ Choose Start⇨Run and type GPEDIT.MSC. Navigate to the Security Policy node and clear the policy named Disable Ctrl+Alt+Del Requirement for Logon.

D ❑ Open the Administrative Tools folder and double-click Local Security Policy. Navigate to the Security Policy node and clear the policy named Disable Ctrl+Alt+Del Requirement for Logon.

6 **Jim has Full Control access to a shared folder on Jill's machine. Jim also belongs to a group for which the Full Control NTFS permission has been denied on that same shared folder. What effective permissions does Jim have on the folder?**

A ❍ Full Control

B ❍ Read

C ❍ Modify

D ❍ None

7 **You decide to restrict access to your Windows 2000 Web server by excluding all traffic except Web traffic and all protocols except ICMP. What TCP/IP port number would you permit using packet filtering? (Choose the best answer.)**

A ❍ 21
B ❍ 23
C ❍ 40
D ❍ 60
E ❍ 80

8 **The NTFS "Modify" permission includes which of the following permissions? (Choose all that apply.)**

A ❑ Read
B ❑ Write
C ❑ Execute
D ❑ Take Ownership

Answers

1 **E.** Choice A is wrong because shared folder permissions only work across the network, and the question posits local users. Choice B is wrong because the question asks about file system directories, not printers (read those questions carefully). Choice C, file-and-folder permissions, is another name for NTFS permissions and those aren't available on a FAT32 disk. Access Control Lists are associated with NTFS permissions, ruling out choice D. *See* "Access Permissions Overview."

2 **D.** Use Windows Explorer. The procedure is to right-click the folder on which you want to enable auditing; choose Properties; and click the Security tab. Then, click Advanced and click the Auditing tab. *See* "File and folder auditing."

3 **A.** In fact, that's the reason for the COMPATWS template's existence. It relaxes access controls for the Users group and permits members of that group to run applications designed for Windows NT 4.0. *See* "The Security Templates snap-in."

4 **C.** WINS is responsible for mapping the NetBIOS name that you use in a UNC path with the IP address of the remote computer. Therefore, if your computer has an incorrect or missing WINS server address in its TCP/IP property sheet, you can't use NetBIOS names (computer names) to contact machines on a different physical subnet. *See* "Connecting to Shared Resources."

5 **C** and **D.** You can't change policy settings from the Computer Management console, logical though that may seem. You can get to the local security policies either with GPEDIT.MSC or the Local Security Policy console. *See* "Policies and the Local Group Policy console."

6 **D.** A denial overrides everything else. A denial on the Full Control permission means Jim can't do jack with Jill's folder. *See* "Permission Conflicts and Inheritance."

7 **E.** Web traffic uses TCP port 80. *See* "Web Server Access Control."

8 **A, B,** and **C.** Know your NTFS permissions for the exam. *See* "NTFS Permissions."

Chapter 12

IntelliMirror and Roaming Access

Exam Objectives

- Configuring and managing user profiles
- Managing and troubleshooting the use and synchronization of offline files
- Installing applications by using Windows Installer packages

Let me clear up something right away. IntelliMirror *isn't* a technology for automatically positioning outside rear-view mirrors on automobiles, for example by sensing the height of the driver. Instead, it's a semi-catchy name for the Windows 2000 version of some technologies that have actually been kicking around on the Windows platform for a few years now. These technologies include *user profiles, offline files,* and the *Add/Remove Programs* wizard (as enhanced by Windows Installer technology). The common denominator among these technologies, and the reason Microsoft gives them a unifying buzzword, is that they enable users to move from one computer to another with less bother.

The Windows 2000 Server exams address certain aspects of IntelliMirror — specifically, publishing and assigning applications in the Active Directory hierarchy — that the Windows 2000 Professional exam does not. Even so, the three aspects of IntelliMirror that this chapter addresses are likely candidates for Exam #70-210 because they're new (sort of) and they make users' lives easier (sometimes). Now, for you mechanical engineers: Drop me an e-mail if you want to work together on that rear-view mirror idea. I think it could be patentable. We could start with a small proximity sensor above the driver's head. . . .

Quick Assessment

Configuring and managing user profiles

1 The Registry component of user profiles exists in two files, ______ and ______.

2 Two items not in the Registry that also make up a user's profile are ______ and ______.

3 You can control what parts of a user's profile roam the network by modifying ______.

4 Delete, copy, and change user profiles using the User Profiles tab of the ______ control panel.

Managing and troubleshooting the use and synchronization of offline files

5 When working with an offline file, the file appears to be in the same network ______ and it has the same ______.

6 What does Microsoft call the kind of logoff synchronization in which Windows 2000 doesn't guarantee that your local copy of offline files is up-to-date? ______

7 (True/False) Windows 2000 offline files work with Novell servers if they are running NetWare version 4.0 or greater.

8 The default idle time Windows 2000 waits before starting synchronization is ______ minutes of inactivity.

Installing applications by using Windows Installer packages

9 As opposed to INF files, Windows Installer packages use ______ files.

10 The executable program that installs, repairs, and removes Windows Installer packages is ______.

Answers

1 *NTUSER.DAT, USRCLASS.DAT.* If you just got the first one right, don't feel bad, I pick nits when it comes to the Registry. See the "File structure" section.

2 *Network connections, printers, My Documents folder, Start menu shortcuts, Favorites, History.* If you didn't choose two of these, read "User Profiles" in this chapter.

3 *Group policies.* The section "What roams, what doesn't" explains.

4 *System.* See "Managing profiles" if you missed this answer.

5 *Location, access restrictions.* If you said "location, name" you would also be correct, just less of a show-off. See "The offline concept" for explanations.

6 *Quick.* See the section "Client-side setup."

7 *False.* Offline files don't work with NetWare servers at all; "Offline in practice: A mixed blessing" mentions other limitations.

8 *15.* That's the computer's inactivity, by the way, not yours. See the "Client-side setup" section for this tidbit.

9 *MSI.* Stands for Microsoft Software Installer; see "Windows Installer Service" for more.

10 *MSIEXEC.EXE.* Again, "Windows Installer Service" has this detail plus a few others you should know.

Registry 101

To really understand how user profiles work (and group policies, for that matter), you should understand at least the most basic basics of the Registry. The Registry is the central store of information that Windows 2000 and Windows 2000 programs use to track all the software and hardware on the machine, including details about how that software and hardware are configured.

The Registry isn't the brain of Windows 2000, but it's a lot like its spine: that is, where most of the nerve endings come together. And, like your spine, the Registry is vitally important. Windows 2000 can't even roll out of bed without the clues that Microsoft has tucked away inside the Registry. After startup, Windows 2000, and the programs you run with it, use the Registry many thousands of times in a typical computing session — to find necessary files, recall user preferences, enforce security restrictions, and perform hundreds of other actions.

If something goes wrong with your Registry, you may not be able to use your computer until you fix it. If something goes wrong with a program you're running, or with Windows 2000 itself, you may need to use the Registry to repair it. If a hacker knows more about the Registry than you do, you could be at risk for some of the more insidious viruses around, like the "I Love You" bug that kissed tens of millions of PCs in May 2000.

Microsoft is moving away from the concept of having the Registry contain every possible configuration setting. Windows 2000 Server uses a separate database, *Active Directory,* which maintains information about how the network is organized. Most of the low-level details about network nuts and bolts remain in the Registry, though.

The Windows 2000 Registry shares many similarities with NT 4.0, which incidentally is why the upgrade path from NT 4.0 is much smoother than from any other Windows version. Some companies are even finding that a two-stage migration, from Windows 9*x* to NT 4.0 to 2000, works more reliably than a "leapfrog" migration (Windows 9*x* to 2000). Others prefer to back up data files, wipe the disk, and do a clean install followed by a restore.

The exam is sure to include one or two questions about the Registry. Also be aware that you'll spend way more time mucking about with the Registry in the real world than the exam leads you to believe.

File structure

The Registry appears as a single, unified database when you view it with either Registry Editor (REGEDIT.EXE or REGEDT32.EXE), but it doesn't reside in a single file on disk. Most of the Registry's several files live in `C:\WINNT\SYSTEM32\CONFIG`, but some live in the profile folders under `C:\Documents and Settings`.

Why not just have one big meaty file with everything in it? Although the "one monster file" design has a certain aesthetic appeal, a few very good reasons exist for separating the Registry into multiple files:

- Different users can create and see different user-specific settings (NTUSER.DAT, USRCLASS.DAT) based on their logon names, but all users on a machine can share the same machine-specific settings.
- On a network, the user-specific settings (NTUSER.DAT, USRCLASS.DAT) can live on a network server and "follow a user around" as he or she logs onto different machines.
- You can maintain a separate group of default settings (the NTUSER.DAT that lives in the `Default User` profile folder) for any new user who logs on, while keeping every existing users' settings intact.
- The security-related parts of the Registry (SECURITY and SAM) can be restricted from view and protected against modification.
- The machine-specific parts of the Registry (HARDWARE, SOFTWARE, SYSTEM) stay with the machine.
- If something goes haywire, you may be able to restore part of the Registry from an earlier backup, instead of restoring all of it. The benefit of such a "surgical restore" is that you may lose less work.

Database structure

When you view or edit the Registry with REGEDIT.EXE, you see a hierarchical database structure in the left windowpane, as shown in Figure 12-1. This structure expands before your eyes when you click the little plus signs, just as a directory tree does in Windows Explorer. Also as in Explorer, the right windowpane displays the contents of whatever item you highlight in the left pane.

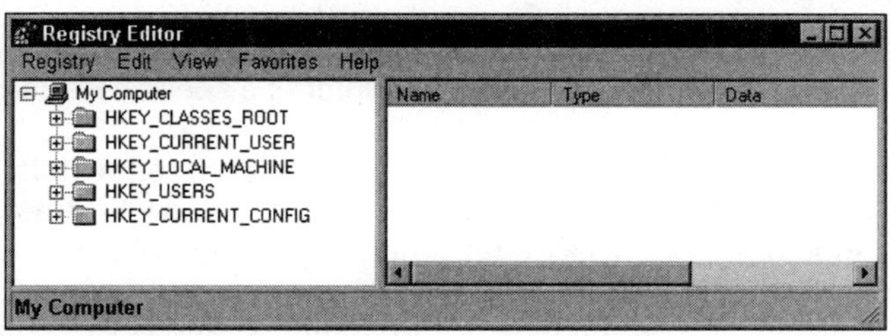

Figure 12-1: Primary Registry branches, or "root keys."

Root keys

The display in Figure 12-1 is a little misleading in that of the five root keys, three are aliases, or pointers, to subkeys of the two "real" root keys.

For example, *HKEY_CURRENT_USER* (abbreviated *HKCU*) contains all the user-specific Registry settings for the currently logged-on user. Saying (and writing) *HKCU* is easier than figuring out the current user's Security ID and specifying a key such as *HKU\S-1-5-21-448539723-842925246-2089417427-500* (where HKU is short for *HKEY_USERS*). Also, Windows 9*x* programs don't know about Security IDs, and therefore need to see *HKCU* to run under Windows 2000.

Here's another example. You often spend time in *HKEY_CLASSES_ROOT* (abbreviated *HKCR*) because it contains information about how different file types behave. Saying (and writing) *HKCR* is easier than *HKLM\SOFTWARE\Classes* (where *HKLM* is short for *HKEY_LOCAL_MACHINE*). The two locations contain pretty much the same information, though. Check it out yourself.

HKCR and *HKLM\SOFTWARE\Classes* contain *pretty much* the same information because *HKCR* now contains a merged view of information in *HKLM\SOFTWARE\Classes* and *HKCU\Software\Classes*. Therefore, HKCR is actually an alias for the combination of those two keys, when in prior versions of Windows it was an alias for the *HKLM* key only.

HKCC, HKCR, and *HKCU* just point to other places in *HKLM* and *HKU.* The "core" branches *HKLM* and *HKU* actually contain the entire Registry contents. (For the curious, *HKLM* corresponds to the physical files SAM, SECURITY, SOFTWARE, and SYSTEM, while *HKU* corresponds to the physical files NTUSER.DAT, USRCLASS.DAT, and DEFAULT.)

Keys and values

Beneath the five root keys, you find keys and values.

- *Keys* are just named containers that can contain other keys, values, or both. The Registry Editors display keys as folder icons in the left windowpane. Sometimes, the exam refers to top-level Registry branches as "keys," and that's technically what they are, so don't be confused.
- A value is a "leaf" element in the Registry database tree; that is, it can't contain anything else, but rather is an endpoint of a specific Registry path.

A typical value has both a name and some data associated with it. The name and data columns appear in the right pane of the Registry Editors. Values usually take one of three forms, determined by the type of data they contain:

- A *string* value can contain letters and numbers, and is by far the most commonly encountered value type.

- A *binary* value is numeric and consists of a series of two-digit, one-byte hexadecimal (that is, base 16) numbers separated by spaces.
- A *DWORD* value is a four-byte (or "double word") binary value, that appears in REGEDIT as "0x" plus eight hexadecimal bytes with no spaces.

Like the NT Registry, the Windows 2000 Registry also permits *multi-string* values (that basically contain a list of strings) and *expandable-string* values (that use replaceable parameters like *%systemroot%*). However, you don't see these often.

Do *not* waste time memorizing particular Registry settings. If you can remember the names and primary functions of the five main branches, and if you understand the differences between branches, keys, and values, you are good to go.

Two editing tools

Windows 2000, unlike Windows 9*x*, provides two Registry Editors:

- REGEDIT, which descends from the Windows 9*x* product line
- REGEDT32, which derives from early versions (3.5*x*) of Windows NT

Rather than provide a unified Registry Editor that can do all the things REGEDIT and REGEDT32 can do, Microsoft provides both these tools with the suggestion that we use the appropriate one for the job at hand.

Table 12-1 presents a summary of the differences between these two tools.

Table 12-1 The Two Registry Editors

Feature	*REGEDIT Operation*	*REGEDT32 Operation*
User interface	Windows 9*x* style	Windows 3.1 style
Registry search capabilities	Almost the entire Registry: key names, value names, value contents	Key names only
Display	Whole Registry in one window	Separate windows for each root key
Display style	Like Windows 9*x* Registry Editor	Like Windows NT 4.0/3.51 Registry Editor
Text file access	Export and import	Export only

(continued)

Table 12-1 *(continued)*

Feature	***REGEDIT Operation***	***REGEDT32 Operation***
Binary file access	None	Export and import
Read-only mode	None	Optional
Security features	None	Supports full Windows 2000 access control and auditing
Location	C:\WINNT	C:\WINNT\SYSTEM32 folder

Don't use REGEDIT or REGEDT32 unless no other way exists for you to make the setting you need. The Windows 2000 control panels, consoles, and property sheets are always preferable to directly editing the Registry, for two main reasons:

- The Registry Editors have no "undo" feature.
- Changes you make in a Registry Editor take effect immediately, unlike the control panels and property sheets, which let you think about your change (and maybe reverse it!) before clicking OK or Apply.

If you want more information about the Registry and what you can do with it, check out *Windows 2000 Registry For Dummies* by yours truly (IDG Books Worldwide, Inc.).

User Profiles

User profiles in Windows 2000 still do what they've always done on the Windows 9*x* and NT platforms. They let different users maintain their own individual settings and preferences — desktop icons, Start menu, application settings, network connections, and so on. User profiles make it possible for different users to share the same computer while each keeps his own settings; profiles also enable a user to log on to different computers and still see his usual desktop environment.

You can think of a user profile as containing two big categories of information: Registry stuff and non-Registry stuff.

- **Registry stuff:** This is basically everything in the *HKCU* branch of the Registry (Windows customizations, such as Control Panel settings; Explorer viewing options; printer connections; Dial-Up Networking connections; command prompt window settings; and any user-specific settings for Windows applications).

Those settings include stuff like whether your word processor checks your spelling as you type, whether you want your spreadsheets to print with gridlines, and so on.

- **Non-Registry stuff:** This is everything in the subfolders under `C:\Documents and Settings\<username>`. (If you upgraded from Windows NT 4.0, your profile folders live in `C:\WINNT\PROFILES`.) You mostly see shortcuts in these folders, but some contain actual data files, most notably the My Documents folder. Non-Registry stuff includes the recently used documents list, user-specific Start menu shortcuts, Internet Explorer cookies, contents of the Network Neighborhood and Printers folders, lists of favorite documents or Web sites, history lists, and so on.

Every time you add a user to a Windows 2000 system, Windows 2000 creates these resources:

- Subdirectory under `C:\Documents and Settings`.
- NTUSER.DAT file in the new subdirectory.

  The file is based on the default user information in `C:\Documents and Settings\Default User\NTUSER.DAT`.
- USRCLASS.DAT file.

  The file is buried in `C:\Documents and Settings\<username>\Local Settings\Application Data\Microsoft\Windows`. This file contains any per-user file type association information, such as the fact that Emily wants to run Photoshop rather than Internet Explorer when she opens a JPG file.

The virtual folder *Desktop\My Documents* is actually an alias, pointing to *C:\Documents and Settings\<username>\My Documents* where *<username>* is the name of the currently logged-on user. Therefore, the "My Documents" folder changes if a user logs off the system and logs on again using a different account. Similarly, the virtual folder *Desktop\My Documents\My Pictures* is an alias pointing to *C:\Documents and Settings\<username>\My Documents\My Pictures*. Certain applications from Microsoft and other vendors use this virtual folder as the default save directory for image files.

You should see an "All Users" folder in the main profile folder of your machine. The contents of this folder — usually some Start menu shortcuts and other scattered miscellany — *combine* with the contents of a user's individual profile folders to create the actual user profile. So, for example, the actual Start menu that you see is really the sum of all the shortcuts in `C:\Documents and Settings\<username>\Start Menu`, plus all the "community" shortcuts in `C:\Documents and Settings\All Users\Start Menu`. Only administrators can add, change, or delete contents of the All Users folder.

You may see an exam question scenario in which a PC's Administrator configures the desktop a certain way (Start menu options, desktop shortcuts, and so on), but another user (who may have Administrator privileges but has a different account) logs on later and doesn't see those configured changes. The reason, as you now know, is that each user has a separate profile. You can solve the problem by copying the Administrator's profile into the other user's profile folder via the System control panel's User Profiles tab.

Roaming versus local profiles

User profiles have two flavors:

- Local
- Roaming

The test expects you to understand both.

Local profiles

Local profiles are user profiles that live on a particular PC, as opposed to a network location. To clarify, a *local* profile doesn't mean that the user *account* must be on a standalone, non-networked PC. You can have a local profile for a network user account as well as for a standalone user account.

A local profile stays on the local hard drive of a single PC. If you take a local profile for a network user account and then give it a new home so that it lives on the network instead of solely on the local hard drive, then it becomes a "roaming" profile, as described in the next section.

With Windows 2000, unlike Windows 95/98, you don't have to take a separate step to activate user profiles; the feature is already "on," you just have to create the user accounts and log on with them. Also unlike Windows 9*x,* you can't necessarily just log on with a new user name and have Windows 2000 create an account for you automatically. You have to create the account ahead of time and then log on.

Which tool you must use and which procedure you must follow to create a local profile depends on your circumstances, as follows:

- On a machine that's *not* on a network domain, you have two options:
  - Fire up the Users and Passwords control panel.
  - Run the Computer Management console from the Administrative Tools control panel and select the Users and Groups snap-in.

- On a machine that *is* on a network domain where you want to add a user who's already defined on the domain, you have three choices:
  - Run the Users and Passwords control panel.
  - Start the Users and Groups snap-in to the Computer Management console.
  - Simply log on to Windows 2000 Professional as that user.
- On a machine that *is* on a network domain where you want to add a local (non-domain) user, run the Users and Passwords control panel and use the Advanced tab.

To run the Users and Passwords control panel or the Computer Management snap-in, you must log on as Administrator. Windows 2000 cares about security, so only an Administrator can create a new user account.

Roamin' profiles (or, "Caesar, who broke your nose?")

Creating a roaming profile allows a user to log on to any PC on the domain and have a server download his settings to that PC immediately after logon. So the procedure for creating a roaming profile is to create a folder on the server for profile data; point the user's account to that folder; and (optionally) load that folder with customized profile information that Windows 2000 will download the next time the user logs on at any PC.

Lab 12-1 presents more detailed steps for creating a roaming profile (this example assumes the user's domain account already exists):

Lab 12-1 Creating a Roaming User Profile

1. **Log on to a Windows 2000 Server domain controller as Administrator.**
2. **Using Windows Explorer, create a new profiles folder on the server (such as C:\PROFILES).**
3. **Right-click the new folder, choose Sharing, share the folder as "PROFILES," and give the Everyone group the Full Control permission.**

   Each user's individual profile folder will live beneath the main C:\PROFILES folder.
4. **Run the Active Directory Users and Computers plug-in from the Control Panel's Administrative Tools folder.**
5. **Navigate to the user's icon, right-click it, and choose Properties.**
6. **On the Profiles tab, type the path to the user's profile folder, such as** \\server1\profiles\christine.
7. **Optionally, run the System control panel, click User Profiles, and copy a template profile to the user's profile folder to "preload" it.**

On a networked PC with roaming profiles enabled, Windows 2000 maintains a user-specific copy of NTUSER.DAT under C:\Documents and Settings\<username> just as it does with local profiles, but Windows 2000 keeps a copy on the network, too.

Here's what happens on the network:

1. When you log on, Windows 2000 checks for an NTUSER.DAT file on your local hard drive in C:\Documents and Settings\<username>, and it also checks for an NTUSER.DAT file in the user's profile directory on the server.
2. If either copy of NTUSER.DAT is newer than the other, Windows 2000 updates the older version and then starts up. Ditto with USRCLASS.DAT.

Windows 2000 performs a similar comparison with all the non-Registry user profile stuff, too, including the My Documents and My Pictures folders. If a file hasn't changed, Windows 2000 doesn't download it — and that's a good thing, because otherwise network performance would really suffer from all the unnecessary file transfers.

When you log off, Windows 2000 copies any changed profile settings back to your profile folder on the network, so the latest settings and documents are available next time you log on — wherever you log on.

What roams, what doesn't

By default, the folders History, Local Settings, Temp, and Temporary Internet Files do not "roam" with the user. They typically contain too much stuff; having these files roam would bog down the network. You can specify additional files that you'd like to exclude from the roaming profile. Run the Group Policy utility and modify the Exclude Directories in Roaming Profile policy. You can find it under User Configuration\Administrative Templates\System\Logon-Logoff. This policy modifies the text file C:\Documents and Settings\<username>\NTUSER.INI.

Mandatory profiles

You can replace the NTUSER.DAT file that resides in the user's network directory with an NTUSER.DAT file that you want to make mandatory and unchangeable.

1. **Create a roaming profile folder as you would normally.**
2. **Copy the NTUSER.DAT file you want to use into that folder.**
3. **Rename it NTUSER.MAN, and you've created a mandatory user profile.**

In the case of NTUSER.MAN, Windows 2000 never copies an NTUSER.DAT on the user's PC hard drive back to the network location, as it does with regular user profiles. Instead, Windows 2000 always uses the NTUSER.MAN file. It's as though you've made the file read-only.

If you're planning to use this feature, point a whole group of users to the same roaming profile folder, so you only have to manage one copy of NTUSER.MAN for the entire group. For example, you could make periodic changes to the mandatory profile by modifying the profile settings on a test PC, logging off, logging on again as an Administrator, copying the profile back up to the network location using the User Profiles tab on the System control panel, and renaming the file NTUSER.MAN.

Mandatory user profiles don't provide any control over the settings in the other Registry hives. You may be able to use group policies in combination with mandatory user profiles, but doing so creates a security environment that's so complex that not many organizations would want to manage it. So, organizations typically choose group policies to impose restrictions on users, rather than mandatory user profiles. However, if you want to freeze user settings for application programs and if those programs don't come with policy templates that let you use group policies to impose restrictions, then you may need to consider mandatory user profiles.

Managing profiles

On a Windows 2000 Professional machine, you manage user profiles with the Users and Passwords control panel described earlier in this chapter, and with the System control panel's User Profiles tab (see Figure 12-2). Use the latter to delete a user profile, copy a profile from one location to another (you can't use Windows Explorer for this task), and change the type of profile from local to roaming or vice versa.

If you want to change a roaming profile back to a nonroaming profile, or (for that matter) vice versa, run the System control panel's User Profiles tab and click the Change Type button to display the Change Profile Type dialog box (see Figure 12-3). If the "roaming profile" choice appears dimmed, as in the figure, then the user account is probably not a domain account — or no profile directory was set up for it.

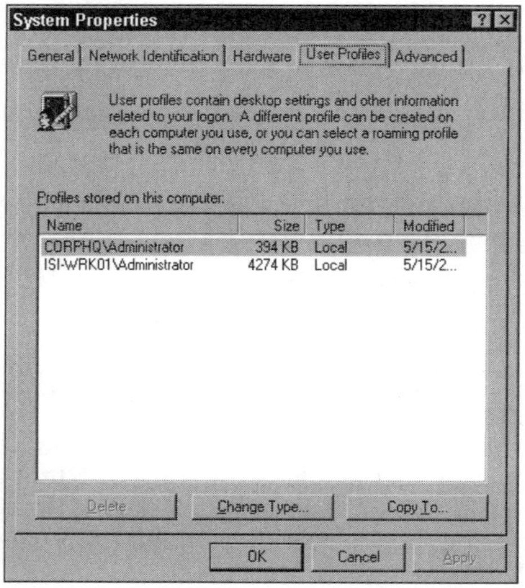

Figure 12-2: The System control panel's User Profiles tab.

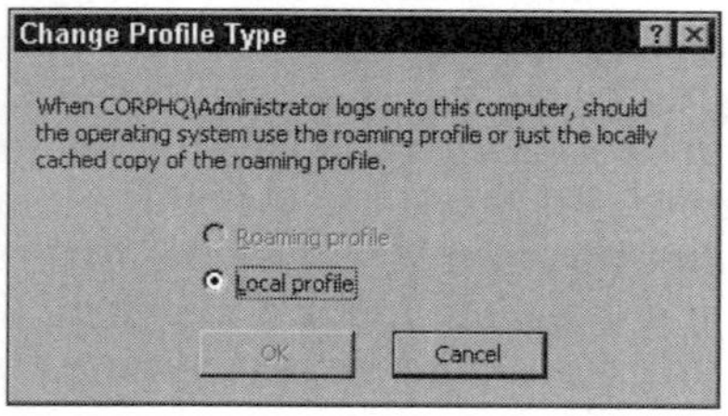

Figure 12-3: Changing a profile's type.

Folder redirection: An alternative to roaming profiles

Roaming user profiles are cool, but they can add a lot of traffic congestion to a busy network. Every time you log on to a particular network computer for the first time, all your roaming profile data flows across the wire. A good way to work around that problem is to use *folder redirection*. Files in redirected folders only travel across the wire if and when the user works with them.

You have to set up folder redirection on a Windows 2000 server machine, using the Group Policy tools. The process is pretty easy. You simply choose an organizational structure, such as a domain, and open the Group Policy editor for that structure. (I'm omitting the boring details; they won't be on Exam #70-210.) Then you navigate your way to a policy node named Folder Redirection. There, you can specify that (for example) when any domain user logs on, the user's My Documents folder doesn't live on the workstation hard drive, but rather on a network server — for example, in \\srv01\redirect\ *%username%*, where *%username%* is a variable corresponding to the user's logon name.

You can use folder redirection as a way of providing personal documents to users if you find that roaming profiles put too much traffic on the network.

Home folders

The *home folder* (or *home directory,* as we called it in Windows NT 4.0) is an alternative to the My Documents folder as a place for users to keep their data files.

Microsoft prefers that you use My Documents, but it continues to provide home folders — mainly for organizations that have used them in the past and are happy with them, or that have decided against roaming profiles for some reason.

Home folders typically live on a network server, where users can get to them from any workstation, although technically home folders can live on client PCs. Microsoft recommends putting them on an NTFS disk for the greater control over access permissions that such disks provide. Microsoft also suggests putting all home folders under one "umbrella" folder, which makes your server's file structure cleaner and easier to manage.

After the home folders are set up on the server, all you have to do at the user's workstation is run the Computer Management console, open Users and Groups, right-click the user name, choose Properties, and (on the Profile tab) point a drive letter with the home folder (see Figure 12-4). Users can then save their data files to that drive letter without worrying about specifying a long and involved network path.

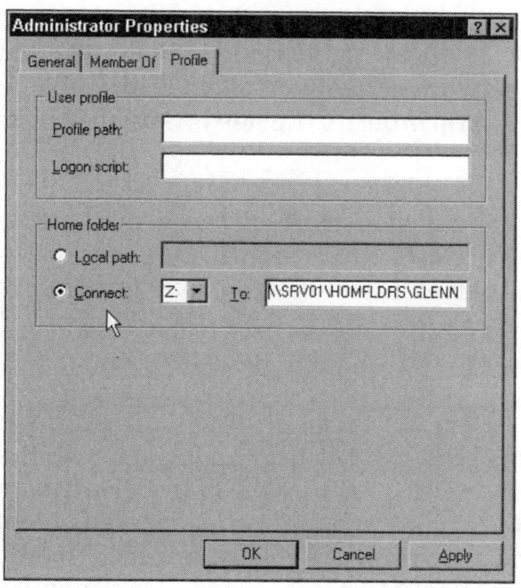

Figure 12-4: Pointing a drive letter at a home folder on a server.

Offline Files and Folders

Windows users have been able to "work offline" to some degree for quite a while now — the "Briefcase" concept debuted in Windows 95, as did offline printing — but Windows 2000 extends the capability and makes it more convenient for network users. (That convenience may not extend to network administrators, who must deal with the extra traffic burden that synchronization can bring!)

The venerable, little-used Briefcase is still present, by the way, and recommended for situations where you use a Zip disk or Direct Cable Connection (parallel or serial) to reconcile notebook files with those on a desktop machine. If you use a network connection to synchronize versions of files that you take away from the office, then Offline Files and Folders is the preferred choice.

The offline concept

Offline files and folders are similar in many ways to roaming user profiles. However, while roaming user profiles let you work with your settings and documents regardless of what PC you log onto, offline files and folders are intended to let you work with your network documents regardless of whether the network's available or not.

The basic concept is that administrators and, optionally, users can designate network files and folders to be *cached* (copied) to the local workstation. Why would users want to do this? If a network connection breaks, the affected user can keep working with the designated files and folders as if the network connection were still present — the view of the network stays the same, file and folder access permissions stay the same. (When the server is down, the user is working with the local copies, or "working offline," whether she knows it or not.) Then, when the network connection again is available, Windows can automatically update, or *synchronize,* the network copies of any changed files and folders.

Savvy network users have effectively performed this same function with critical documents well before Windows 2000's arrival, by periodically copying server-based files down to their workstations to protect against server unavailability, or to get ready for a road trip with their notebook PCs. Windows 2000 makes such manual "caching" unnecessary.

The synchronization can work in the opposite direction, too. If a user connects to the network and the network version of a file is newer than the user's local version, then Windows 2000 can download the network version to the user's PC. Also, if a user or administrator has marked an entire network folder to be made available offline, then any new files that others may have saved to that folder since Joe User last logged off will copy over to Joe's local PC at synchronize time, too (say, his next logon).

Setting up offline files and folders

As the offline files and folders feature involves network machines and local machines, you'd expect to have to do some configuration on servers as well as clients, and you'd be right.

Server-side setup

The first step in setting up offline folders is telling the server that you want them. That's a network administrator's job, and the tiny details are more important for the server exam than for this one. Suffice it to say here that you right-click the shared folder of interest, choose Sharing, click the Caching button, and check the box that reads Allow Caching of Files in This Shared Folder. You can also specify one of three settings: Automatic Caching For Documents (which caches all files in the folder as users open them); Manual Caching For Documents (which lets the user choose which files to make available offline); and Automatic Caching For Programs, for folders containing read-only applications that run from the server.

Client-side setup

On the client side (where you're running Windows 2000 Professional), you also have to enable the offline files and folders feature. You can do so two ways:

- Choose Tools⇨Folder Options.
- Choose Start⇨Settings⇨Control Panel and double-click Folder Options.

Either way, click the Offline Files tab to see a screen like the one in Figure 12-5.

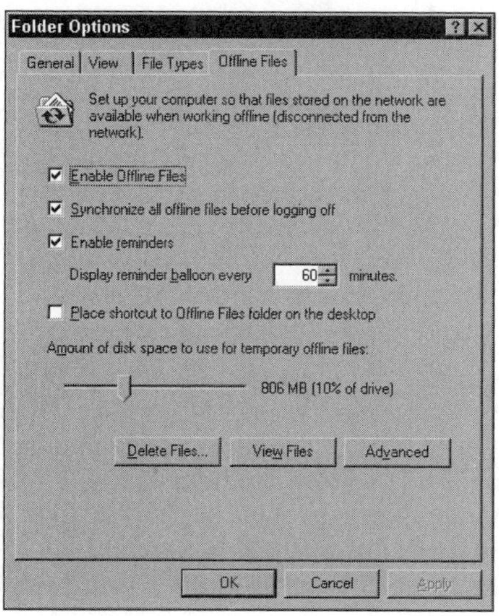

Figure 12-5: The Offline Files tab is one of two places you must visit.

Here are the things you should know about the Offline Files property sheet:

- Check Enable Offline Files to turn on the feature for the client PC.
- Checking Synchronize all offline files before logging off ensures that when you log off, your locally-cached files are completely up-to-date. This is "full" synchronization in Microspeak.

  If you clear this check box, Windows 2000 makes sure you have all the files you should have offline, but doesn't guarantee that they're the latest versions; this is the "quick" synchronization option. It's unclear to me why this feature appears both here and in Synchronization Manager (discussed in a minute), but it does.
- Enable reminders turns on the display of a Taskbar balloon when a network server is unavailable and you're working offline.
- The disk space slider specifies what percent of the drive you want to permit Windows 2000 to use for files that your network administrator wants you to have offline, but that you haven't specifically designated to be made available offline. (These are "temporary offline files" in Microsoft lingo.)
- The Delete Files button deletes the local, cached copy of offline files, but not the network copy.
- The Advanced button lets you designate how Windows 2000 behaves when different servers become unavailable.

  For example, you may want to "go offline" and continue working with locally-cached documents in most cases. But if a particular server goes down, you may not want to use in an offline manner the files that it shares — say, highly time-sensitive data such as stock quotes, which could do damage if they aren't current but appear to be so! You can specify normal behavior and a list of exceptions to achieve the desired configuration.

After you've set your preferences using Folder Options, you simply open My Documents or Windows Explorer, find the folder you want to make available offline, right-click it, and choose the menu option "Make Available Offline." If you've never made this folder available offline before, a wizard activates to walk you through the process. A dialog box appears saying "Synchronizing..." as Windows caches the network copy to your local disk.

Finally, you can go back at any time and modify your settings with something that Microsoft calls *Synchronization Manager* (although you'll never see that designation in the user interface). Get there one of two ways: Open My Computer or Explorer and choose Tools⇨Synchronize, or choose Start⇨Programs⇨Accessories⇨Synchronize. From the Items to Synchronize dialog box that appears, you can manually synchronize any offline files or folders, change certain of their synchronization settings by clicking the Properties button, or click Setup to display the Synchronization Settings dialog box as shown in Figure 12-6.

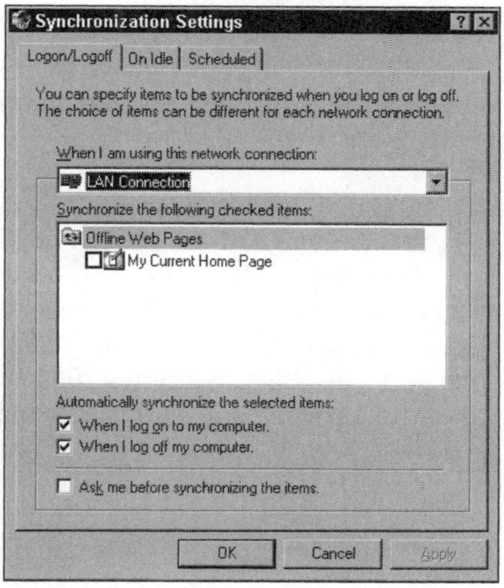

Figure 12-6: Yet more synchronization settings.

Here are a few notes regarding the Synchronization Settings dialog box:

- The Logon/Logoff tab lets you control which items synchronize at logon and/or logoff, and whether the user gets prompted before synchronizing. The behavior must be the same for any single network connection (LAN or dial-up).
- The On Idle tab lets you specify that Windows should synchronize offline files and folders after a period of inactivity, which you can define. You can also specify the synchronization repeat frequency for continued idle states, and whether to disable synchronization if your machine's running off a battery.
- The Scheduled tab lets you add or edit schedules for synchronization events ("sync this network connection every Friday at 1:00 am"). Scheduled jobs appear in the Control Panel's Scheduled Tasks folder.

Offline in practice: A mixed blessing

The first drawback to using offline files and folders is that they can dramatically increase network congestion. I've heard from a few corporate IS managers that the additional traffic from frequent offline file synchronization can bring a busy network to its little silicon knees.

The next drawback has to do with ease of use. The concept is that the offline files and folders feature works transparently. However:

- Someone has to set up the feature on each network server that shares folders containing files to be cached, as I explain in the previous section.
- Cases can often crop up in which the user must resolve a conflict and perform file reconciliation manually.

That last item deserves attention, as it may well appear on the exam. Suppose, for example, that Forsberg has designated a shared network file as cached, and Roy has done so, too. Forsberg undocks his notebook computer, goes on a trip, and makes some changes to the file. Roy undocks his notebook, also goes on a trip, and makes some changes of his own. Forsberg gets back to the office first, and hooks up to the LAN. Windows 2000 sees that his cached (local) copy is newer than the network copy, so synchronizes by copying the cached copy to the server. Roy then arrives at the office, docks his notebook, and — sacré Bleu, a dilemma! If Windows 2000 copies Roy's version to the server, it will overwrite Forsberg's changes. But if it *doesn't* copy Roy's version, then Roy's work never gets put up onto the server.

What happens in this situation is that Windows 2000 asks Roy to decide whether to nuke Forsberg's file, save Roy's file to the server under a different name, or do nothing. The second choice is usually the safest, but someone must then manually merge Forsberg's changes with Roy's to create a properly updated file that reflects both their work. Not exactly transparent.

Clearly, the offline files and folders feature works best if each user has his or her own data area on the server and only makes those files available offline. And yes, such an arrangement defeats the purpose of network file sharing to some extent! So the offline files and folders feature isn't as cool as it seems at first glance. (Learn it anyway.)

One final drawback: The offline files and folders feature only works on Microsoft networks, so Novell shops can't use it.

Windows Installer Service

Microsoft's published exam objectives specify that you be able to install applications onto a Windows 2000 Professional machine by using the Windows Installer service. Happily, that's about the easiest objective in the entire list! In general, all you need to do is double-click an MSI file — it doesn't get much simpler than that! (MSI files are associated in the Registry with MSIEXEC.EXE.) Alternatively, you can right-click an MSI file and choose Install from the context menu.

Another alternative if you need more control is to invoke the Microsoft Software Installer Executive, or MSIEXEC.EXE, at a command prompt or Run dialog box. For example, if H: is your local CD-ROM drive containing the Windows 2000 Professional CD, then this command installs the Windows 2000 Resource Kit Support Tools onto your machine:

```
MSIEXEC  /I  H:\SUPPORT\TOOLS\2000RKST.MSI
```

You may need to know some of the other MSIEXEC command-line qualifiers, so here are a few besides /I for Install:

- **/F** means "Fix" and has several variations, which you don't need to memorize.
- **/L** means "Log" and has several variations specifying just what exactly the log file should contain (again, don't memorize 'em). Note that Windows Installer logs significant events to the Application event log by default. You can view this log with Event Viewer.
- **/P** means "Patch" and modifies an existing administrative image, usually on a server, from which the application installs to client machines.
- **/X** means "eXtract," or uninstall.

Installing MSI packages from the Active Directory gets a bit more complex. For example, using Group Policies, you can specify that a particular application is to be *published* to users, that is, made available to any user who wants it. Such an application appears in users' Add/Remove Programs control panel. Or, you can specify that the application is to be *assigned* to a particular user or computer, that is, installed onto the client machine in such a way that it can't easily be removed. However, beyond understanding these terms, you don't need to master the intricacies of assigning and publishing applications (at least, not for this exam!).

The impact of Windows Installer on the Add/Remove Programs wizard is significant for two reasons:

- The wizard lets users "repair" an installation that may be damaged in some way.

  Select the program from the list, click the Support link, and you usually see the repair option. This option is a graphical front end to the MSIEXEC /F command.
- The wizard performs a more complete "uninstall" because the MSI file lets the wizard see exactly what needs to be removed — including Registry entries, shortcuts, the whole ball of wax.

  This option is a graphical front end to the MSIEXEC /X command.

Incidentally, the exam may expect you to know that MSIEXEC shows up as a service named "Windows Installer" in the list that you can display via the Services icon in the Administrative Tools folder.

Prep Test

1 **In the lingo of Active Directory and Windows Installer, what does it mean to publish an application to a computer?**

A ❍ To make that application available to all users on the computer

B ❍ To make that application available to the currently logged-on user on the computer

C ❍ To initiate an automatic installation of the application the next time the computer is rebooted

D ❍ Nothing

2 **Lloyd is a tech support guy for your non-profit organization. As such, he hops around from one PC to another on a regular basis. Often, he has to log on to the Windows 2000 domain using his own account, so that he can run special tools, such as various troubleshooting tools, consult his own private online documentation, log trouble calls, and so forth. You have configured Lloyd with a roaming user profile.**

Lloyd complains to you that his profile takes a while to download from the network when he logs on at a machine that is not his own. He also tells you that he doesn't really use his Favorites folder when away from his usual PC. How would you modify Lloyd's profile behavior to exclude the Favorites folder from roaming? (Choose the best answer.)

A ❍ Modify the list of roaming folders in the Registry.

B ❍ Edit the file NTUSER.DAT in Lloyd's profile folder.

C ❍ Edit the file NTUSER.INI in Lloyd's profile folder.

D ❍ Set Favorites as an exclusion in the Local Group Policy editor.

3 **You set up roaming user profiles, but you find that network performance has become unacceptably slow. What other options does Windows 2000 Professional give you for providing users with network-based access to documents and settings, without imposing as much of a traffic burden on the network infrastructure? (Choose all that apply.)**

A ❑ Home folders

B ❑ Redirected folders

C ❑ Mandatory profiles

D ❑ Dynamic disks

4 Which of the following file names contains a mandatory user profile? (Choose one.)

A ❍ NTUSERMAN.DAT

B ❍ NTUSER.MAN

C ❍ USER.MAN

D ❍ PROFILE.MAN

5 Bertram calls you for help in troubleshooting user profiles on his machine. When you arrive at his side and take over the keyboard after he logs on, you notice that the `C:\Documents and Settings` **folder does not exist. Bertram mentions that he upgraded to Windows 2000 Professional from Windows NT 4.0 Workstation. Where are Bertram's profiles? (Choose the best answer.)**

A ❍ `C:\WINNT`

B ❍ `C:\WINNT\PROFILES`

C ❍ `C:\PROFILES`

D ❍ `C:\WINNT\SYSTEM32\PROFILES`

6 You decide to implement offline files on your Windows 2000 Professional PC. How can you make sure that your locally cached versions are always in full synchronization with the network versions of your offline files? (Choose the best answer.)

A ❍ In the Folder Options control panel's Offline Files tab, check the box labeled Synchronize All Offline Files Before Logging Off.

B ❍ In the Folder Options control panel's Offline Files tab, check the box labeled Synchronize All Offline Files Before Logging On.

C ❍ In the Synchronization Manager's General tab, check the box labeled Synchronize All Offline Files Before Logging Off.

D ❍ This setting is only available on a Windows 2000 Server PC and must be set by an administrator.

7 You are preparing a master disk image for the cloning and deployment of Windows 2000 Professional. Your plan is to use the Sysprep utility in combination with a disk cloning utility. When you configure the machine, you do so while logged on as the Administrator. You install applications, configure desktop shortcuts, and tailor the Start menu.

When you perform a small-scale test deployment, you discover that when users log on with their own network accounts, they don't see the tailoring that you performed. What can you do to fix this problem before you deploy Windows 2000 to the entire department? (Choose the best answer.)

A ❍ Using the User Profiles control panel, copy the Administrator's user profile to the Default User profile.

B ❍ Using the System control panel, copy the Administrator's user profile to the Default User profile.

C ❍ Using the System control panel, copy the Administrator's user profile to the All Users profile.

D ❍ Create a home directory on the network server.

8. **A software vendor advises you that you must modify the access control list for a specific Registry key in order for that vendor's application to work properly under Windows 2000. Which of the following Registry tools should you use to make the modification?**

A ❍ REGEDT32.EXE

B ❍ REGEDIT32.EXE

C ❍ REGEDIT.EXE

D ❍ REGEDIT.MSC

Answers

1 **D.** Tricky question, this. The statement means nothing because you can't publish an application to a computer; you can only publish applications to users. You can, however, assign applications to computers — or to users, as you choose. See "Windows Installer Service."

2 **D.** Choice C isn't as good an answer, because whenever you have a choice between using a management console or editing a text file (or the Registry) directly, you should use the console for safety and reliability. Note that you'd use the Local Group Policy tool (GPEDIT.MSC) here, rather than a domain-based policy, because you only want to change the behavior for Lloyd's account. See "What roams, what doesn't."

3 **A** and **B.** Both home folders and redirected folders permit users to keep documents on network servers without moving them across the wire unless users need them. Microsoft would prefer that you use folder redirection, which is a component of IntelliMirror, because it's transparent and makes use of the My Documents and My Pictures desktop elements. See "Folder redirection: An alternative to roaming profiles" and "Home folders."

4 **B.** One more fact to memorize. See "Mandatory profiles."

5 **B.** Microsoft made a command decision to leave profiles in its Windows NT 4.0 location if a user upgrades to Windows 2000 Professional from NT. The idea is that one or more applications may expect to see profile data in the old location. See "User Profiles."

6 **A.** If you clear the check box, then you are sure to have all your files on the local disk, but you can't be sure that they're all up-to-date. See "Setting up offline files and folders."

7 **B.** Choice B is the best answer. But it isn't perfect. For example, the Administrator's profile may contain some programs that others can't execute because of user rights issues. See "User Profiles."

8 **A.** REGEDT32.EXE is the tool that understands NT-style security; REGEDIT.EXE is best for searching the Registry. The Registry Editors are not management consoles and so don't have the suffix MSC. See "Two editing tools."

Chapter 13

Dial-Up Networking and Remote Access

Exam Objectives

- Creating a dial-up connection to connect to a remote access server
- Connecting to computers by using a virtual private network (VPN) connection
- Connecting to the Internet by using dial-up networking
- Configuring and troubleshooting Internet Connection Sharing

Setting up a dial-up connection was always a bit of a headache in Windows NT Workstation 4.0. Windows 98 handled the task more intuitively, but even there, creating a "DUN connectoid" was still fraught with opportunity for error and confusion. Even the terminology was weird (whoever came up with the word "connectoid"?).

Microsoft has revamped the dial-up networking user interface in Windows 2000 in an effort to make creating a connection more straightforward. For example, the company has lumped dial-up connections into the same folder as LAN and WAN connections, reinforcing the concept that a modem works just like a slow network adapter. The Make New Connection wizard is significantly more capable, versatile, and (therefore) useful. You can create secure computer-to-computer dial-up links using the Internet as a communications medium. And you can now set up a single workstation computer so that it shares its Internet connection with other connected computers — something that you could also do with Windows 98 Second Edition if you read all the tech notes ahead of time and the wind was blowing just right that day.

Remote network access is a traditional favorite topic of Microsoft workstation exams, so (bad news coming) you should probably memorize just about everything in this chapter. As usual, if you can also practice building remote links in real life, so much the better; if not, please read this chapter twice, and when you're done, read it again.

Quick Assessment

Creating a dial-up connection to connect to a remote access server

1 If you're creating a link to a remote network and you want to use encryption for the entire communications session, the protocols that you can use are ______, ______, and ______.

2 When you create a link to a remote computer, you can specify whether the link should be available to you only, or to ______.

3 The precise name of the folder where all dial-up connections reside is ______.

Connecting to computers by using a virtual private network (VPN) connection

4 Create a VPN connection by choosing the option named "Connect to a ______ network through the Internet."

5 The two communications protocols you can use with VPN links are ______ and ______.

Connecting to the Internet by using dial-up networking

6 (True/False) A connection that links to the Internet must have the Client for Microsoft Networks component installed and checked on the connection's Network property sheet.

7 When you choose to "Dial up to the Internet" in the Network Connection wizard, that wizard hands you off to another program named ______.

8 You connect to two different ISPs with different modem error control requirements, so you must modify the ______ tab on the connection icons' property sheets.

Configuring and troubleshooting Internet Connection Sharing

9 You should not use Internet Connection Sharing on a network that also has one or more PCs running ______ or ______.

10 When you enable ICS on a PC, Windows 2000 assigns it the IP address ______.

Answers

1 *MS-CHAP, MS-CHAPv2, and EAP/TLS.* The section "Security tab" in this chapter helps explain the alphanumeric gobbledygook.

2 *All users of the PC.* The section "Creating a connection" offers this tidbit and many others.

3 *Network and Dial-Up Connections.* This is different from previous Windows versions. See the "Central control" section.

4 *Private.* Or, the "P" in "VPN." See "Setting up a VPN link" in this chapter.

5 *PPTP, L2TP.* If this alphabet soup tastes strange, read "VPN protocols."

6 *False.* The Internet isn't a Microsoft network (at least not yet). See "Networking tab" for more.

7 *Internet Connection wizard.* Sort of a wizard baton race. "Creating a connection" is worth your inspection.

8 *General.* Then you click the "Configure" button. See the section titled "General tab" for other "generalities."

9 *Windows 2000 domain controller, DNS server, DHCP server, TCP/IP with a static IP address.* If you didn't get two out of these four possibilities, read the "Internet Connection Sharing" section.

10 *192.168.0.1.* If you got this difficult question right, you don't need to read the "Internet Connection Sharing" section. In fact, you should probably just stop reading right here and take the exam tomorrow.

Configuring for Remote Access

This "get ready" section discusses hardware, software, and configuration preparations for remote access with dial-up connections.

Hardware prep

If you're looking to make connections to remote computers, you need some sort of hardware connection to those computers. Configuring your PC for remote access involves one or more of the following:

- A modem and phone line
- An ISDN (Integrated Services Digital Network) adapter and ISDN phone line
- A network interface card (NIC) and connection to a Local Area Network (LAN)
- A parallel or serial cable configured for bidirectional communication, or an infrared port (for Direct Cable Connection, a modemless approach)

Software prep

On the software side, the components that you need depend on the kind of system you're connecting to. For example:

- If you need to connect to the Internet with a Web browser, all you need is the TCP/IP protocol. You don't need a networking client, such as the Client for Microsoft Networks. However, you do need a Web browser. Internet Explorer 5 comes with Windows 2000, and you can add other browsers to your system as well.
- If you need to connect to a corporate network, then you need a transport protocol (the same as your corporate network uses) plus a networking client.
- If you need to share resources with the computer or computers you're connecting to, then you need the File and Printer Sharing for Microsoft Networks service.

Typically, the Network Connection wizard handles these details for you when you first create the connection. You may need to make some manual changes, however, if you create a new connection by copying and renaming an existing one.

Configuration prep

You should configure Windows 2000 properly for your *dialing location* or locations. You normally perform this task when adding a modem driver via the Modems control panel or the Add New Hardware wizard, but you need to come back to it any time your dialing properties change, or if you want to add new dialing locations.

To configure dialing location information, open the Phone and Modem Options control panel and click the Dialing Rules tab. Click on the location of interest (only one may appear) and click the Edit button. A dialog box similar to Figure 13-1 appears.

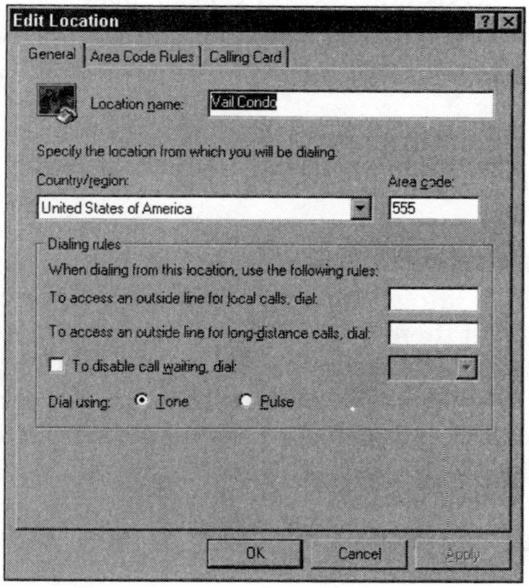

Figure 13-1: The Edit Location box lets you set dial-out options.

Here's what you need to remember about dialing rules:

- Change dialing rules whenever you move your PC to a new location that has different ones (for example, a different area code, which you may find yourself in after a crosstown relocation).
- Dialing rules are available to all Windows applications that support TAPI (Telephony Application Program Interface). Other TAPI-compliant programs are Outlook Express and MSN (Microsoft Network).
- Dialing rules are *global*. That is, if you change the location in the Phone and Modem Options control panel, the dialing rules change for all dial-up connections that you may have created.

- On a location-by-location basis, you can specify whether Windows 2000 needs to dial an area code for local calls (an increasingly common situation) via the Area Code Rules tab.
- On a location-by-location basis, you can specify calling card information via the Calling Card tab.

Network and Dial-Up Connections: First Principles

The Network and Dial-Up Connections software (we used to call it DUN, for Dial-Up Networking, or RAS, for Remote Access Services) lets you connect a Windows 2000 PC to a remote computer or to a remote network over a telephone line (be it regular analog or ISDN) or cable, or infrared link.

Central control

In Windows 2000, Microsoft decided to lump all connections — local and remote, regardless of media — into a single folder, which I abbreviate henceforth as NDUC (ENN-duck). Get there by choosing Start⇨Programs⇨Accessories⇨Communications⇨Network and Dial-Up Connections, or (more quickly) by choosing Start⇨Settings⇨Network and Dial-Up Connections, or (most quickly) by right-clicking My Network Places and choosing Properties. You see a window that looks something like the one in Figure 13-2. No more bouncing around between a Dial-Up Networking folder and a Network control panel; all connection settings are here in one place.

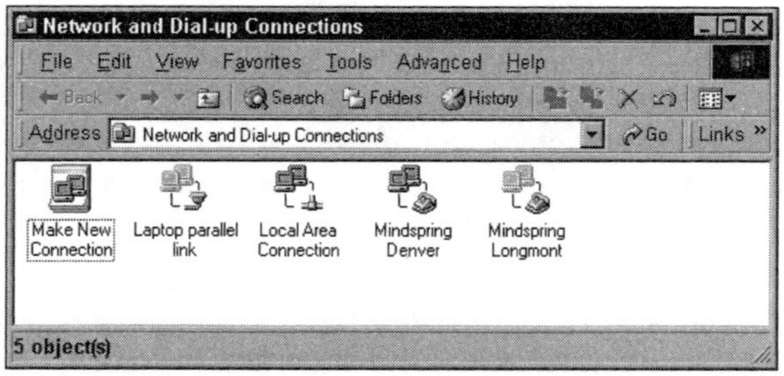

Figure 13-2: The Windows 2000 connectivity folder.

NDUC is where you configure both inbound and outbound connections, for Windows 2000 Professional can host incoming sessions as well as dial out to other networks.

The NDUC folder, which replaces the Network control panel in earlier versions of Windows, is very "deep" — that is, it has lots of settings and options. Thankfully, Microsoft has provided a Make New Connection wizard that gets you through most of the initial configuration.

Also, certain aspects of this folder's setup are automatic. For example, you can't manually create an icon for a LAN connection; Windows 2000 creates one for you automagically, when it detects a network interface card. (Windows 2000 does *not* automatically create an icon for a dial-up connection if the operating system detects a modem, however, for the good reason that a human being must supply a phone number to create a dial-up link.)

Why create a connection?

You would create an NDUC link in the following situations:

- Employees need Internet access from the workplace, but your organization doesn't have a constant Internet connection.
- Employees in your organization travel and need to be able to "dial in" to the LAN at headquarters.
- Employees in your organization travel and need to be able to connect to the Internet (for example, to check e-mail).
- Your organization has telecommuters who need to be able to "dial in" to a single PC at the office.
- You have a notebook PC with no network card, and you need to exchange files with a desktop PC.
- You're planning to take an MCSE test and you decide to practice with the software. (Smart.)

Connection independence

With some exceptions (such as dialing rules, rules for how Windows "fills in" partial DNS names, and so on), each connection that you create has its own communications settings. That is, one connection can have a different set of DNS server addresses on its TCP/IP property sheet than another connection. (I know, it sounds obvious, but it didn't work that way in Windows 95!) Generally, if a given setting isn't connection-specific but instead is global, the relevant property sheet advises you of the fact.

Creating a connection

A *connectoid* is Microspeak for a connection icon. You create connectoids by using the Network Connection wizard in the Network and Dial-Up Connections (NDUC, my abbreviation not Microsoft's) virtual folder, as Lab 13-1 demonstrates. You can create as many connections as you want; each time you create a new connection, a new connectoid appears in the NDUC folder.

The procedure for creating a dial-up connection is similar whether you're creating a "regular" dial-up link, a virtual private network link, or a direct cable connection. Lab 13-1 demonstrates the procedure for a plain vanilla modem link and assumes that you've installed a modem.

Lab 13-1 Creating a Connectoid

1. **Right-click My Network Places and choose Properties.**
2. **Double-click the Make New Connection icon.**

   An explanatory screen appears. Note its title, Network Connection Wizard. The exam may refer to this program as the "Network Connection Wizard" *or* as the "Make New Connection" wizard; they mean the same thing. (User interface screwup #1,274.)
3. **Click Next to get past the verbiage.**

   The screen shown in Figure 13-3 appears.

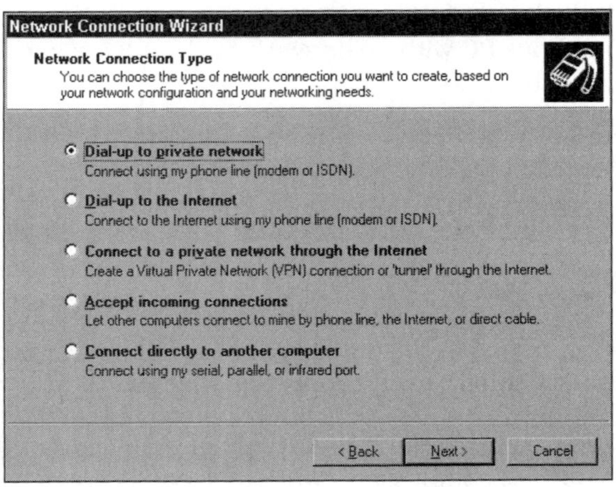

Figure 13-3: You can create just about any kind of connection here.

4. **Click the Dial-Up To Private Network button and click Next.**

   If you choose Dial-Up To The Internet, then Windows 2000 hands you off to the old *Internet Connection Wizard*, which is largely the same as it was in earlier Windows versions. You can create a new ISP account, move an existing account's settings to this PC, or specify details for a LAN-based Internet connection.

5. **If you have more than one dial-up device, choose the one you want for this connection and click Next.**
6. **Enter a phone number to dial and click the check box if you want this connection to follow the dialing rules you set in the Phone and Modem Options control panel. Click Next.**
7. **Specify whether you want all users of this PC to have access to the connection, or only you. Click Next.**
8. **Type a name for the new connection. Check the check box if you want Windows to add a shortcut icon to your desktop.**
9. **Click Finish and marvel as Windows creates a new icon in the Network and Dial-Up Connections folder.**

   You're not really finished, of course. You probably need to configure your network protocol settings and modem settings, for example. The procedures for doing all of that appear in the next section.

Anatomy of a Connection

The Make New Connection wizard automates only a fairly small part of the connection creation procedure, leaving a lot of settings for you to configure manually after the wizard has left the scene in a flash of orange smoke. Access these settings by right-clicking your freshly minted "connectoid" and choosing Properties. The ensuing dialog box has five tabs, redesigned somewhat from earlier Windows versions:

- **General:** Settable options.
- **Options:** General settings. (Sorry, but these generic names are so lame.)
- **Security:** Authentication options.
- **Networking:** Network modules, bindings, and data required for this link.
- **Sharing:** Whether, and how, to implement Internet Connection Sharing (ICS).

The following sections elaborate on each tabbed dialog box.

General tab

The General tab (see Figure 13-4) and the Options tab are just two dialog boxes full of settings that Microsoft couldn't figure out how to categorize.

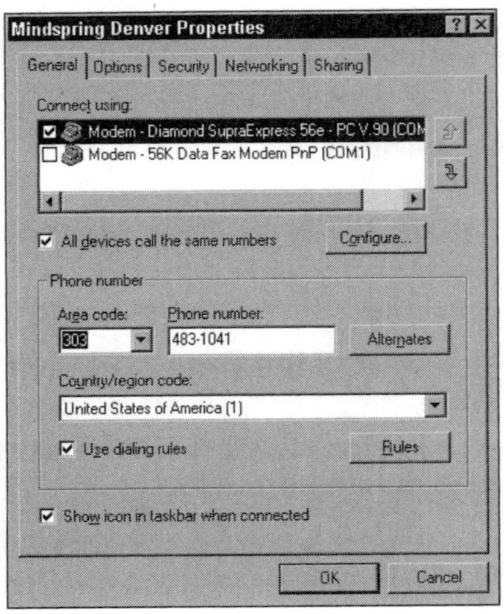

Figure 13-4: The General tab.

Notice that you can specify more than one hardware device for the connection. You could use two modems to create a *multilink* connection, by checking both of them in this dialog box. (Other multilink settings, however, live on the Options tab — go figure.) If the two modems should both call the same phone number, click the All Devices Call the Same Numbers check box. Otherwise, clear the check box, and enter the appropriate phone number for each modem by highlighting the modem and filling in the Phone Number fields.

Speaking of the Phone Number area, you can also specify whether the connection should follow your global dialing rules, and whether you want to key in one or more alternate phone numbers in case the first number is busy.

You can modify several modem settings by clicking the Configure button. (Again, in a multilink setup, click the modem of interest first and then click Configure.) The settings that you make sound like the same ones that you set in the Phone and Modem Options control panel, but these settings apply only to the connection icon that you're configuring. That is, they're local rather than global. You can tailor them to the characteristics of the servers you're dialing up. For example, one information service may support error correction, while another may not. These settings include:

- Maximum speed, in bits/second
- Hardware flow control (on or off)
- Modem error control (on or off)
- Modem compression (on or off)
- Whether to show a terminal window before making connection
- Run a script before dialing
- Modem speaker (on or off)

After you create a connectoid, if you later make a change to the Phone and Modem Options control panel, don't assume that that change automatically propagates to your NDUC icons. Some changes do, but most don't. Verify the change by checking the NDUC icon properties, and make the change there again, if necessary.

Options tab

Whatever miscellany didn't fit on the General tab, Microsoft put on the Options tab (see Figure 13-5). This section runs through the options, which are *highly likely to be on the exam.*

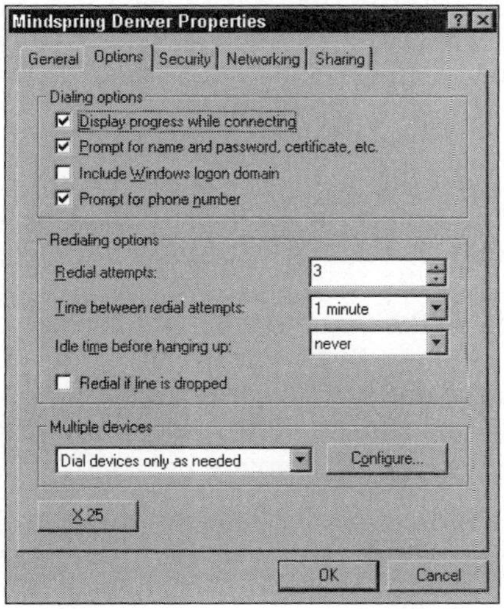

Figure 13-5: The Options tab.

"Prompt for name and password, certificate, etc." is an important setting. If you clear this check box, Windows won't give you the chance to enter a username or password the next time you run it (see Figure 13-6). Windows just assumes the previous settings you used, or pulls your authentication data from a smart card reader if you have one. Check this option if you want to ensure maximum security in case someone steals the PC.

"Include Windows logon domain" lets you choose a domain if you're also prompting for username and password. Use this if you're dialing into a Microsoft network and you want users to be able to choose different domains into which to log on. Clear it if you're dialing into an ISP for Internet access.

"Prompt for phone number" is mighty handy for notebook users in that it lets them choose a different phone number and/or dialing location before making the connection.

Figure 13-6: You can set Windows to display this dialog box or to bypass it.

Redialing options are self-explanatory so I will not explan them. However, it may be worth knowing that Internet Explorer overrides the connectoid's redial settings with its own redial settings, which you reach via the Internet Options control panel. (Microsoft, your slip is showing.)

TIP

If you want Internet Explorer to use the modem to automatically connect you to the Internet, you can make that setting in the Internet control panel's Connection tab. (Outlook Express shares that setting, by the way.)

If you selected multiple devices on the General tab, then you can configure the multilink connection. If you choose Dial Devices Only As Needed, then you can click the Configure button and set your BAP and BACP options (see Figure 13-7). Bandwidth Allocation Protocol (BAP) and Bandwidth Allocation Control Protocol (BACP) let you save cash if you're paying by the minute.

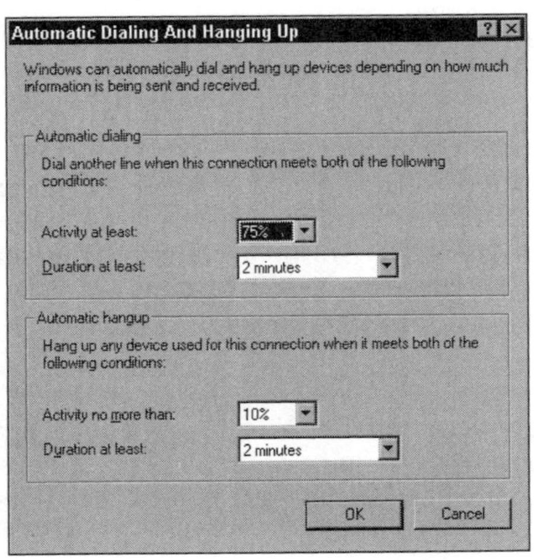

Figure 13-7: Windows can dynamically add or drop multilink devices as needed.

Security tab

The Security tab (see Figure 13-8) lets you specify how Windows 2000 should handle the authentication, or logon, phase of the connection.

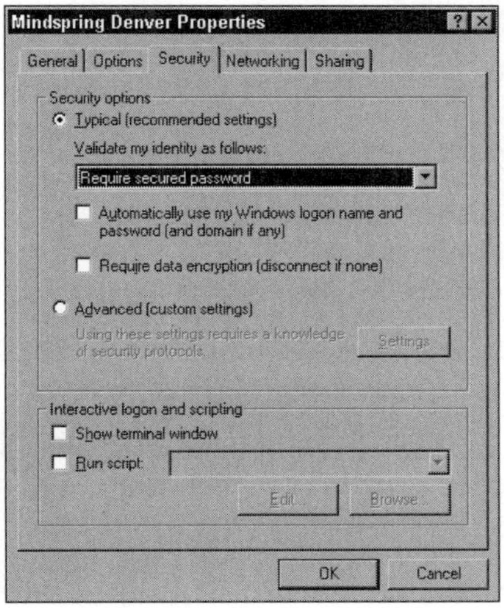

Figure 13-8: The Security tab.

If you choose Allow Unsecured Password in the Security options part of the dialog box, then the other two settings just below the list box appear grayed-out, as they are irrelevant. (Many ISPs require unsecured passwords, rendering this dialog box very simple for those kinds of links.) If you choose Require Secured Password, which only lets you make a connection if the remote computer also supports encrypted passwords, then you can set both of these settings. If you choose Use Smart Card, you can set the data encryption check box only.

- The setting "Automatically use my Windows logon name and password (and domain if any)" is appropriate if you're dialing into a Microsoft network. Your domain user name and password will authenticate you to the remote server.
- The Require data encryption (disconnect if none) check box means that if the remote computer supports Data Encryption Standard, or DES, then the entire communications session is encrypted and secure. The protocols that support encryption are MS-CHAP, MS-CHAPv2, and EAP/TLS; see below for more on this acronymania.

For organizations with very specific security requirements, the Advanced (Custom Settings) radio button leads to the dialog box in Figure 13-9.

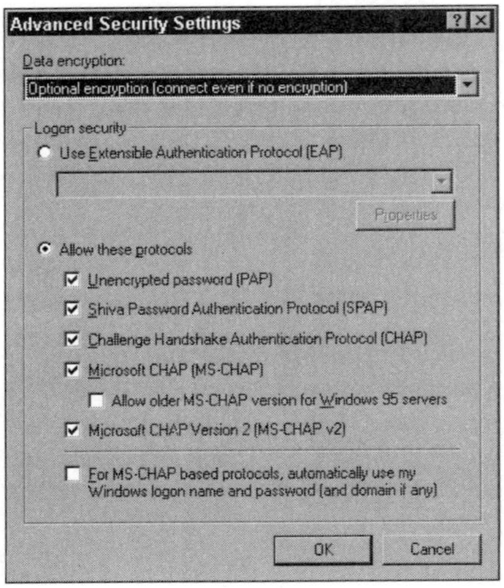

Figure 13-9: Getting secure, in great detail.

The top of the dialog box lets you choose one of three data encryption settings that apply to the entire communications session: require encryption, use it if it's available, or require that it *not* be used.

The Logon Security area throws a lot of alphabet soup at you. Here's what you need to know about logon authentication protocols. It's awfully dry, I know, but you should just memorize all this stuff:

- **PAP (Password Authentication Protocol)** uses no password encryption and may be required for dialing up non-Windows systems.
- **MS-CHAP (MicroSoft Challenge-Handshake Authentication Protocol)** works with Windows 9*x* and NT 4. It authenticates the client and uses one-way encryption.
- **MS-CHAPv2** is another Microsoft protocol; this extension of MS-CHAP authenticates both client and server.
- **SPAP (Shiva Password Authentication Protocol)** is used for dialing into and out of Shiva (that's a brand name) communication products. It doesn't support data encryption.
- **EAP (Extensible Authentication Protocol)** is an extension to PPP and evolved to support smart cards and other related devices. With EAP, client and server negotiate an authentication method — such as Transport Level Security (TLS), a smart card authentication standard.

INSTANT ANSWER

If you're setting up a smart card, when you choose EAP on the Advanced Security Settings dialog box, you must also choose Smart Card Or Other Certificate from the drop-down list; that's the TLS part. Also notice that as soon as you choose EAP, the other options — PAP, SPAP, MS-CHAP, and so on — aren't available. If you see a question that asks you which settings you must make on this dialog box, EAP is all the alphabet soup you need!

Networking tab

After the connection is made, your computer can communicate over the modem in exactly the same ways that it communicates over a NIC: Sending and receiving TCP/IP packets, NetBEUI packets, IPX/SPX packets, and so on. Your network link is just a communications device that connects to a cable — never mind that for a modem, the communications device is slow, and the cable is very long. (This method of networking goes by the moniker *remote node,* as opposed to *remote control,* in which keyboard, mouse, and display data travel the phone lines.) Figure 13-10 shows the Networking tab of a dial-up connection's property sheet.

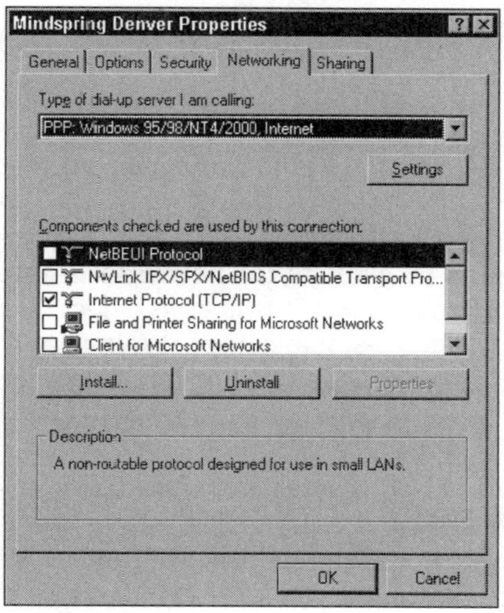

Figure 13-10: The Networking tab.

Connection protocols

The first decision you must make is the "Type of Dial-Up Server I Am Calling" at the top of the Networking tab. This setting is actually something called a *connection protocol,* or *communications protocol.* It's basically an extra network protocol that you need for dial-up lines, but that you don't need for hardwired LAN links.

The choice you make for your connection protocol is determined by the kind of computer (server) you're dialing into. Choose one that the server doesn't support, and you won't connect.

- **PPP:** Point-to-Point Protocol is the default choice for dial-up connections because it's the most reliable, secure, and efficient connection protocol. Unlike SLIP, PPP supports error checking. It works with NetBEUI, IPX/SPX, and TCP/IP network protocols.

- **SLIP:** This is a UNIX server running Serial Line Interface Protocol. SLIP is old, slow, and a bad choice unless you're calling up an old, slow UNIX server that doesn't work with PPP. No error correction, no encrypted passwords, no automatic IP address assignment.

Network bindings and protocol settings

You create and destroy *bindings* on this tab by checking and clearing check boxes in the central scrolling list (a much simpler way to do it than on the Network control panel of previous Windows versions, by the way — kudos to Microsoft on this one). A binding is nothing more than an active connection between two different layers of network software: for example, between a network interface adapter (modem) and any installed network protocols (such as TCP/IP), or between a protocol and a service (such as File and Printer Sharing for Microsoft Networks).

One way to improve a connection's logon speed is to uncheck the protocols, clients, and services you know you won't use over a given connection. Rule to live by: Activate only one network protocol for any given connectoid.

You can configure each active (checked) network protocol, service, or client for this specific dial-up connection by clicking the network component in the list and then clicking the Properties button. This is convenient. Some ISPs (Internet Service Providers), for example, may support dynamic IP address assignment via DHCP or some similar mechanism; others may require you to set up a static IP address.

Much of the time, especially with a PPP connection protocol, you'll choose "Obtain an IP address automatically" and "Obtain DNS server address automatically," because most ISPs and TCP/IP hosts provide this information automatically after you connect. However, you have the flexibility to "hard-code" specific IP addresses for your computer, for multiple DNS servers, and for multiple WINS servers, via the Advanced button on the TCP/IP configuration property sheet.

Note that if you're connecting to the Internet to browse the Web, you use domain names, so you don't need a WINS server.

The upper check box on the General tab of the TCP/IP Advanced settings property sheet, "Use default gateway on remote network," tells Windows 2000 not to use the default gateway you may have configured on your local TCP/IP LAN, if both it and your dial-up connection are live. As with the check box "Use IP header compression," which improves performance, you normally leave this option checked.

It's highly likely that the exam will ask you about protecting the security of a dial-up connection. Disabling the binding to File and Printer Sharing for Microsoft Networks is one way to do that, as you don't want other people on the remote network or computer to see, read, modify, or even delete resources that you've shared on your PC. You would also disable this binding if you wanted to create an incoming connection on a PC that should only act as a gateway to a network, but that should not share any of its own resources to users dialing in.

Sharing tab

Here's where you set up Internet Connection Sharing, which is important enough to warrant its own section — coming up next.

Internet Connection Sharing

If you create an Internet link (see "Creating a connection" earlier in this chapter) and you want to share that link with other computers on the same local area network, you can now do so, with some significant limitations. For example, the Windows 2000 PC you configure to share an Internet connection must be the only computer on the network that provides an Internet gateway.

Internet Connection Sharing (ICS) made its debut in Windows 98 Second Edition, and it works similarly in Windows 2000. (You may also see the acronym NAT, for Network Address Translation, used in the context of ICS. NAT is the Windows 2000 Server service that provides ICS-type capabilities for larger networks.)

Here's what you must know for the exam:

- Enable the feature by checking the Enable Internet Connection Sharing for this connection box on the Sharing tab of the connection's property sheet (see Figure 13-11). You must be an Administrator to do this.
- If your connection isn't an "always-on" type, then you can check Enable on-demand dialing so that your PC calls up the ISP when any networked PC tries to access the Internet.
- This feature is for SOHO (Small Office/Home Office) applications.

  Microsoft warns against using it on networks that have Windows 2000 Server domain controllers, DHCP servers, DNS servers, or any computers with static IP addresses. Such networks should use NAT instead of ICS.

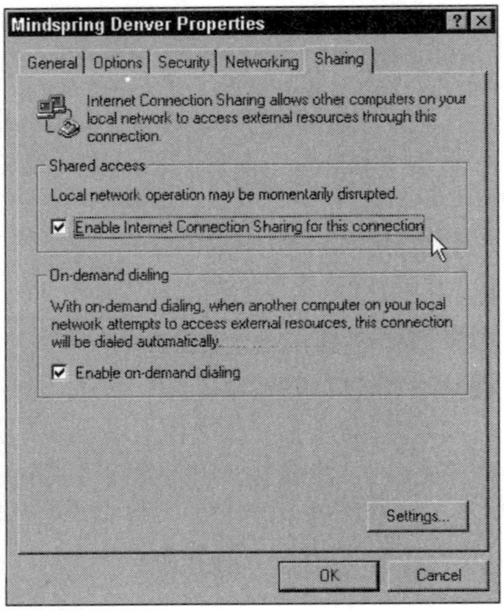

Figure 13-11: Set up your ICS server machine here.

- When you create a shared Internet connection, Windows 2000 assigns your PC network card a static IP address (192.168.0.1, subnet mask 255.255.255.0), and all present TCP/IP connections between your PC and other network PCs are lost.
- Other computers on the network that will use the ICS link must be set up to obtain IP addresses automatically on their TCP/IP property sheet.

  The PC you're configuring to connect to the Internet effectively becomes a DHCP server, allocating IP addresses to other PCs on the local network.
- Those other computers must also configure their Internet Options control panel's Connection tab to never dial a connection; to automatically detect LAN settings; to use an automatic configuration script; and to use a proxy server.

Creating Inbound Connections

The Network and Dial-Up Connections folder also contains icons for any inbound connections you may want to create. Lab 13-2 goes through the steps.

Lab 13-2 Creating an Inbound Connection

1. **Log in as Administrator and start the Make New Connection wizard as usual.**
2. **Choose Accept Incoming Connections on the Network Connection Type screen.**
3. **Choose the device (modem and parallel port are the usual choices) and configure it, if you want, by clicking the Properties button.**
4. **Tell Windows to accept incoming VPN connections, as long as your computer has a unique Internet domain name or IP address.**
5. **Specify who can have access to this inbound connection, and set *call-back* options for each user.**

   Callback simply means that your computer authenticates the incoming caller, hangs up, and calls him back at a predefined phone number. This method increases security and localizes long distance or other carrier charges.
6. **Select the network components that you need for the inbound connection.**

   Choose only the minimum components (protocols, services, and clients) necessary to provide the required connectivity.
7. **Name your connection, and you're done.**

Virtual Private Networking

One of the nifty features that Windows 2000 offers is *Virtual Private Networking,* or *VPN* for short. VPN is a private network link that isn't really private and doesn't use a normal network connection (hence the "virtual"). VPN creates a secure tunnel through an intermediary network, such as the public Internet, through which two computers can communicate privately and securely.

Think of VPN as using the Internet as the communications medium instead of a traditional web of leased lines and Wide Area Network (WAN) carriers. The speed of a VPN is always subject to the speed of the various intervening Internet links, but if that's not a big deal, then a VPN can save a company some money.

VPN protocols

The protocols that VPNs use are *PPTP,* or *Point-to-Point Tunneling Protocol,* and *L2TP,* or *Layer 2 Tunneling Protocol.* Here's what you must know about these communications protocols:

- Both PPTP and L2TP work over dial-up lines, local network links, wide area network links, and public TCP/IP networks such as the Internet.
- L2TP provides tunneling but not encryption. You would therefore normally use L2TP in combination with *IPsec* (Internet Protocol Security, a set of security protocols to protect the privacy of IP communications). PPTP provides encryption via PPP.
- L2TP uses header compression for lower overhead; PPTP doesn't.

Setting up a VPN link

You create a VPN link in Windows 2000 by starting the Make New Connection wizard in the Network and Dial-Up Connections folder. Choose the Connect To A Private Network Through The Internet option.

Typically, to use the Internet to make a VPN connection, you use one icon to establish the Internet link, and another to establish the VPN tunnel. The first icon may already exist, in which case you should select it and click Automatically dial this initial connection (see Figure 13-12). If you don't need to create an ISP link (for example, because an always-on link already exists), click Do not dial the initial connection.

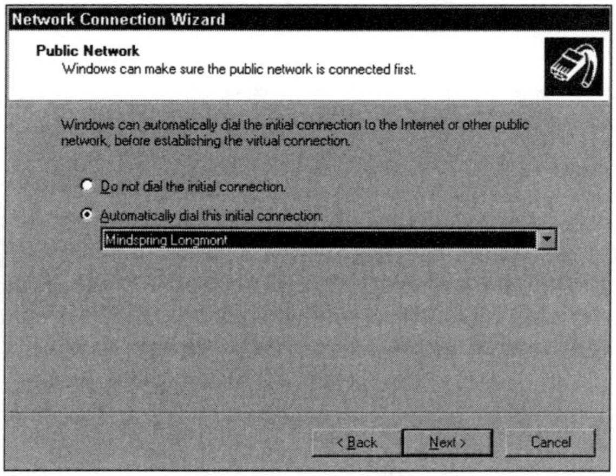

Figure 13-12: Telling Windows how to start your VPN session.

Follow the wizard and specify the domain name or IP address of the VPN server. As usual, you can also specify if you want the connection all to yourself or if you prefer to share it with other users of that PC. Name the connection and you're done.

Placing a VPN call

Establishing a VPN link via the Internet is easier than it is in Windows 98. Just double-click the connectoid that you created in the previous section. After Windows establishes the link, your PC behaves just as if it were logged on to the private network, rather than to the public Internet.

Prep Test

1 **Bob is setting up his Windows 2000 Professional machine to access the Internet via a dial-up connection. He goes through the Make New Connection wizard and answers the questions. When finished, he looks at the connection's networking property sheet to confirm his choices. Which elements should he make sure are present and activated?**

A ❍ Microsoft TCP/IP
B ❍ Client for Microsoft Networks
C ❍ File and Printer Sharing for Microsoft Networks
D ❍ Microsoft NetBEUI

2 **Jeannie has installed an additional network card in her Windows 2000 Professional computer, for a total of two network cards. She goes to the Network and Dial-Up Connections folder to configure her second network card; however, it doesn't appear as an icon. What should Jeannie do to add the icon to the folder? (Choose the best answer.)**

A ❍ Open Device Manager and drag the second network card's icon into the Network and Dial-Up Connections folder.
B ❍ Open My Network Places and drag the second network card's icon into the Network and Dial-Up Connections folder.
C ❍ Run the Add New Network Adapter wizard from the Network and Dial-Up Connections folder's Advanced menu.
D ❍ Run the Add New Hardware wizard from the computer's Control Panel.

3 **You're configuring a Windows 2000 Professional machine for a user who needs dial-up access to the corporate LAN. This user has a "smart card" authentication device. On the Advanced Security Settings dialog box for the connection, which items should you select? (Choose all that apply.)**

A ❑ MS-CHAP Version 2 (MS-CHAPv2)
B ❑ For MS-CHAP-based protocols, automatically use my Windows logon name and password (and domain if there is one)
C ❑ Unencrypted password (PAP)
D ❑ Use Extensible Authentication Protocol (EAP)
E ❑ Smart Card or other certificate (encryption enabled)

4 **You're configuring a Windows 2000 Professional home machine for a telecommuter who plans to work from home 50 percent of the time. Your company is a government contractor and this employee works with sensitive military information. Therefore, you must provide a secure connection. Your boss tells you to set up a VPN link. Which protocol or protocols would be appropriate?**

A ○ IPsec and NWLink

B ○ PPTP and NWLink

C ○ L2TP and IPsec

D ○ PPTP and L2TP

5 **You administer a Windows 2000 network that contains both Professional machines and Server machines in a domain-based network using Active Directory. You consider activating Internet Connection Sharing (ICS) in order to avoid having to run high-speed DSL lines to every user in the Research department, which has its own domain. How should you proceed? (Choose the best answer.)**

A ○ Create an Internet connection using the Make New Connection wizard, then access the icon's property sheets, click the Sharing tab, and check the Enable Internet Connection Sharing check box.

B ○ Create an Internet connection using the Make New Connection wizard, answering "yes" to the question "Do you wish to enable Internet Connection Sharing?".

C ○ Create an Internet connection using the Make New Connection wizard, then access the icon's property sheets, click the ICS tab, and check the Enable Internet Connection Sharing check box.

D ○ Configure the NAT service on a Windows 2000 Server computer.

6 **You travel frequently and you want to set up your Windows 2000 Professional notebook computer so that you can dial up your corporate network while you're on the road. What step or steps should you take to increase security, in case your notebook is stolen? (Choose all that apply.)**

A ❑ Configure Windows 2000 for autologon via the Users and Passwords control panel.

B ❑ Configure Windows 2000 for interactive logon via the Users and Passwords control panel.

C ❑ Enable callback security on your corporate communications server.

D ❑ Encrypt important files using EFS.

7 **You use your Windows 2000 Professional machine to dial up two different Internet Service Providers. These two ISPs require you to enter different IP addresses for DNS servers. Assuming that you have already created connection icons for each account, how can you configure them for different DNS server addresses? (Choose the best answer.)**

A ❍ Open the Network control panel, right-click the connection icon for the first ISP account, click TCP/IP, click Properties, and enter the DNS server address. Repeat for the connection for the second ISP account.

B ❍ Create a separate hardware profile for each configuration. Reboot into the first profile, right-click the connection icon for the first ISP account, click TCP/IP, click Properties, and enter the DNS server address. Reboot into the second hardware profile and repeat.

C ❍ Open the Network and Dial-Up Connections folder, right-click the connection icon for the first ISP account, choose Properties, click Networking, click TCP/IP, click Properties, and enter the DNS server address. Repeat for the connection for the second ISP account.

D ❍ You can't take advantage of this action. Windows 2000 Professional supports just a single DNS configuration for the computer.

8 **You configured a dial-up connection to an Internet Service Provider. When you double-click the connection icon, Windows 2000 Professional seems to dial the remote host and initiate a connection, but it hangs up shortly after you see the dialog box saying "Verifying username and password." After a couple of minutes, you see a dialog box stating "Error 619: The specified port isn't connected." Another user with a notebook computer running Windows 98 can use your phone connection to browse the Web with no problem. What could be the problem? (Choose the best answer.)**

A ❍ The phone line is noisy.

B ❍ Your ISP doesn't support Windows 2000.

C ❍ Your connection is set up to require an encrypted password.

D ❍ Your modem speed setting is too high.

9 **You have created a dial-up connection to a private network using the Make New Connection wizard. Three other people use your computer. None of them can see the connection that you created. Why? (Choose the best answer.)**

A ❍ When you ran the wizard, you checked the box that says "Only for myself" in the Connection Availability dialog box.

B ❍ The default setting on the connection icon's Sharing property sheet is for new connections to apply to your user profile only.

C ❍ You were logged on as an administrator when you created the connection. No non-administrators can see a connection created by an administrator.

D ❍ The three other people have poor vision.

10 **You want Windows 2000 Professional to dial into your corporate network at 6 a.m. and trigger a program on a Windows 2000 Server to power up the coffeemaker by your office. Which coffeemaker is compatible with Windows 2000 Server? (Choose the best answer.)**

A ❍ Mr. Coffee

B ❍ Ms. Coffee

C ❍ The "Java Virtual Machine"

D ❍ Any coffeemaker would work

Answers

1 **A.** All Bob needs to connect is TCP/IP and a Web browser. The browser's included with Windows 2000. The Client for Microsoft Networks is needed only if Bob is connecting to a Microsoft network, but just needs to connect to the Internet. File and Printer Sharing isn't needed and is, in fact, good to avoid. Finally, NetBEUI isn't the language of the Internet; TCP/IP is. See "Software prep."

2 **D.** The absence of the card's icon means that Windows 2000 hasn't automatically detected the card's presence. That could happen with an older card that doesn't support Plug and Play, for example. In order to detect the new hardware, Jeannie must run the Add New Hardware wizard, at which point the icon appears automatically in the Network and Dial-Up Connections folder. See "Central control."

3 **D** and E. If you choose D, options A, B, and C aren't available! Note that choice E also goes by the name of Transport Level Security, or TLS. See "Security tab."

4 **C.** The combination of L2TP, which provides tunneling but not encryption, and IPsec, which provides encryption, would create a secure connection capability. Choices A and B are wrong because you wouldn't use NWLink for a VPN connection; VPN connections use TCP/IP. Choice D is wrong because you wouldn't use PPTP and L2TP together; PPTP provides both tunneling and encryption. See "VPN protocols."

5 **D.** This is the only correct answer, because you are not supposed to enable ICS in a domain environment. The NAT service (Network Address Translation) on Windows 2000 Server provides the same functionality that ICS does on a workgroup network. See "Internet Connection Sharing."

6 **B** and **D**. You don't want automatic logon, because that means a thief doesn't need to know your user name and password. You can't use callback security for a traveling user, because the user isn't at a predetermined phone number. Encryption is a good idea, because if a thief figures out how to log on (say, as Guest) but can't guess your particular user name and password, he or she can't open your encrypted files. This last tidbit isn't in this chapter, but it's an example of the sort of cross-topic question you are likely to see on the exam. See "Creating Inbound Connections."

7 **C.** Choice A is wrong because Windows 2000 doesn't have a Network control panel. B is wrong because you don't have to create a separate hardware profile to accomplish the goal, and because even if you did, the two dial-up connections probably use the same hardware device (modem) so there would be no point. Choice D is wrong because choice C works just fine. See "Connection independence."

8 **C.** The most likely cause is that you've set the Security dialog box for your connection to require an encrypted password, but the ISP only supports unencrypted passwords. Choice A is unlikely, because the other user connects just fine. Choice B is also unlikely, because Windows 2000 can connect to any ISP that Windows 98 can connect to. Finally, D is wrong because even if your modem speed setting is too high, Windows 2000 negotiates a proper speed based on line conditions and the capabilities of the remote host. See "Security tab."

9 **A.** The default selection at this dialog box is "For all users." Choice B is wrong because the Sharing tab is only for Internet Connection Sharing (ICS). Choice C is wrong because it's not true; as long as you choose "For all users," you can share a connection with others, even if you create it when logged on as an administrator. D could be correct, but the odds are against it. See "Creating a connection."

10 **D.** All you'd need is an output controller in the Windows 2000 Server machine that would flip a relay sending power to the coffeemaker. The brand of coffeemaker doesn't matter. Yes, this is a gag question, but it could be done! (Now you'd probably also want to build a robot to pour freshly ground beans into the filter. . . .)

Part V

Tuning and Troubleshooting Windows 2000

"Well kid, if your certification is as impressive as your cover letter, you've got a big future with this gang."

In this part . . .

The PC operating system that tunes itself, and fixes itself, isn't quite here yet. (Heck, we still don't even have a file system that automatically defragments itself. Ten years ago, I wouldn't have dreamed we'd still be running defrag utilities in the year 2000! And where are those personal jetpacks and flying cars that we were all supposed to be zipping around the metropolis with, anyway? Someone needs to get busy.)

So, performance tuning and problem-solving remain essential skills for computing professionals, and favorite topics for MCSE questions. Chapter 14 looks at how you can make Windows 2000 go faster, and Chapter 15 looks at how you can make Windows 2000 go, period, when it decides to stop.

Chapter 14

Performance Optimization

Exam Objectives

- Optimize and troubleshoot processor utilization
- Monitor and configure multiple processing units
- Optimize and troubleshoot memory performance
- Optimize and troubleshoot disk performance
- Optimize and troubleshoot network performance
- Optimize and troubleshoot application performance
- Configure, manage, and troubleshoot the Task Scheduler

The Microsoft exam objective list combines optimizing and troubleshooting goals, which often fall into two separate mental buckets in the real world of system management. My consulting clients' usual attitude is that a functioning, trouble-free system is *de rigueur,* and performance optimization is nice to have, assuming any money is leftover.

I try to teach my clients that a computer component that's running really slowly may be even *worse* than something that's broken outright. The user may not know about the slow performance problem, while she'd certainly know about (and fix) the catastrophic failure. So a big part of being a computer pro is knowing how to use the various stethoscopes and thermometers at your disposal. (It also helps to be handy with analogies, such as driving your expensive car around town with the parking brake on all the time.)

The good news is that Windows 2000 provides some fairly good tools "out of the box" to monitor performance. The exam expects you to be quite familiar with these tools. The bad news is that with this operating system, optimizing and troubleshooting computer performance often involves the injection of cold, hard cash in the form of beefier hardware!

Quick Assessment

Optimize and troubleshoot processor utilization

1 The two common ways to add CPU horsepower are ______ and ______.

2 You could have a processor bottleneck if the queue length is greater than ______.

Monitor and configure multiple processing units

3 Windows 2000 Professional supports a maximum of ______ CPUs.

4 After adding a second processor, you may be able to update the computer driver in ______ instead of reinstalling Windows.

Optimize and troubleshoot memory performance

5 A "hard page fault" is a situation where the computer must access ______.

6 The pagefile name is ______.

Optimize and troubleshoot disk performance

7 Before you defragment a disk, press the ______ button in Disk Defragmenter.

Optimize and troubleshoot network performance

8 (True/false) Network Monitor is a utility that comes with Windows 2000 Professional.

Optimize and troubleshoot application performance

9 The setting for whether foreground applications should get more CPU time is found on the ______ tab of the System control panel.

Configure, manage, and troubleshoot the Task Scheduler

10 The command-line version of the Task Scheduler is ______.

Answers

1 *Replace the processor with a faster one, add a second processor.* The "Processor Tuning" section explains.

2 *2.* See "Processor monitoring" for more.

3 *2.* The Server product supports 4. "Adding a second processor" has details.

4 *Device Manager.* Again, see the section "Adding a second processor."

5 *The disk.* See "Performance console method" for more.

6 *"Mr. Pagefile."* No, I'm kidding, it's PAGEFILE.SYS. See the "Location" section.

7 *Analyze.* The disk may not need defragging. See the "Defragmenting" section if you missed this one.

8 *False.* This utility comes with Windows 2000 Server, and with Systems Management Server. See "Network Monitor."

9 *Advanced.* The "Foreground/background adjustment" section has more.

10 *AT.EXE.* See "Disk maintenance and Scheduled Task" for this and other riveting tidbits.

Monitoring Tools

This first section introduces the performance monitoring tools that come with Windows 2000, along with a primer on their operation. In later sections, you can apply this knowledge to specific troubleshooting and optimization areas, such as disk, CPU, and memory.

INSTANT ANSWER

The very running of a performance monitoring tool has an effect on performance, because the tool has its own CPU, memory, and graphical requirements.

Performance Monitor

The fanciest performance monitoring tool in Windows 2000 is the Performance console, which you can get to by choosing Start⇨Settings⇨Control Panel, opening Administrative Tools, and opening the Performance icon. (Alternatively, you can create a desktop shortcut to `C:\WINNT\SYSTEM32\PERFMON.MSC` or just choose Start⇨Run and type **PERFMON.MSC**.)

The two main snap-ins to this console are *System Monitor* and *Performance Logs and Alerts*. (Note that you can also view Performance Logs and Alerts on the Computer Management console.)

Objects, counters, and instances

In the Performance console's System Monitor snap-in, an *object* is a computer component to measure, and a *counter* is a specific performance measurement. Any given object may have more than one associated counter. For example, in a track meet, a runner would be an object, and that runner's times in the hundred-yard dash and in the mile would be two separate counters for the runner object.

Objects and counters often appear together, separated by a backslash or hyphen. For example, *Runner\100yarddash* would mean the counter "100yard-dash" for the object "Runner."

An *instance* identifies which object the Performance console should monitor when more than one such object exists in the system. If, at the track meet, four runners are competing in each race, you will have four instances of the Runner object: Runner(1), Runner(2), Runner(3), and Runner(4). So the counter that reports how quickly Runner 2 performs in the mile race would appear as *Runner(2)\mile*. Note that not all objects in a computer system have multiple instances; memory is an example.

Add counters by right-clicking anywhere in the System Monitor display area and choosing Add Counters, or by clicking the + button on the toolbar. You should see a dialog box similar to the one shown in Figure 14-1. You choose an object first and then a counter. The Explain button opens a window of text that elaborates on the counter you highlight.

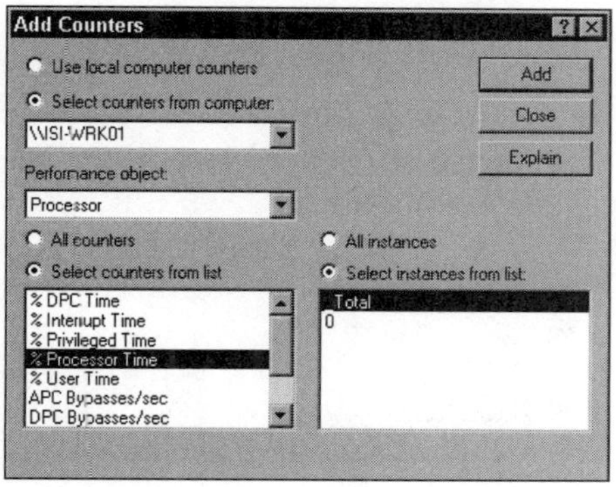

Figure 14-1: Adding a counter to an object in the Performance console's System Monitor.

TIP

Notice in Figure 14-1 that you can monitor remote computers with System Monitor, which is very handy for technicians and troubleshooters. Just keep the update frequency as low as you can while still capturing the data you need.

Views

System Monitor offers a variety of ways to view data, controllable via three toolbar buttons:

- **Chart:** What we used to call "line chart" in college; the most useful general-purpose view.
- **Histogram:** Ten-dollar term for bar chart.
- **Report:** Text mode only, for those who like decimal places.

If you choose Action⇨Properties with System Monitor highlighted, you see an absolutely useless display (try it); ditto if you right-click System Monitor in the snap-in tree on the left. Oops! However, if you click the Properties toolbar button (normally fourth from the right), you get a proper Properties window. This window (see Figure 14-2) lets you control the update frequency (default 1 second), colors, fonts, scaling, and what the histogram and report modes actually show: current data, an average, maximum, minimum.

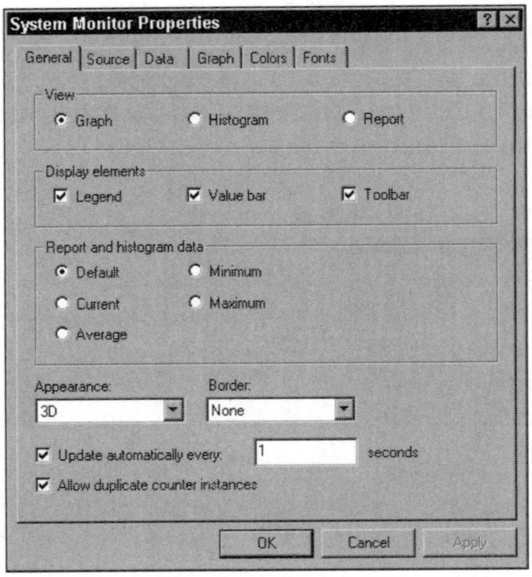

Figure 14-2: A proper Properties sheet.

Performance logs and alerts

If you have a heart problem, the doctor may put you on a heart monitor that tracks cardiac activity for a 24-hour period or longer. That monitoring device may also have an alarm that sounds when the patient's heart rate strays outside safe limits, for example, when watching *Baywatch.*

The Performance console's Performance Logs and Alerts snap-in can generate log files that you can collect over a reasonable time period and then view at your leisure later, using the same System Monitor display that you use to watch real-time data. You can also configure performance alerts that trigger events or messages when certain threshold levels are violated.

Here's what you must know about the Performance Logs and Alerts snap-in:

- **Counter logs** let you create disk files that record the state of object counters you specify, at a frequency you specify. The default format is *.BLG, for Binary LoG.
- **Trace logs** monitor a particular value continuously, rather than at sampling intervals. You can't trace every object counter that you can run counter logs for.
- **Alerts** can specify a minimum or maximum threshold for any counter, and can generate an application log entry, send a message to any computer on the network (see Figure 14-3), start a log file, and/or run any program you specify.
- **Create** a new log or alert by selecting the appropriate branch under the Performance Logs and Alerts snap-in in the left window pane, and by right-clicking the right (details) window pane and choosing New Log Settings or New Alert Settings. Give the log or alert a name and set its properties.

- All logs go by default to the `C:\PERFLOGS` folder.
- You need to be an Administrator to set logs and alerts, or at least have specific Registry access rights that you don't need to memorize here!
- If you set the sampling frequency or number of counters too high, you can run out of disk space in a major hurry.
- You can use the Schedule tab on the property sheets of logs and alerts to set begin and end times, or you can start and stop logs and alerts manually by right-clicking the icon in the details pane and choosing Start or Stop.

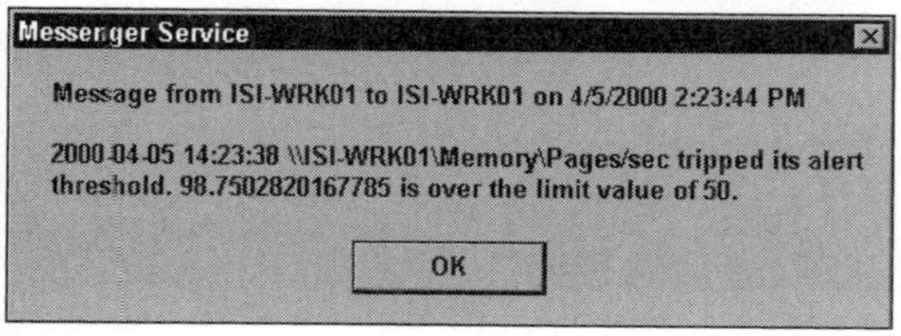

Figure 14-3: An alert message stating that lots of disk paging is going on.

Task Manager

If the Performance console is like a $500 oscilloscope, Task Manager is like a $50 handheld voltmeter. Less complete than the Performance console, but also easier to understand and use, Task Manager comes in handy for taking a quick look at key system performance variables. Activate Task Manager by pressing Ctrl+Alt+Del and clicking the Task Manager button. (I know, it seems like a weird way to get to a program. A faster way is to choose Start⇨Run and type **TASKMGR**.) You should see a screen similar to the one shown in Figure 14-4, with the three tabs Applications, Processes, and Performance.

The Applications tab has the simplest display and shows a list of running programs and their status (usually either "running" or "not responding"). The Processes tab shows not only programs but also services and operating system executables, along with CPU and memory usage by process. The Performance tab (see Figure 14-5) shows overall figures for CPU and memory usage, along with rolling line graphs.

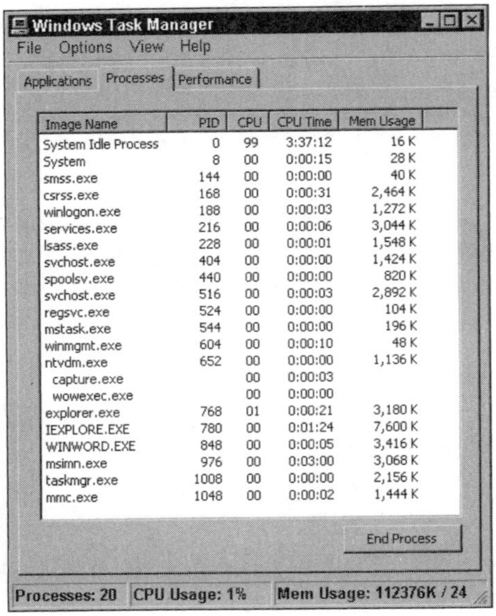

Figure 14-4: The Task Manager Processes display.

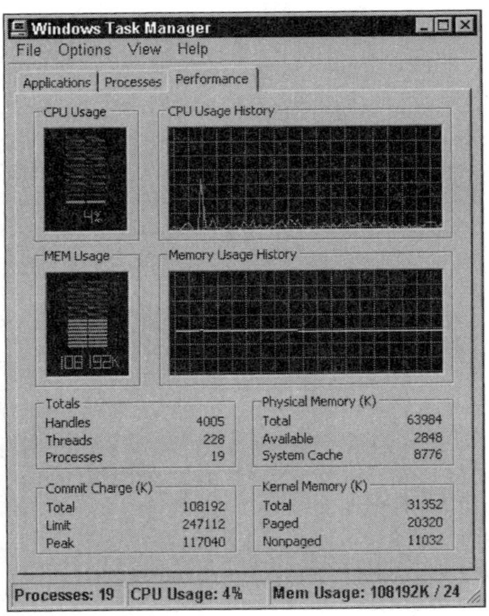

Figure 14-5: The Task Manager Performance display.

Network Monitor

Windows 2000 Server comes with a tool named *Network Monitor,* which permits analysis of frames (network packets) sent and received using the server's network interface card(s). The BackOffice product Systems

Management Server comes with an industrial strength version of Network Monitor that can monitor packet traffic at client workstations as well as servers. Windows 2000 Professional doesn't come with either version of Network Monitor, but it does come with a Network Monitor driver that permits SMS to watch traffic on a Windows 2000 Professional PC. Install the Network Monitor driver as you would any network protocol.

Processor Tuning

Processor tuning falls into three categories: monitoring existing CPU usage, adjusting the foreground-to-background CPU time split, and adding a second CPU. The next sections deal with each topic in turn.

Microsoft specifies a Pentium 166 CPU for running Windows 2000 Professional. As a practical matter, you want a more powerful CPU than that. A Pentium II class processor running at 200 megahertz is a more realistic minimum level.

Processor monitoring

You can perform some quick-and-dirty CPU monitoring in Task Manager. The Applications and Processes tabs let you see which applications and processes are using the most CPU time, while the Performance tab lets you watch total CPU usage via a graphical display. You can keep an eye on the Performance tab while opening and running typical applications on the system to get a sense of whether the CPU may be a bottleneck. You may find that one application in particular is a CPU hog and you may be able to modify its default settings to reduce the performance drain it causes.

If a quick analysis suggests a closer look, then you can collect and analyze more detailed data on CPU usage with the Performance console. Here are some of the counters to watch:

- **Processor\% Processor Time.** What percent of total time the CPU is busy doing useful work. Periodically pegging out at 100% is okay, but long stretches over 85% indicate a bottleneck (or a misbehaving application).
- **Processor\Interrupts\Sec.** How many hardware interrupts the CPU deals with per second. Hardware interrupts come from devices rather than from programs. Microsoft says watch out if you have more than 15 here.

- **Processor\% Privileged Time.** What percent of the CPU's busy time (or "non-idle time" as Microsoft likes to put it) is spent in *privileged mode,* that is, handling operating system and hardware requests (as opposed to *user mode,* which applications typically use). If this value goes up suddenly and dramatically, you may have a failing network card or other device; adapters sometimes flood the CPU with interrupts when they go bad.
- **System\Processor Queue Length.** How many threads are waiting around in line to be handled by the CPU (or CPUs, in a two-processor system). Any number greater than two may mean processor bottleneck.

On a multiple-processor system, you can specify which processor you want to measure by making a selection in the instances list of the Add Counters dialog box. You can specify that you want to measure all processors, in aggregate, by choosing the *_Total* instance.

Foreground/background adjustment

You can make a very broad adjustment to modify whether Windows 2000 pays more CPU attention to the *foreground* program (the application you're running in an open, active window with a highlighted title bar) or pays equal attention to foreground and background programs (background programs being applications and services that are not running in the "top window").

Windows 2000 Professional defaults to the traditional Windows behavior of favoring the foreground program, but you may prefer a more UNIX-like, egalitarian distribution of processor power if you often run background programs (such as backup or printing operations) and if those programs run poorly. To make such a change, follow the steps in Lab 14-1.

Lab 14-1 Adjusting Processor Behavior

1. **Right-click My Computer and choose Properties.**

   The System control panel appears.
2. **Click the Advanced tab.**
3. **Click the Performance Options button.**
4. **In the Application Response dialog box, click the Background Services radio button under the Optimize Performance For: heading.**
5. **Click OK and click OK again to close the dialog boxes.**

Adding a second processor

Based on monitoring as discussed earlier in this section, you may find that you need to add processing power to a PC for which the CPU has become a bottleneck. If you run graphics-intensive applications, engineering design software, or scientific analysis programs, then you may be a candidate for CPU turbocharging. You can add processing power two ways: by replacing your CPU with a faster one (assuming the particular PC supports such replacement), or by adding a second CPU to a single-processor machine (again, assuming your PC has the expansion socket available).

Windows 2000 supports up to two processors in a single PC, using a scheme called *symmetric multiprocessing* or *SMP*. If you install Windows 2000 onto a PC with two processors, the setup program should automatically detect them and install SMP support. However, if you install Windows 2000 onto a PC with only one CPU installed and then add a second CPU later, Windows 2000 doesn't automatically detect the change and make adjustments. Adding a second processor fundamentally changes how Windows 2000 deals with your hardware, and it's not an action that a mere Plug and Play device detection can handle. For one thing, Windows 2000 uses a different HAL (Hardware Abstraction Layer) for an SMP machine than for a single-CPU machine.

So, the multiple-CPU upgrade requires one of two actions: You can either reinstall Windows 2000 over itself, or you can update the driver for the Computer object in Device Manager. The first method is preferable, but you can try the second method in Lab 14-2 and see whether it works for you.

WARNING! The second method may render your PC unusable if you haven't actually installed a second CPU!

Lab 14-2 Reconfiguring for Multiple Processor Support

1. **Run the System control panel by right-clicking My Computer and choosing Properties.**
2. **Click the Hardware tab.**
3. **Click the Device Manager button.**
4. **Double-click the Computer icon at the top of the tree.**
5. **Right-click your computer model (just under the Computer icon) and choose Properties.**
6. **Click the Driver tab.**
7. **Click the Update Driver button and click Next.**
8. **Click Display A List Of The Known Drivers For This Device So That I Can Choose A Specific Driver and click Next.**
9. **Click Show All Hardware Of This Device Class.**
10. **Select the new driver based on your best educated guess.**

    For example, in Figure 14-6, you would upgrade from ACPI PC to ACPI Multiprocessor PC.
11. **Agree with the warning message and step through the remaining dialog boxes until you restart the PC.**

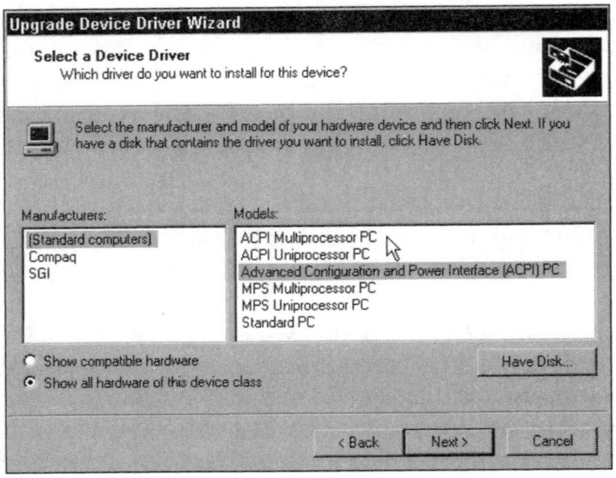

Figure 14-6: Upgrading to multi-processor support.

Before considering a processor upgrade, use Task Manager to make sure you aren't running any unnecessary services on your PC. Check your startup group and system tray for any utilities that may be loading at boot time but that you may not need. Modify the settings of any loaded programs (such as antivirus utilities) and see whether the changes reduce the burden on the CPU. And make very sure that you don't have a PCI or ISA card that's flooding the CPU with interrupts in a failure mode.

On a dual-processor PC, you can specify that a particular process run on a particular CPU! Open Task Manager, click the Processes tab, right-click the process of interest, choose Set Affinity, and specify the CPU.

Memory Tuning

Windows 2000 Professional memory tuning is vital to the performance of your PC. Optimizing memory has two components: tuning RAM and tuning the pagefile.

Determining the right amount of RAM

Windows 2000 Professional is more of a memory hog than Windows 95, 98, or NT Workstation 4.0. When Windows 2000 runs out of physical RAM, it uses the disk-based *pagefile,* at a serious performance penalty. (You may see the word *swapfile* on the exam; it's synonymous with *pagefile* for all intents and purposes.) So the best action you can take for improved memory performance is to add RAM so that Windows 2000 doesn't need to use the pagefile much, if at all.

Task Manager method

One quick way to see how much more memory you may need in a given PC is to load the applications you usually run, open some typical size data files in each application; then run Task Manager and click the Performance tab. Look at the graph titled Mem Usage. You see that the number shown is the same as the Total Commit Charge in the lower left of the display.

REMEMBER

"Commit" memory is the sum of memory used by all the software on the computer: operating system, applications, services, the lot.

Task Manager also shows the Commit Charge Limit (which is RAM plus pagefile size), and Commit Charge Peak (maximum commit charge since last reboot).

Diagonally up and to the right of the Commit Charge memory figures is the Physical Memory area. Total Physical Memory is how many kilobytes of RAM the PC has. If you subtract Total Physical Memory from Total Commit Charge, you can see how much more RAM you need at that moment to avoid paging. Taking things one step further, if you subtract Total Physical Memory from Peak Commit Charge, you can see how much more RAM you'd need to avoid paging during the entire computing session since the last reboot.

Now go buy your RAM expansion module, and enjoy a faster PC.

Performance console method

In the Performance console, the two most relevant counters for the Memory object are:

- **Pages/second.** This number is how many "hard" page faults occur, that is, cases when a program needs data that isn't in RAM but resides on disk in the pagefile. Hard page faults slow down the system, so bigger numbers are bad. Frequent peaks over 20 indicate a potential problem.
- **Available MBytes.** How much physical RAM is available for use by the operating system or programs. If this value falls below 4 on a regular basis, you need more RAM.

Figure 14-7 shows a System Monitor display for a 64MB computer running a couple of applications (Word 2000 and Outlook Express). See why most consultants recommend 128MB for Windows 2000 Professional?

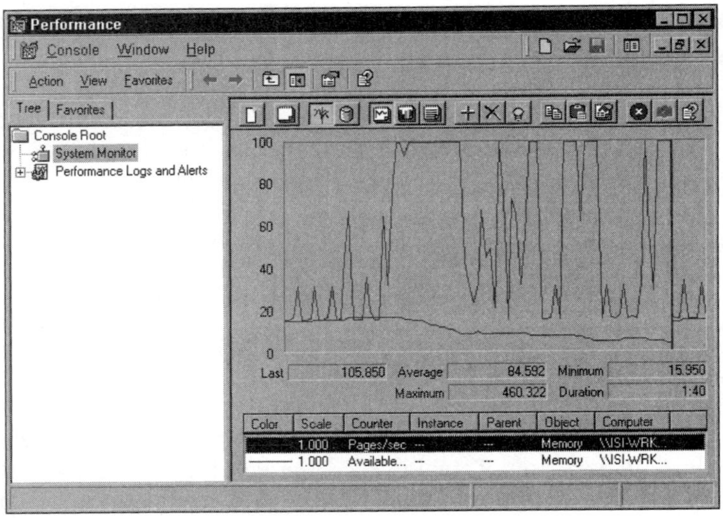

Figure 14-7: Frequent hard page faults and low available RAM mean trouble.

Optimizing the pagefile

If you can't put as much RAM into your system as the previous section indicates, the next best thing is to optimize the pagefile. You can modify the pagefile's size, location, and fragmentation level to improve virtual memory performance.

You must be logged on as an Administrator to change pagefile settings.

Size

By default, the pagefile size is 1.5 times the amount of installed RAM. You may need to increase that if you work with a lot of applications loaded into memory at the same time and get "out of memory" errors. The maximum pagefile size is the sum of available disk space on all local hard drives, but you would usually increase the size in reasonable increments (for example, 32MB) until the error messages go away, so you don't tie up disk space needlessly.

Increasing the pagefile size doesn't generally require a restart, but decreasing it does.

If the preset pagefile size is too small, overall performance is likely to suffer. When Windows must increase pagefile size to meet memory demand, the system practically comes to a halt during the resizing operation.

You can use the Performance console to check pagefile usage. The object is Paging File and the counter is % Usage.

TIP

Normally, Windows dynamically increases pagefile size from the Initial Size up to the Maximum Size on the dialog box, depending on system requirements. By setting the Initial Size to be the same as the Maximum Size, you reduce the operating system overhead associated with dynamic size adjustment. This is a good performance tip if you have plenty of disk space.

Location

The default location for the pagefile (PAGEFILE.SYS) is on the root of the boot drive, but you can change that. For example, you could set up the pagefile to live on a second physical hard drive, in order to perform some rudimentary load balancing.

You don't even have to limit yourself to a single pagefile: You can create several of the rascals and put 'em onto different drives. In fact, the more hard drives on which you have pagefile fragments living, the better Windows 2000 performs.

Fragmentation

Okay, this probably won't be on the exam and my friendly and sensible editors didn't want me to include it, but it's a real-world performance tip that I've found helpful enough to sneak into a test-prep book. Disk Defragmenter doesn't defragment the pagefile, but you can work around that limitation! Using the System control panel's Performance tab, set the pagefile to a really low value, such as 4MB, and reboot. Next, run Disk Defragmenter on the disk(s) where the pagefile lives. Finally, set the pagefile back to the value you want, and reboot. This method helps ensure that the pagefile has as few performance-sapping fragments as possible. When Windows 2000 rebuilds the bigger pagefile, it does so on a defragmented disk, so Windows doesn't need to fragment the new file. Sneaky, eh?

Disk Tuning

Hot on the heels of CPU and memory optimization comes disk tuning, which typically involves monitoring, defragmenting, and scheduled periodic cleanup.

Disk performance monitoring

Task Manager isn't much help when it comes to disk performance monitoring, so you should use the Performance console here. (Note that if you want to monitor disks by volume or logical drive letter, rather than by physical disk, you must activate the necessary counters by typing the **DISKPERF –YV** command.) The values to watch for the PhysicalDisk object include the following:

- **% Disk Time.** 90 percent or more for extended periods, and your disk is a bottleneck. Adding a hard drive could help, as could replacing the existing one with a faster unit.
- **Current Disk Queue Length.** If this value is over 2 + the number of physical disks, your disk is a bottleneck.
- **Disk Reads/Sec and Disk Writes/Sec.** If the total of reads and writes is up around 40 or so and you have an EIDE disk, consider replacing it with a new Ultra SCSI one.

TIP

Adding RAM, if necessary, and optimizing the pagefile can dramatically reduce disk activity. Take those steps before deciding that you need a newer, faster hard drive. (There's a reason I put these topics in a certain order!) Also, you may find that defragmenting your disk can bring the counter values down, too, as the next section explains.

Defragmenting

Unlike Windows NT Workstation 4.0, Windows 2000 Professional comes with a simple disk defragmenter. Defragmenters improve performance by undoing the fragmentation or "chopping up" that operating systems typically perform as they allocate space for files. That is, defragmenters realign all the bits and pieces of a file so that they are adjacent, or *contiguous,* meaning that the disk drive's read/write heads have to do less bouncing around to read or write the file. Whatever file system you use, NTFS, FAT32, or FAT, the Disk Defragmenter utility can consolidate most of the fragmented files. (The utility doesn't defragment the pagefile, however, or the Master File Table, or the Registry. You need to buy the full Diskeeper product for those benefits.)

In what can only be explained as an attack of Overly Obsessive Paranoia Syndrome (OOPS), Microsoft programmers decided that you need to be logged on as an Administrator before you can defragment your disks. Having done so, you access Disk Defragmenter (DFRG.MSC) by right-clicking a drive in My Computer, choosing Properties, clicking the Tools tab and then clicking the Defragment Now button. Defragment Now doesn't "defragment now," it just opens the Disk Defragmenter window (see Figure 14-8).

The suggested approach is to analyze a disk before defragging it, as Windows 2000 may advise you that the disk doesn't need optimizing. I recommend that you close all applications before running this utility; open files may not be able to be consolidated. Disk Defragmenter doesn't have any options that you can set.

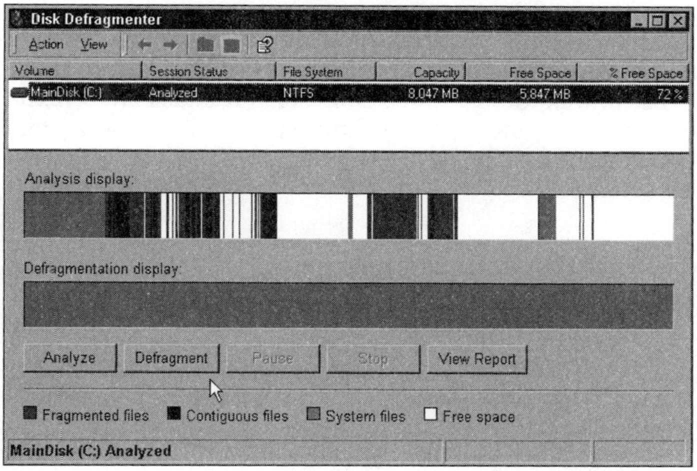

Figure 14-8: The colored regions show optimized and fragmented areas.

You need to have about 15 percent free disk space for this utility to do its job properly. Therefore, on a really full disk, you may enjoy better performance if you use the Cleanup Wizard (CLEANMGR.EXE) before running Disk Defragmenter.

You can run Disk Defragmenter only on local drives. And you can have only one instance of the program going at a time.

Disk maintenance and Scheduled Tasks

If remembering to defragment your disks once in a while is helpful, having Windows 2000 automatically defragment them on a regular basis is more helpful. This is as good a time as any to introduce the Scheduled Tasks utility (which is similar to the utility of the same name in Windows 98). Microsoft sometimes calls this utility the Task Scheduler, so don't be confused.

Get to Scheduled Tasks through the Control Panel and run the wizard by double-clicking the Add Scheduled Task icon. You can specify a program to run, a descriptive name for the task, how often the task should run (daily, weekly, monthly, at each reboot, at each logon, or once), when the task should run (time and date), and the name and password of the user under whose account the task should run.

This last item is important because many tasks (such as defragmenting a disk) require administrative rights. If you configure several scheduled tasks and a single task doesn't run but others do, you may have a problem with user rights. If you configure several scheduled tasks and none of them run, then you may suspect that the Task Scheduler service itself has been stopped, paused, or never started. (You can manually restart the service by using the Services console in the Administrative Tools folder.)

After you create a scheduled task, you can view its property sheet from the Scheduled Tasks folder to modify it further. For example, the Settings tab (see Figure 14-9) provides additional options for starting and stopping tasks, such as whether to wait for idle time before starting a task and whether to run a task when the computer is using battery power. The Security tab lets you define NTFS permissions for the scheduled task object, which is actually a file with the suffix .JOB.

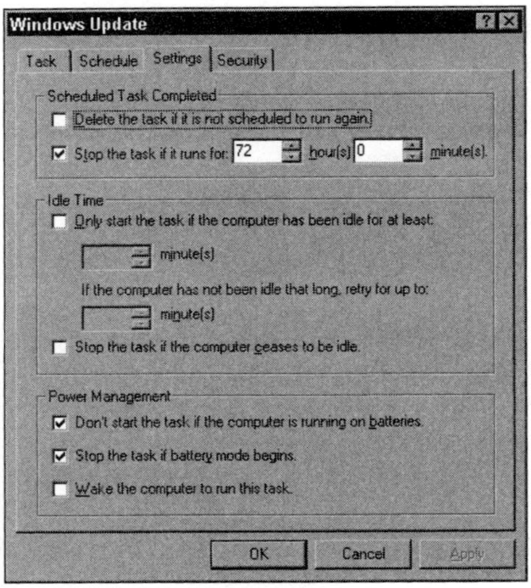

Figure 14-9: Set configuration options for scheduled tasks here.

INSTANT ANSWER

You should know for the exam the meaning of the various options on the Scheduled Tasks folder's Advanced menu, as follows:

- **Stop Using Task Scheduler.** This one's self-explanatory.
- **Pause Task Scheduler.** This one morphs into "Continue Task Scheduler" if you choose it. If the time specified for a task comes and goes while the scheduler is paused, the task doesn't run until its next scheduled time (if any).
- **Notify Me of Missed Tasks.** Oddly, the default for this toggle setting is off (cleared). You may see an exam question that expects you to know this fact.
- **AT Service Account.** Here, you name the user account for all tasks created with the command-line utility, AT. (See this section's last paragraph for more on AT.)
- **View Log.** This command runs Notepad with a log of the utility's actions (the file SCHEDLGU.TXT in `C:\WINNT`). The Windows 2000 help system is wrong when it refers to the file as SCHEDLOG.TXT.

Use the task scheduler tool to schedule recurring maintenance tasks, such as running the "full" Diskeeper disk defragmenter product or running the Disk Cleanup wizard. (Alas, Scheduled Tasks doesn't work with the "baby" Disk Defragmenter included with Windows 2000.) Scheduled Tasks is also handy for running resource-intensive programs when you don't need the computer, for example at night.

Make sure your PC's system date and time are set correctly via the Date/Time control panel. If this information is inaccurate, any tasks you have scheduled won't run when you expect them to.

You may need to modify the command line to accomplish an automated task. For example, when scheduling the Backup program, you would normally specify a backup job name on the command line so that the program knows what files you want to back up, and where they should go.

A command-line version of the graphical Scheduled Tasks utility is AT.EXE. All tasks that you create by using this program must run under the same user security context, which you set in the Advanced menu of the graphical utility. The graphical utility is more flexible than AT.EXE, in that each task can run in a different user security account context.

Network Tuning

The Windows 2000 Server exam covers network tuning more thoroughly than Exam #70-210. However, you should know about one Performance console metric for a Windows 2000 Professional network client, and that's the % Net Utilization counter for the Network Segment object. More than 30 percent on an Ethernet network means a potential bottleneck at the client machine's network interface card. The value varies for other network types.

The Remember icon at the end of Chapter 6 addresses the topics of disabling unused network bindings and putting active bindings in an optimum order in order to enhance network performance. Clearly, adding a faster network adapter can help, too. Cards that work in full duplex mode (send and receive at the same time) can be faster than those limited to half duplex mode.

Application Tuning

The method for tuning application performance that's likely to be on the exam is the foreground/background split adjustment for CPU time, which this chapter explains earlier in the section "Foreground/background adjustment."

You may also need to know that you can set the priority levels of individual processes by using the Task Manager's Processes tab. That's a bit risky, but you can experiment with the technique if you like. Just right-click a process and choose Set Priority, followed by the value you want. The values are, from highest priority to lowest, realtime; high; abovenormal; normal; belownormal; and low. Note that any priority changes you make in Task Manager remain in effect only while the process is running; if you stop and restart the process, it reverts to the default base priority level that its programmer originally coded for it.

Prep Test

1 **You install Windows 2000 Professional onto 14 computers using a disk cloning technique. You discover that (unbeknownst to you) the 14 machines have dual Pentium processors. However, the machine you used to make the master disk image only has one CPU. As a result, the cloned systems are not using their second CPUs. You do not want to re-clone the operating system onto the 14 computers if you can help it. What can you do? (Choose the best answer.)**

A ❍ Go to each machine's System control panel. Click the Advanced tab and check the box labeled "Enable SMP."

B ❍ Go to each machine's System control panel. Click the Hardware tab and check the box labeled "Enable SMP."

C ❍ Go to each machine's System control panel. Click the Hardware tab, open Device Manager, and update the driver for the Computer device to a multiprocessor version.

D ❍ Go to each machine and enable multiprocessor support in the BIOS.

E ❍ Go to each machine and remove the second CPU.

2 **What is the default size of the pagefile? (Choose one answer.)**

A ❍ 1.0 times installed RAM

B ❍ 1.5 times installed RAM

C ❍ 2.0 times installed RAM

D ❍ 256MB minus (installed RAM)

3 **On a multiprocessor machine, Windows 2000's Performance console lets you use System Monitor to track activity on each CPU separately. In this situation, the graph for each CPU's "percent processor time" would correspond to a separate:**

A ❍ Object

B ❍ Counter

C ❍ Instance

D ❍ Module

4 **You set up a Windows 2000 Professional computer in a small workgroup. You decide to dedicate this particular computer to sharing files for the group, and you put all the shared files onto this machine. You're aware that no more than 10 computers can access these files simultaneously, but that's not a problem because your workgroup consists of 8 computers. You install the File and Printer Sharing service and bind it to the local area connection.**

Before you lock away the monitor in a closet, what performance setting should you change from the default value? (Choose the best answer.)

A ❍ Optimize Performance For Background Services, in the System control panel.

B ❍ Optimize Performance For Foreground Tasks, in the System control panel.

C ❍ Optimize Performance For Applications, in the System control panel.

D ❍ Optimize Performance For Workgroup Services, in the System control panel.

E ❍ Increase the priority of the LSASS.EXE process, in Task Manager.

5 **While logged on as an Administrator, you set up Scheduled Tasks to run the Backup program every night at 2 a.m. to perform a data folder backup from your C drive to your D drive. For the task's security context, you specify a member of the Users group. The next day, you find that Backup did not execute. Why not?**

A ❍ You must create the task when logged on as a Backup Operator.

B ❍ You must specify a different security context.

C ❍ You must use the AT.EXE command to run Backup.

D ❍ NTBACKUP does not perform disk-to-disk backups.

6 **You run System Monitor on a PC whose user is complaining of poor performance. You add counters for Available MBytes and Pages/second for the Memory object. After watching these values while the user performs normal daily tasks, you see that Available MBytes frequently drops below 16 but never drops below 8. The Pages/second graph shows frequent spikes in the range from 5 to 10. What do these monitoring statistics indicate? (Choose the best answer.)**

A ❍ The user's pagefile is heavily fragmented.

B ❍ The user's disk is heavily fragmented.

C ❍ The user needs more RAM.

D ❍ The user has enough RAM.

E ❍ The foreground/background setting needs adjusting.

F ❍ The maximum pagefile size is set too low.

7 **Bob comes to you with a problem. He has 920MB used on a 1000MB hard drive that is formatted with NTFS. When he runs DFRG.MSC, he receives a warning message. Bob knows he has too many files on his system. Of the following values, which is the smallest amount of additional space that Bob can free up in order to make the error message go away? (Choose the best answer.)**

A ❍ 120MB

B ❍ 100MB

C ❍ 80MB

D ❍ 60MB

E ❍ 40MB

8 **Task Manager's Performance tab; what's the commit charge limit?**

A ❍ The current pagefile size

B ❍ The minimum pagefile size

C ❍ The maximum pagefile size

D ❍ The maximum pagefile size plus installed RAM

E ❍ The maximum pagefile size minus installed RAM

Answers

1 **C.** By "updating" the driver for the computer itself, you're actually changing the Hardware Abstraction Layer (HAL), which you must do if the multiprocessor machines are to recognize the second processor. See "Adding a second processor."

2 **B.** So, the more RAM you have, the larger your swapfile — which doesn't necessarily make sense, so you should remember it! Also remember that too small a swapfile hurts system performance. See "Optimizing the pagefile."

3 **C.** The object is "processor," the counter is "% processor time," and the instances are processor #1 and processor #2. See "Objects, counters, and instances."

4 **A.** This computer won't be running any foreground applications, so a bit more CPU time should go to programs running in the background, such as the Server service (File and Printer Sharing). As for choice E, modifying the priority of a process is a temporary setting, not a persistent one. See "Foreground/background adjustment."

5 **B.** The user account that you specify as the task's security context must have appropriate user rights to perform the task — in this case, you should specify a member of the Backup Operators group or a member of the Administrators group. Choice A is incorrect, because you can specify a security context for the task that is different from the account you used to log on. Choices C and D are simply inaccurate. See "Disk maintenance and Scheduled Tasks."

6 **D.** This user probably has enough RAM for the application mix. The general rules are that Available MBytes shouldn't fall below 4 on a regular basis, and Pages/second shouldn't have sustained rates above 20. As for choices A and B, memory counters don't tell you anything about pagefile fragmentation. See "Determining the right amount of RAM."

7 **C.** 920 minus 80 is 840, leaving 16 percent of the drive free; the Disk Defragmenter needs to see 15 percent free in order to perform optimally. See "Defragmenting."

8 **D.** The commit charge limit is effectively the maximum amount of memory, whether RAM-based or pagefile-based, available to the system. See "Determining the right amount of RAM."

Chapter 15

Troubleshooting and Recovering Windows 2000 Systems

Exam Objectives

- Troubleshooting failed installations
- Updating drivers
- Managing and troubleshooting driver signing
- Recovering systems and user data by using Windows Backup
- Troubleshooting system restoration by using Safe Mode
- Recovering systems and user data by using the Recovery Console

Anybody could be a Windows 2000 expert if things always went right. When trouble strikes, the pros rub their hands together with relish (the attitude, not the condiment), while the amateurs bolt for the phone. Your days of bolting are about to be over.

The certification exam expects you to know what to do when Windows 2000 goes awry, and specifically how to use new features — signed drivers, safe mode, the new backup program, and recovery console — to resuscitate a dead or dying PC.

Unlike many of the problems in the previous chapter, the ones this chapter deals with typically require restarting Windows 2000 in a different "mode" or restoring data from backup. Interestingly, during the beta program, Microsoft documents discussed an "Automatic System Recovery" program that was supposed to bring several recovery options — the ones this chapter examines — into a single handy utility. Microsoft never followed through on ASR, though, so now you have to learn about when and how to use several completely different system recovery approaches.

Maybe we'll get an ASR application in Windows 2010. Then again, the more complex a chore Windows system recovery remains, the greater the demand will be for MCPs and MCSEs who know all the secret handshakes. . . .

Quick Assessment

Trouble-shooting failed installations

1 If Windows 2000 Professional is having trouble installing network components, make sure that a ______ and a ______ are online.

2 If the setup program fails during the graphical phase, a good log file to check would be ______.

Updating drivers

3 Probably the most convenient way to update device drivers is via the ______ display.

4 Vendors sometimes provide driver updates in the form of an ______ file which you can right-click and choose Install.

Managing and trouble-shooting driver signing

5 The three options for driver signing are ______, ______, and ______.

6 (True/false) To set the driver signing option for all users of the PC, you must log on as Administrator.

Recovering systems and user data by using Windows Backup

7 The set of files that Windows Backup calls the ______ contains by default the Registry and protected system files.

Troubleshooting system restoration by using Safe Mode

8 The name of the log file created during a Safe Mode boot is _____.

Recovering systems and user data by using the Recovery Console

9 You can install the Recovery Console "permanently" by running WINNT32 with the ______ option.

10 (True/false) The Recovery Console commands are the same that you would type in a regular command prompt window.

Answers

1 *Domain controller, DNS server.* See "Setup lockups" for more on installation woes.

2 *SETUPACT.LOG.* The section "The trail of crumbs" lays out log file details.

3 *Device Manager.* The "Driver updating" section has more on the different methods.

4 *INF.* Again, check out "Driver updating."

5 *Ignore, warn, and fail.* The section "Driver signing (not by famous golfers)" elaborates.

6 *True.* You have to be an Administrator to set darned near anything on this operating system. See "Driver signing (not by famous golfers)."

7 *System state.* The section "System state backups" has more.

8 *NTBTLOG.TXT.* See "Safe Mode" for details if you missed this one.

9 */CMDCONS.* The section "Installing Recovery Console onto the hard disk" includes this important detail.

10 *False.* See the section entitled "Recovery Console" for more.

Installation Irritations

Your first introduction to Windows 2000 system recovery may be an early one if the setup process fails to complete correctly.

Setup lockups

Several situations or conditions can cause the Windows 2000 setup program to fail at various different points. The following list describes common failure modes along with recommended fixes.

- **Inadequate disk space.** The general rule is that you should have 1GB of free space on the partition (not necessarily disk!) to which you are installing Windows 2000 Professional.
- **Failure to detect essential hardware.** For example, if the setup program doesn't recognize your CD-ROM drive, you can start an upgrade from Windows 95 but you may not be able to continue it after the first reboot. In such a case, you may need to use a different drive (one that's on the Hardware Compatibility List) or install Windows from a network distribution server.
- **Conflicts with running applications.** If you're upgrading from an earlier version of Windows, you may need to disable any third-party power management, antivirus, disk quota, and networking software before running setup. (Note that this includes BIOS-based antivirus software!)
- **Failure to find server(s).** If you tell setup that you want to join an existing domain, a domain controller and DNS server (they may be the same machine) must be up and connected to the PC where you're installing Windows 2000 Professional. You also have to get the domain name correct when running the setup program and make sure the local computer name is unique among other computer names, domain names, and workgroup names.
- **Flaky hardware.** If a disk controller, memory module, or other essential piece of hardware isn't performing up to spec, Windows 2000 Professional may consistently fail to install. Any newly-added hardware is suspect. Consider updating device firmware (such as a SCSI controller's BIOS) before tossing the hardware in the trash bin.

The trail of crumbs

The setup program makes a number of plain-text log files as it goes along, recording the things that go right as well as those that go wrong. You don't have to memorize all of these. Here are the key log files you should know for the exam (the list assumes you install Windows 2000 into the default folder C:\WINNT):

- `C:\WINNT\SETUPACT.LOG` is a chronological list of pretty much every action the setup program takes, after its graphical mode begins, and any errors that the program encounters. Microsoft sometimes calls this the "action log."
- `C:\WINNT\SETUPERR.LOG`, or simply the "error log," just has the errors in it, along with severity codes.
- `C:\WINNT\WINNT32.LOG` records the checking of available disk space and the copying of temporary boot files (for example, from the installation CD-ROM to the hard drive's system partition).
- `C:\WINNT\DEBUG\NETSETUP.LOG` covers network connection steps.
- `C:\WINNT\MMDET.LOG` covers multimedia detection steps.
- `C:\WINNT\SECURITY\LOGS\SCESETUP.LOG` includes details of access control settings on Registry keys and files. (The "SCE" part of the filename stands for Security Configuration Editor.)
- `C:\WINNT\SETUPAPI.LOG` includes details on processing of *.INF files, that is, a whole lot of hardware device driver information.
- `C:\WINNT\COMSETUP.LOG` includes details on installation of COM+ (Component Object Model) modules.

WARNING!

Most of the log files live in `C:\WINNT` but a few live elsewhere. Don't ask me why, just memorize the exceptions.

Application conflicts

Sometimes Windows 2000 installs okay, but one or more applications that worked under Windows 95, 98, or NT don't work right anymore. Four ideas:

- You may be able to fix such problems with *upgrade packs,* which are typically DLL files that you get from the application supplier.
- You can also experiment with the Resource Kit utility APCOMPAT.EXE, which lets you "fool" the application in various ways to think it's running on an earlier operating system.

- The application may expect users to have rights and access permissions that they no longer have, because the Windows 2000 "Users" group is more tightly restricted than in Windows NT 4.0. Try running the application when logged on as a member of the Power Users group.
- If the application is consistently crashing, check the file `C:\Documents and Settings\All Users\Documents\DrWatson\DRWTSN32.LOG`. If the log mentions an executable file that's part of your cranky application, e-mail the log to the software manufacturer for analysis and (perhaps) a fix.

Boot Blunders

Separate from setup problems are problems that occur when Windows 2000 boots. True, these may occur immediately after a fresh installation, but they may also crop up at later dates, and they often require different troubleshooting approaches.

A normal boot

To understand abnormal psychology, you first must understand normal psychology. In this sense, (and perhaps this sense only!) dealing with Windows is similar to dealing with humans.

Typical sequence of events

Here's what happens (or should happen) when you turn on your Windows 2000 Professional PC, in more detail than you ever wanted to know:

1. The Power-On Self Test (POST) runs, under control of BIOS.
2. The Plug and Play BIOS performs enumeration of (that's a fancy way of saying "finds") system board hardware devices.
3. The BIOS finds and runs Master Boot Record (MBR) program.
4. The MBR finds the boot sector on the active partition and loads the superhidden file NTLDR on the root directory. (*Superhidden* just means that NTLDR has both of the file attributes System and Hidden.)
5. NTLDR throws the CPU into 32-bit mode and loads FAT and NTFS file drivers. (Without these, it couldn't go any further.)
6. NTLDR reads BOOT.INI, also in the root directory, to see whether any other operating systems live on the machine. If so, NTLDR asks the user to pick one, please. If you pick an older operating system, NTLDR then runs BOOTSECT.DOS, which contains the boot sector from the system before Windows 2000 was installed onto it. For example, BOOTSECT.DOS

might start Windows 95. Note that BOOT.INI also contains details on where the operating system(s) reside (typically C:\WINNT for Windows 2000).

7. If you choose Windows 2000 in Step 6, or if that's the only operating system on the PC, then the next program to take the baton is NTDETECT.COM. This program, as its name suggests, performs a good deal of hardware detection (but not for network cards).
8. NTLDR steps back in and presents you with a list of hardware profiles, along with an option to use the Last Known Good Configuration, assuming you've defined more than one hardware profile. If not, you'd have to tap F8 at boot time to see this menu.
9. The kernel load phase is next, displaying the "Starting Windows 2000" text message at the bottom of the screen. NTOSKRNL.EXE loads, the Hardware Abstraction Layer (HAL) loads, the control set (essentially a Registry-based list of device drivers, services, and settings) loads, and low-level device drivers load.
10. Kernel initialization follows, displaying the graphical boot progress screen. NTOSKRNL.EXE takes over from NTLDR here, building the HKLM\HARDWARE Registry key, initializing the low-level device drivers, loading more device drivers, and starting services via the Session Manager (SMSS.EXE).
11. The logon dialog box shows up (it's associated with WINLOGON.EXE and LSASS.EXE) and a last set of high-level services starts (such as the Workstation service).
12. Post-logon, Windows creates a new version of the Last Known Good control set based on the current control set.

After putting this list together, I admit feeling a little bit sheepish complaining about how long my system takes to boot.

ARC path nomenclature

In Windows 2000, ARC (Advanced RISC Computing) paths in BOOT.INI help NTLDR figure out where the heck the operating system is. I may as well go on record as saying that I don't like ARC nomenclature. It's obscure and inconsistent and the chances are good that you'll never need it. However, Microsoft loves to put it on the exam, so here are a couple of examples, with explanations following:

```
multi(0)disk(0)rdisk(0)partition(3)
scsi(0)disk(0)rdisk(0)partition(1)
```

- In the first of the examples above, multi(0) refers to the first disk controller, which can be an IDE type or a SCSI type with SCSI BIOS enabled; disk(0) doesn't mean anything, but the number must be zero if the path uses the "multi" designation instead of "scsi"; rdisk(0) means the first disk on the controller; and partition(3) means the third partition, where the numbering starts with the primary partition and continues with logical drives defined on an extended partition (if present).

- In the second example, scsi(0) refers to the first SCSI disk controller whose BIOS is disabled; disk(0) refers to the SCSI ID of the disk drive; rdisk(0) doesn't mean anything; and partition(1) refers to the first partition. Because most SCSI controllers work best with their own BIOS enabled — for example, the BIOS must generally be enabled to boot from a disk on that controller — the SCSI nomenclature has become rather rare. Learn it anyway.

WARNING! In ARC nomenclature, controllers and disks start counting at zero, but partitions start counting at one. I *told* you I hate this stuff.

TIP: If, for some obscure reason, you want to modify BOOT.INI, you must first make it viewable (use the Folder Options control panel to see hidden files and folders) and then turn off the read-only attribute (use the file's property sheet). In real life, you rarely need to modify this file directly; for example, you can change the operating system menu selection delay (the "timeout=xx" line) via the System control panel.

Boot logging

If you want to create a text file listing the events that occur (mainly drivers loading) during a normal boot, press F8 at the "Starting Windows" prompt and choose Enable Boot Logging. The log file is NTBTLOG.TXT and it typically lives in C:\WINNT.

Device derailments

One of the common reasons for a boot problem is a device driver problem. A driver may conflict with another device driver, be corrupt or buggy, doesn't let itself be detected by the operating system, point to a device that isn't working right, or tries to work in a way not supported by Windows 2000. The following sections cover these situations.

Resource conflicts

You can discover resource conflicts quickly in two ways — by using Device Manager and by using the System Information console. You can get to both of these utilities quickly by right-clicking the My Computer icon and choosing Manage.

Here's how to use these utilities:

- Device Manager typically shows devices with resource conflicts by using a yellow-and-black exclamation point.
- System Information has a separate category for "Conflicts/Sharing" (see Figure 15-1). Note that it is not abnormal to see several devices sharing the same interrupt on a PCI-bus computer.

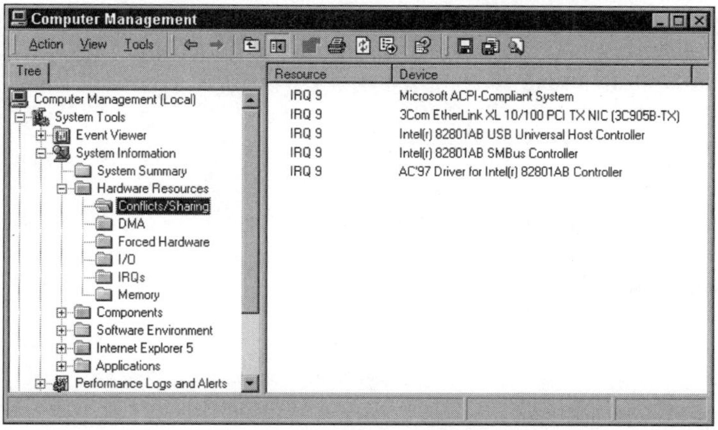

Figure 15-1: System Information combines conflicts and resource sharing data.

You must use Device Manager to manually correct a resource conflict. The typical procedure is as described in Lab 15-1.

Lab 15-1 Correcting a Resource Conflict

1. **Right-click My Computer and choose Manager.**
2. **In the tree pane, click the Device Manager icon under the System Tools node.**
3. **Find the device with a problem in the details pane and double-click it.**
4. **Click the Resources tab.**
5. **Clear the Use Automatic Settings check box, if it lets you.**

   If you can't modify the check box's setting, Windows 2000 doesn't permit you to configure the device manually. You may be able to use a third-party utility in this case.
6. **Manually set interrupts and memory ranges that don't display a conflict in the Conflicting Devices window.**
7. **Click OK and close the Computer Management console.**

STOP screens and crash dumps

A "STOP" screen is something you'd really rather not see. It's a fatal error (fatal to Windows 2000, at least) indicating that something has gone so horribly awry that Windows 2000 believes it should shut itself down, before anything on disk gets messed up worse than it already is.

The exam doesn't expect you to know all the different hexadecimal STOP screen codes, so don't memorize them. What you *do* need to know is how to configure Windows 2000's behavior in the event of a stop screen.

Click the Advanced tab of the System control panel, and then click the Startup and Recovery button to see the dialog box shown in Figure 15-2. The System Failure box is where you can tell Windows 2000 how to act if and when it encounters a STOP screen.

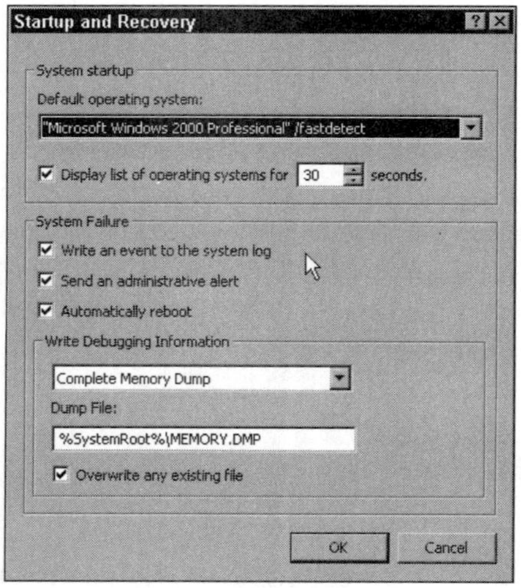

Figure 15-2: Setting crash options in the System control panel.

If you specify that you want to "Write Debugging Information," Windows 2000 creates a memory dump file (with suffix .DMP) containing the contents of RAM when the crash occurred. You would then typically send this file to Microsoft, or a third party software vendor, for detailed analysis. You have three choices for a crash dump, in decreasing order of size: complete, kernel, and small.

You must have enough disk space to hold the whole contents of RAM, plus 1MB breathing room, for a complete dump. The kernel dump is smaller but varies in size, and the small dump is about 64K in size.

Note also that you can specify whether Windows should automatically reboot upon encountering a stop screen. If yes, then you may never get to see the blue stop screen with its various details. Automatic reboot is a better idea for a server than for a workstation.

Detection woes

A device or driver may not be Plug and Play compatible, meaning that Windows 2000 cannot automatically load the correct driver for the device. In such situations, use the Control Panel's Add New Hardware wizard to install the driver. (It should really be called "Add Old Hardware" but we won't quibble.)

USB problems

By far the most common USB snafu is having too many bus-powered devices on the chain. Replace some of the devices with powered versions, or plug in their power supplies if they have them. If the bus comes back to life after you disconnect one or more devices, then current drain may well be the problem.

The second most common USB snafu is that support for USB hasn't been enabled at the BIOS level. In this case, Windows 2000 doesn't even see the USB host controller in the Device Manager tree.

For more on USB configuration rules, please see Chapter 8.

Multi-display problems

The problems you're likely to run into here usually result from one of three things:

- The display adapters aren't on the right bus or buses. AGP and PCI are the only ones that work. No way around this one.
- The BIOS is trying to set your secondary display as the system's primary display. A simple BIOS setting change should fix this one in short order.
- You're trying to use an adapter for a secondary display when that adapter is only certified by Microsoft for use with a primary display. Check the Hardware Compatibility List (HCL) for details.

Curing and preventing device problems

As seasoned Windows troubleshooters have known for years, many problems find their solution in an updated or patched device driver. In Windows 2000 Professional, you can update device drivers several different ways, and — even better — you can control whether non-Microsoft drivers can even infiltrate your PC in the first place.

Driver updating

Here are some of the more common ways that you can update a device driver:

- Double-click a driver in the Device Manager display (get to Device Manager via the System control panel or the Computer Management console), click the Driver tab and then click the Update Driver button. This procedure activates the Driver Update Wizard, which gives you various choices for hunting new drivers (see Figure 15-3).
- Open the relevant control panel for the device you want and update the driver from there. For example, choose the Settings tab of the Display control panel, and then click Advanced, Adapter, Properties, Driver, and Update Driver. (As an exercise, try finding the driver update option in the Sounds and Multimedia control panel.)
- Choose Windows Update from the Start menu to connect to Microsoft's update Web site, and follow the prompts to update a driver if one's available. This method is really intended primarily for updating Windows 2000 system files as opposed to device drivers, but you can update select drivers this way. Note that you can't use Netscape or any other non-ActiveX browser to use Windows Update, because it uses an ActiveX control to inventory your machine and recommend updates.
- Run a vendor-supplied EXE program or INF file (which you would right-click and choose Install).

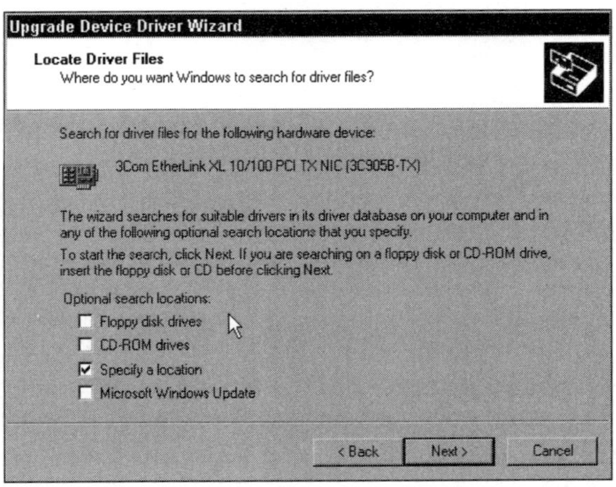

Figure 15-3: The Driver Update Wizard lets you choose where to look.

Driver signing (not by famous golfers)

Microsoft brands a *digital signature* into the core operating system files and drivers that it ships with Windows 2000, as well as files and drivers released subsequently that have passed testing at Windows Hardware Quality Labs (WHQL). That way, Windows 2000 can "tell" when a program installation tries to replace one of those core files with a version not "signed" by Microsoft. (Microsoft has stated that all files that appear on the Windows Update Web site will be cryptographically signed, too.)

The Registry contains settings that govern how Windows 2000 behaves with respect to driver signing. If you want to see the settings in the Local Security Policy utility, look up *Unsigned driver installation behavior* and *Unsigned non-driver installation behavior* under *Security Settings\Local Policies\Security Options*.

You can set the behavior options on an individual PC through the System control panel's Hardware tab by clicking the Driver Signing button to display the dialog box shown in Figure 15-4. If you have administrative privileges on the machine, you can make one setting the default for all users who log on to the PC. The three behaviors, which activate upon an attempt to install a new driver or software component, are as follows:

- **Ignore:** Unsigned drivers may load without notification.
- **Warn:** Unsigned drivers prompt a warning message to the user.
- **Fail:** Unsigned drivers may not install.

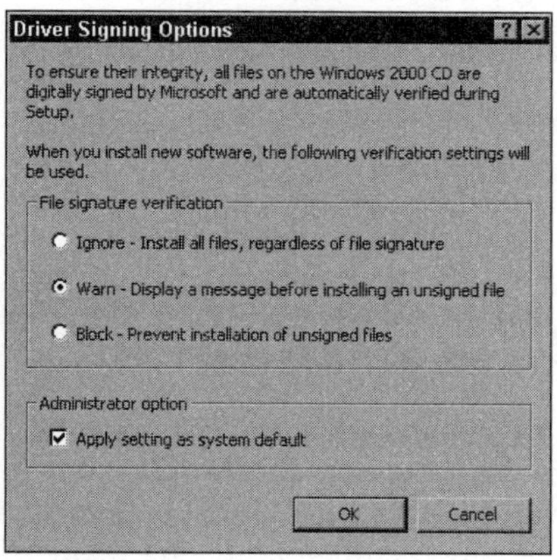

Figure 15-4: Setting options for driver signing.

If a domain-based policy exists for driver signing, it takes precedence over any setting you may make with the Local Security Policy console.

Drivers aren't the only files that have digital signatures in Windows 2000. *System protected files* are the 1600-plus files for which the Windows File Protection system keeps duplicates in the `C:\WINNT\SYSTEM32\DLLCACHE` folder. The idea is that Windows can restore the original copies from the DLLCACHE folder if the "live" ones become corrupted, overwritten, or destroyed. Two utilities let you explore signed system files: SIGVERIF and SFC.

- **SIGVERIF.EXE,** the Signature Verification tool, lets you quickly scan protected system files and verify that their digital signatures are intact. This utility produces a log file, SIGVERIF.TXT, showing the version, modification date, and signed-or-unsigned status of each file. Using the utility's advanced settings dialog box, you can set the program to scan non-system files in any location you specify.
- **SFC.EXE,** the System File Checker, also lets you check the digital signature of system protected files. It works from a script, batch file, or command prompt. SFC doesn't show you the file details that SIGVERIF does, and it doesn't let you scan non-system files. However, SFC does two things that SIGVERIF doesn't: It repopulates the DLLCACHE folder if it detects system files added since Windows was installed, and it offers to replace any system files that it determines are missing or different from their original versions.

The key parameters for SFC.EXE are as follows:

- **/CACHESIZE** lets you specify the maximum size of the DLL cache.
- **/PURGECACHE** clears the DLL cache, and then repopulates it.
- **/SCANNOW** initiates an immediate scan of system protected files.
- **/SCANONCE** sets SFC to perform a scan at the next reboot.
- **/SCANBOOT** sets SFC to perform a scan at every reboot.
- **/CANCEL** deactivates any pending scans.
- **/QUIET** automatically replaces system files without prompting.

Windows 2000 Recovery Methods

In times of serious trouble, when you can't even get Windows 2000 Professional to start properly, you're looking at performing some system recovery. Windows 2000 offers various degrees of recovery, and this section treats them in the same order I usually recommend trying them: from simplest (Last Known Good boot) to most complex (Recovery Console).

Last Known Good boot

When you log on successfully to Windows 2000 Professional, the operating system assumes a "good" boot and writes the control set information to the Registry as the "Last Known Good" control set. (Remember, a control set is a collection of device drivers and their settings.)

Later, if you add a device that interferes with Windows' ability to start normally, you can apply the Last Known Good boot technique, as described in Lab 15-2.

Lab 15-2 Using the Last Known Good Configuration

1. **Restart the system after the failed boot by pressing F8 at the "Starting Windows" text mode prompt.**

   You can also boot while holding down the Ctrl key, if you're worried about tapping the F8 key quickly enough.

2. **At the text mode boot menu, choose Last Known Good Configuration.**

   Doing so instructs Windows to use the last known good control set instead of the current, or default, control set. Because the last known good control set doesn't call the new device driver, it should let you boot normally.

If you suspect a device problem, restart the computer, and forget to choose Last Known Good Configuration, don't log on. The moment you do, the current control set becomes the Last Known Good control set, and you'll have to figure out some other way to exorcise the evil device driver.

Safe Mode

Windows 9*x* offers a Safe Mode boot option that doesn't activate the Registry and that loads only a minimal set of device drivers (basic VGA, mouse, keyboard, disk). Safe Mode has been a boon to troubleshooters, and its absence in NT 4.0 prompted a great deal of pressure from corporate customers for Microsoft to implement something similar in its next operating system.

As a result, Windows 2000 also offers a Safe Mode boot option (press the F8 key at the text-mode boot menu and select Safe Mode, Safe Mode Command Prompt, or Safe Mode with Networking), but it differs from the Windows 9*x* Safe Mode in some key ways. The most important distinction is that Windows 2000 Safe Mode activates the Registry, meaning that you can't back up or restore the Registry using file copy commands in Windows 2000 Safe Mode.

When you're running in Safe Mode, the words "Safe Mode" appear in all four corners of your display. Windows 2000 doesn't load network software in the basic Safe Mode, nor does it load any system services beyond the bare necessities. If you need network access, you can choose Safe Mode with Networking. The Safe Mode with Command Prompt option is sort of a silly one; all it does differently from regular Safe Mode is (you guessed it) display a command prompt without your having to choose Start⇨Run and type **CMD**.

So what would you actually *do* in Safe Mode? Typically, you'd open up Control Panel and undo whatever setting you recently made which may be causing Windows to start abnormally or hang up at boot time. For example, you could remove a newly installed device driver, or start or stop a system service. Then you'd restart normally and see if everything looks fine. If not, you may have to move to the next recovery option, the Recovery Console (coming up soon).

Safe Mode in any of its three flavors automatically creates a boot log named NTBTLOG.TXT in the Windows folder (usually C:\WINNT). See the section, "Boot logging," earlier in this chapter.

You may be curious about the boot menu options "Directory Services Restore Mode" and "Debugging Mode." April Fools! These options don't apply to Windows 2000 Professional, only to the Server product! (You'd think Windows would know which version of itself was installed on a given PC, but apparently it doesn't, at least not this early in the boot process.)

Emergency Recovery Diskette (ERD)

The Emergency Recovery Diskette (ERD) contains a list of system files and their checksums. (*Checksums* are just numerical values based on the contents of a file.) If any system files are damaged to the point that you can't boot to Safe Mode, you can try using the ERD to fix your system. (Assuming, of course, that you've actually *made* an ERD, which you do by clicking a button on the initial screen of the Windows Backup program.)

Start Windows 2000 with the installation CD-ROM, if your PC can boot from the CD (using the "El Torito" specification), or with the four diskettes that you may have created when originally installing Windows 2000. Type **R** for Repair Options and then **R** again for the Emergency Repair process. Pop the ERD into the drive, and Windows compares the system file checksums on your hard drive with the list and the checksums on the diskette. If any don't match, the system prompts you to install the Windows 2000 CD if it's not already present, and copies "good" versions of the corrupted or missing files onto your hard drive.

The ERD repair process can also fix problems with the boot sector. If you see a message like "Operating system not found" when you try to boot, use Emergency Repair to fix the boot sector.

You can't boot a Windows 2000 system from the ERD.

In Windows NT 4.0 the ERD contains part of the Registry, but not in Windows 2000. However, when you make the ERD, you get the opportunity to make a backup copy of the Registry files to a special folder on your hard drive,

`C:\WINNT\repair\RegBack`. You can then restore the Registry from that folder at a later date, if necessary, using the Recovery Console.

Recovery Console

Okay, Last Known Good didn't work, and neither did Safe Mode. Time to bring out a bigger hammer. Recovery Console is new to the NT platform. It lets you start Windows 2000 Professional when Professional won't start otherwise, and it provides a limited number of command line utilities for repairing a damaged system. (Note that these commands are not identical to the commands you can type in a "regular" command prompt running under Windows 2000 Professional in normal operation.) One of the nice aspects of Recovery Console is its capability of working with NTFS drives in a command-line environment.

TIP

Recovery Console doesn't start the Registry, so you can copy backed-up Registry files from (for example) `C:\WINNT\REPAIR` to `C:\WINNT\SYSTEM32\CONFIG` to do a brute-force Registry restore.

Running Recovery Console

Here's the weird part. You run the Recovery Console by starting Windows 2000 setup. You can do this with the installation CD-ROM, if your PC can boot from the CD (using the "El Torito" specification), or by booting with the four diskettes that you may have created when originally installing Windows 2000.

When you get to the Welcome to Setup screen, type **R** to open the Repair Options screen. Then, type **C** to activate the Recovery Console. The computer asks you which Windows 2000 installation you want to work with (usually there's only one, but the program is too dumb to figure this out). Finally, you have to log on with the Administrator password. (If the system is so fouled up that it doesn't recognize this password, you're looking at a restore from a previous backup, as you can't use Recovery Console.)

INSTANT ANSWER

Type **help** at the command prompt to see a list of Recovery Console commands. Here are a few you should know:

- Many viruses infect a hard drive's Master Boot Record, or MBR. You can often clear out such infections by using the Recovery Console's FIXMBR command.
- LISTSVC lists services.
- The DISABLE and ENABLE commands let you start and stop system services and device drivers.
- FDISK lets you do some partitioning work (be careful! this option deletes data!).

- EXIT ends your Recovery Console session.
- COPY lets you copy files, but only from and to the hard disk or disks. You can't copy to or from a diskette or Zip drive.

Installing Recovery Console onto the hard disk

If you find yourself doing a lot of Recovery Console work on a particularly troublesome system, you may want to speed up the load time by installing it onto your hard drive as a boot option on the "choose an operating system" menu. Doing so is easy: Just run the setup program WINNT32.EXE with the /CMDCONS qualifier (it stands for "command console"). You can find WINNT32.EXE on the Windows 2000 Professional CD-ROM, or on the network server from which you installed the operating system.

Don't worry: In spite of the fact that you're running WINNT32, this command doesn't reinstall Windows 2000 Professional onto your system.

Windows Backup

Sometimes even Recovery Console isn't enough to resuscitate a Windows 2000 Professional system. In such cases, you can turn to the backup-and-restore program that comes with Windows 2000, NTBACKUP.EXE or Microsoft Windows Backup. This program is significantly different from the backup utility included with previous versions of Windows. It's actually a scaled-down version of the popular Veritas (formerly Seagate Software) program, Backup Exec.

Advantages

- NTBACKUP can compress files on the fly.
- If you have to use a diskette drive as your target device, NTBACKUP has no trouble creating a multiple-diskette backup to deal with files that are typically too large to fit on one diskette.
- NTBACKUP can also back up to a good variety of target devices, including Zip, Jaz, and writeable optical drives, as well as the more traditional tape drives and network directories. Unlike the Windows NT 4.0 backup program, NTBACKUP can back up to another hard drive (hurrah!).
- NTBACKUP logs its activites (typically in `C:\Documents and Settings\<username>\Local Settings\Application Data\Microsoft\Windows NT\NTBackup\data`).
- NTBACKUP is able to make a backup of your Registry even though the files are open and "in use." That is, NTBACKUP can copy Registry files even when COPY and XCOPY and drag-and-drop can't.

Disadvantages

NTBACKUP requires Windows 2000 to be running in order to restore the files. So, if you experience total hard disk failure and you have to replace the drive, you first have to reinstall Windows 2000 onto the drive before you can run NTBACKUP in order to restore the files you backed up earlier. True, you can specify a minimum install and save some time, but doing so is still a chore and adds an hour or so to your recovery time.

If your system is so damaged that you can't boot Windows 2000 at all, even in "Safe Mode," then you can't run NTBACKUP to restore your system. Here again, you may be faced with a reinstall (and, in extreme cases, a reformat before the reinstall) before you can restore your backup.

Another drawback of NTBACKUP is that you can't save all your backup settings and options to a disk file so that you can run NTBACKUP with a single click. All you can save is the list of files you want to back up. This limitation is all the more limiting in that the command line version of the program doesn't offer every option that the graphical version does.

Procedure

Lab 15-3 shows the basic steps to running Windows Backup.

Lab 15-3 Running Windows Backup

1. **Choose Start⇨Programs⇨Accessories⇨System Tools⇨Backup to start running the program.**

   The initial screen that says "Welcome to the Windows 2000 Backup and Recovery Tools" appears.

2. **Select the Backup Wizard radio button to use the built-in wizard, or click the Backup tab and design your backup job in the utility's main window.**

   The latter method is a little more flexible.

3. **Choose which directories or files you want to back up in the two Explorer-like windows that occupy most of the main screen (see Figure 15-5).**

   When you're done choosing files and folders, you can choose Job⇨Save Selections As, which lets you create a disk file such as FILELIST.BKS containing your file selections. You can later load those file selections in one fell swoop by choosing Job⇨Load Selections.

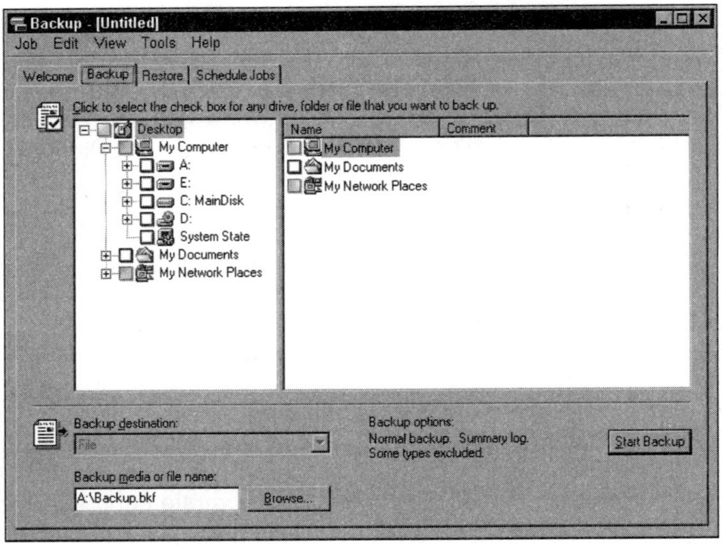

Figure 15-5: The main window of Windows Backup.

4. **Choose Tools➪Options to set your preferences for this backup job.**
5. **Pick a target device in the lower-left corner of the window.**
6. **Click the Start Backup button in the lower-right corner, set a few final options, and you're done.**

   You can't save all those option choices along with your file list, as you can, for example, with a Windows 98 Backup job file. In NTBACKUP, you have to choose your backup options each time you back up (although you can, at least, save a file list with the Job➪Save Selections command).

To restore a backup set with this program, you must first install Windows 2000 Professional (if it isn't already present), and then run NTBACKUP and click the Restore tab. As the saying goes, "installation is the reverse of removal."

Scheduling backups

You can schedule your backups from within the Backup program. When you do so, a new icon appears in your Scheduled Tasks folder. (Microsoft Backup, Scheduled Tasks, AT.EXE, and WINAT.EXE all rely on the *Task Scheduler* service, which normally starts automatically at boot time. You can check the status of this service with the Services control panel.)

The online help for the Scheduled Tasks program lays out the details for specifying the file you want to run (it doesn't have to be Microsoft Windows Backup) and how often you want to run it (every Friday night at 2 a.m., for example). Access the Scheduled Tasks utility by choosing Start➪Programs➪Accessories➪System Tools➪Scheduled Tasks, or Start➪Settings➪Control Panel➪Scheduled Tasks. (For more details on Scheduled Tasks, please refer to Chapter 14.)

System state backups

When you use NTBACKUP, you're likely to see the term *system state* in the hierarchical tree listing of things you can back up (or restore). Microsoft defines the system state to include the following specific elements:

- **The Registry.** Actually, you don't quite get all the Registry, but you do get most of it.
- **The boot files.** Specifically, NTLDR and NTDETECT.COM. These are the minimum files that you need to boot Windows 2000.
- **The COM+ Class Registration Database.** This has to do with software components that may be accessed over a network.
- **All the system files in the C:\WINNT folder.** These files (which have the suffixes DLL, EXE, FON, OCX, SYS, and TTF) amount to at least 200 megabytes. Thankfully, you can exclude them when backing up the system state, at least from NTBACKUP's graphical interface. (You don't have the option to exclude them using NTBACKUP's command-line interface.)

The only way you can back up the local Registry in Microsoft Windows Backup is to select the System State check box in the directory tree on the main backup window. (Checking the folder `C:\WINNT\SYSTEM32\CONFIG`, or checking the individual files therein, works when you back up a remote Registry but doesn't work when you back up your own Registry. NTBACKUP lets you check them, but it won't back them up. These aren't ordinary files, so ordinary procedures don't apply.)

When you do choose to back up the system state, NTBACKUP gives you the opportunity to exclude the system files in the `C:\WINNT` folder, because they occupy so much space (see Figure 15-6).

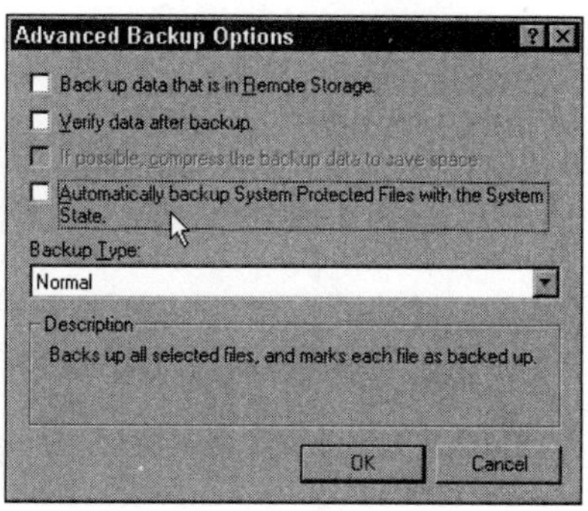

Figure 15-6: Tell Backup that you don't want to back up system files.

Even the system state backup bypasses the multiple possible copies of NTUSER.DAT and USRCLASS.DAT that make up the user-specific Registry files. So, if you want to create a backup job that includes all of these (strongly recommended), go check them as well. These files will either live under the `C:\Documents and Settings\<username>` folder, or under the `C:\WINNT\PROFILES\<username>` folder, depending on whether Windows 2000 is an upgrade of an earlier Windows system or not.

Prep Test

1 **You decide to perform a Registry backup before installing the latest game program from Superego Software. First, you check the current Registry size via the System control panel, and see that it is about 14 MB. Then, you fire up NTBACKUP and click the System State checkbox. You choose a Zip drive as your target device. When you make the backup, however, you find that you need three 100 MB Zip disks. Why is the Registry backup so much larger than you anticipated? (Choose the best answer.)**

A ❍ The System State includes every file on the C drive.
B ❍ The System State includes every EXE, DLL, and OCX file on the C drive.
C ❍ You didn't click the checkbox excluding protected files.
D ❍ You didn't click the checkbox excluding the pagefile.

2 **You're running Recovery Console in order to stop a service that has rendered your PC unbootable. You don't know the exact name of the service, but you think that you would know it if you saw it. Which two Recovery Console commands would you use? (Choose the best answer.)**

A ❍ LIST, STOP
B ❍ LISTSVC, STOPSVC
C ❍ SERVICES, DISABLE
D ❍ LISTSVC, DISABLE
E ❍ SVCLIST, HALT

3 **You install Windows 2000 Professional as a fresh installation onto a new PC. The installation fails repeatedly. Where is the first place you would look to get more information on what's going wrong? (Choose the best answer.)**

A ❍ ERROR.LOG
B ❍ SETUPERR.LOG
C ❍ WINNTERR.LOG
D ❍ WINNTERR.DAT
E ❍ The Event Log

4 **What does the command WINNT32.EXE /CMDCONS do? (Choose the best answer.)**

A ❍ Installs the Command Console
B ❍ Installs Windows 2000 Professional, with the Recovery Console option on the text mode boot menu
C ❍ Installs Windows 2000 Professional, with the Safe Mode option on the text mode boot menu
D ❍ Installs the Recovery Console onto the local hard disk

5 **All the PCs in your office come equipped with built-in removable disk devices (100MB Zip drives). Al, a user in Marketing, is having a problem getting Windows 2000 Professional to start properly. You decide to try booting into Safe Mode, and you're able to get the system running. You have a diagnostic tool (which occupies 35MB) on your server-based home directory, and you want to run that tool next in order to zero in on Al's problem, but you can't seem to access the network. What should you do? (Choose the best answer.)**

A ❍ Load real-mode network drivers. Then you can copy the diagnostic tool from the network share.

B ❍ Reboot and choose Safe Mode With Networking. Then you can copy the diagnostic tool from the network share.

C ❍ Reboot and run the Recovery Console. Then you can copy the diagnostic tool from the network share.

D ❍ Log on to another computer and copy the diagnostic tool to a Zip disk. Load it onto Al's computer.

6 **At which point does Windows 2000 Professional write the current control set into the Last Known Good control set? (Choose the best answer.)**

A ❍ When the "Welcome to Windows" screen appears

B ❍ When the "Starting Windows" text message appears

C ❍ When any user logs on

D ❍ When the Startup folder is processed

7 **Andrea wants to update a device driver on her system. She downloads a new driver from the device manufacturer's Web site (the manufacturer is not Microsoft). She tries installing the driver, but the process fails. She then logs on to her PC as Administrator, opens her System control panel, and changes the Driver Signing setting from Block to Ignore. Upon attempting to install the driver again, the process fails once more. What could be causing the installation to fail?**

A ❍ Andrea belongs to a domain that includes a Group Policy that sets driver signing behavior to Block.

B ❍ Andrea hasn't run the local Group Policy editor, GPEDIT.MSC, to set the local policy for driver signing to Ignore.

C ❍ Andrea needed to set Driver Signing to "Warn" in the System control panel.

D ❍ Windows 2000 Professional does not permit third-party device drivers to run in any circumstance.

8 **A Windows 2000 Professional PC isn't booting all the way to the logon prompt. You enable boot logging by holding down the Ctrl key at startup and choosing the option from the text mode boot menu. Where can you typically find the boot log file? (Choose one answer.)**

A ❍ `C:\WINNT\NTBTLOG.TXT`

B ❍ `C:\WINNT\SYSTEM32\NTBTLOG.TXT`

C ❍ `C:\WINNT\BOOTLOG.TXT`

D ❍ `C:\WINNT\SYSTEM32\BOOTLOG.TXT`

9 **An application is creating fatal crashes and the vendor advises you to submit a complete memory dump. You enable the feature on the System control panel, but after the next crash, you discover that a complete memory dump was not created. What could be the problem? (Choose all that apply.)**

A ❑ You didn't have Administrative rights when you enabled the memory dump.

B ❑ You didn't have Backup Operator rights when you enabled the memory dump.

C ❑ Available disk space is less than (RAM + 1MB).

D ❑ Available disk space is less than 64KB.

10 **You work in an office out of your home in the Yukon ("Great White North"). You have Windows 2000 Professional installed on your PC. One night at 3 a.m., you sit down in front of the screen. All you see is static or "snow." What should you do? (Choose the best answer.)**

A ❍ Boot to the Recovery Console and run FIXMON.

B ❍ Boot to Safe Mode.

C ❍ Boot the PC out the window.

D ❍ Get up and move over to your computer. You're sitting in front of the TV.

Answers

1 **C.** The default behavior of the System State backup is to include all system protected files, that is, system files (mostly DLLs) under *%SystemRoot%*. You must clear the check box that reads Automatically Backup System Protected Files With The System State before making your Registry backup. See "System state backups."

2 **D.** Recovery Console commands are likely subjects for an exam question or two. If you have access to a Windows 2000 machine, boot to the Recovery Console and type HELP to see a list of commands. See "Running Recovery Console."

3 **B.** The error log `C:\WINNT\SETUPERR.LOG` is probably the best place to start. Because Windows hasn't fully installed, the event logs are not likely to contain any useful information. The SETUPACT.LOG file may also contain some hints. See "The trail of crumbs."

4 **D.** This command lets you run Recovery Console from the hard drive instead of by booting the Windows 2000 CD. Note that despite the syntax, nothing called a "Command Console" exists. Also note that this command does ***not*** install the operating system itself. See "Installing Recovery Console onto the hard disk."

5 **B.** The "regular" Safe Mode excludes network support, but you can also choose Safe Mode With Networking, which is easier than choice D, although D would work. See "Safe Mode."

6 **C.** Therefore, if you don't notice a device driver problem until you've restarted and logged on, you can't use the Last Known Good boot option to recover. You would most likely try Safe Mode next in that circumstance. See "Last Known Good boot."

7 **A.** A domain-based policy always overrides a local policy in a Windows 2000 network, so it doesn't matter what Andrea sets on her local PC if her domain policy contradicts the local setting. Choice B is wrong for the additional reason that the System control panel setting is enough to make the behavior change for the local PC, if no domain setting overrides it. C is wrong because "Warn" and "Ignore" both permit third party drivers. D is wrong because it is wrong. See "Driver signing (not by famous golfers)."

8 **A.** Some other versions of Windows use BOOTLOG.TXT and I guess Microsoft wanted to distinguish the NT-platform version of the file. It's a normal ASCII text file that you can view with Notepad. See "Boot logging."

9 **A** and **C.** Only Administrators can set crash dump options, and a complete memory dump requires enough disk space to contain the entire contents of RAM plus an extra megabyte for safety. See "STOP screens and crash dumps."

10 **D**. No TV shows are on at 3 a.m in the Canadian wilderness, explaining the static. FYI, just so I don't get any e-mail from humor-impaired readers, the Recovery Console does ***not*** include a FIXMON command.

Part VI
The Part of Tens

The 5th Wave By Rich Tennant

"OH, I THINK WE'VE FOUND OUR MAN."

In this part . . .

The famous "Part of Tens" is a fixture of the For Dummies books, and one of my favorite aspects of the series. (I admit to turning directly to The Part of Tens whenever I buy a new Dummies book. After reading the cartoons, that is.) So here's Chapter 16, with ten valuable test-taking tips to help speed you on your way to certification.

I thought about including one more chapter in this part, but that would mean a total of 17 chapters, and the idea of a computer book having exactly 16 chapters has a sort of nerdy elegance to it. (I also have 2 dogs, a family of 4, and we live off highway exit 256. Coincidence, you say? Then explain my 65,536 computer magazine subscriptions!)

Chapter 16

Ten Test-Taking Tips

In This Chapter

- Discovering great resources (free and otherwise) to help you prepare
- Getting both your brain and body fired up for the exam
- Finding out tips on answer changing and checking
- Staying cool under pressure

Knowing a few test-preparation tricks can give you a bit of an edge on the exam, so here are ten suggestions that may help rocket you to a passing grade after you've dutifully studied the core material.

Do Your Homework

The best single bit of advice I can give you for passing the Windows 2000 Professional exam is *use the product.* Even if you normally work with Windows 98 or NT 4.0 at work or at home, consider switching to Windows 2000 for the weeks prior to the MCSE test. Set up a dual-boot machine if you need to; use an alternate PC if one is available. (See Chapter 4 for more information on setting up a dual-boot system.) Whenever you have a few minutes free during the day or night, experiment with the Windows 2000 control panels, property sheets, and system utilities. If you can practice using Windows 2000 in a network environment, so much the better: Map drives, print to printers, configure TCP/IP, and try out Dial-Up Networking. The more you use the software, the easier the exam becomes.

Having said that, here's a bushelful of resources that can help you with the book learnin', whether you can wangle access to a Windows 2000 machine or not.

Windows 2000 Professional Resource Kit

Yes, it's expensive. Yes, the documentation really should come with the operating system, especially for what Microsoft is charging for the software. And yes, it's still not a bad idea to go out and buy it, especially if you plan to use Windows 2000 after you take the exam. You're not going to read all 1,792 pages cover to cover (at least I hope not), and you really don't need it to pass the exam. However, for dipping in and out of various technical subjects that you may need to understand more thoroughly, this hefty tome is a smart addition to your bookshelf.

As I write this, the best price on this product is at `www.provantage.com`, but you may want to check other online bookstores as well; the list price is US$69.99, which is fairly appalling (although marginally less appalling than the $79.99 the publisher charged for the *beta* version of this book!). The ISBN number is 1-57231-808-2.

Here's some happy news for those who aren't independently wealthy: You get a subset of the full Resource Kit product "free" on the Windows 2000 Professional CD. Install the Resource Kit tools, which take about 20MB of disk space, as follows:

1. **Log on as a member of the Administrators group.**
2. **Run SETUP.EXE from the** `\SUPPORT\TOOLS` **folder of your setup CD.**
3. **Restart the system.**

The tools install onto your local hard drive, typically `C:\Program Files\Support Tools`. The tools appear on the taskbar as Start⇨Programs⇨Windows 2000 Support Tools. Be aware that although most of the software resides in a cabinet file (SUPPORT.CAB), merely extracting the files from the cabinet file does not perform a complete installation of the Resource Kit tools.

You can also install the tools from the command prompt. Microsoft has packaged them using the Windows Installer methodology, so you can use MSIEXEC.EXE with the appropriate options. For example, if H is your local CD-ROM drive, you could use a command such as the following:

```
MSIEXEC /I H:\SUPPORT\TOOLS\2000RKST.MSI
```

The Resource Kit Tools consist of two categories of software: documentation and utilities. The documentation files include:

- **The Deployment Planning Guide** (DEPLOY.CHM) is a compiled HTML file with a fair amount of information on rolling out Windows 2000.
- **Error and Event Messages** (W2000MSGS.CHM) is a compiled HTML file listing Windows 2000 messages that may appear in the event logs, in

dialog boxes displayed by the operating system itself, in control panels, in utilities, during installation, and so on.

- **Tools Help** (W2RKSUPP.CHM) is a compiled HTML file detailing functions and command-line qualifiers for the utilities. This well-designed module is your most convenient single point of reference for all the support tools, both GUI and command-line varieties. It provides syntax and (even better) examples.
- **Release Notes** (SREADME.DOC) is a Word/WordPad file providing the most current details on installing the support tools software.

The Resource Kit Support Tools package contains GUI-mode utilities and command-line utilities.

- You can view the list of GUI-mode utilities in the menu structure at Start➪Programs➪Windows 2000 Support Tools➪Tools.
- You can view information about the command-line utilities in the Tools Help file (Start➪Programs➪Windows 2000 Support Tools➪Tools Help).

Many of the utilities are holdovers from the Windows NT 4.0 Resource Kit. In fact, some utilities haven't even been modified from their NT 4.0 versions. Note also that some of the support tools pertain to specific environments. For example, Active Directory Administration Tool, Active Directory Replication Monitor, and ADSI Edit are not relevant for an environment that does not use AD.

Finally, you should also know that some of the support tools duplicate functions that already exist in the user interface. KILL.EXE and MEMSNAP.EXE, for example, overlap with the Windows Task Manager display (Ctrl+Alt+Del➪Task Manager).

IDG Books Worldwide

IDG Books Worldwide has some great Windows 2000 books at reasonable prices (in contrast to Microsoft Press, which generally offers average books at high prices). The list is evolving as I write this, so check out `www.idgbooks.com` and `www.dummies.com` to see the most current listing. One in particular that I can vouch for (shameless plug ahead) is my own *Windows 2000 Registry For Dummies*.

Microsoft TechNet

Whether you subscribe to the CD-ROMs (recommended; $295 per year) or simply patronize the Web site (`www.microsoft.com/technet`), TechNet is a good reference for common problems and their solutions. However, it has expanded considerably beyond its early scope of presenting the Microsoft knowledge base in CD format. Now it includes selected resource kits, service packs, online seminars, white papers, walkthroughs, client and server utilities.

As I write this, you get a year's complimentary subscription to TechNet when you get your MCSE.

Internet search engines

Internet search engines are great for finding Windows 2000 information; choose "Windows 2000" as a search phrase and go wild, or get more specific with a query such as ("Windows 2000 Professional" and "Plug and Play"). Here are some of the more popular search services:

- All the Web (`www.alltheweb.com`)
- Altavista (`www.av.com`)
- Excite (`www.excite.com`)
- Google (`www.google.com`)
- HotBot (`www.hotbot.com`)
- Lycos (`www.lycos.com`)
- Northern Light (`www.northernlight.com`)
- Yahoo! (`www.yahoo.com`)

Usenet newsgroups

Usenet newsgroups are like Internet bulletin boards. Some contain lots of information about Windows 2000. These groups can also be good places to post a question when you can't get an answer anywhere else, or when you just want to read what other Windows 2000 users are saying. Newsgroups also often post FAQs (Frequently Asked Questions documents) within the newsgroups themselves and on related Web sites; such FAQs can be good sources of distilled information on specific subjects.

Newsgroups are public. Any sloppy, lazy, uninformed, or even malicious bozo can post to them. Use newsgroups for clues, ideas, and potential problem solutions, but check every tip yourself before you use it or pass it along to others.

Some newsgroups of interest include:

- alt.certification.mcse
- alt.os.windows95.crash.crash.crash (It's not Windows 2000 but it's so funny I had to throw it in.)
- comp.os.ms-windows.misc
- microsoft.public.cert.exam.mcse
- microsoft.public.certification.mcse
- microsoft.public.win2000.enable
- microsoft.public.win2000.activedirectory
- microsoft.public.win2000.applications
- microsoft.public.win2000.dns
- microsoft.public.win2000.filesystem
- microsoft.public.win2000.general
- microsoft.public.win2000.group_policy
- microsoft.public.win2000.hardware
- microsoft.public.win2000.msi
- microsoft.public.win2000.multimedia
- microsoft.public.win2000.netware
- microsoft.public.win2000.networking
- microsoft.public.win2000.printing
- microsoft.public.win2000.registry
- microsoft.public.win2000.security
- microsoft.public.win2000.setup
- microsoft.public.win2000.setup_deployment
- microsoft.public.windows.inetexplorer.ie5.browser

Software is required to read postings from these newsgroups. Windows 2000 comes with Outlook Express 5, formerly Microsoft Internet Mail and News. If you use America Online to access the Internet, you can't use Outlook Express, but you can use AOL's built-in newsreader. Just choose keyword *newsgroups,* click the Expert Add button, and type in the newsgroup name.

Exam simulations

Some companies make a business of providing exam simulations. The fees for these tests have gone down somewhat in recent years, and you can often download demos from the Web before shelling out cash. Here are a couple to check out:

- Transcender (www.transcender.com) — A Transcender demo accompanies this book, on the CD-ROM.
- Self-Test Software (www.stsware.com/microsts.htm).

Microsoft Web sites

Microsoft has hundreds of pages on its own Web site that pertain to Windows 2000. Here are a few to get you started:

- www.microsoft.com/mcp/certstep/mcse.htm
- www.microsoft.com/windows/professional/default.asp
- www.microsoft.com/windows/server/default.asp
- http://resourcelink.mspress.microsoft.com/reslink
- www.microsoft.com/mcp
- www.microsoft.com/technet/
- www.microsoft.com/trainingandservices/default.asp
- www.microsoft.com/windows2000/default.asp
- http://support.microsoft.com/support

Third-party exam information sites

Dozens of non-Microsoft sites offer aid and sustenance to the MCP-seeker. Here's a small sample:

- www.certificationshack.com (that's Certification Shack, not Certifications Hack) is a pretty useful site with details on most Microsoft exams.
- www.cramsession.com has some good overview pages for review the day or two before you take the exam, just to make sure you have all the important bases covered.
- www.mcsedirectory.com is an MCSE smorgasbord, featuring everything from sample exams to online books. A really useful site.

- `http://209.207.167.177` is "Braindump Heaven," where test-takers unload their memories right after exam time. The site warns that some of the information is inaccurate, so *caveat dumpee*. I find that most of it is good stuff.

Magazine Web sites

Here are a few "webzine" sites that are worth a visit. Most have their own keyword search facilities:

- PC World (`www.pcworld.com/pcmag`)
- InfoWorld (`www.infoworld.com`)
- PC Magazine (`www.zdnet.com/pcmag`)
- PC Computing (`www.zdnet.com/pccomp`)
- PC Week (`www.zdnet.com/pcweek`)
- Windows 2000 Magazine (`www.winntmag.com`)

For ongoing technical education, I recommend a print subscription to Windows 2000 Magazine. Call 800-621-1544 or 970-663-4700, or write P.O. Box 447, Loveland, CO 80539-0447 USA.

Leverage Your Biorhythms

Do you experience a lull in alertness in midafternoon, anywhere between 1:30 p.m. and 3:30 p.m.? If so, don't schedule the exam to fall during this time period! For most people, midmorning is best.

You know your own body. If you're an evening person rather than a morning person, slate the exam for as late in the day as you can arrange it. The point is to take the test at a time of day when you normally feel productive and energized.

Get Fired Up

When taking the timed exam, you don't have the luxury of breaks, making a phone call or two to interrupt the tedium, or walking around the building in midtest to get the blood flowing. So you put yourself in a good position to sit down for 100 minutes or so and focus like a laser beam the entire time.

What helps you focus? People are different, but here are some suggestions:

- **Get plenty of sleep the night before.** Don't party hardy on Exam Eve. You know how much sleep you need to be at your peak; for most people, the amount is between seven and eight hours.
- **Exercise.** The morning of the test, oxygenate your brain cells. Run, swim, walk, pump iron, or just do some jumping jacks and running in place. For most people, a little exercise improves alertness.
- **Eat light.** Don't chow down on heavy food before the exam. A full stomach means naptime. Eat a light breakfast or lunch that won't weigh you down. And avoid fast-food burgers. They induce drowsiness.
- **Drink a caffeinated beverage.** If a mug of java or a can of soda (Mountain Dew is said to have high caffeine content) revs your engine, go for it. However, keep the quantity low, so that you don't have to waste valuable exam time on an unplanned biological imperative.
- **Eat cinnamon.** No one knows why, but cinnamon seems to be an energizing spice. A suitably sinful cinnamon roll half an hour before the test may be your tasty ticket to alertness. If that would weigh you down too much, go for a slice of cinnamon toast, or just sprinkle some in your coffee (see previous tip).
- **Try herbal remedies.** Some people like the effects of herbal remedies such as ginkgo and ginseng, which claim to increase mental clarity and boost energy. Just don't try something new on test day.

One substance you *don't* want swimming through your veins on test day is alcohol. If you're taking an afternoon exam, the lunchtime martini, beer, or glass of wine slows you down. Celebrate after you pass, not before.

Get Warmed Up

Whether you believe that "cramming" is a good idea, warming up shortly before the test seems to help most of the people I talk with about the exam. I always do it. The difference between cramming and warming up is one of degree. You don't want to be exhausted before you start the exam, but you do want to get your brain going so you don't have to shift from first gear into fifth as you enter the testing center.

Spend some time before you go to the test center shifting your mental momentum. You can do this several ways: with the CD-based material in this book, with the sample tests, by running through some of the labs, or simply by flipping through the book looking for points that you highlighted and making sure you understand them.

My advice is to spend between one and two hours on your warmup. Too little time doesn't do you any good; too much makes you tired.

TIP

Reread Chapter 1 as part of your warmup. It'll remind you of what to expect regarding the mechanics of the exam.

Kill a Tree

The testing centers I've visited are strangely stingy about the amount of scratch paper they provide. Some just give you a small whiteboard.

If you don't get at least a dozen sheets of paper, ask for more. If you aren't comfortable with the whiteboard, ask for paper. (Bring your own pad just in case. I did that once, and after the administrator looked it over to be sure I hadn't written notes on a tiny sheet tucked up by the adhesive strip, or scratched answers onto the pages with a leadless mechanical pencil, I was allowed to use my pad. Good thing, too; all the center provided was the markerboard, which I hate. Why waste time erasing that thing every 20 seconds?)

Your own mini-diagrams can be a great help, especially in the "scenario" questions that tell a rather long story. The last thing you want between you and a successful exam is a problem as mundane as not having enough paper.

Jump the Gun

TIME SHAVER

Remember that the exam clock doesn't start running until you click the button that displays the first exam question. Here's a clever trick: Write down any charts, mnemonic devices (such as the OSI model), or other memory-joggers (such as the address ranges of different IP address classes) on your scratch paper before starting the exam. Why use up valuable exam time for this sort of thing if you don't have to? True, you may not use all the bits and pieces that you jot down ahead of time, but, on the other hand, it doesn't cost you anything and it can't hurt.

Don't Reinvent Wheels

TIME SHAVER

When I take a non-adaptive multiple-choice certification test, I mark off a half-page on the first sheet of scratch paper to keep track of eliminations: answers I know are wrong on questions I plan to review later. If you study question #19, for example, and you're not quite sure what the answer is but you know it isn't B or C, you mark "19. A B C D" on the scratch paper and cross out the B and C. When you review tough questions after your first pass through the exam, you don't waste time figuring out all over again that B and C aren't correct answers. Putting this "record of eliminations" on the first sheet of your scratch paper means that you don't have to hunt for these notes.

Trust Your Gut

You should certainly review questions that you have doubts about, and check your reasoning twice on every question if you have the time. (In a non-adaptive test, you can mark questions for review as you go along, then go back and study them after you reach the end of the test.) But if you're tempted to change an answer, be sure you have a compelling reason.

Although the exam questions can be tricky on occasion, most of them are fairly straightforward, which means that you should give some extra weight to your first reaction. I've found from taking lots of MCSE assessment tests that my gut instinct is more often right than wrong.

Check the Numbers

The most frustrating missed answers are those in which you click one answer when the question really calls for two or three or "as many as apply." Therefore, I double-check whether the question asks for a single answer or multiple ones. Although I'm aware of the pitfall, I usually catch one or two questions where I didn't pay enough attention and omitted a relevant answer.

Keep Your Head

You certainly want to pass the test on the first try. However, don't get worked up about it. Worry can become a self-fulfilling prophecy: If you agonize over whether you're answering enough questions right instead of answering the questions themselves, you're likely to create cause for worry!

Remind yourself of the following, and you're more likely to succeed:

- The exam fee is the equivalent of six loaded pizzas. Even if you have to retake the exam, your $200 investment comes back to you many times as you progress in your career. (If your company is paying, pay the retest fee out of your own pocket if you feel awkward asking the boss again.)

- The exam is *not* a measure of how smart you are! It's a measure of how well you know what Microsoft thinks you need to know Windows 2000, how well you take tests, and how sharp you feel on exam day.
- Microsoft, the testing center, the test, and this book aren't going anywhere anytime soon. If you don't pass today, you can pass next week, or next month, or whenever you feel ready.
- These MCSE tests are designed so that almost nobody gets a perfect score, and darn few people get an "A" (90 percent or above). An MCSE with a 71 percent average in six exams gets the same letters after his or her name as an MCSE with a 95 percent average.
- Rumor has it that even Bill Gates has trouble passing some of the MCSE tests. Of course, he has a more impressive credential: MSCEO.
- You already have a great advantage over most exam-takers by virtue of having read this book. You can feel confident because of that edge.
- Don't tell everyone you know that you're taking the exam. The fewer who know you're taking it, the less you'll worry about what they will think of you if you fail. Tell the world afterward, preferably with a poetic flair. "Pizza's on me, I'm an MCSE!" (Substitute "MCP" as appropriate.)

Part VII
Appendixes

The 5th Wave — By Rich Tennant

"ACCORDING TO THIS RESUME YOU'VE DONE A LOT OF JOB-HOPPING."

In this part . . .

The four appendixes (and before you defenders of the English language fire up your e-mail programs to send me a message, let me assure you that it is just as correct to say "appendixes" as it is to say "appendices") in this part can be critically important parts of your successful path to MCSE-dom.

The practice test in Appendix A gives you a very good flavor of the actual exam while also pointing out any knowledge gaps you may have. Appendix B helps you map out your MCSE certification program and discusses other Microsoft certification options you may want to pursue. The glossary (Appendix C) may come in handy as you read the main body of this book and bump into words that are foreign to you. Finally, the CD-ROM Appendix explains the various goodies on the enclosed disk, which are well worth a chunk of your time.

Appendix A

Practice Exam

- Practice Exam Rules
- 90 minutes
- 50 questions
- At least 62 percent to pass
- Treat this test as closed-book: Don't look ahead (to the answers) or behind (to the chapters)

Here's a sample exam to help prepare you for the real deal.

The actual passing percentage is 62 percent as I write this, but Microsoft can change it at any time. Also, the passing percentage is likely to change for adaptive versions of the test. If you get 80 percent or better on this sample exam, you should be in good shape for the real thing. If you get 100 percent, I salute you.

I cover the same topics that the Microsoft exam covers, but it's unlikely that any of the questions in this sample exam appear verbatim on the Microsoft exam. If you miss a question, reread the section in the book that covers that topic. The answers guide you to the correct chapter and objective.

The actual exam includes the occasional simulation and graphical exhibit. I dispense with these here; if you can understand the word questions, the graphical simulations and exhibits will actually be easier for you.

REMEMBER

Like the actual exam, you have circles to mark your answer when only one answer can be correct, and square boxes when there may be more than one correct answer.

The test questions in this sample exam are different than the ones in the prep tests at the end of each main chapter. Therefore, even if you've gone through each chapter's prep test, the sample exam is worth taking. Good luck!

Prep Test

1 **You are a network administrator at a medium-sized company. Bob in Sales comes to you with a complaint: A print job he started never finished. Upon further investigation, you discover that several users have submitted print jobs that never finished. It turns out that the printer, connected to the PC named PSERV, has malfunctioned and you can't restart it. There's another identical printer on the network, but you don't want to have to tell 20 users to resubmit their print jobs to that other printer. What's your best approach to solve this problem?**

A ❍ Go to the Printers folder on the machine sharing the printer and choose File➪Pause Printing. Then physically move the identical network printer to the PSERV machine. Choose File➪Pause Printing again to clear the toggle.

B ❍ Open the spool folder on the PSERV machine and drag-and-drop all the spooled files to the icon in the Printers folder for the identical network printer.

C ❍ Right-click the stalled printer's icon and choose Properties, and then Ports. Choose Add Port, Local Port, New Port, and type the UNC name for the functioning network printer.

D ❍ Right-click the stalled printer's icon and choose Properties, and then Ports. Choose Redirect Port, Local Port, Network Port, and type the UNC name for the functioning network printer.

2 **Donna comes to you wanting more disk space on her Windows 2000 Professional computer. Specifically, she has a folder on her C drive named DONNA_DATA, where she stores all her data files, and her C drive (formatted with NTFS) is nearly full. All of Donna's programs are configured to save files to C:\DONNA_DATA. Donna works with sensitive information, so the entire DONNA_DATA folder uses NTFS encryption.**

What solution could you implement that would minimize the impact on Donna's daily work habits and, at the same time, be easy for you? (Choose the best answer.)

A ❍ Do a full backup with NTBACKUP.EXE. Install a larger hard drive. Reinstall Windows 2000 Professional onto the fresh drive and then do a full restore.

B ❍ Copy the contents of Donna's C drive to the network. Install a larger hard drive. Copy all the files back from the network to the C drive.

C ❍ Activate NTFS compression on the DONNA_DATA folder.

D ❍ Move Donna's data files to the network. Install a second hard drive and mount it to C:\DONNA_DATA. Move the files back.

3 You're installing Windows 2000 Professional onto a brand new computer that will become a member of a domain having both Windows 2000 and Windows NT servers. Which of the following statements is true regarding the computer name? (Choose all that apply.)

A ❑ It should contain no more than 15 characters.

B ❑ It should be unique among all other NetBIOS computer names in the domain.

C ❑ It should not have the same name as the domain.

D ❑ It should use the 8+3 naming convention if it will share resources to Windows 95 clients.

4 As a software application developer, you need to set up a dual-boot machine that can run Windows NT Workstation 4.0 and Windows 2000 Professional. After you install NT onto an NTFS partition, you install Windows 2000 into a separate NTFS partition, per Microsoft's advice. However, you notice immediately after installing Windows 2000 that you are no longer able to boot to Windows NT! What gives?

A ❍ Windows 2000 automatically upgraded the NT partition to NTFS version 4, and you didn't have Service Pack 3 installed.

B ❍ Windows 2000 automatically upgraded the NT partition to NTFS version 5, and you didn't have Service Pack 4 installed.

C ❍ You must run the NT Emergency Recovery process and restore the boot sector.

D ❍ You must use FAT for the system partition on a dual-boot machine with NT 4.0 and Windows 2000.

5 You decide to roll out Windows 2000 Professional using RIS, or Remote Installation Service. You use RIS to install Windows 2000 Pro onto the client computer you will use as a "master" image. Then you install the user applications you want to roll out along with Windows 2000 Professional.

What utility do you need to run in order to copy the master image to the network server?

A ❍ The Remote Installation Preparation wizard

B ❍ The Remote Image Replication wizard

C ❍ The System Preparation program

D ❍ Systems Management Server (SMS)

6 Which of the following network services must be available somewhere on the network for RIS installations to work?

A ❑ Active Directory

B ❑ DHCP

C ❑ DNS

D ❑ WINS

7 **You're creating a new user account on a Windows 2000 Professional PC, and you want to make it a member of one of the built-in local groups. Which of these groups most nearly approximates a standard user account in Windows NT Workstation 4.0?**

A ❍ Users
B ❍ Restricted Users
C ❍ Power Users
D ❍ Administrators

8 **You want to connect to a networked TCP/IP printer on your corporate intranet. Which of the following statements about the Add Printer wizard is correct? (Choose all that apply.)**

A ❑ You can specify the printer using a Uniform Resource Locator.
B ❑ You can specify the printer using its share name.
C ❑ You can specify the printer by browsing the network for it.
D ❑ You can specify the printer using its SID.

9 **You install a USB speaker system on your Windows 2000 Professional computer. However, it doesn't work, even after you restart the computer. You open Device Manager, and you expand every node but you cannot find an entry for the USB host controller. What should you do next?**

A ❍ Enable the USB controller in the BIOS.
B ❍ Run the Add New Hardware wizard.
C ❍ Enable the USB controller in the System control panel.
D ❍ Reinstall Windows 2000 with a different HAL.

10 **Wilma is an employee of your company. She gets a sweet job offer from an Internet startup and quits your brick-and-mortar business faster than you can say "dot com." Your company hires a replacement, Betty. What's the easiest way for you to disable Wilma's local user account and create a local user account for Betty that has the exact same access rights as Wilma's old account?**

A ❍ Delete Wilma's account and create Betty's account using the Users and Passwords control panel. Recreate any special file and folder access permissions manually, using Windows Explorer.
B ❍ In the Local Users and Groups console, copy Wilma's account to create a new account for Betty, and then delete Wilma's account.
C ❍ In the Local Users and Groups console, rename Wilma's account to Betty, and then change the account password.
D ❍ In the Users and Passwords control panel, click on Wilma's account, type **Ctrl+V**, and then click anywhere in the user list and type **Ctrl+P**.

11 **You convert a FAT disk to NTFS on a Windows 2000 Professional computer. Later, the user asks you to convert it back to FAT, as he needs to be able to boot to a DOS diskette and access the hard drive. Which of the following methods can accomplish the conversion?**

A ❍ Right-click My Computer, choose Manage, and click Disk Management in the left windowpane. Right-click the disk in the right windowpane, choose Properties, and change the file system from NTFS to FAT.

B ❍ Right-click My Computer, choose Manage, and click Disk Management in the left windowpane. Right-click the partition in the right window-pane, choose Properties, and change the file system from NTFS to FAT.

C ❍ Back up the disk, reinstall Windows 2000, format the disk to NTFS during the first part of the installation procedure, and restore the disk backup after Windows 2000 is installed.

D ❍ Back up the disk, boot to a DOS diskette, run FDISK to format the disk to NTFS, then install Windows 2000 and restore the disk backup after Windows 2000 is installed.

E ❍ Open a command prompt and type **CONVERT /FS:FAT**. Then, reboot in order for the conversion utility to activate.

12 **How can you use NTBACKUP.EXE to back up the local Registry? (Choose all correct answers.)**

A ❑ Check the C:\WINNT\SYSTEM32\REG folder.

B ❑ Check the C:\WINNT\SYSTEM32\CONFIG folder.

C ❑ Check the System State check box.

D ❑ Click the Emergency Repair Diskette button and check the optional check box.

13 **You have to use the Registry to troubleshoot a device driver problem. The device manufacturer's tech support person tells you to open windows in REGEDT32 for the "two main Registry keys" and minimize the other windows.**

Which of the following Registry main keys is merely a pointer to a subkey of one of the other main keys, and therefore not one of the "two main" keys? (Choose all that apply.)

A ❑ HKEY_CLASSES_ROOT

B ❑ HKEY_CURRENT_USER

C ❑ HKEY_LOCAL_MACHINE

D ❑ HKEY_DYN_DATA

14 **Emily recently upgraded her Windows NT 4.0 Workstation computer to Windows 2000. She discovers that she can now specify a password for her account that is shorter than ten characters, something she was not able to do under NT. She comes to you, the PC administrator, to reset her system so that it again requires at least ten characters for the account password. Which of the following actions accomplishes this goal?**

- **A** ❍ Open the Computer Management console, choose the Local Security Policy snap-in, and set Minimum Password Length under the Password Policy node.
- **B** ❍ Open the Administrative tools console, choose the Local Security Policy snap-in, and set Minimum Password Length under the Password Policy node.
- **C** ❍ Open the Users and Passwords control panel, click Emily's account in the list, click the Properties button, choose the Passwords tab, and enter the number 10 in the Minimum Password Length field.
- **D** ❍ Open the Computer Management console, choose the Local Users and Groups snap-in, and set Minimum Password Length under the Password Policy node.

15 **Mary is an Administrator of her own Windows 2000 Professional PC. She runs the Local Security Policy console and enables the Security Options policy "Disable CTRL+ALT+DEL Requirement for Logon." However, the next time she restarts, she still has to press Ctrl +Alt+Del to log on. Why? (Choose the best answer.)**

- **A** ❍ A Group Policy setting that overrides Mary's local setting has been made at the domain level.
- **B** ❍ A Group Policy setting that overrides Mary's local setting has been made at the site or domain level.
- **C** ❍ A Group Policy setting that overrides Mary's local setting has been made at the site, domain, or organizational unit level.
- **D** ❍ Mary forgot to choose File⇨Save to commit her changes to disk.

16 **A remote network user is having application problems. Which of the following utilities can you use to diagnose and/or troubleshoot remote computers?**

- **A** ❑ REGEDIT
- **B** ❑ REGEDT32
- **C** ❑ Event Viewer
- **D** ❑ System Monitor

17 **You install a new device driver, reboot Windows 2000 Professional, log on, and discover that the system is no longer working correctly. What should your first system recovery step be? (Choose the best answer.)**

A ❍ Restart, press F8, and specify Last Known Good Configuration.

B ❍ Restart, press F5, and specify Last Known Good Configuration.

C ❍ Restart, press F8, specify Safe Mode, and remove the driver.

D ❍ Boot your Emergency Recovery Diskette and remove the driver.

E ❍ Boot from the Windows 2000 CD and choose Recovery Console.

18 **Georgina complains that she is unable to access the BUDGET folder on Jim's Windows 2000 Professional computer from her Windows 2000 Professional machine. Jim has shared the folder using shared folder permissions as follows: Read access allowed to the Sales group; Change access allowed to the Managers group; and Full Control access denied to the Staff group. She belongs to both the Sales and Staff groups. What can you do to give Georgina access to the BUDGET folder? (Choose one answer.)**

A ❍ Make Georgina a member of the Managers group.

B ❍ Have Jim add Georgina's individual user account to the BUDGET folder's permission list, with Full Control access allowed.

C ❍ Make Georgina a member of the Power Users group.

D ❍ Remove Georgina from the Staff group.

19 **You are configuring a notebook computer to dial up a private LAN. The notebook computer is equipped with a smart card. Which dial-up security protocol are you most likely to use? (Choose the best answer.)**

A ❍ MS-CHAP

B ❍ MS-CHAPv2

C ❍ SPAP

D ❍ EAP

E ❍ SCSP

F ❍ IPsec

20 **You're in charge of securing your company's Windows 2000 network. You decide to study the various settings in the predefined security templates, so that you can determine which one is the best fit for your organization. What's the best tool for you to use when studying the settings in the INF template files?**

A ❍ The Security Templates snap-in

B ❍ The Security Configuration and Analysis snap-in

C ❍ The Local Security Policy console

D ❍ The Local Group Policy console

E ❍ The SECEDIT program

21 **You just added a network adapter to your Windows 2000 Professional workstation, and installed the Client Service for NetWare (CSNW). How would you configure that machine to access a NetWare 5 server running IP only?**

A ❍ Choose Start⇨Settings⇨Control Panel⇨CSNW, click the Advanced button, and click the radio button labeled "Access NetWare servers using TCP/IP only."

B ❍ Choose Start⇨Settings⇨Control Panel⇨Administrative Tools⇨CSNW, click the Advanced button, and click the radio button labeled "Access NetWare servers using TCP/IP only."

C ❍ Right-click the LAN connection icon in the Network and Dial-Up Connections folder. Click the Networking tab, clear the IPX/SPX checkbox, and check the TCP/IP checkbox.

D ❍ You can't configure the workstation this way without third-party software.

22 **You get a complaint from Baxter, who believes that another user of his PC, Frieda, is meddling with Baxter's files. You decide to enable auditing on the file system in order to see if Baxter's claims have merit. Which of the following audit policies should you enable in the Local Security Policy console?**

A ❍ Audit system events

B ❍ Audit account management

C ❍ Audit process tracking

D ❍ Audit object access

23 **Your organization has a TCP/IP network of Windows 2000 workstations and Windows 2000 Server computers. One of the servers is set up to provide a link to the Internet. Emily complains that she can connect to any of the local servers on her subnet, but not to the public Internet. What's the most likely cause of the problem? (Choose the best answer.)**

A ❍ Emily's PC has an incorrect IP address on the General tab of the TCP/IP property sheet for the LAN connection.

B ❍ Emily's PC has an incorrect IP address for the default gateway on the IP Settings tab of the TCP/IP property sheet.

C ❍ No Windows 2000 server is running WINS.

D ❍ No Windows 2000 server is running DHCP.

24 **You install Windows 2000 Professional onto a PC that supports Advanced Power Management and used to run Windows 98. Although the "shut down" command would power off your PC under Windows 98, it does not do so under Windows 2000. How can you fix this problem? (Choose the best answer.)**

A ❍ You can't fix it. APM machines don't support power-down on shutdown.

B ❍ In the Power Options control panel, choose the Shutdown tab, and click the check box labeled Power Off at Shutdown.

C ❍ In the Power Options control panel, choose the APM tab, and click the check box labeled Enable Advanced Power Management Support.

D ❍ Enable support for APM in the BIOS.

25 **What's the default file extension for a Windows Installer package?**

A ❍ MSI
B ❍ WMI
C ❍ INF
D ❍ WSI

26 **Bertie is an employee at your company and says his dial-up link to an ISP is too slow. He works in an office that has a spare phone line, and you decide to implement a multilink setup. Which of the following statements are true about multilink connections in Windows 2000 Professional? (Choose all that apply.)**

A ❑ Both modems must be the same speed.
B ❑ You can combine a modem and an ISDN line.
C ❑ The ISP must support multilink connections.
D ❑ Both modems must be internal.

27 **You're working on a network-connected Windows 2000 Professional notebook machine and you've made a particular file on a Windows 2000 Server "available offline." You synchronize files and leave on a trip. While you're away, you make changes to the file, but another user makes changes to the copy on the server machine, too. When you return, and attempt to synchronize with the network, what happens with this file?**

A ❍ Windows 2000 detects that both copies have been edited and asks you what you want to do.
B ❍ Windows 2000 detects that both copies have been edited and automatically saves your version to the server but with a different file name.
C ❍ Windows 2000 doesn't detect that both copies have been edited, and simply replaces the older file with the newer one. Changes made to the older file are lost.
D ❍ You receive an Error 601 from the Synchronization Manager.

28 **You need to access the C:\WINNT folder of a remote Windows 2000 Professional computer on your company's local area network. However, the user has not shared any folders. What "secret" share name can you use to connect to this folder? (Choose the best answer.)**

A ❍ ADMIN$
B ❍ C$\ADMIN
C ❍ C$\WINNT
D ❍ WINNT$

29 **You need to set up a Virtual Private Network connection over the public Internet. How should you proceed? (Choose the best answer.)**

A ❍ Start the Make New Connection wizard in the Network and Dial-Up Connections folder. Choose the Connect To A Private Network Through The Internet option.

B ❍ Start the Make New Connection wizard in the Network and Dial-Up Connections folder. Choose the Create a Virtual Private Network Link option.

C ❍ Start the Make New Connection wizard in the Administrative Tools folder. Choose the Create a Virtual Private Network Link option.

D ❍ You can't do this. You can only create VPN links across private networks.

30 **Which of the following statements is true about Disk Defragmenter?**

A ❍ It only works with NTFS volumes.

B ❍ It only works with local volumes.

C ❍ Microsoft recommends you have 5 percent or more free space on disk before using it.

D ❍ It defragments the Windows page file.

31 **Your boss tells you that he is sick and tired of PCs crashing due to buggy third-party device drivers and he wants you to make sure that users can't install any unsigned drivers onto their Windows 2000 Professional machines. The network you manage has 100 PCs and 3 servers, all running Windows 2000 Server (2 are domain controllers). What is your best move to meet your boss's demand?**

A ❍ Set a "block" value for the policy "Unsigned driver installation behavior" at the domain level.

B ❍ Use the Local Security Policy console to set a "block" value for the policy "Unsigned driver installation behavior" on each local workstation.

C ❍ Log on as an administrator and run the System control panel on each local workstation. Choose the Hardware tab and the Driver Signing button. Click "Block – Prevent installation of unsigned files" and check the box labeled "Apply setting as system default."

D ❍ Do nothing. This is Windows 2000 Professional's default behavior.

32 **When setting up roaming user profiles on Windows 2000 Professional computers in a network whose servers are running Windows 2000 Server, you decide that you want to limit the profile data that is stored on network servers. Which file on each user's local hard drive contains information about roaming profile exclusions?**

A ❍ C:\PROFILES*<username>*\EXCLUSIONS.TXT

B ❍ C:\WINNT\PROFILES*<username>*\EXCLUSIONS.DAT

C ❍ C:\DOCUMENTS AND SETTINGS*<username>*\NTUSER.INI

D ❍ C:\DOCUMENTS AND SETTINGS*<username>*\EXCLUSIONS.TXT

33 **You receive Service Pack #14 for Windows 2000 Professional. You want to apply this service pack to your master distribution server, so that all subsequent installations of Windows 2000 Professional from the server will incorporate the service pack. What command should you use?**

A ❍ UPDATE.EXE /SRV

B ❍ UPDATE.EXE /SLIP

C ❍ UPDATE.EXE /IMG

D ❍ PATCH.EXE /IMG

34 **Raymond has encrypted a sensitive file on his Windows 2000 Professional machine's C drive, which uses NTFS. He makes regular backups by copying the file to his D drive, which uses FAT32. In order to protect against physical damage to his computer, he also occasionally copies the file to an NTFS network drive on a Windows 2000 server. Which of the following statements is true? (Choose all that apply.)**

A ❍ The file on Raymond's D drive is encrypted.

B ❍ The file on the network drive is encrypted.

C ❍ Windows 2000 does not permit copying encrypted files to FAT32 disks.

D ❍ Windows 2000 does not permit copying encrypted files over the network.

35 **You're setting up some PCs for international language support because your company is managing an international research project. You know that Windows 2000 Professional supports Unicode, an international-standard character set that has extra characters above and beyond those that appear in the ASCII character set. However, one of the applications you run doesn't support Unicode, and menus and dialog boxes don't appear correctly in that application.**

How can you change the default language that Windows 2000 uses for non-Unicode applications on a single Windows 2000 machine?

A ❍ In the Regional Options control panel, choose the General tab and the Set Default button to change the System Locale.

B ❍ In the Regional Options control panel, click the appropriate language in the list titled Language Settings for the System.

C ❍ In the Regional Options control panel, click the appropriate language in the list titled Language Settings for the System, then click the Set as Default button.

D ❍ Windows 2000 doesn't support applications that don't support Unicode.

36 **Ralph has shared a folder, RALPHSTUFF, on his NTFS drive with the share permission Full Control to EVERYONE. Later, Ralph sets the NTFS permission, Read & Execute, to the same folder for the group TEMPS. Ralph also removes inherited NTFS permissions for the group EVERYONE, so the only NTFS permissions for RALPHSTUFF apply to the group TEMPS. Francine is a member of TEMPS but also (naturally) a member of EVERYONE, which still has the share permission of Full Control. Can she delete a file in the RALPHSTUFF folder? (Choose the best answer.)**

A ❍ Yes. The share permission "Full Control" overrides the NTFS permission "Read & Execute."

B ❍ No. When NTFS permissions exist, share permissions are ignored.

C ❍ Yes. Just because Francine can Read and Execute files at the NTFS permisison level doesn't mean she can't delete files at the share permission level.

D ❍ No. Francine's effective permissions are the most restrictive combination of share permissions and NTFS permissions.

37 **You have just graduated from business school. Your boss asks you to analyze the costs and benefits of using multiple displays as opposed to very large single displays, so you begin gathering facts that may affect the overall cost of multiple display setups. Which of the following statements about Windows 2000 Professional's multiple display support are correct?**

A ❑ You can have a maximum of three simultaneously active displays.

B ❑ All video adapters in a multiple display setup must use the PCI bus.

C ❑ All video adapters in a multiple display setup must use the PCI bus or the AGP bus.

D ❑ Some video cards work as a primary display but not as a secondary display.

E ❑ Some computers automatically disable onboard video circuits when one or more plug-in adapters are detected.

38 **You want to test 200 PCs for compatibility with Windows 2000 Professional before you upgrade them. You have several options for performing this test. Which files could you use? (Choose all that apply.)**

A ❑ CHKUPGRD.EXE

B ❑ WINNT32.EXE

C ❑ UNATTEND.TXT

D ❑ APCOMPAT.EXE

39 **Which of the following accessibility settings helps users who may tap keyboard keys unintentionally and involuntarily? (Choose the best answer.)**

A ❍ ToggleKeys

B ❍ FilterKeys

C ❍ StickyKeys

D ❍ QuickKeys

40 **You've enabled Automatic Private IP Addressing on a Windows 2000 Professional workgroup. Which of the following is a valid address for a computer in that workgroup?**

A ❍ 169.254.10.10

B ❍ 127.0.0.1

C ❍ 169.10.10.2

D ❍ 255.255.0.0

41 **You come to work one morning and discover that your PC won't boot to Windows 2000, but hangs at the graphical startup splash screen (you know, the one that's mostly white and flickers like crazy). You think about using the Recovery Console, but you realize that your boss is on vacation and she's the only one with a Windows 2000 Professional CD. Thankfully, you remember that you installed the Recovery Console from the Windows 2000 CD onto your computer's hard disk.**

Assuming that your CD drive uses letter E, what command did you use to install the Recovery Console onto your hard disk?

A ❍ WINNT32.EXE /CMDCONS

B ❍ WINNT.EXE /CMDCONS

C ❍ CMDCONS.EXE C:

D ❍ CONSOLE.EXE E: C:

E ❍ RECOVER.EXE /S:E /T:C

42 **You have a portable computer that can have a diskette drive or a CD-ROM drive in the internal drive bay, but not both. You need to create two hardware profiles under Windows 2000 Professional for this situation. How do you begin?**

A ❍ Run the System control panel. Choose the Hardware tab. Click the Hardware Profiles button. Copy the current profile and give the copy a new name.

B ❍ Run the System control panel. Choose the Hardware tab. Click the Hardware Profiles button. Click the New button and give the new profile a name.

C ❍ Run the Add New Hardware wizard. Specify "Hardware Profile" as the device type to add.

D ❍ Right-click the Computer icon in Device Manager. Choose Add Hardware Profile from the context menu.

43 **Which of the following security templates provides the strictest security for a Windows 2000 Professional workstation?**

A ❍ BASICWK
B ❍ HISECWK
C ❍ HISECWS
D ❍ SECUREWS
E ❍ SECUREWK

44 **Jennifer, an employee at Acme Widgets, is concerned that she doesn't have enough RAM in her Windows 2000 Professional computer, which runs a manufacturing program essential to the operation of your plant. You decide to use the Performance Logs and Alerts console snap-in to track page faults per second. However, you can't slow down her computer excessively. Which option would you choose? (Pick the best answer.)**

A ❍ Alert
B ❍ Trace log
C ❍ Counter log
D ❍ Message

45 **What information about your TCP/IP configuration can you gather from the IPCONFIG utility? (Choose all that apply.)**

A ❑ IP address
B ❑ Subnet mask
C ❑ IP address of DHCP server
D ❑ MAC address of network card (if present)

46 **A user comes to you with performance complaints about his Windows 2000 Professional computer. He has 64 MB of memory and about 75 MB of free disk space. What steps would you suggest he take? (Choose all that apply.)**

A ❑ Defragment the hard disk.
B ❑ Run the Disk Cleanup wizard.
C ❑ Set the pagefile to 32 MB.
D ❑ Add another 64 MB of memory.

47 **WINS is the name of a network service that matches up which of the following?**

A ❍ NetBIOS names with domain names
B ❍ Domain names with IP addresses
C ❍ IP addresses with workgroup names
D ❍ NetBIOS names with IP addresses

48 **You set up a single Scheduled Task on your computer to run at 2 a.m. You find out the next day that it didn't execute. What could be possible reasons for this?**

A ❑ Someone has stopped the Task Scheduler service.

B ❑ You didn't specify a proper security context for the task.

C ❑ You didn't log on as Administrator when creating the task.

D ❑ No one was logged on to the PC at 2 a.m.

49 **You have a notebook computer that has a PC Card USB host adapter. You use the USB controller when the notebook is at your office in its docking station. However, while you're on the road, you don't use any USB peripherals. How can you reduce the computer's power consumption while on battery power? (Choose the best answer.)**

A ❍ Run the System control panel, click the Hardware tab, and click the Hardware Profiles button. Double-click the profile corresponding to the undocked state. Go to Device Manager and disable the USB controller.

B ❍ Run the System control panel, click the Hardware tab, and click the Hardware Profiles button. Right-click the profile corresponding to the undocked state and choose Properties. In the device list, clear the check box for the USB controller.

C ❍ Undock the computer, reboot it, and choose the undocked profile if Windows doesn't select it automatically. Remove the USB controller in Device Manager.

D ❍ Undock the computer, reboot it, and choose the undocked profile if Windows doesn't select it automatically. Disable the USB controller in Device Manager.

50 **You're using System Monitor to track CPU utilization, specifically, interrupts per second. At what value of sustained interrupt activity do you begin to suspect that a second processor is necessary to optimize system performance?**

A ❍ 5

B ❍ 10

C ❍ 15

D ❍ 50

Answers

1 **C.** By adding a port to the existing printer definition, you allow Windows to automatically redirect all existing print jobs. Choice A is wrong because you could strain your back moving the printer. Choice B might work, but some of those files may be incomplete (in the process of spooling). Choice D is wrong because no such option exists. Objective: Manage printers and print jobs (Chapter 7).

2 **D.** This way, Donna doesn't have to reconfigure any of her applications to save files somewhere else. A and B are both fairly major chores. Choice C would work if not for the fact that the data folder uses encryption, and you can't have both encryption and compression active for the same folder. Objective: Monitor and configure disks (Chapter 7).

3 **A, B,** and **C.** Choice D would be true if it said "Windows 3.1" instead of "Windows 95," but Windows 95 can understand computer names that are longer than the 8+3 convention allows. Objective: Configure and troubleshoot domain user accounts (Chapter 10).

4 **B.** Windows 2000 doesn't ask you about performing the file system upgrade, nor does it check to verify that your currently installed version of NT can handle NTFS 5. Choice C isn't correct, because it's not just the boot sector that's causing the problem, it's the whole doggoned file system. And choice D just isn't true. Objective: Configure file systems by using NTFS, FAT32, or FAT (Chapter 3).

5 **A.** The Remote Installation Preparation Wizard also goes by the name of its executable file, RIPREP.EXE, which resides on the Windows 2000 server where you have installed the RIS service. Objective: Install Windows 2000 Professional by using Windows 2000 Server Remote Installation Services (RIS) (Chapter 4).

6 **A, B,** and **C.** The network PC gets its own IP address, and that of the RIS server, via DHCP. DNS and Active Directory are necessary for Windows 2000 to locate the directory service, computer accounts, and the RIS server itself. Objective: Install Windows 2000 Professional by using Windows 2000 Server Remote Installation Services (RIS) (Chapter 4).

7 **C.** The regular Users group in Windows 2000 is more restrictive than the regular Users group in Windows NT 4.0 Workstation. Applications written for Windows 2000 should work fine with the built-in Users group, but older applications may need users to be members of the built-in Power Users group. Objective: Implement, configure, manage, and troubleshoot user rights (Chapter 10).

8 **A, B,** and **C.** To browse the network for the printer, leave its name blank in the wizard and click the Next button. You can't find a printer in the wizard by using its security ID. Objective: Connect to an Internet printer (Chapter 7).

9 **A.** If the controller doesn't appear in Device Manager, then Windows 2000 isn't seeing the controller, much less the speakers. Because the controller is typically a motherboard device, the best guess is that it isn't enabled in the BIOS. Because USB is a Plug and Play bus, Windows should autodetect it, therefore running the Add New Hardware wizard would typically not be necessary. Objective: Install, configure, and manage USB devices (Chapter 8).

10 **C.** No command exists for copying a user account in the Users and Passwords control panel, or the Local Users and Groups console (which you access via the control panel's Advanced tab). By renaming the account and immediately choosing a new password, you create a secure account with the same security identifier as the old one — and therefore all the same access permissions, group memberships, and rights. Objective: Create and manage local users and groups (Chapter 10).

11 **C.** You can't convert from NTFS back to FAT using the Disk Management snap-in or the CONVERT.EXE utility; the only method available (at least, with the supplied Microsoft software!) is a backup, reformat, and restore cycle. In real life, use Partition Magic. Objective: Convert from one file system to another file system (Chapter 3).

12 **C** and **D.** You can't simply back up the Registry by checking the folder that contains the Registry files (which by the way is C:\WINNT\SYSTEM32\CONFIG), because the files are in use by the system. The System State backup lets you specify any target folder; the ERD backup forces the Registry backup to C:\WINNT\REPAIR\REGBACK. Objective: Recover systems and user data by using Windows Backup (Chapter 15).

13 **A** and **B.** In fact, the only two "real" root keys are HKLM and HKU. HKEY_DYN_DATA is not present in Windows 2000. Objective: Monitor, configure, and troubleshoot I/O devices (Chapter 8).

14 **B.** The Local Security Policy console in the Administrative Tools folder is what you want; note that the policies you set under the Account Policies node apply to all local user accounts on that computer. You can't get to the account policy settings via the Computer Management console or the Users and Passwords control panel, although you can set some user-specific password options there, such as whether to prevent a given user from changing his or her password. Objective: Implement, configure, manage, and troubleshoot account policy (Chapter 10).

15 **C.** You may also want to remember that the order of precedence for the processing of policies in Windows 2000 is, from lowest to highest, local — site — domain — organizational unit. Incidentally, no File⇨Save command exists in the Local Security Policy console. Objective: Implement, configure, manage, and troubleshoot local Group Policy (Chapter 11).

16 **A, B, C,** and **D.** Using these tools remotely assumes that you and the computer you're trying to administer share at least one network protocol in common. Objective: Optimize and troubleshoot application performance (Chapter 14).

17 **C.** You should use Safe Mode. You can't use Last Known Good configuration, because you already logged on after installing the driver, making the LKG setup a defective setup. (By the way, F5 is the wrong function key to use at startup.) As for choice D, the Emergency Recovery Diskette isn't bootable. Choice E is more of a last resort; Safe Mode is much easier and faster. Objective: Troubleshoot system restoration by using Safe Mode (Chapter 15).

18 **D.** Denials override all other permissions, so the only way to let Georgina into the company budgets is to remove her from the Staff group, which has been denied the Full Control permission. Objective: Control access to shared folders by using permissions (Chapter 11).

19 **D.** The Extensible Authentication Protocol is your best bet for smart card authentication; the exam may also refer to EAP/TLS. Objective: Create a dial-up connection to connect to a remote access server (Chapter 13).

20 **A.** The Security Templates snap-in (which you must add to a new, custom console of your own devising) presents all the security settings of each available template in a handy hierarchical structure. Objective: Implement, configure, manage, and troubleshoot a security configuration (Chapter 11).

21 **D.** The Microsoft-supplied Client Service for NetWare (CSNW) doesn't support accessing NetWare servers using IP, it only works if the NetWare servers are running IPX/SPX. Objective: Install, configure, and troubleshoot network adapters (Chapter 6).

22 **D.** Object access permits auditing the file system and the Registry. Objective: Implement, configure, manage, and troubleshoot auditing (Chapter 10).

23 **B.** If the IP address for the default gateway is wrong or missing, then Emily's PC has no way to connect to the Internet via the gateway. If her own PC's IP address were wrong or missing, she couldn't see local Windows 2000 servers. WINS doesn't enter into the equation, because the gateway is specified in Windows 2000 using a numeric IP address, not a NetBIOS computer name. And DHCP doesn't have to be running for Emily to access the Internet. Here's a tip to remember: If Emily connects to the Internet or other subnets via a router, the default gateway is the IP address of the network port on the router that communicates with her subnet. Objective: Configure and troubleshoot the TCP/IP protocol (Chapter 6).

24 **C.** Note that the APM tab does not appear in the Power Options control panel for ACPI machines, so looking for it is a quick way to tell whether your machine is APM or ACPI. If your machine uses APM, Windows 2000 doesn't support APM features by default; you have to check the check box. Objective: Configure Advanced Power Management (Chapter 9).

25 **A.** It stands for Microsoft Software Installer, never mind that the technology goes by the name of Windows Installer just about everywhere in the Microsoft documentation. The associated executable is MSIEXEC.EXE. Objective: Install applications by using Windows Installer packages (Chapter 12).

26 **B** and **C**. The modems can be different speeds, and can be either internal or external devices. Objective: Install, configure, and manage modems (Chapter 8).

27 **A**. Then you have the option of deciding whether to overwrite the server-based copy, or save your file to a different name (which you must specify). Objective: Manage and troubleshoot the synchronization of offline files (Chapter 12).

28 **A**. This is a so-called "administrative share." The root directory of each hard drive is also shared (as C$, D$, and so on). Objective: Create and remove shared folders (Chapter11).

29 **A**. This wizard is sort of a one-stop shop for all types of network and dial-up connections (hence the name of the folder in which it lives!). Objective: Connect to computers by using a virtual private network (VPN) connection (Chapter 13).

30 **B**. Choice A is wrong because the defragger works with all the file systems that Windows 2000 supports. B is true: You can't run this utility to defragment a server disk, for example. As for choice C, the figure is 15 percent, and D is (unfortunately) not true. Objective: Optimize and troubleshoot disk performance (Chapter 14).

31 **A**. Generally, the easiest way to assign any networkwide setting is to set a policy at the network level, rather than run around and make each setting at the local workstation. Choice C is the correct procedure for blocking unsigned drivers on a single local PC. Choice D is simply wrong. Objective: Manage and troubleshoot driver signing (Chapter 15).

32 **C**. You would actually set the exclusion list using Group Policies, most likely on a server acting as a domain controller. Note that on a PC upgraded from Windows NT 4.0 Workstation, user profiles reside under C:\WINNT\PROFILES\ <username>. Objective: Configure and manage user profiles (Chapter 12).

33 **B**. The command is simply UPDATE.EXE to apply the service pack to a standalone PC. Objective: Deploy service packs (Chapter 4).

34 **B**. As long as Raymond copies or moves the encrypted file to an NTFS disk on a Windows 2000 system, the file retains its encryption. Windows 2000 lets you copy encrypted files to any storage device without any warnings about potential loss of security. Objective: Encrypt data on a hard disk by using Encrypting File System (EFS) (Chapter 3).

35 **A**. The System Locale setting lets non-Unicode applications display menus and dialog boxes in the language in which they were created. Objective: Configure multiple-language support for users (Chapter 5).

36 **D**. You must remember that when both share level permissions and NTFS permissions have been set for the same resource, any restrictions at either level do apply. Objective: Control access to files and folders by using permissions (Chapter 11).

37 **C, D,** and **E.** Windows 2000 actually supports up to ten simultaneously active displays. Because choice C is true, choice B is not. Objective: Configure multiple-display support (Chapter 8).

38 **A, B,** and **C.** Note that the qualifier you'd use with WINNT32.EXE is /CHECKUPGRADEONLY. You could add the line ReportOnly in UNATTEND.TXT to create a log file of compatibility issues without actually installing the operating system. Objective: Prepare a computer to meet upgrade requirements (Chapter 4).

39 **B.** No such setting as QuickKeys exists. StickyKeys lets you type key combinations, such as Ctrl+Alt+Del, in sequence instead of all at once. ToggleKeys makes sounds when you hit NumLock, CapsLock, or ScrollLock. Objective: Configure and troubleshoot accessibility services (Chapter 5).

40 **A.** The range for APIPA addresses is 169.254.0.1 through 169.254.255.254. Yes, this question is nitpicky. So is the exam. Objective: Configure and troubleshoot the TCP/IP protocol (Chapter 6).

41 **A.** The Recovery Console takes 5 to 7 megabytes, but it sure could come in handy in a situation such as this. The PC is apparently booting far enough to get to the splash screen, meaning that you should have the chance to choose Recovery Console from the text menu that appears earlier. Objective: Recover systems and user data by using the Recovery Console (Chapter 15).

42 **A.** You can also specify which profile should be the default, and how long Windows 2000 should wait before it chooses the default profile. Objective: Manage hardware profiles (Chapter 9).

43 **C.** You just gotta memorize these. Watch out, the spelling isn't consistent; sometimes the workstation templates use "WS," sometimes "WK." *Objective: Implement, configure, manage, and troubleshoot a security configuration (Chapter 11).*

44 **C.** A counter log has less impact on system performance than a continuous trace log, especially if you set the counter interval to a fairly long value. Alerts are for sending messages regarding one-time threshold events. Objective: Optimize and troubleshoot memory performance (Chapter 14).

45 **A, B, C,** and **D.** Note that in order to see some of this information, you must invoke IPCONFIG with the /ALL qualifier. Objective: Configure and troubleshoot the TCP/IP protocol (Chapter 6).

46 **A, B,** and **D.** The system is low on disk space, which means fragmentation is likely to be a problem. The Disk Cleanup wizard gets rid of unnecessary files, and allows the Disk Defragmenter tool to work more effectively. More RAM helps, as Windows 2000 itself typically needs around 50 to 55 MB before you load any programs or data files. However, setting the pagefile size to a low value (the default is 1.5 times RAM) hurts performance as Windows dynamically resizes the pagefile upward. Objectives: Optimize and troubleshoot memory performance, optimize and troubleshoot disk performance (Chapter 14).

47 **D.** Remember also that the NetBIOS name is the same as the computer name. You don't need WINS in a pure Windows 2000 network, just for networks that include "legacy" computers (everything prior to Windows 2000!). Objective: Configure and troubleshoot the TCP/IP protocol (Chapter 6).

48 **A** and **B.** You don't have to log on as an Administrator to schedule a task, nor do you have to be logged on when the task is due to execute. You do, however, have to specify a user account that has appropriate rights to execute the program, when you create the task. FYI: If you schedule lots of tasks, and none of them run, the Task Scheduler service is likely stopped. If some run but others don't, you probably have a security issue. Objective: Configure, manage, and troubleshoot the Task Scheduler (Chapter 14).

49 **D.** If you removed the device driver, as choice C suggests, you wouldn't have it available in any hardware profile, and you'd have to reinstall the driver next time you used your docking station. Objective: Configure and manage card services (Chapter 9).

50 **C.** Also watch out if % processor time is over 85 percent for long stretches of time. You should probably just memorize some of the performance guidelines in Chapter 14. Objective: Optimize and troubleshoot processor utilization (Chapter 14).

Practice Exam

Appendix B

About the CD

On the CD-ROM:

- The QuickLearn game, a fun way to study for the test
- Practice and Self-Assessment tests, to make sure you are ready for the real thing
- Practice test demos from Transcender, QuickCert, and Super Software

System Requirements

Make sure that your computer meets the minimum system requirements listed below. If your computer doesn't match up to most of these requirements, you may have problems using the contents of the CD.

- A PC with a Pentium or faster processor.
- Microsoft Windows 95 or later or Windows NT 4.0 or later.
- At least 16 MB of total RAM installed on your computer. For best performance, we recommend at least 32 MB of RAM installed.
- A CD-ROM drive — double-speed (2x) or faster.
- A sound card for PCs.
- A monitor capable of displaying at least 256 colors or grayscale.
- A modem with a speed of at least 14,400 bps.

Important Note: To play the QuickLearn game, you must have a 166 or faster computer running Windows 95 or 98 with SVGA graphics. You must also have Microsoft DirectX 5.0 or later installed. If you do not have DirectX, you can install it from the CD. Just run D:\Directx\dxinstall.exe. Unfortunately, DirectX 5.0 does not run on Windows NT 4.0, so you cannot play the QuickLearn Game on a Windows NT 4.0 or earlier machine.

Using the CD with Microsoft Windows

To install the items from the CD to your hard drive, follow these steps.

1. **Insert the CD into your computer's CD-ROM drive.**
2. **Click Start⇨Run.**
3. **In the dialog box that appears, type** D:\IDG.EXE.

   Replace *D* with the proper drive letter if your CD-ROM drive uses a different letter. (If you don't know the letter, see how your CD-ROM drive is listed under My Computer.)
4. **Click OK.**

   A license agreement window appears.
5. **Read through the license agreement, nod your head, and then click the Accept button if you want to use the CD — after you click Accept, you'll never be bothered by the License Agreement window again.**

   The CD interface Welcome screen appears. The interface is a little program that shows you what's on the CD and coordinates installing the programs and running the demos. The interface basically enables you to click a button or two to make things happen.
6. **Click anywhere on the Welcome screen to enter the interface.**

   Now you are getting to the action. This next screen lists categories for the software on the CD.
7. **To view the items within a category, just click the category's name.**

   A list of programs in the category appears.
8. **For more information about a program, click the program's name.**

   Be sure to read the information that appears. Sometimes a program has it's own system requirements or requires you to do a few tricks on your computer before you can install or run the program, and this screen tells you what you might need to do, if necessary.
9. **If you don't want to install the program, click the Back button to return to the previous screen.**

   You can always return to the previous screen by clicking the Back button. This feature allows you to browse the different categories and products and decide what you want to install.
10. **To install a program, click the appropriate Install button.**

    The CD interface drops to the background while the CD installs the program you chose.

11. **To install other items, repeat Steps 7 – 10.**

12. **When you've finished installing programs, click the Quit button to close the interface.**

    You can eject the CD now. Carefully place it back in the plastic jacket of the book for safekeeping.

In order to run some of the programs on this *MCSE Windows 2000 Professional For Dummies* CD-ROM, you may need to keep the CD inside your CD-ROM drive. This is a good thing. Otherwise, the installed program would have required you to install a very large chunk of the program to your hard drive, which may have kept you from installing other software.

What You'll Find

Shareware programs are fully functional, free trial versions of copyrighted programs. If you like particular programs, register with their authors for a nominal fee and receive licenses, enhanced versions, and technical support. Freeware programs are free, copyrighted games, applications, and utilities. You can copy them to as many PCs as you like — free — but they have no technical support. GNU software is governed by its own license, which is included inside the folder of the GNU software. There are no restrictions on distribution of this software. See the GNU license for more details. Trial, demo, or evaluation versions are usually limited either by time or functionality (such as being unable to save projects).

Here's a summary of the software on this CD.

Dummies test prep tools

This CD contains questions related to MCSE Windows 2000 Professional administration. Most of the questions are topics that you can expect to be on the test.

QuickLearn Game

The QuickLearn Game is the ...*For Dummies* way of making studying for the Certification exam fun. Well, okay, less painful. OutPost is a DirectX, high-resolution, fast-paced arcade game.

Answer questions to defuse dimensional disrupters and save the universe from a rift in space-time. (The questions come from the same set of questions that the Self-Assessment and Practice Test use, but isn't this way more fun?) Missing a few questions on the real exam almost never results in a rip in the fabric of the universe, so just think how easy it'll be when you get there!

Please note: QUIKLERN.EXE on the CD is just a self-extractor, to simplify the process of copying the game files to your computer. It will not create any shortcuts on your computer's desktop or Start menu.

Note: Don't forget, you need to have DirectX 5.0 or later installed to play the QuickLearn game; and it does not run on Windows NT 4.0.

Practice Test

The Practice test is designed to help you get comfortable with the certification testing situation and pinpoint your strengths and weaknesses on the topic. You can accept the default setting of 60 questions in 60 minutes, or you can customize the settings. You can choose the number of questions, the amount of time, and even decide which objectives you want to focus on.

After you answer the questions, the Practice test gives you plenty of feedback. You can find out which questions you answered correctly and incorrectly and get statistics on how you did, broken down by objective. Then you can review the questions — all of them, all the ones you missed, all the ones you marked, or a combination of the ones you marked and the ones you missed.

Self-Assessment Test

The Self-Assessment test is designed to simulate the actual certification testing situation. You must answer 60 questions in 60 minutes. After you answer all the questions, you find out your score and whether you pass or fail — but that's all the feedback you get. If you can pass the Self-Assessment test regularly, you're ready to tackle the real thing.

Links Page

I've also created a Links Page, a handy starting place for accessing the huge amounts of information on the Internet about the certification tests. You can find the page at D:\Links.htm.

Screen Saver

A spiffy little screen saver that the Dummies team created. Maybe, like sleeping with the book under your pillow, this can help you learn subliminally! Screen shots of test questions will fill your screen, so when your computer is not doing anything else, it can still be quizzing you! And if you'd like to visit the *Certification ...For Dummies* Web site, all you have to do is press the space bar while the screen saver is running — your default browser will be launched and send you there! (You might want to keep this in mind if you're the kind of person who hits the space bar to get rid of your screen saver. . . .)

Commercial demos

QuickCert Exam Simulator, from QuickCert, Inc.

This package from QuickCert offers practice tests for several Certification exams. Run the QuickCert IDG Demo to choose the practice test you want to work on. For more information about the Exam Simulator, visit the QuickCert Web site at `www.quickcert.com`.

Windows 2000 Professional Flash, from Transcender Corporation

Another demo from the good folks at Transcender, this one is designed to help you learn the fundamental concepts and terminology behind SQL Server. You provide short answer-type explanations to questions presented in a flash card format, and grade yourself as you go. To learn more about what Transcender has to offer, check out their Web site at `www.transcender.com`.

Transcender Demo Sampler, from Transcender Corporation

Transcender's demo tests are some of the most popular practice tests available. The Certification Sampler offers demos of many of the exams that Transcender offers.

Transcender SQLFlash, from Transcender Corporation

Another demo from the good folks at Transcender, this one is designed to help you learn the fundamental concepts and terminology behind SQL Server. You provide short answer-type explanations to questions presented in a flash card format and grade yourself as you go.

W2000 Prof. MCSEprep, from Super Software

This demo, designed to help you prepare for the Windows 2000 Server exam, gives you another 20 practice questions. Get lots more by ordering the software. Learn more by visiting the Web site, `www.mcseprep.com`.

Self Test Software for MCSE Windows 2000, from Self Test Software

Self Test Software's demo is designed to help you learn more about the Windows 2000 Professional exam by giving you extra practice questions. Learn more by visiting the Web site, `www.selftestsoftware.com`.

If You've Got Problems (Of the CD Kind)

I tried my best to compile programs that work on most computers with the minimum system requirements. Alas, your computer may differ, and some programs may not work properly for some reason.

The two likeliest problems are that you don't have enough memory (RAM) for the programs you want to use, or you have other programs running that are affecting installation or running of a program. If you get error messages like `Not enough memory` or `Setup cannot continue`, try one or more of these methods and then try using the software again:

- **Turn off any antivirus software that you have on your computer.** Installers sometimes mimic virus activity and may make your computer incorrectly believe that it is being infected by a virus.
- **Close all running programs.** The more programs you're running, the less memory is available to other programs. Installers also typically update files and programs; if you keep other programs running, installation may not work properly.
- **In Windows, close the CD interface and run demos or installations directly from Windows Explorer.** The interface itself can tie up system memory, or even conflict with certain kinds of interactive demos. Use Windows Explorer to browse the files on the CD and launch installers or demos.
- **Have your local computer store add more RAM to your computer.** This is, admittedly, a drastic and somewhat expensive step. However, adding more memory can really help the speed of your computer and enable more programs to run at the same time.

If you still have trouble installing the items from the CD, please call the Customer phone number: 800-762-2974 (outside the U.S.: 317-572-3993).

Index

• Numbers •

• A •

• B •

• C •

• D •

• F •

• G •

• H •

• I •

• J •

• K •

• L •

• M •

• N •

• O •

• P •

• S •

• T •

• V •

• W •

• Y •

• Z •

Notes

Notes

Notes

Notes

Notes

Hungry Minds, Inc., End-User License Agreement

READ THIS. You should carefully read these terms and conditions before opening the software packet(s) included with this book ("Book"). This is a license agreement ("Agreement") between you and Hungry Minds, Inc. ("HMI"). By opening the accompanying software packet(s), you acknowledge that you have read and accept the following terms and conditions. If you do not agree and do not want to be bound by such terms and conditions, promptly return the Book and the unopened software packet(s) to the place you obtained them for a full refund.

1. **License Grant.** HMI grants to you (either an individual or entity) a nonexclusive license to use one copy of the enclosed software program(s) (collectively, the "Software") solely for your own personal or business purposes on a single computer (whether a standard computer or a workstation component of a multi-user network). The Software is in use on a computer when it is loaded into temporary memory (RAM) or installed into permanent memory (hard disk, CD-ROM, or other storage device). HMI reserves all rights not expressly granted herein.

2. **Ownership.** HMI is the owner of all right, title, and interest, including copyright, in and to the compilation of the Software recorded on the disk(s) or CD-ROM ("Software Media"). Copyright to the individual programs recorded on the Software Media is owned by the author or other authorized copyright owner of each program. Ownership of the Software and all proprietary rights relating thereto remain with HMI and its licensers.

3. **Restrictions On Use and Transfer.**

   (a) You may only (i) make one copy of the Software for backup or archival purposes, or (ii) transfer the Software to a single hard disk, provided that you keep the original for backup or archival purposes. You may not (i) rent or lease the Software, (ii) copy or reproduce the Software through a LAN or other network system or through any computer subscriber system or bulletin-board system, or (iii) modify, adapt, or create derivative works based on the Software.

   (b) You may not reverse engineer, decompile, or disassemble the Software. You may transfer the Software and user documentation on a permanent basis, provided that the transferee agrees to accept the terms and conditions of this Agreement and you retain no copies. If the Software is an update or has been updated, any transfer must include the most recent update and all prior versions.

4. **Restrictions on Use of Individual Programs.** You must follow the individual requirements and restrictions detailed for each individual program in Appendix B of this Book. These limitations are also contained in the individual license agreements recorded on the Software Media. These limitations may include a requirement that after using the program for a specified period of time, the user must pay a registration fee or discontinue use. By opening the Software packet(s), you will be agreeing to abide by the licenses and restrictions for these individual programs that are detailed in Appendix B and on the Software Media. None of the material on this Software Media or listed in this Book may ever be redistributed, in original or modified form, for commercial purposes.

5. **Limited Warranty.**

   (a) HMI warrants that the Software and Software Media are free from defects in materials and workmanship under normal use for a period of sixty (60) days from the date of purchase of this Book. If HMI receives notification within the warranty period of defects in materials or workmanship, HMI will replace the defective Software Media.

   (b) HMI AND THE AUTHOR OF THE BOOK DISCLAIM ALL OTHER WARRANTIES, EXPRESS OR IMPLIED, INCLUDING WITHOUT LIMITATION IMPLIED WARRANTIES OF MERCHANTABILITY AND FITNESS FOR A PARTICULAR PURPOSE, WITH RESPECT TO THE SOFTWARE, THE PROGRAMS, THE SOURCE CODE CONTAINED THEREIN, AND/OR THE TECHNIQUES DESCRIBED IN THIS BOOK. HMI DOES NOT WARRANT THAT THE FUNCTIONS CONTAINED IN THE SOFTWARE WILL MEET YOUR REQUIREMENTS OR THAT THE OPERATION OF THE SOFTWARE WILL BE ERROR FREE.

   (c) This limited warranty gives you specific legal rights, and you may have other rights that vary from jurisdiction to jurisdiction.

6. **Remedies.**

   (a) HMI's entire liability and your exclusive remedy for defects in materials and workmanship shall be limited to replacement of the Software Media, which may be returned to HMI with a copy of your receipt at the following address: Software Media Fulfillment Department, Attn.: *MCSE Windows 2000 Professional For Dummies,* Hungry Minds, Inc., 10475 Crosspoint Blvd., Indianapolis, IN 46256, or call 1-800-762-2974. Please allow four to six weeks for delivery. This Limited Warranty is void if failure of the Software Media has resulted from accident, abuse, or misapplication. Any replacement Software Media will be warranted for the remainder of the original warranty period or thirty (30) days, whichever is longer.

   (b) In no event shall HMI or the author be liable for any damages whatsoever (including without limitation damages for loss of business profits, business interruption, loss of business information, or any other pecuniary loss) arising from the use of or inability to use the Book or the Software, even if HMI has been advised of the possibility of such damages.

   (c) Because some jurisdictions do not allow the exclusion or limitation of liability for consequential or incidental damages, the above limitation or exclusion may not apply to you.

7. **U.S. Government Restricted Rights.** Use, duplication, or disclosure of the Software for or on behalf of the United States of America, its agencies and/or instrumentalities (the "U.S. Government") is subject to restrictions as stated in paragraph (c)(1)(ii) of the Rights in Technical Data and Computer Software clause of DFARS 252.227-7013, and in subparagraphs (a) through (d) of the commercial Computer-Restricted Rights clause at FAR 52.227-19, and in similar clauses in the NASA FAR supplement, when applicable.

8. **General.** This Agreement constitutes the entire understanding of the parties and revokes and supersedes all prior agreements, oral or written, between them and may not be modified or amended except in a writing signed by both parties hereto that specifically refers to this Agreement. This Agreement shall take precedence over any other documents that may be in conflict herewith. If any one or more provisions contained in this Agreement are held by any court or tribunal to be invalid, illegal, or otherwise unenforceable, each and every other provision shall remain in full force and effect.

Installation Instructions

Make sure that your computer meets the minimum system requirements listed in Appendix B. If your computer doesn't match up to most of these requirements, you may have problems using the contents of the CD.

Using the CD with Microsoft Windows

1. **Insert the CD into your computer's CD-ROM drive.**
2. **Click Start⇨Run.**
3. **In the dialog box that appears, type** D:\setup.exe.

   Replace *D* with the proper drive letter if your CD-ROM drive uses a different letter.
4. **Click OK.**

   A license agreement window appears.
5. **Read through the license agreement, nod your head, and then click the Accept button if you want to use the CD — after you click Accept, you'll never be bothered by the License Agreement window again.**
6. **Click anywhere on the Welcome screen to enter the interface.**
7. **To view the items within a category, just click the category's name.**
8. **For more information about a program, click the program's name.**
9. **If you don't want to install the program, click the Back button to return to the previous screen.**
10. **To install a program, click the appropriate Install button.**
11. **To install other items, repeat Steps 7 – 10.**
12. **When you've finished installing programs, click the Quit button to close the interface.**

FOR DUMMIES BOOK REGISTRATION

Register This Book and Win!

We want to hear from you!

Visit **dummies.com** to register this book and tell us how you liked it!

- Get entered in our monthly prize giveaway.
- Give us feedback about this book — tell us what you like best, what you like least, or maybe what you'd like to ask the author and us to change!
- Let us know any other *For Dummies* topics that interest you.

Your feedback helps us determine what books to publish, tells us what coverage to add as we revise our books, and lets us know whether we're meeting your needs as a *For Dummies* reader. You're our most valuable resource, and what you have to say is important to us!

Not on the Web yet? It's easy to get started with *Dummies 101®: The Internet For Windows® 98* or *The Internet For Dummies®* at local retailers everywhere.

Or let us know what you think by sending us a letter at the following address:

For Dummies Book Registration
Dummies Press
10475 Crosspoint Blvd.
Indianapolis, IN 46256

...FOR DUMMIES™
BESTSELLING BOOK SERIES